The Russian Threat

THE RUSSIAN THREAT

Its Myths and Realities

Jim Garrison & Pyare Shivpuri

Gateway Books, London

Published by

GATEWAY BOOKS
37 Upper Addison Gardens
London W14 8AJ

© *1983, Jim Garrison & Pyare Shivpuri*

Hardcover ISBN 0 946551 00 6
Paperback ISBN 0 946551 01 4

First Published 1983

Maps and drawings by Jan Hoult
Cover design by Humphrey Stone

Set in Palacio 10 on 11pt by
Mathematical Composition Setters Ltd.
7 Ivy Street, Salisbury, Wilts

Printed and bound by
The Pitman Press
Lower Bristol Road, Bath, Avon.

British Library Cataloguing in Publication Data
Garrison, Jim, 1951-
The Russian Threat
1. World Politics 1975–1985
2. Soviet Union—Foreign Relations—1975–
I. Title   II. Shivpuri, Pyare
327·470171'3   D849

Contents

for you
Claire
and
Emma-Vidya

Acknowledgements

Innumerable people on five continents have helped, encouraged, guided and assisted us in shaping this book. We are specially grateful to Dr. David Ashead + Vladimir Bukovsky + Prof. John Burton + Christopher Cornford + Arthur Cox + Malcolm Dando + Dr.Vera Dunham + Dhirubhai Ganatra + Richard Hauser + Edward Heath, MP + Jane Hewer + Prof. John Humphrey + Msgr. Bruce Kent + Frieda Knight + Inder Malhotra + Margaret Masterman + Joe and Judy Montville + Damaris and Frederick Parker-Rhodes + Paul Ostreicher + Brain Revell + Ann Robinson + Dr. John A. T. Robinson + Paul Rogers + Nial Ross + Sunil Roy + Sir Martin Ryle + Bob Smith + John Steiner + Jenny Sturtridge + E. P. Thompson + Vera Trail + Dr. Aruna Vasudev + Liz Walmsley + Sir John Whitmore and many Polish and Soviet citizens whom discretion does not permit to name.

Preface

Cambridge, England, is a quiet sheltered sort of University town to live in. That does not mean it is also calm. Under the upper veneer of almost disconcern for the rest of the mundane world, the academic community, it seemed to both of us, has been looking for a new role in the societal structures of the future. That, of course, is a perennial human occupation. The present difficulty is that this generation has not been able to anticipate, let alone find the societal structures of the future. It cannot relate to anything. The British Empire is no more. The elite of the biggest empire known in human history does not even accept that after the fall of the British Empire, there could be others. Hence, while it sees the uncertainty, it does not apprehend the danger.

Oh, yes! it sees the dangers of unemployment and the resultant corrosion of social and moral values. It recognises the dangers of disaffection and alienation. It is prepared—and preparing—to fight against the decay. But it is not capable of struggling for rejuvenation. It does not anticipate events. It is a system which merely reacts. Against the future. Against the unknown. Against its disenchanted.

It was in this rarified atmosphere that we both worked for a while and discovered that it is the plutonium culture—our insistence on increasing our nuclear destructive capability—that is sucking away at all our resources—physical, mental, psychological, emotional and spiritual. Unfortunately, our society does not fully understand that. If we did, we would not be groping. We would be grappling.

This vacuum is cleverly filled by official propaganda presenting the Russians as the greatest threat to human society and urging any sacrifice to combat their onslaught. The President of the United States keeps telling us that the Russians intend to take over the world. Other heads of state in the West, echoing his words, point to the tyranny of the Soviet system and the air of liberty that we breathe. They tell us that that air must be protected at all costs whether or not we live to breathe it. Our way of life, we are told, is threatened by the Russian bear and we must put it in a cage.

Even in that cage, it is argued, the bear presents an increasing threat. He may break open the door or bend the rods and escape. We need something more than a cage. Something stronger. More durable. Safe. A coffin, for instance. Then we can get on with our liberty and democracy and constitutions and human rights.

Yet, the very administration that tells us that the Russians are so greedy that they want our piece of globe and so strong that they might just snatch it away, also tells us that it is necessary to sell wheat to the Russians. So that they can live. So that they can continue to be the greatest threat to humankind. So that the cage can constantly be fortified. So that the cage-fortification industry which supports the administration and its trappings can thrive, and in thriving continue to take liberties with our liberty and democracy and constitutions and human rights.

We are both simple people and to our minds there seems to be no logic in this argument. If the Russians are, in fact, the greatest threat to humankind, then selling wheat to them in preference to Central Africa or Latin America is an act of high treason. On the other hand, if the sale of wheat to the Russians is even marginally important for our own well-being, then the Russians are not, in fact, the greatest threat to humankind.

Wheat and gold—in Sanskrit both are called 'kanak'—elicit cooperation between the Soviet Union and the United States of America directly or via 'friendly' nations. There are other areas of cooperation between the Kremlin and the White House. And this cooperation is not limited to the surface of our planet. It reaches beyond. Into space. This cooperation extended by the United States makes the Russians stronger. Slowly but certainly. It makes them more able to destroy the cage. Even able to rip open the coffin.

In this baffling situation two main issues arise. Are the Russians really bent upon dominating the world? Or is the White House using the *threat* of Russian domination to *itself* dominate the world? There are only two punters in this race and both can lead us all to our annihilation. Both must know, whatever their public postures, that there cannot be any victors in a nuclear conflict. Perhaps no survivors. So what kind of games are they playing? The Soviet leader, can he dream of becoming the King of Ashes one of these days? Or does the American President entertain the ambition of commanding a corps of radio-active corpses? Or are they together playing a very closed hand of poker taking the rest of us for a ride? In spite of the loud trumpets of liberty blown in the West and of equality in the East, there is precious little of either available to people anywhere. In the West, we elect an individual to be the protector of our democracy. In the East, the protector of equality is imposed upon the people. All we are really doing is erecting crosses to crucify our duty of vigilance which is an essential part of both liberty and equality. To this process of abnegation, we all give high-sounding labels of 'education and information'. We two discovered, when we dug a little deeper, that there is a lot of 'mis' in both the education and the information about the Russians and about ourselves. If all this is laid bare and co-related properly, and more importantly, honestly, one finds that the Russians, very much like Americans, are not such a bad lot after all. It is fear on both sides that compels the Russians to brand the Americans as the Imperialists and compels the Americans to paint the Russians as the Expansionists. Both are divided by ignorance but deep down, they are both united in their fear. Both want their fear to be shared universally.

We are both convinced that if this divisive fear can be removed or even be understood—for which eliminating ignorance is essential—the human race would not need to subsidise its death dealing industries with deprivation and misery and exploitation and hunger and poverty. As a matter of fact, we would not need to amass the destructive power with which we can literally undo creation.

For that understanding, we must trace our steps back to the day when history fired its own shot at its own head. We must travel back to 6 August 1945 at 8.15 in the morning.

Jim Garrison
Pyare Shivpuri

Cambridge, England.

1 'The Russians Are Coming'

Hiroshima was a thriving Japanese city of 400,000 people. There were 90,000 buildings in the city. It boasted of 45 hospitals and 298 doctors. There were 1,780 nurses to take care of the sick and the infirm. Thirty-three fire-stations, working 24-hours a day, guarded the city against fires.

On 6 August 1945 at 8.15 a.m., time stopped its indifferent flow. History, tired of its march through blood and tears, paused.

A US Air Force bomber flying overhead dropped a single bomb. The bomb detonated 1,800 feet above the city centre. Within three miles of the explosion, 62,000 buildings were immediately pulverised. All utilities and transportation services were demolished. Forty-two hospitals were destroyed. Two hundred and seventy doctors and one thousand six hundred and forty-five nurses were immolated in that single blast. Twenty-six fire-stations were reduced to cinders. Hiroshima became the graveyard of our age.

Savants of many climes had forged a chain of discoveries to create the chain-reacting explosion of the split atom. A desert in New Mexico was made to blossom into a city for the atom bomb to be born. And when the bomb burst, a city of unsuspecting men and women and children in Japan was ground into a desert.

Floods, earthquakes and fires of all history were jealous of the atom bomb for its record toll in record time. The sun envied the human-made sun which imprinted permanent shadows of men and things after destroying them. "Such weapon has power to make everything into nothing", said an unfortunate one who survived.[1] Unfortunate, because for those who died in the blast it was only a second of sun's heat and a gale of lightning speed. Those who survived lived on in the 'Ashes of Death'.

Almost a world away, in Washington DC, a statement was issued in the afternoon of 6 August 1945. It announced that a bomb with a yield of 12,000 tons of TNT had been dropped on Hiroshima. It stated simply: "It is an atomic bomb. It is a harnessing of the basic powers of the universe. The force from which the sun draws its power has been let loose against those who brought war to the Far East".

Three days later, the Americans did it again. On 9 August 1945 they let loose "the force from which the sun draws its power" on Nagasaki.

This raw display of power shocked the world. The magnitude of its destructiveness was such that Arthur Koestler was compelled to record, "If I were asked to name the most important date in the history of the human race, I would answer without hesitation, 6 August 1945. From the dawn of consciousness until 6 August 1945, man had to live with the prospect of his death as an individual; since the day when the first atomic bomb outshone the sun over Hiroshima, he has had to live with the prospect of his extinction as a species".[2]

The tragedy of the post-war world is that we have not paused to reflect on the fact that Hiroshima and Nagasaki were potentially the death-knell of our species. Rather, the Americans first and the Russians later, sought to translate all this 'kill power' into political strength, believing that if somehow one could threaten one's enemy with enough devastation one's own interests might be better protected. The Russians were followed by the British, the French, the Chinese, the Indians and the Israelis.

By 1958, both the US and the Soviet Union had exploded, in tests, single bombs which were at least a thousand times more deadly than the ones dropped on Japan. The largest explosion was of a 57 megaton device in Siberia. Khrushchev bragged at the time that Soviet scientists could have made the bomb bigger but that would have shattered every window in Moscow, 4,000 miles away.

By 1978, the US had enough nuclear explosive power to destroy completely forty-one times over, all 229 Soviet cities with a population over 100,000; the Soviets could do the same to similar American cities twenty-three times over. The spiral, nevertheless, continued until the multiplicity of weapons systems, delivery systems and satellite systems co-ordinating the entire complex of nuclear 'preparedness' became truly staggering. The Stockholm International Peace Research Institute 1978 Yearbook, *World Armaments and Disarmaments*, listed five different nuclear weapons categories, twenty-one different nuclear weapons types, with thirty-seven different maximum ranges and thirty-four different kiloton/megaton yields, just for the nuclear weapons deployed in Europe by the North Atlantic Treaty Organisation (NATO) and the Warsaw Treaty Organisation (WTO).

It was in 1978 that the United Nations Special Session on Disarmament was convened. In that conference all nations pledged themselves to work for peace. Between the end of that Special Session and the beginning of 1982, the world that had pledged itself to peace spent *$1.6 trillion* ($1,600,000,000,000) on military

expenditure. In 1982 alone, $600 billion was spent for world arma-
ments, $100 billion of which went into the growing stockpile of
nuclear weapons.

The magnitude of what our money has bought can best be
understood by a comparison. All the gunpowder that has been
used in wars since it was invented could be carried in a train 50
miles long, if the freight cars were 40 feet long and carried 50 tons
each. Our nuclear stockpile now stands at 16 billion tons of TNT
equivalent. We would need a train 2,424,242 miles long. Such a
train would encircle the earth at the equator over ninety-seven
times or cover the distance to the moon and back five times. If we
could compress our nuclear stockpile into bombs of the size dropped on Hiroshima and exploded one bomb every day, it would
take us 4,600 years to get rid of them all.

Have we accomplished anything by this? Yes, we have. We have
a matrix of buttons which can be pressed to blow up our world
with the underlying assumption that the need to press them will
not arise if one threatens clearly enough to press them. Through
these buttons we have perverted the very word 'peace' to mean
little more than a balance of terror. We have even anaesthetised
this terror by a new vocabulary of word-groups like 'credible
first-strike capability', 'surgical strikes', 'limited theatre nuclear
forces', 'reciprocal fear of surprise attack', 'calculated pre-emption'
and even 'striking second-first'. Nuclear weapons with their
fail-safe systems and built-in controls have created a world almost
devoid of chance. The new computerisation of nuclear weapons
technology is even relegating the human factor to near obsoles-
cence. If the end comes, it may well not be by our decision but by
the malfunction of a silicon chip. Yet, it is we who fashion these
chips and design these computers. It is we who continuously increase suspicion and fear between the nations. The East or the
West, each side can feel its 'national security' assured only when
the 'enemy' has been convinced of not only the MEANS but also
the WILL to destroy utterly; and, in the process, be itself utterly
destroyed. We have created a recipe for annihilation and validate
it by arguing that only thus the nuclear weapons will remain un-
used. We have poisoned human trust so much that it is only out
of the thicket of mutual assured destruction (aptly shortened to
MAD) that we feel secure enough to pick the flower of safty.

Yet, perhaps because of the all pervasive nature of the danger
around us, nothing seems to be frightening. The levels of destructiveness have already ceased to be meaningful. Yet we go on piling
weapon after weapon, missile after missile, bomber after bomber.
It would not be wrong to say that we have been mesmerised by the
dream-like quality of our ability to push all life into the abyss of

death. Lemmings would be pleased to know how much human beings have learnt from them.

The tragedy of the situation deepens when one realises that the arms race between the NATO and the Soviet bloc is dragging down the rest of the world. The poor nations of Asia, Africa, and Latin America have an average per capita income of $400 per year. Yet between 1970 and 1979, they spent over $64 billion on foreign weapons. The US has the lion's share in this business. In 1970, the sale of US weapons was worth only $1 billion. Ten years later, in 1980, it was worth $16 billion. Countries on the American 'friendly list' are furnished with the most advanced equipment whether or not they need it. Arms sales fuel the arms race. When Reagan decided to sell F-16 jet fighters to Pakistan, India bought an equivalent force of Mirage 2000s from France. The Soviet Union is never far behind. Along with its Warsaw Pact allies, the Soviet Block accounts for nearly 40% of all arms exports.

No area is more inundated with weapons than the Middle East. Israel and its Arab adversaries now have virtually as many conventional weapons as are deployed by both NATO and the Warsaw Pact countries in Europe. Military expenditures in the Middle East are five times larger than those in Europe when calculated on a per capita basis. Much of this money is being spent on the development of nuclear weapons, particularly in Israel and Iraq. It is a singularly expensive process because the countries involved must first establish a 'civil' nuclear capacity before they can obtain the plutonium or enriched uranium to make nuclear weapons. In the case of Israel, this meant building several 'research' reactors. In the case of Iraq, it meant the Osiris nuclear plant which the Israelis blew up in May 1981. The Iraqis are rebuilding it. Fifty-three other countries either have or are building nuclear industries. Twelve of them, including Israel, have refused to sign the Nuclear Non-proliferation Treaty. Argentina, Brazil, India, Pakistan, South Africa and Taiwan are close to having their own nuclear weapons.

Chemical warfare preparations are also dramatically increasing. Although there is a treaty renouncing the use of chemical and bacteriological weapons, signed by both the US and USSR, there are allegations that the Soviets have been using chemicals in Afghanistan and giving them to the Vietnamese to use in Kampuchea. The US is rapidly stockpiling chemical weapons and keeps a store of such weapons in West Germany. It must not be forgotten that the US used chemical defoliants in the Vietnam war.

We are allowing all this to happen while at the same time there are around the world

870,000,000 adults who cannot read and write

500,000,000 people who have no jobs or are less than fully
  employed
130,000,000 children who are unable to attend primary school
450,000,000 people who suffer from hunger or malnutrition
12,000,000 babies who die every year before their first
  birthday
42,000,000 people who are blind or nearly so
2,000,000,000 people who do not have safe water to drink
250,000,000 people who live in urban slums or shantytowns

It is estimated that only two weeks' worth of worldwide armaments expenditure would be enough to feed, house and clothe
every single human being on the planet, such is the level of our
'defence' spending.

Yet the world we live in is a world which, for the most part, is
either arming itself to death or being starved to death. With all the
alternative futures possible and available it is highly likely that the
industrialised and Third World countries alike will spend the rest
of this century bleeding themselves to death with escalating
military expenditures that are slowly but surely wrecking their
economies and devastating their people. The chaos and dislocation
this will cause makes it highly probable that the human race will
blow itself to smithereens.

Why are we doing this to ourselves? Why have we created a
world in which 'peace' can only be forged through threat of war?
Why have we permitted our rulers to become the ultimate terrorists? Why have we amassed the instruments and capacity of such
mass destruction that we can now annihilate all planetary life? And
why are we content to continue arming ourselves while the world
around us starves?

The answer given most frequently in the West, believe it or not,
is 'because of the Russian threat'. British Prime Minister Margaret
Thatcher explained it by wishing to God that nuclear weapons did
not exist but went on to say, "But they do, and the fact is that the
Soviet Union has some of the most sophisticated nuclear weapons
in the world, more advanced than the Americans. The SS-20 is
targeted on Europe, and if you really value your way of life and
wish to pass it on to your children, you'll do everything possible
to see that the Soviet Union does not use those on us. The only
way to ensure that is to make certain that if she did the
consequences for her would be so catastrophic that she would not
do it."[3]

Margaret Thatcher is not alone. This mentality also dominates
the thinking of President Reagan. From the first day in office he
has sought and he has been given evidence to convince him that
the Caribbean is being stirred into revolution by the agents of

Havana and Moscow, and that the Central American nations are being penetrated by the Communists. He has placed his faith in the CIA Director, William Casey, who tells him how the Soviet Union has exploited food, technology and credit from the West. He has watched the CIA 'horror show' of satellite pictures of Soviet ships and submarines coming down the sea-lines, bow to stern, like cars rolling off the production line. Reagan's advisers have outlined for him how captured American M-16 rifles, their serial numbers clumsily altered, have been shipped from Vietnam to El Salvador. They have shown him what purports to be the evidence indicating that Moscow's clients have used poison gas—the lethal 'yellow rain'—in Cambodia and that the Soviets have themselves used chemical weapons in Afghanistan. Reagan has been tutored by his experts into believing that the USSR is in 'historic decline' and is in a state of 'systemic failure'. As a result, his advisers tell him, the Soviets are more unpredictable and dangerous than ever.

Not surprisingly, the President of the United States has concluded that the 1980s will be the most perilous decade in modern times. Hence it is imperative that the US 'catch up with the Russians' and remain strong. The President believes that the only way that strength can be created and maintained is by pouring literally billions of dollars into defence. In the President's mind, dollars first translate into guns, tanks and nuclear weapons; then into confidence and courage; and finally into victory over the 'red menace'.

There is a thirty minute film that has been showing all across Europe and the US for several years. It is called *The Salt Syndrome*. It is produced by a group that proclaims itself to be the 'American Security Council'. The film argues for a military doctrine of 'peace through strength'. The assertion is made that the US and its NATO allies are in bad military shape, and only a continuous massive armament programme will inhibit the Soviet Union from invading the West. The film reports that the Soviet Union spends three times as much as the US on nuclear weapons, indicating an arms build up paralleled only by Nazi Germany in the 1930s. It is also claimed that the Soviets have a six-to-one advantage over the West in nuclear missile fire-power; a three-to-one advantage in attack submarines; a 93-to-41 superiority in all types of ballistic missile submarines; and a vast superiority in troop numbers and in conventional armaments.

In the film, General Alexander Haig comes on camera to charge that the West's defence policies have been "immoral, self-defeating and devastating". Former Secretary of State Henry Kissinger testifies that "rarely in history has a nation so passively accepted such a radical change in military balance". Admiral

Thomas H. Moorer, former Chief of Naval Operations and now on
the board of directors of the Texaco Corporation, states, "We're
already behind. We must accept either disaster through weakness
and disarmament or peace through strength". It is argued that
only a bigger nuclear arsenal, only a massive defence budget, and
only the willingness to push the nuclear button first will prevent
a Russian invasion.

The facts about the Russians do seem stark. A 1982 Pentagon
booklet, *Soviet Military Power*, reports the following:

*Soviet Ground Forces have grown to more than 180
divisions. They are stationed in Eastern Europe, in the USSR, in
Mongolia and in Cuba.

*The Soviet Union can field 50,000 tanks, 20,000 artillery
pieces, and over 5,200 helicopters.

*There are more than 3,500 Soviet and Warsaw Pact tactical
bombers and fighter aircraft located in Eastern Europe alone.
Since 1972 the Soviets have produced over 1,000 fighter aircraft.

*The Soviet arsenal of deliverable nuclear warheads against
Western Europe, China and Japan is increasing. The number of
launchers grows, with some 350 mobile SS-20 Intermediate
Range Ballistic Missile launchers already in the field, each with
three warheads.

*The Soviet intercontinental strategic arsenal includes 7,000
nuclear warheads; 1,398 Intercontinental Ballistic Missile
(ICBM) launchers; 950 Submarine Launched Ballistic Missiles
(SLBM); and 156 long-range bombers.

*The Soviets have eight classes of submarines and eight
classes of major surface warships, including nuclear-powered
cruisers and aircraft carriers. The Soviet Navy is deployed in
every major ocean of the world.

*Soviet Air Defence Forces operate 10,000 surface-to-air
missile launchers at 1,000 fixed missile sites across the USSR.

*This growth in military might is made possible by the
existence of 135 major military industrial plants covering over 40
million square metres of floor space, a 34% increase since 1970.
These plants produce more than 150 different types of weapons
systems both for Soviet use and for export to allied states and
developing countries.

*85,000 Soviet troops are currently engaged in actual combat
in Afghanistan.

The entire edifice of Western defence and foreign policy rests on
the central notion of protecting the West against these formidable
capabilities of the Soviet Union. The Russians have become the

people that the Western public loves to hate. They are the modern devils. They personify in the public mind all that is evil and to be feared. It is against them that the United States, Britain, France and China direct their nuclear arsenals and the vast preponderance of their conventional forces. This is done with urgency because for many in the West the Russian threat is so imminent that the question is not *whether* they will invade but *when*.

Militarism is as central to communism as the pursuit of profit is to capitalism, runs the argument. The USSR is bent on world domination and will not rest until it has subjugated all of us under its red banner. The victory of the Marxists in nations as diverse and far-flung as Nicaragua, the Seychelles, Angola, Mozambique, Ethiopia, and South Yemen, and the presence of Cuban troops in different parts of Africa support this belief. It is said that the Soviet Union is behind most Third World insurrections and may even be co-ordinating and funding an international network of terrorism. World War III has already begun, warns former President Richard Nixon, and the other side may be winning.

Raymond Aron, a French political philosopher, observes that throughout human history those empires and alliances which enjoyed political and military influence abroad invariably had robust economies at home and dynamic international commerce. He notes that for the Soviet Union this is not the case, indeed the reverse may be true. The Soviet economy is in shambles, and the collective gross national product of the Eastern bloc is far less than that of the West; yet Western leaders often seem on the defensive against Soviet strength. Since World War II, 15 more countries have unfurled the banner of the hammer and sickle. Communism covers over a quarter of the earth's surface and dominates a third of the world's population.

Many people believe that Soviet military strength and the expansion of Marxism around the world is due to the complete ruthlessness of the Communist Party. "The dictatorship of the Communist Party is maintained by recourse to every form of violence", Leon Trotsky, Lenin's Commissar of War, once declared. Indeed, despite all its schisms and internal feuding, world communism remains a Soviet phenomenon in one clear respect: all Marxist regimes, from China in the East to Angola in the South and Cuba in the West, seem to maintain their power by a bureaucratic state socialism in which the Communist Party ensures centralised and absolute power. Violence is institutionalised internally by an extensive secret police network, giving rise to such phenomena as the Gulag Archipelago in the USSR and the 'detainment camps' in Poland. Violence is projected externally by a heavily armed and politically motivated Red Army.

The combined spectre of advancing Red Army units with a ruthless Communist Party behind it frightens us all, particularly when we are told that the Soviets are even willing to unleash *nuclear war* to attain their goal of world conquest.

The question we must ask ourselves now is whether this apprehension about Soviet intentions and capabilities is justified by facts. Is it based on objective assessment or is it a misplaced hysteria that is being whipped up by sources within our own countries for purposes that we need to understand?

Robert McNamara denies the assertion that the Soviet Union has grown stronger and has been making gains all over the world.[4] "They have grown weaker", he says. "They have grown weaker because economically and politically there have been some very serious failures ... they are in a weaker position today than they were 14 or 15 years ago". Those who raise the alarm of 'Russian threat' are exaggerating. "We overstate the Soviets' force and we understate ours, and we therefore greatly overstate the imbalance. Moreover, this is not something new. It has been going on for years".

To understand this claim, Mr McNamara suggests that we go back to 1960 when many in the US believed there was a missile gap favouring the Soviets. "With hindsight", he says,

it became clear there wasn't any missile gap. But Kennedy had been told that there was. What actually happened was this: in the summer of 1960, there were two elements in the US intelligence community disagreeing on the relative levels of the US and the Soviet strategic nuclear forces. One element greatly overstated the level of the Soviet nuclear force. When one looked over the data, it didn't justify the conclusion.

And within two years of that time,. the advantage in the US warhead inventory was so great vis-a-vis the Soviets that the Air Force was saying that they felt we had a first-strike capability and could, and should, continue to have one. If the Air Force thought that, imagine what the Soviets thought. And assuming that they thought that, how would you expect them to react? The way they reacted was by substantially expanding their strategic nuclear weapons programme.

Now, when they did that we sat back here and saw the way they were moving—and we always had to take account of their capability more than their intentions, because we were not sure of their intentions—we looked at their capability—and they were building submarines, missiles and planes, and experimenting with new warheads, at such a rate that we had to respond. We probably over-responded because it is likely that their capability, which we observed, exceeded their intentions. So you have an action-reaction phenomenon. And the result is that during the last twenty-five years, and particularly during the last fifteen, there has been a huge build-up, much more than people realise, in the nuclear strength of these two forces. That has changed the nature of the problem and increased the risk greatly. I have read that the inventory of nuclear warheads in the two arsenals is of the order of 50,000.

Mr McNamara ought to know. He was the US Secretary of Defense during that crucial summer of 1960. It was only in the summer of 1982 that he told us what actually happened. But it was not until 1983 that the two main intelligence agencies, the CIA and the Department of Defense began to differ on their respective estimates of Soviet military expenditure. According to CIA figures the Pentagon was overestimating Soviet expenditure by 30%, which had been confirmed a few months earlier by Robert McNamara.

What confuses the issue for many is that there are so many contradictory pieces of information available. The US Department of Defense says that the Soviets spend more on defence than the Americans. The Stockholm International Peace Research Institute maintains that the Americans spend more than the Soviets, although there is rough parity. The British Ministry of Defence asserts the Soviet Union has more troops than NATO. The International Institute on Strategic Studies indicates that NATO forces actually outnumber the forces of the Warsaw Treaty Organisation.

What is to be believed? Who is lying?

There is an old saying that 'figures lie and liars figure'. In no area

"Well, I'm sure the Prime Minister and all those Generals must know more about it than we do ...."

(*Arthur Horner* © *The Guardian*)

is this more true than in trying to discern the truth about the Soviet Union. Yet this is the task of this book, to seek that thread to truth which will help us to discern between the myths and realities of the 'Russian threat'.

We will use the format of answering the numerous questions people have about the Soviet Union. This will allow us to deal specifically with different areas of concern. It is hoped that what emerges is an overall perspective of the Soviet Union as it relates to the West.

2 Know Your Enemy

IS THE SOVIET UNION PREPARING TO START A NUCLEAR WAR?

It was on the fourth day of the nuclear crisis when hundreds of Soviet missiles hit their targets in the United States.

The President died where he was sitting, in the cramped 'Situation Room' beneath the White House, obliterated along with the rest of Washington, D.C. after the blast of a 20 megaton Soviet warhead. Instantaneously, command over the nation's remaining civilian and military resources shifted to his successor. In retaliation a nuclear strike was launched against the Soviet Union. Meanwhile, critical functions of the federal government continued, operating from hundreds of underground locations scattered throughout the United States.

This was the scene in a massive world-wide nuclear war game, code-named 'Ivy League', that was secretly directed from the White House during early March 1982. It was the first complete exercise of the military and civilian command structures and communications systems to be used in all-out nuclear war with the Soviet Union since 1956.

During the last week of February 1982, the 'President' and the 'Vice-President', along with the officials of the game's mock National Security Council, were told that the world situation had seriously deteriorated. The response of both the USA and the USSR to the deepening crisis was to mobilise for war. The Soviet Union launched the first attack, against US forces in Europe, Korea and South-east Asia. The US declared war.

The players in the Situation Room were then told that the Soviets had attacked a US ship in the North Atlantic using tactical nuclear weapons. The Soviets had also fired chemical munitions at US troops in Europe, causing massive casualties.

After studying various options provided by the Joint Chiefs of Staff, the 'President' decided to use tactical nuclear weapons in response to the Soviet chemical attack. He then gave permission for the release of tactical warheads elsewhere, on a case-by-case basis, as the Soviet attacks intensified.

The 'Ivy League' players simulated the use of the 'hot line', the teletype link between the White House and the Kremlin, in an attempt to alleviate the deepening crisis. All these attempts were rebuffed by the Soviet leaders. They escalated the conflict by shooting US satellites out of the sky with their secretly developed 'killer satellites'.

The ultimate moment came late on the fourth day. The North American Air Defense Command reported a major Soviet nuclear missile attack. At that point, 'Ivy League' technicians began switching off major pieces of the US military and civilian communications systems used by the Pentagon and the Federal Emergency Management Agency to simulate the resultant destruction.

'Ivy League' posited a 'worst-case' Soviet nuclear strike of over 5,000 megatons raining down across the United States. This is the equivalent of 425,000 Hiroshima bombs. The game also assumed that the Soviet Union had planned a 'decapitation strike', an effort to destroy Washington and the entire federal command structure.

At that point in the game, with the 'President' dead, authority shifted to the 'Vice-President', who had been dispersed to the National Emergency Airborne Command Post, a specially equipped Boeing 747 known as the 'Doomsday Plane'. Later, authority shifted to each of two Cabinet officers, one in a secret federal facility in Massachusetts and the other at a similar facility in Texas. There, the two men, accompanied by 'core teams' of officials from key government agencies, took command of what little remained of America's resources.

A fourth 'miniature White House' was established in a US embassy in Europe to simulate what might happen if a successor to the President, such as the Secretary of State, was consulting with NATO allies when a nuclear war broke out.

The ground rules of the game called for the President and his successors to use what is called the Single Integrated Operations Plan, developed by the Joint Chiefs of Staff for conducting an all-out nuclear war with the USSR.

'Ivy League' had an all-star cast. Former Secretary of State William Rogers played the President. Former CIA Director and Ambassador to Iran Richard Helms played the Vice-President. Members of the mock National Security Council included former Secretary of the Air Force Thomas Reed; Deputy Secretary of State Walter Stoessel; Under-Secretary of Defense Fred Ikle; and the Staff Director of the office of the Joint Chiefs of Staff James Dalton. Former Hollywood actor, President Ronald Reagan, watched the 'Ivy League' war game. With him were Vice-President George Bush, Secretary of State Alexander Haig, Secretary of Defense

Caspar Weinberger, National Security Adviser William Clark, and other members of the National Security Council.

The purpose of Ivy League? "To make sure the other side is aware we have the capability",[1] said one of the team players. He explained that the exercise was devised to act on the philosophy of President Reagan and other top US officials, that 'protection of key government functions during a crisis is as much of a deterrent to nuclear war as building new strategic nuclear weapons systems'. The President evidently believes that knowing how to *fight* a nuclear war is as good as *preventing* one. He believes this because he is convinced, rightly or wrongly, that the Soviet Union has nuclear superiority over the United States and will attack unless the US demonstrates both the capability and the will to fight back with nuclear weapons.

Many people share the President's conviction. This conviction seems to be supported by the fact that the published writings of several Soviet military officers emphasise nuclear 'war-fighting' rather than 'war-deterring'. NATO and US strategists interpret this to mean that the USSR is aggressively preparing to wage and win a nuclear war against the United States and its NATO allies. The rationale offered is that the Soviet military strategists have not progressed beyond the 19th century German philosopher Karl van Clausewitz's enunciation that "war is the continuation of policy by other means". The late Soviet Marshall V. D. Sokolovosky is often cited. He said in his book *Military Strategy* that "the essential nature of war as a continuation of politics does not change with changing technology and armaments".[2] Several other Soviet writers are said to dismiss as 'idealism' and 'metaphysics' the American notion that nuclear is a qualitatively different mode of war than conventional combat. "As long as the Soviets persist in adhering to the Clausewitzian maxim on the function of war, mutual deterrence does not really exist",[3] says Prof. Richard Pipes of Harvard University. In March 1981, he went so far as to say that war with the Soviet Union was "inevitable" unless the Soviets stopped their aggressive military strategy.[4]

This assessment of Soviet military doctrine indicates a misunderstanding in the West of both Clausewitz and Soviet strategy. It is true that Marxists who study war do so with an ear sympathetic to Clausewitz. Marx, Engels and Lenin were all impressed with his thinking. What is often ignored by the Western analysts who point to Clausewitz in alarm, however, is his central theme:

> Since war is not an act of senseless passion but is controlled by its political objects, the value of this object must determine the

sacrifice to be made for it in magnitude and also in duration. Once the expenditure of effort exceeds the value of the political object, the object must be renounced and peace must follow.[5]

This point is well taken by current Soviet strategists. "That war is a continuation of politics even in the nuclear era is not the same thing as to argue that nuclear war can serve as a practical instrument of policy", writes Soviet Colonel Ye Rybkin. "War is always the continuation of politics, but it cannot always serve as its weapon."[6]

This is an issue of utmost importance. No one in the NATO Alliance has yet suggested a Soviet political objective that would be worth the risk of a US and NATO nuclear retaliation. The US arsenal alone can destroy each of the 229 Soviet cities with over 100,000 people *41 times over*. Could any political goal be worth that risk?

Despite this fact, some NATO and US analysts argue that the Soviets would not mind a nuclear retaliation from the US and/or NATO. T. K. Jones, Deputy Under-Secretary of Defense for Theatre Nuclear Forces, stated in Congressional testimony, "I firmly believe that the present Soviet leadership would have no qualms in risking the loss of 20 million or so of its population . . .".[7] Professor Pipes argues that the Soviets would risk even 30 million dead.[8] After all, he says, they lost a similar percentage of their population during World War II. This is like saying that if one's pocket has been picked once, one would welcome it being picked again. And again.

Apart from the fallacy of this number—it is more likely that *100 to 175 million* Soviets would die in the event of a nuclear war—there are several historical circumstances that need to be considered. First, the Soviet Union entered the Second World War in self-defence against the Nazi invasion; it did not attack first. Second, the Soviets did not estimate the loss of life at 20 million and *then* decide whether fighting the Nazis was worth this 'price'. Third, these deaths were spread over a period of four years while a nuclear war would inflict the same loss of life, and more, within the space of minutes. Fourth, the Soviet Union was able to rescue much of its industrial capacity by transporting it eastward after the Nazi invasion had begun. It would be impossible to do so in the event of a nuclear war. Fifth, it is highly unlikely that any one could do much rebuilding after a nuclear war as the Soviets were able to do after World War II.

Far from thinking a nuclear war to be an acceptable instrument of policy, or that the losses would be worth certain political risks, the Soviets are clear in their writings that nuclear war cannot and must not serve as a means of solving international disputes.

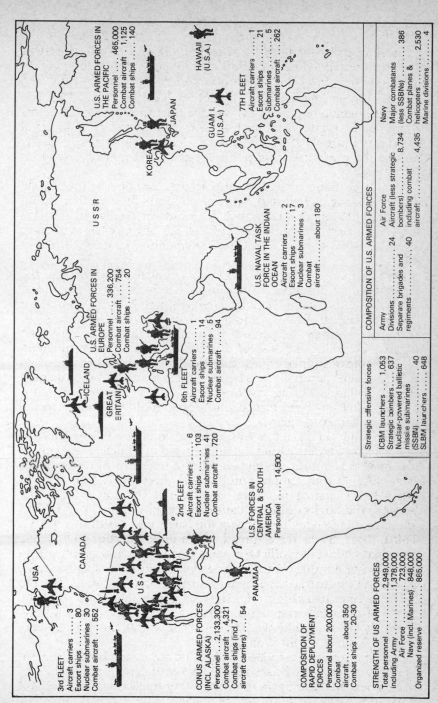

The Soviet estimate of the US Armed Forces (*Source: Whence the Threat to Peace*)

President Leonid Brezhnev said, "The starting of a nuclear missile war would spell inevitable annihilation for the aggressor himself, to say nothing of the vast losses for many other countries perhaps not even formally involved in the war. It would be a tragedy the like of which has not been seen in the history of mankind".[9] Soviets know that just *two* US or British Polaris submarines—each loaded with 160 Poseidon warheads—are capable of obliterating 150 million Soviet citizens, and devastating 75% of the Soviet economy. With nuclear weapons there can be no winners. There can only be annihilation.

The Harvard economist Professor Kenneth Galbraith recently pointed out that in the event of nuclear war, "not even the most passionate ideologue will be able to tell the ashes of capitalism from those of communism for, among other reasons, he too will be dead".[10]

What has caused so much confusion in the West about Soviet intentions is the fact that they see the problem of nuclear weapons in dramatically different ways than we do. Geography is an important element in determining definitions. Hence the terms 'strategic weapons', 'deterrence', and 'theatre war' mean something different to them than they do to us.

Soviet nuclear strategic doctrine began in the aftermath of World War II. The Soviets found themselves the dominating conventional power in Europe, particularly with Hitler defeated, Soviet troops stationed throughout Eastern Europe, and the withdrawal of most of the US troops from Western Europe. With the defeat of Nazi Germany, however, the Soviet Union found itself facing an even more formidable adversary in the United States. The seeds of this conflict were sown even as the two fought together in the United Front against the Nazis. After the war, their grand alliance cracked up as each found itself to be a 'superpower' in a devastated world.

The US, nevertheless, had a substantial advantage over the Soviet Union. It had emerged from the war with its industrial might unblemished and had suffered only half a million casualties. On the other hand, the Soviets had paid a heavy price because of their geographic position, with some twenty million dead and most of their industry destroyed. The US, as a symbol of its technical and strategic superiority, had the monopoly over atomic weapons at the end of the war. The Soviets joined the nuclear club only in 1949.

Moreover, the US quickly developed several alliance structures which virtually encircled the USSR on all sides: the Western Hemisphere Defence Treaty Organization in 1947, establishing US alliances throughout North and South America; the North Atlantic Treaty Organization (NATO) in 1949, allying the US with 12

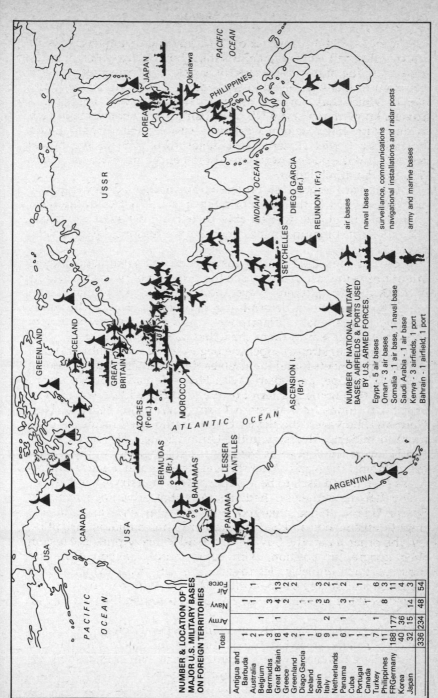

NUMBER & LOCATION OF MAJOR U.S. MILITARY BASES ON FOREIGN TERRITORIES

	Total	Army	Navy	Air Force
Antigua and Barbuda	1			1
Australia	2		1	1
Belgium	1	1		
Bermudas	3		3	
Great Britain	18	1	4	13
Greece	4		2	2
Greenland	2			
Diago Garcia	1		1	
Iceland	6		1	
Spain	6		3	3
Italy	9	2	5	2
Netherlands	1		1	
Panama	6	1	3	2
Cuba	1		1	
Portugal	1			1
Canada	1		1	
Turkey	7	1		6
Philippines	11		8	3
FRGermany	188	177		11
Korea	40	36		4
Japan	32	15	14	3
	336	234	48	54

NUMBER OF NATIONAL MILITARY BASES, AIRFIELDS & PORTS USED BY U.S. ARMED FORCES.

Egypt - 5 air bases
Oman - 3 air bases
Somalia - 1 air base, 1 naval base
Saudi Arabia - 1 air base
Kenya - 3 airfields, 1 port
Bahrain - 1 airfield, 1 port

air bases
naval bases
surveillance, communications
navigational installations and radar posts
army and marine bases

Major U.S. military Bases on Foreign Territories, according to Soviet sources. (*Source:* Whence the Threat to Peace) nations of Western Europe; the Australia-New Zealand-United States Treaty (ANZUS) in 1951; The South-East Asia Treaty Organization (SEATO) in 1954 bringing together Philippines, Thailand, Pakistan, Australia and New Zealand with Britain and France; and the Central Treaty Organization in the Middle East (CENTO) in 1959 linking Turkey, Iraq, Iran, Pakistan and Britain. In a little more than a decade after the Second World War in which the US and USSR had fought as allies, the US surrounded the USSR with 400 major as well as 2,000 auxiliary bases spread around the world.

The 'Cold War' that gripped the world during the late 1940s and 1950s was largely fanned in the East by a growing alarm of US global power. In the West it was fuelled by the depiction of the Soviet Union as ruthlessly seeking to expand the perimeters of its influence. Contrary to popular belief, there was no Soviet or US masterplan for expansion and world domination. The reality was that both the Russians and the Americans were gripped in such mutual suspicions and misunderstandings that they soon divided the world in two, the symbol of which was Winston Churchill's famous image of the 'iron curtain'.

The catalyst for the initial tensions seems to be the determination of the USSR to hold onto the land it had occupied in defeating Germany, thereby securing a vital buffer zone. That the Soviets would retain a 'sphere of influence' between themselves and Germany had been agreed upon during the wartime conferences between Roosevelt, Stalin and Churchill. Stalin believed that "whoever occupies a territory also imposes on it his own social system".[11] When this reality began to emerge in Eastern Europe, divisions began to harden. The West began to perceive Stalin's post-war emphasis on heavy industry and armaments with suspicion. The Truman Doctrine of March 1947 and the Marshall Plan of June 1947, were believed by many to be necessary if communism was to be 'contained'. The Soviet reply was the *Zhdanovshchina* of 1947–8. This period was marked by severity of political purges within the Soviet Union, by militancy in foreign relations, and by the consolidation of Soviet control of Eastern Europe, including the establishment of Cominform, the *coup* in Czechoslovakia, and the Berlin blockade.

It is an open question whether this period was objectively one of militant probing on the part of Stalin or of a feigned bellicosity to hide Soviet weakness in the face of the US monopoly of atomic weapons, or a combination of both. Western leaders interpreted it at the time as militant probing; consequently, they moved towards the formation of NATO, the unification of the zones of occupation in West Germany, and, at the outbreak of the Korean War, the rearming of West Germany.

The decision to rearm West Germany, less than ten years after the Nazi invasion of the Soviet Union, reopened an old wound for the Russians. The Soviet response was to further tighten its control over Eastern Europe, thus bringing the cold war spiral full circle. Whether or not the Soviets intended to invade Western Europe, the Western leaders believed they had sufficient evidence to cause anxiety and therefore to legitimise further military preparations. Conversely, whether or not the US was seeking to 'roll back communism', the Soviets dug into Eastern Europe, quelling the 1953 disturbances in East Germany and Poland and the 1956 revolt in Hungary with heavy handed military reprisals. They formed the Warsaw Treaty Organization in 1955.

Despite the many post-war crises and the fact that Europe was sharply divided into two camps orbiting around hostile superpowers, a strange stability was established. It was a balance characterised by an 'asymmetrical deterrence'. The US had superiority in air and naval power as well as monopoly control of atomic weapons. This was countered by the deployment of Soviet troops in superior numbers in Eastern Europe. For the Soviets, these forces served a direct deterrent role against US global superiority by holding Western Europe 'hostage' in the event of a US attack. As long as the US homeland remained inviolate from Soviet attack this was the only option open to the USSR.

However, once the Soviets successfully concluded their own atomic tests, they began to feel less insecure. What emerged in the 1950s, was the beginning of a multi-layered Soviet strategy. Conventional forces in Eastern Europe were maintained and trained for speed and offensive operations in the belief that a good offense is the best defence. More directly, Soviet security was reinforced with expanded naval protection and air defence systems. Simultaneously, a nuclear deterrent force was developed based on bombers and an intercontinental ballistic missile (ICBM) force, thereby threatening the US heartland directly for the first time in history. These military aspects were supported by a campaign to reduce political tensions by pursuing a policy of peaceful coexistence. The horrors of nuclear war were clearly understood by the leaders in both the Kremlin and the White House. Fears of nuclear proliferation, especially to China and West Germany, gave the Soviets a genuine interest in arms control negotiations.

Between late 1959 and mid 1961, the USSR unilaterally reduced its conventional forces and laid emphasis on its ability to hit the US directly with its intercontinental missiles. With President Kennedy's dramatic expansion of America's nuclear arsenal, however, the Soviets changed their strategy. They embarked on a campaign to establish a deterrent strategy based on *war fighting*. Its

momentum is still with us. This is to be understood in contrast
with the deterrent policy of the US, which is based on the ability
to inflict *unacceptable damage* upon the enemy.

This basic difference in nuclear strategy requires examination, for
it colours the two superpowers' perceptions of the very meaning
of the word 'deterrence'. The fundamental US view, pressed upon
NATO, is that deterrence involves threatening the Soviet Union
with unacceptable damage to its cities and industrial base. In
effect, the US has a deterrence-through-possible-punishment
policy, which consists of letting the Soviet Union know that if it
attacked, the US and NATO will be able to counterattack with such
devastating ferocity that the Soviets will not dare attack in the first
place. The classic formulation of US deterrence doctrine was the
Eisenhower policy of Mutual Assured Destruction known by its
appropriate acronym MAD.

Under President Kennedy, US nuclear strategy began to change.
By the end of President Johnson's administration it had been
modified to include the notion of 'flexible response'. While
ultimately holding a MAD scenario over the Soviets, US strategy
sought to emphasise the 'certainty of uncertainty' of response,
thereby giving the President a variety of options over military and
civilian targets rather than the stark options of surrender or global
holocaust.

This strategy was taken to its logical conclusion by Carter's
Presidential Directive 59, issued in 1980. Now official US policy
enunciates the twin notions of *'limited'* nuclear war and
'counterforce'—the attacking of selected targets in particular
'theatres' of war such as Europe or the Middle East. Moreover,
because of the size, sophistication and accuracy of US nuclear
warheads, American planners now threaten the Soviets with
unacceptable damage in an unanswerable *first strike*. In his
National Security Decision Document 16, President Reagan gives
official sanction to not only waging nuclear war but *fighting to win*.

While the Americans have a deterrence based on possible
punishment, the USSR has a deterrence based on denial. By
'deterrence-through-denial' the Soviets seek to convince the US
that it cannot carry out an attack against the USSR with impunity.
The US, it is hoped, would be deterred by the knowledge that no
military advantage will be gained by striking first. The Americans
can be so convinced only as long as the Soviets can limit any
American inflicted damage. Moreover, by their visible capacity to
paralyse the US, at least partially, the Soviets hope to keep the US
at bay. A deterrence-through-denial strategy, therefore, clearly requires a *war fighting* nuclear strategy, one that can simultaneously
provide adequate measures for one's own protection as well as to
destroy the military force of the enemy.

These two notions of deterrence reflect the respective historical experiences of the Americans and the Russians. The Americans are surrounded by two vast oceans and have traditionally had to rely on an effective naval power to secure markets, keep trade lines open, and deploy troops to theatres of war. Since 1945, the US Air Force has joined the navy in projecting US military might abroad. Besides the geographic immunity the Pacific and Atlantic oceans have provided, the single most important fact that colours US military perceptions is that the US has not had hostile foreign troops on its soil since 1812. For over a century and a half it has fought its wars by attacking the enemy in the enemy's heartland; inflicting crippling blows on the enemy; and then withdrawing across the two oceans that protect it. It is easy to understand, therefore, how the Americans would see their nuclear arsenal as a way to inflict a crippling blow on their enemy in a lightning first strike.

Now, what about the Russians? What is necessary to produce a strategic doctrine of deterrence-through-denial? Two things: first, a sense of vulnerability chiselled by history; and second, a belief that the enemies of the Soviet Union are out to destroy it.

Even a brief overview of Russian history reveals a sobering experience of isolation, encirclement, and repeated invasions, all of which have produced in the Russian consciousness a sense of that vulnerability to attack. The Mongol tribes conquered them in the 13th century and kept them in subjugation for 250 years. Since then they have been both invading and being invaded in conflicts with the Swedes, the Lithuanians, the Poles, the Germans, the French, the Turks, the Persians, the Japanese and the Chinese. Since the Mongol period, the most celebrated invasions of Russia have been by Napoleon in 1812, who burned Moscow to the ground, and by the Nazis from 1941 to 1945, who devastated most of the USSR west of the Ural Mountains and drew it into a war that caused the deaths of 20 million Soviet citizens. These experiences have engrained in the Russian psyche not only a fear of invasion but an *expectation* of it. They have been repeatedly attacked, conquered and exploited. They have a heightened sense of vulnerability to military onslaughts. Consequently, they are naturally predisposed to think in terms of frustrating, negating, or pre-empting enemy attacks. Their expansion has been invariably characterised as 'defensive', the result of trying to put as much land as possible between themselves and their enemies—real or imagined. The Russians are compelled to use land as the Americans use the oceans.

These feelings of mistrust and suspicion grew to fears bordering on panic with the Bolshevik seizure of power in 1917. The Soviets were the first country in the world to experiment with socialist economy. They believed and hoped socialism would spread throughout Europe, indeed throughout the world. They soon found themselves to be an island in an ocean of capitalist states actively hostile to what they were trying to achieve. Beginning in May 1918, the new state was subjected to intervention and invasion numerous times as foreign powers such as the USA, Britain, France, Germany, Poland, Turkey and Japan tried to take advantage of the chaotic situation Russia was caught in. That period is known in Soviet history as the Wars of Intervention (see p. 190–199).

Soviet people have been inculcated with the belief that the Western 'imperialists' are inherently hostile toward socialism; that they will continually seek to 'reverse the course of history' the Bolsheviks set in motion with their 'Great October Revolution'; and consequently, that the danger of war will persist as long as the differing social systems exist. "History teaches us that while imperialism exists, the danger of new aggressive war remains,"[12] is a phrase Brezhnev liked to repeat often. Lt. General Zhilin puts the matter in even stronger terms: "So long as imperialism and armed adventurism exist," he says, "they will inevitably, if only by virtue of their own momentum, unleash armed actions...."[13]

In addition to the threat of capitalism and imperialism in general, Soviet leaders also believe that the West has isolated the USSR as 'enemy number one' to be destroyed at all costs. This belief is coupled with the Marxist-Leninist assertion that the Western imperialists will not be restrained from war by either moral or political considerations. Indeed, they will be *compelled* to go to war as the crisis of capitalism deepens. In these circumstances, it is not surprising that the Soviets have little faith in a deterrent policy based on mutual assured destruction or threatened punishment. The only effective way they see for deterring the West from going to war to destroy the USSR is by having such an effective war fighting capability known to the West that it will conclude the futility of achieving any goal by military means.

This doctrine has resulted in not only massive military expenditure on the part of the Soviet Union but also in an emphasis on large numbers of troops and hardware. They seem to entertain the belief that the *more* military power they have the *better prepared* they will be against the war they believe the West seeks to wage against them. Like the Czarist governments before them, the Soviet government has 'over-insured' in military affairs. As former CIA Chief William Colby testified before the Senate Foreign Relations Committee:

> You will find a concern, even a paranoia, over their own security. You will find the determination that they shall never again

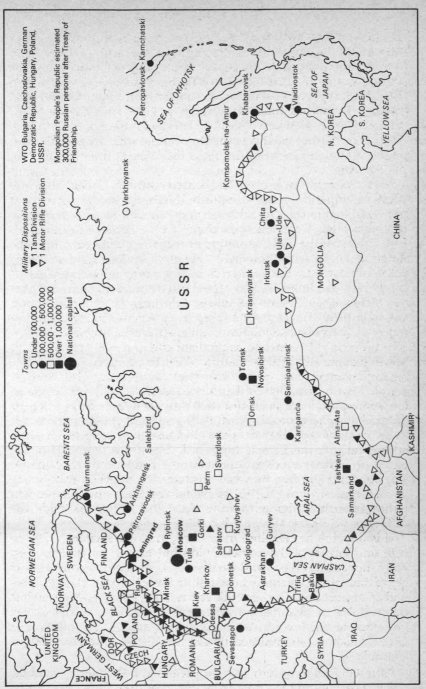

Deployment of Soviet military might, according to Western sources.

be invaded and put through the kind of turmoil that they had been under (with) many invasions ... they ... want to *overprotect* themselves to make certain that that does not happen, and they are less concerned about the image that that presents to their neighbors, thinking that their motives are really defensive and pure and therefore other people should not be suspicious of them.[14]

What needs to be pointed out, however, is that over-insurance is not a uniquely Soviet attribute. It is inherent amongst all the major powers of the world, particularly in nuclear matters. Until the late 1960s, the United States held tenaciously to the doctrine of nuclear superiority and even though it was clear that just two Polaris submarines, each with their 160 Poseidon warheads, could inflict more than unacceptable damage to the USSR, it went on to build a fleet of *dozens*. Britain, too, over-insures. Not content with having Polaris-class submarines, which it claims are becoming 'outdated', it seeks to acquire a fleet of Trident submarines. Each one is capable of unleashing not a 'mere' 160 nuclear warheads like the 'old' Polarises, but *408*. Each warhead is 39 times more powerful than the Hiroshima bomb, giving each Trident the explosive power of 10,506 Hiroshimas. And Britain wants at least four, possibly five, of these 'insurance policies'.

Over-insurance is the inevitable outcome of strategic planning based on 'worst case' scenarios, such as 'Ivy League'. It has brought about a situation in which the world's stockpile of nuclear weapons equals more than 2,000,000 times the destructive force of the Hiroshima bomb. And yet the USA and the USSR continue to spend over $100,000,000 *per day* to 'upgrade' their arsenals. During the same 24 hours, the President's Commission on Hunger estimates, 50,000 people in other parts of the world either starve to death or die of hunger-related diseases. This means that in the year 1982 alone, while the governments of the world spent $600 billion arming themselves, approximately 18,250,000 people died of hunger.

It is this over-insurance mentality as well which keeps 25 million men and women permanently under arms, 45 million in paramilitary and reserve units, a number exceeding the combined work force of the European Economic Community. Finally, this 'over-insurance' profits the 30 or more governments in the business of selling arms to countries either insuring or over-insuring themselves. Selling of arms totals £25–35 billion a year and is the most influential and profitable business in the world.

Therefore, when people in the West see the Soviet Union over-insuring, they should pause and wonder how their own over-insurance is affecting the Soviet Union. This they seldom do. The walls we have built between East and West prevent us from seeing much further than our own borders, if at all.

Edward Crankshaw, in his book *Khrushchev's Russia*, emphasises this point:

> One of our difficulties when it comes to understanding foreign countries is that we think of them almost exclusively in terms of foreign policy, whereas they are thinking of themselves much more in terms of domestic policy. It means, for example, that the Soviet Union is seen by us always in relation to our problems and hardly at all in relation to its own. To hear people talk, to read the Western newspapers, one would think that the Soviet Government devotes nine-tenths of its energies and ingenuity to making trouble for us, whereas in fact it is spending most of its time in trying to make the Soviet Union work.[15]

With this in mind, it is easier to come to terms with and choose between the two opposing views on the significance of Soviet strategy for the West. The first view refuses to accept the historic and geographic differences between the Soviet and US strategies. It stresses the importance of accepting the Soviet war fighting capabilities in purely offensive terms. Such a line of thought assumes the worst about Soviet capabilities and intentions and argues the American and NATO response accordingly. Seeing any Soviet build-up in terms of how it threatens the West, or *could* threaten the West, this view generally concludes that only further US and NATO military build-ups will deter the Soviets from going to war. Such is the mentality of those who designed and 'fought' the 'Ivy League' war game.

But another view is possible. It maintains that the Soviet nuclear weapons programme is not driven by a doctrinal imperative to wage nuclear war. Rather, the Soviets have basically been trying first to catch up and then keep abreast with US and NATO nuclear capability in a manner consistent with the Russian experience of history. Essentially, their nuclear programme is motivated by such factors as programme momentums, bureaucratic policies, technical breakthroughs, and perceptions of 'enemy' intentions. These factors by and large, shape the defence policies of all modern industrial powers, including the United States. They, like us, are locked in a state of paranoia that only seems to be eased if there is enough 'over-insurance' to cover the worst conceivable scenario.

While the first line of thought can only lead to more tensions, more over-insurance, and probably, in the end, to annihilation, the second one need not. Rather, it urges that the Soviet strategy be seen and understood as the way the Soviets ensure stability. Such a view accepts Soviet intentions and capabilities as being primarily defensive. Their war-fighting doctrine needs to be assessed realistically and not as a justification for increased Western armament.

Were we to show our readiness to understand their problems and indicate our willingness to negotiate sincerely for disarmament, it is likely they would respond in equal measure. If we were to be wrong, our current over-insurance would more than give us the capacity to deter any attack.

WHY IS THE USSR IN EASTERN EUROPE?

Soviet troops are stationed along the Chinese border and, since 1979, in Afghanistan, but it is primarily towards Europe that the Soviets direct their concern. Since a large part of the Soviet Union is in Europe, and the rest is a continuation of the same land mass, high priority directed towards Europe is understandable, especially when it is noted that the most devastating invasions of the Soviet Union originated in Europe. Today NATO exists. It was formed in 1949 at the US initiative. It brought Western Europeans (initially Belgium, France, Holland, Italy and Britain) into an explicitly anti-Soviet alliance with the United States.

On 5 May 1955, West Germany was also made a member of NATO. The Soviet Union reacted quickly to the rearming of Germany so soon after the war, and, within a fortnight, signed an "Agreement on Friendship, Co-ordination and Mutual Assistance" with Albania, Bulgaria, Czechoslovakia, East Germany, Hungary, Poland and Romania. The term 'Warsaw Treaty Organisation' (WTO) was soon adopted as the name of the new alliance and it became the primary focus of the Soviet military forces in Europe.

By the middle of 1956, these countries had also signed separate bilateral treaties with the USSR. Yet their alliance has been a fragile one. Romania showed signs of being reluctant to be dominated by the Soviet Union and during 1958, just a year after signing a treaty with the Soviets, allowed the agreement to lapse. Soviet forces were withdrawn in June 1958, although Romania did not leave the Pact. Albania expelled all Soviet forces in 1961. Czechoslovakia did not sign an agreement with Moscow allowing Soviet troops on Czech soil until October 1968, two months after the Soviet invasion. Since then, Soviet soldiers have never left Czechoslovakia. The Albanians left the WTO in September 1968 in protest over Soviet actions in Czechoslovakia. With time, however, the WTO has taken on a life of its own and despite its fragility, seems durable enough to continue indefinitely.

Although it is commonly claimed that the Soviet Union and the Warsaw Pact countries are preparing to attack the NATO Alliance at the first opportunity, the facts do not support this view. The primary function of the WTO is not to prepare for war with NATO but to deny to Eastern Europe exclusive control over its military and politcal structures. The WTO is the mechanism through which the USSR ensures continued imperial control over its European 'allies'. The USSR justifies this system as being necessary to defend Eastern Europe against NATO, just as the US justifies NATO for defence against the WTO. But this is clearly a secondary consideration. Even a cursory look at the map of Europe indicates that it is largely divided between two 'spheres of influence'. The one dominated by the Soviet Union; the other by the United States.

Dr Christopher Jones of the Harvard Russian Research Center has pointed to three ways through which the Soviets have used the institutional mechanism of the Warsaw Pact to maintain hegemony: 1) through the Eastern European military officers who sit on party committees, politburos, etc.; 2) through the defence industry agencies which play a key role in integrating the Soviet and East European countries; and 3) through the military agencies which have become involved in the efforts to integrate the scientific, technical and educational activities of the Soviet and Eastern European nations.[1]

Jones offers two important clarifications about these observations: first, that the system of control testifies as much to its cohesion as to its diversity, i.e. the primary purpose of the WTO is to resist centrifugal forces within the Pact rather that to integrate WTO into a multinational fighting force capable of attacking NATO; and second, Romania stands outside the system. Although nominally a member of the Pact, Romania neither participates in the Warsaw Pact manoeuvres nor allows Soviet troops on its soil.

The WTO staff is the most important agency in the Pact. It plans and evaluates the training programmes and joint military exercises of the Pact and maintains direct links with the militaries of the member countries. Thus a military doctrine is standardised which emphasises speed, offensive operations and the use of nuclear weapons. This standardisation has had the effect envisaged by the Soviet Union, i.e. subordinating the national Defence Ministries under the central Pact infrastructure, and depriving the individual member countries of the doctrinal and military capability of waging a defensive war under its own exclusively national command. The result is that no Warsaw Pact state except Romania has a doctrine that can serve as the basis for national resistance to a WTO or Soviet military intervention. This has been made painfully clear by events in Hungary in 1956 and Czechoslovakia in 1968. WTO doctrine specifically states that Pact officers and troops should be

ready for the defence of socialism in each WTO country, whether
from external or internal enemies.

This doctrine was offered as justification for the quelling of riots
in East Berlin in 1953 and the crushing of the Hungarian rebellion
in 1956. It is also the essence of the Brezhnev Doctrine, proclaimed
to justify the invasion of Czechoslovakia.

In contrast, Romanian military doctrine emphasises massive
guerilla resistance by both regular and paramilitary units.
Romanian doctrine does not even mention participation with or
assistance of WTO forces. Moreover, Romanian doctrine provides
for the acquisition of weaponry from outside the WTO countries.

Besides integrating military doctrine, a WTO agency also co-
ordinates officer training and plays a major role in officer promotions. The system has three levels, the highest of which is the
Voroshilov General Staff Academy in Moscow. Voroshilov has
secured a virtual monopoly on the training of WTO officers destined for senior positions. The course is four years long and to
complete it, an East European officer must pass the same state
examination as required of Soviet officers. Every WTO country
with the exception of Romania has officers in training at
Voroshilov. So pervasive is Voroshilov's influence that of the
fifteen top posts in the WTO forces, thirteen are currently held by
Voroshilov graduates.

The second level consists of post graduate academies for mid-
career officers. Excluding Romania, there are 9 such academies in
the Pact countries: there are 24 in the USSR, 13 of which are
attended by East Europeans. Degrees from the Soviet academies
are much more valuable than degrees from the East European
ones. Promotions seem to come faster and admittance into
Voroshilov is easier. The Soviet academies also offer courses not
offered in East Europe, particularly in military communications,
the study of transport and logistics and chemical warfare
techniques.

The third level of officer training consists of the undergraduate
military schools. Almost all East European military officers are
trained in their own countries but their schools co-ordinate their
curricula with their Soviet counterparts and exchange both faculty
and textbooks.

Besides integrating doctrine and co-ordinating training, the
WTO also links the political administrations of the member states,
except for Romania. In every WTO military unit and institution,
political administrations have agencies. These agencies serve the
purpose of disseminating the official political line and to gather
information on the politcal reliability of both officers and troops.

For all joint military exercises, joint political directorates are formed.

Perhaps the single most important way in which the USSR dominates the Warsaw Pact countries is through the joint military training programmes and exercises. If one merely examines the numbers of weapons, the troop levels and the battlefield tactics of the WTO it would be easy to conclude that the WTO is preparing

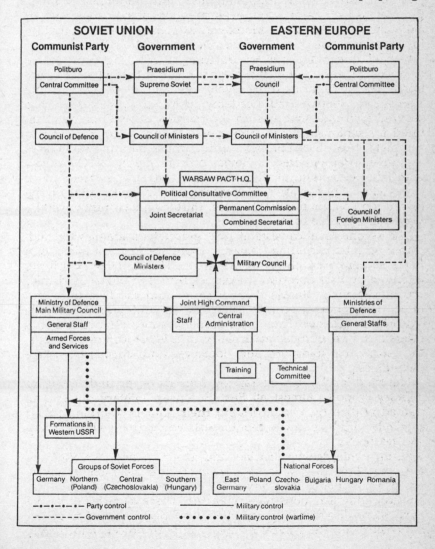

to attack the West. But if one examines the military exercises the WTO troops actually engage in, they seem to be designed much more for maintaining Soviet domination.

WTO exercises last up to two weeks and have two phases. The first phase generally consists of rapid and offensive military actions, frequently with the simulated use of nuclear weapons. The second phase consists of a series of 'friendship meetings' between the participating forces midst the fanfare of multi-lingual speeches, political orations and field publications. The military units visit cultural and historical sites, joint concerts and sporting events, farms, factories and villages. The military and political phases alternate with one another during the exercises.

In terms of actual command, the Soviets have exclusive control over the nuclear arsenal of the WTO. They also control most technical aspects of the exercises: air defence, naval and air force manoeuvres and communications and logistics. However, the overall commanders of the joint exercises are generally East European. Their operational staffs tend to be multinational. At the troop level, WTO forces are organised so that Soviet units work side by side with their East European counterparts.

The joint exercises of the WTO ensure that no individual military develops an independent capability, particularly a defensive one. They also ensure that both Soviet and other Eastern European forces practice frequent, rapid and offensive operations into each other's countries, including Bulgaria, where Soviet troops are not permanently based. The political administrations continually emphasise the importance of defending the Pact against internal and external enemies. Through these exercises, large numbers of Soviet troops moving in and out of individual countries has become a familiar sight and publicly acceptable. The Soviet presence is made more legitimate by assigning important roles to East European officers and troops in the exercises themselves. Finally, these joint exercises allow the WTO General Staff to evaluate and pass judgement on the careers of individual officers as well as upon the fighting capabilities of the respective countries. This fact has become obvious to even NATO military experts. Colonel Jonathan Alford, for instance, who is Deputy Director of the International Institute of Strategic Studies, wrote in the June 1980 issue of *NATO Review* that

> Frightening though the twenty ready divisions of the Group of Soviet forces in Germany may appear to us, I find it hard to believe that such a force would appear to them to be anything like sufficient to secure Western Europe or even West Germany ... On the other hand it is clearly enough to strike out at the West if the West appeared to be preparing for war ... When one

adds the continuing Soviet need to subjugate the countries of Eastern Europe by force in order to stifle dissent, the rationale for Soviet Forces is sufficiently defined and its size and shape adequately explained.

It is important to understand that the Soviet Union has enforced an oppressive system upon Eastern Europe, not a progressive one. The successful empires in history, particularly those of Rome and Britain, brought not only technology to the peoples they conquered but also a period of peace. The *Pax Romana* lasted for centuries. Within this peace, the freedom of many individuals was enhanced. The Soviet Union, on the contrary, installed a totalitarian system upon nations which before the Second World War had experimented with democracy. Moreover, they were nations who for the most part were traditionally hostile to Russia. The Soviet Union was technologically more backward than they were. Thus, in trade, the Soviet Union has found itself in the position of furnishing Eastern Europe with raw materials in exchange for manufactured goods, rather than the opposite.

Since the primary purpose of the WTO is to consolidate Soviet hegemony over Eastern Europe rather than to prepare for an invasion of the NATO Alliance, the presence of US and British forces in Central Europe performs the vital role of justifying WTO activities to the Eastern European countries. To hold WTO together the Soviets need a large US and British commitment to NATO. The current build-up of the NATO forces will not 'deter' a Soviet attack any more than the attack is already deterred. It may well reinforce Soviet domination; it may facilitate the continued Soviet effort to incorporate the military hierarchies of Eastern Europe into a more rigid Soviet military system; and it may contribute to the further build-up of WTO forces, exerting greater pressure—not on NATO—but on Romania and Poland.

This is an important point to note. The feud between 'the US and the SU' imperils the Eastern Europeans most, particularly those seeking greater ties with the West and/or increased internal liberalisation. For all its limitations, the Helsinki Agreement of 1975 did establish a whole network of human interchanges, technical agreements and cultural understandings that would have been unthinkable in the 1950s and 1960s. The result was that the economies of East and West Europe became increasingly complementary. This revealed to people on both sides the degree of superpower domination and indicated a possible way of lessening it.

A pan-European economic community would be more powerful than either the US or the USSR. Both superpowers realise this fact. They know that with economic growth will come political integration. Both fear a United Europe. From the US and Soviet perspective, two superpowers in one world are already one too many.

What emerges from an examination of the WTO is that it is neither completely under Soviet control nor intent on invading the West. The East European countries, as fearful of NATO as NATO is of them, are so primarily because of combined Soviet and US insistence. Left on their own, they would forge greater cooperation than is currently being allowed by either superpower. The West Germans, for instance, negotiated with the Soviets to build a natural gas pipeline that would bring 1.5 trillion cubic feet of gas annually from Siberia to Western Europe. Potential customers besides West Germany include Britain, Austria, Italy, Belgium, Switzerland, Spain, Holland and Sweden. The US opposed the deal. It argued that it will create 'excessive' dependence on Soviet supplies—West Germany would eventually import 6% of its energy from the USSR. Although the countries involved pointed out that so massive an undertaking contributes to a long-term understanding between East and West that could only improve relations, and although US corporations are trying to get into the deal, a senior American diplomat in Brussels complained to a West German: 'we have our wagons in a circle and are fighting the indians while you sell them firewater'.[2] It is interesting to note that while President Reagan embargoed some of the American technology necessary for this pipeline deal, he lifted the grain embargo imposed by President Carter after the Soviet intervention in Afghanistan. The US, while counselling the Western Europeans against trade with the Soviet Union, is itself exchanging hundreds of millions of tons of grains for Soviet gold. The message is quite clear. Do as I say. Not as I do.

What is important to bear in mind here is that even as the USSR has used the Warsaw Pact to maintain political and military control over Eastern Europe, so the US has used NATO for the same purpose. From 1948 when the US deployed strategic bombers in Britain and then decided to maintain a military presence in West Germany, NATO has served to perpetuate the US military occupation of Western Europe. So flagrant were the US intentions that Charles de Gaulle withdrew France from the military wing of NATO in 1967, declaring flatly that France was not willing to become 'America's Algeria'.

The US has maintained hegemony primarily through a monopoly control over the NATO nuclear stockpile and the presence of 250,000 US troops in Europe as well as by its massive technical assistance to the individual NATO militaries. Exercising this control has not been easy nor without its tensions. When the

US first proposed in 1954 that US 'tactical' nuclear weapons be deployed in Europe, the NATO members were reluctant. Aquiescence was obtained by whipping up the 'Soviet threat' to the necessary level of hysteria. NATO has always been reluctant to accept the American strategic doctrine as well. In 1967, when NATO finally approved the flexible-response doctrine, the precursor to the present doctrine of 'limited' nuclear war and first strike, the NATO members demanded that they be given greater influence over the use of the weapons deployed on their soil. The only concession the US would make was to permit the establishment of the NATO Nuclear Planning Group, which would allow for joint consultations on targeting of the weapons. The US retained exclusive control and possession of the warheads themselves. In the case of the Cruise and Pershing II missiles, while Britain, West Germany, Holland, Belgium and Italy have some say on where they might be deployed, the missiles themselves will remain under US control. They can be shot only at US command.

US control over the nuclear weapons stockpile gives it leadership in NATO. Thus NATO unity is based on the supremacy of its superpower. This unity is made tolerable because of the political indoctrination that accompanies the US military presence. Even as the presence of US troops and the NATO alliance offers to the USSR the 'foreign threat' necessary to keep the WTO in line, so the 'Soviet threat' is constantly used to justify, continue and increase US domination.

West Germany is the most firmly controlled NATO member, perhaps because it is 'closest' to the 'Russian threat'. The US domination of Britain, however, is also pervasive and so deeply entrenched as to have become a part of the British way of life. It is commonly referred to as 'the special relationship'.

Although the US forces left Britain early in 1946, they returned in July 1948. The US deployed several squadrons of B-29 bombers in Britain for a 30-day stay. Then the stay was extended to 60 days. In November 1948, the Air Ministry discreetly informed the Americans that their 'temporary' stay might become 'long-term'. Since then, the US presence has grown to include over 100 known bases over the length and breadth of Britain, staffed by nearly 40,000 Americans, with dependents resident in the United Kingdom.

The British public has never been consulted about this US presence, nor has the Government been honest about it even to Members of Parliament. In June 1980, for instance, Bob Cryer MP asked Defence Secretary Francis Pym for a 'total' list of US bases. Pym said there were about a dozen—eleven air bases and one submarine base. Pym also acknowledged that there were a 'few' other bases for 'storage, logistic support, administration and communication'. When pressed about a month later, Pym was forced to acknowledge that there were not 12 but 53 US bases in Britain—and still the list was incomplete. Finally in August, when asked to list any bases he might have 'overlooked', Pym came up with three more, bringing the official total to 56. In fact there were 150 known bases at the relevant time.

The US presence in Britain includes 21 air bases, 9 transportation facilities, 17 weapons storage and dump sites, 38 communication centres and 10 intelligence bases. The majority of these are for use in the global strategy of the US as much as for the defence of Western Europe. Many Royal Air Force (RAF) bases are designated and stocked for US use in crises or war. But not one of the 150 US bases is directly committed to the defence of Britain. Britain is committed by NATO agreement to provide the 'area' defences for US bases on its soil. Yet while the bases are ostensibly for NATO 'protection' the US maintains separate lines of command and control to operate on its own when US interests require. Alert orders to US bases are not necessarily communicated to the host country. During the 1973 Middle East war alert, for example, British bases and facilities were used but neither Britain nor NATO were notified. The same thing happened during the attempt to rescue the hostages in Iran in the summer of 1980.

This is all part of America's 'global options' strategy. US bases

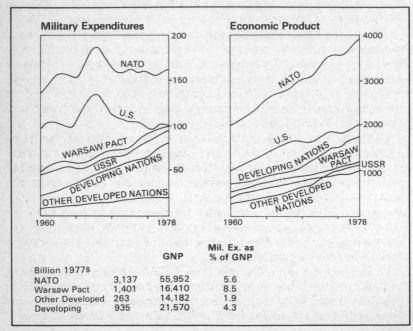

	GNP	Mil. Ex. as % of GNP
Billion 1977$		
NATO	3,137	55,952	5.6
Warsaw Pact	1,401	16,410	8.5
Other Developed	263	14,182	1.9
Developing	935	21,570	4.3

The Distribution of Power and Resources (Figures are in US $ billion)
(World Milit. & Soc. Expand. 1980)

are in NATO to protect members against the 'Russian threat'. They also protect American interests elsewhere. Therefore, unquestioned non-interference with what the US does with its bases and facilities—even though they are in a NATO country—is expected. In most cases, it is given.

Britain has acquiesced to US control almost enthusiastically, particularly since Mrs Thatcher became Prime Minister. The result is that Britain has become something akin to an advance aircraft carrier for the Pentagon. The largest American underwater surveillance station anywhere in the world is located at Brawdy, on St David's Bay, in southwest Wales. It is the largest of the 22 stations in the US Sonar Surveillance System network and is indispensable for any US first strike capability. However, both the US Navy and the Ministry of Defence claim the Brawdy base is an 'oceanographic research facility'.

During the Falklands crisis of May 1982, the US allowed Britain access to many of its facilities. British intelligence had access to the Fleet Ocean Surveillance Information Centre (FOSIC), operated by the US Navy from Grosvenor Square, London. FOSIC analyses data from all US intelligence sources covering the Atlantic ocean. It shares the information with the NATO and Royal Navy centre in Northwood, Middlesex. British Intelligence was also given access to the US Navy's Ocean Surveillance Satellites (OSUS). These satellites fly at a height of 600 miles and orbit the earth every 104 minutes. They use radar and infrared photography to detect ships and also monitor radio and radar signals from ships. One of the stations controlling these satellites is located at Edzell, near Dundee, Scotland. Two other US bases in Britain, Thurso in northern Scotland and Croughton, near Banbury, provide links with the US Defence Satellite Communications System which, in turn, provided reserve communications to the Royal Navy task force surrounding the Falklands.

The US also keeps a massive arsenal of nuclear weapons scattered throughout Britain. The largest concentration of nuclear weapons in Europe is at Mildenhall, near Cambridge. Another main depot is at Welford, where a railroad siding takes the weapons into underground caverns. Because Welford's facilities are so sensitive, British Ordnance Survey maps have helped the Americans camouflage their intentions by erasing everything but the ground contours. The irony is that this erasure only serves to make the area more noticeable.

Welford is the base for the USAF 7234 Ammunition Support Squadron, which has stored nuclear weapons there since 1954. It provides over 700,000 square feet for storage of nuclear weapons. Despite this, it is omitted from public lists of US bases in Britain.

"Pym's Dozen"; American Bases in Britain. This map includes those bases known in October 1980. Up to June 1983 at least a further 53 have come to light. Are there any more in the dark? (©: *The New Statesman*)

US spy planes are also permanently based in Britain. Their presence, of course, is denied. The main spy base is Mildenhall, where secret reconnaissance aircraft are stationed. In 1980, during filming on the base by Thames TV, US officials denied that US spy planes were stationed there. Soon after, the TV crews filmed one landing and being parked in a special hangar.

So important is Britain to US military strategy and preparedness that it stations its 'flying war rooms' here. In times of crisis or war the European Command is to be lifted above the battlefields in specially designed Boeing 707 EC 135s. Called 'Silk Purse', these planes are on continuous alert and are stationed at Mildenhall.

Ignored in all this is the reality that US bases in Britain drastically increase Britain's vulnerability, particularly in a nuclear confrontation. In the Ministry of Defence's war game exercise, Operation Square Leg in 1980, for an anticipated nuclear attack on Britain, 13 of the attacks were on US bases. In fact, the first two sites the Ministry of Defence expected to be attacked were US bases at Greenham Common, where the US plans to begin deployment of its cruise missiles in 1983, and Boscombe Down, where the US has a major intelligence gathering base.

Even Britain's 'independent' deterrent is dependent on the United States. Beginning as early as 1958, the British arsenal was developed only in conjunction with agreements for the large-scale transfer of US technology to Britain. Important V-bomber bases such as Waddington, Marham, Scampton and Wittering have relied largely upon US owned nuclear weapons. In fact, the inner guards at the British nuclear Special Storage areas are US Air Force personnel. Assembled weapons can only be removed with US authorisation, and in many cases the weapons remain under US guard even when aboard British ships and planes.

The RAF nuclear weapons in West Germany remained under US control until well in to the 1970s, and the nuclear weapons of the British Army on the Rhine are still under US control. The 'custodial units' protecting the weapons have explicit orders to shoot any non-American NATO personnel who attempt to assemble a nuclear weapon without US authorisation.

In Britain itself, much of the nuclear weaponry is NATO and US controlled, particularly the nuclear-armed surface-to-air missiles, and the hundreds of air-dropped bombs to be used from Britain and West Germany in the event of a Soviet attack on NATO.

The bombs over which Britain does retain some control have required massive reliance on US technology. The warheads for use in Polaris and Trident submarines, for example, were tested under US supervision in the US Testing Sites in Nevada. They are merely adaptations of US designs.

So integral is Britain's nuclear arsenal to the US nuclear strategy that Britain has been designated as a key ally in which US first-strike weapons are to be deployed. This can be seen with particular clarity in the US decision to sell the Trident II nuclear submarine system to Britain.

The Trident is so deadly that it was described by the *Fiscal Year 1980 Arms Control Impact Statement* President Carter submitted to Congress in the following manner:

> The addition of highly accurate Trident–II missiles with higher yield warheads would give US SLBM (submarine launched ballistic missile) forces a substantial time-urgent hard-target-kill capability for a first strike .... The countersilo capability of a (deleted) KT Trident–II missile would exceed that of all currently deployed US ballistic missiles. Moreover, the additional effects of two potential advances (Trident–II and MX) in US countersilo capabilities by the early 1990s could put a large portion of Soviet fixed ICBM silos at risk. This could have significant destabilizing effects ....[3]

For what on earth could Britain want 4 Trident submarines capable of launching over 1600 first strike nuclear warheads?

While the answer to this question may elude many, the Reagan administration made a unique offer to Britain as an inducement to buy the Trident D-5 missile system. The plan was for British firms to be given the 'chance' to build parts for the missiles, for those that will be used by Britain as well as the hundreds that will be used by the American navy. The Americans offered the British the best nuclear weapons deal they have ever had for a system that would be easily their most lethal. They were offered a system that could obliterate every major city in the Northern Hemisphere, and for this destructive capability Britain could take 21 years to pay.

The British Minister of Armed Forces, Peter Blaker, was jubilant about Reagan's 'bargain'. The Trident system, he said sweetly, would now only cost each man, woman and child in Britain about the price of one chocolate bar per week till 1997. Moreover, the cost of Trident would not hit Britain's conventional forces. "Over the next 15 years we are paying for it, Trident will cost about three pence in every pound spent on defence", he told a youth seminar in London on 5 March 1982. This was enough "to ensure that today's teenagers collect their pensions in the next century after a lifetime of peace".[4]

What a deal.

Although no direct strings were attached, one of the Americans privy to the deal said that "the attitude of the administraiton, and even more that of Congress, is conditioned by the way the UK acts

Airstrip One (© *Richard Willson*)

in the wider defence interest of the alliance and the US".[5] Britain would agree, for example, to continue the patrolling of the Gulf of Oman it has maintained since the start of the Iran-Iraq war in 1981. Britain would also be expected to supply larger quantities of British-made plutonium to the US. On 12 March 1982, the Thatcher Government approved the Trident–II system purchase package.

US arrogance in Europe and British compliance with it are such that in the event of war, the US and Britain are even prepared to invade Sweden, a neutral country. In the event of a war, attack plans call for British based bombers to fly north of Denmark and then low over Sweden to bomb Soviet targets. The reason for this is that US and British war plans anticipate that any war would see intense air and land conflict in Central Europe. By flying north over Sweden the planes would stay out of Soviet and Warsaw Pact airspace for the longest possible period.

Although this is a violation of Sweden's neutrality, Britain and US expect Sweden to 'turn a blind eye'. The Defence Attache at the Swedish Embassy in London, Rear Admiral Rolf Rheborg, categorically asserts that, "Swedish policy will be to prevent anybody passing through our air space. It doesn't matter whether the intruders come from east or west . . . . The Air Force will do its best to shoot them down".[6]

The aircraft the Swedes would be shooting down would include British Vulcans and Buccaneers and US F1–11s and B52s. Sweden possesses a large force of interceptor aircraft and a modern sophisticated air defence system. Although specific defence plans and exercises are kept secret, Rear Admiral Rheborg states that "all borders and all possible invasions" have been provided for.

In case ideological and geopolitical competitions spill over into armed conflict, either in East or West Europe, each superpower will endeavour to expand its vassal states first. Europe thus stands to be the first casualty, particularly in a nuclear conflict, unless Europe can wrest independence from the two conflicting imperiums. Moreover, concurrent with a concern for eliminating the *threat* of nuclear war, must be a concern for converting the *mentality* that demands the existence of nuclear weapons. Indeed, it can be said that nuclear weapons have left the conflict patterns behind, like the sorcerer who has lost control of the monster he had fashioned. The nuclear weapon is a technology out of control which is no longer serving the interests of the superpowers but undermining the very security it is supposed to provide. Yet both sides are forced to interlock with the nuclear arms race because both are obsessed with the anxiety that the other side might outpace them with a 'final' weapon. It is this fear that motivates the domination of their respective sphere of influence in Europe.

This mentality could be ignored so long as military technology was equally primitive. As Einstein pointed out, however, in splitting the atom we changed everything in the world—except our mode of thinking. Thus we drift towards 'unparalleled catastrophe'. We have maintained a primitive mentality based on territoriality, aggression and competition. Yet we have developed weapons which are capable of destroying only in totality. Not having the mentality to recognise that unless we live in peaceful inter-dependence we will all perish, we have permitted the superpowers to carve up Europe—and indeed the world—as well as to create such a balance of terror that annihilation to all life within minutes has come within our reach.

As the potential battleground, Europe has the greatest stake in developing the mentality necessary to prevent an 'overkill' situation. The two superpowers seem incapable of developing a new mentality on their own. Their SALT agreements have only resulted in more arms.

Only if a country can rise above the ideological and geopolitical rivalries that have divided Europe can it perform the catalytic role of peacemaker. Romania offers a possibility. It is a member of the Warsaw Pact but it refuses to allow either Soviet troops or Warsaw Pact manoeuvres on its soil. It remains socialist but trades and exchanges with both the American and Soviet blocs. It also has a credible non-nuclear defence doctrine and military capability. Because of this, Romania has been able to provide a peacemaking role. It was a catalyst for Nixon's first visit to China and for Egyptian President Sadat's historic journey to Jerusalem. Respected by both sides, Romanian diplomats have been able to act as arbiters and catalysts in situations which otherwise would have degenerated into further conflict.

Romania has put forward proposals for European security and arms control at both the Belgrade Conference on Cooperation in Europe and the United Nations Special Session on Disarmament in 1979. The proposals call for reducing the military presence of both the US and USSR in Europe. They also call for greater freedom within WTO and the reduction of Warsaw Pact pressure on Romania. These proposals have been endorsed by Yugoslavia, Austria and Switzerland, i.e. by both Communist and non-Communist states. Why have not Britain, West Germany or Italy endorsed them?

A plural Europe, a nuclear-free Europe would have as a common denominator a desire to survive and a will to experience sovereign freedom from imperial control. Each part must know that it can only survive if the other part does. European survival is dependent on Europe being free.

A call for a free and plural Europe would have several dimensions. First, it would be a call for a continuation of detente between the superpowers rather than the renewal of cold war tensions. Diplomatic negotiations rather than military confrontation is to be stressed as essential for superpower conduct. Secondly, a plural and nuclear free Europe would not be against either superpower nor against the ideological loyalties each superpower requires. Rather, Europe can provide the catalytic presence *between* the superpowers essential to supply that element of peace they themselves are currently unable to generate. Particularly since the decision to deploy the Cruise missiles and the enunciation of the doctrine of 'limited' nuclear war, Europe is faced with the question of survival. It must become a *catalyst* between the superpowers or be a probable *nuclear battleground* between them. Thirdly, and perhaps most importantly, Europe must realise that its survival depends not only on being free of the divisive effects of the superpowers but also in being free from nuclear weapons.

Although a plural and nuclear free Europe could be the catalyst for ensuring human survival and for generating the momentum necessary for disarmament, it is a vision far from completion. Neither superpower wants either a genuine reduction in tensions or the real independence of its European allies. This can be seen with particular clarity in the recent events in Poland.

WHAT ABOUT POLAND?

Joseph Stalin once remarked that bringing Communism to Poland was "like trying to saddle a cow". He would have known. In 1938, he ordered the Polish Party leaders to Moscow for 'consultations'. After 'consultations', he executed the whole lot.

In 1944 a communism agreeable to Stalin finally came to Poland on the backs of Soviet tanks, as the Soviet Army was pushing the defeated Nazis out of the Soviet Union, across Poland, and back into Germany. The 'liberation' of Poland cost the Soviets over 600,000 dead—more than the US lost during the entire war on all fronts. The Soviet military went on from Poland to 'liberate' Romania, Bulgaria, Yugoslavia, Hungary, Czechoslovakia and the eastern part of Germany. Stalin 'liberated' them by imposing a socialist economy. He met with varying degrees of success.

Because Poland was of such strategic importance to the Soviet Union, lying as it does squarely between the Soviet Union and Germany, Stalin was particularly determined to ensure that it became an integral part of the buffer zone the Soviets felt they needed on their Western frontier. In Moscow, on 21 April 1945, the two countries signed a treaty of friendship, mutual assistance, and post-war cooperation. This occurred before the war was over.

The war left Poland the most badly damaged nation in Europe. One out of every four people had been killed. Its industry had been almost completely wiped out. Its capital city of Warsaw, on Hitler's orders, had been levelled to the ground. But the tragedy was not over. The ensuing struggle for control of the country between the Stalinist backed parties and forces wanting to install a Western-style representative democracy left a further 2 million dead. The presence of Soviet troops dictated the outcome: the Polish United Workers Party (PUWP) emerged victorious. As its signpost, it adopted both the theory and practice of Stalinism. At the National Unification Congress in 1948, it declared that the basis for the 'New Poland' would be a 'dictatorship of the proletariat in the form of a people's democracy'. In practice, this meant the Party's total monopoly of power', according to Artur Starewicz, former secretary to the PUWP and for seven years Polish ambassador to the Court of St James's.[1]

The restrictions placed on the 'reactionary' forces, says Starewicz, at the time probably essential if communism was to succeed in Poland, were extended to the whole of society. The monopoly control of the Polish United Workers Party embraced all areas of life: from politics and economics, to the administration and control of propaganda, art, culture, education and scientific research. At one stage, the Party even tried to subordinate the hierarchy of the Roman Catholic church, a battle it quickly realised was untenable. The church provided a unique alternative to an atheistic Marxist regime in a nation of rebellious and romantic anti-Russian catholics. Going to mass became not only a religious act but a quiet sign of rebellion against the State. Considering that over 75% of the 36 million Poles are practising catholics, this made the church a major bastion the Communist Party has never been able to move.

Outside the Church, however, Party control was complete. It made the taking of decisions of all kinds, both important and unimportant, its sole preserve, thus paralysing any initiative from other organs of government, trade unions, cooperative organisa-tions, or voluntary associations. "In the nature of things," says Starewicz, "all these social and representative bodies became mere window dressing. Their role was reduced to rubber-stamping what had already been decided elsewhere." All decisions and policies, he adds, were "reinforced by far-reaching intervention by the security forces".[2]

From the beginning, Stalinism in Poland, just like back in the

USSR, violated all criteria of merit. What was produced was not quality or creativity but conformism on a mass scale. Non-party members, however distinguished, were left out in the cold, the result of the 'negative selection' process the system bred and encouraged.

Monopoly control gave rise to centralism—in the state, in the economy and in the Party. But it was not a democratic centralism. Rather, the very stucture of the Party and the way it functioned resembled an upside-down pyramid. It was not the base—the rank and file—that gave shape to the higher levels, but the tip—the ruling few—which dictated the shape of the base. Even the tip itself was subject to centralisation of power. At the apex stood Moscow.

Thus in Poland, again like in the USSR, where Stalinism had even firmer control, the ruling group chose those they considered 'appropriate' to sit on the Central Committee; and the Central Committee selected, with the aid of the Party apparatus, the delegates deemed 'suitable' for the Congress. Neither meetings of the Central Committee nor meetings of the highest legislative bodies of the land provided an opportunity for discussion of policy. They were usually called only to gain formal acceptance of decisions already made 'higher up'. They served only to demonstrate superficial unanimity and loyalty to the leadership. The countless speeches, broadcast throughout the land, were neither here nor there. Real differences of opinion were left on the doorstep. The overall style of Stalinism in Poland, as elsewhere, was one of commands issued under the facade of unity.

It is in this system of exercising power that we can find the major reasons for a loss of a sense of reality, the isolation of the leadership from the society, and the main source for the degeneration and deformation of socialism that Stalinism represents.

Nevertheless, this monopolist version of the leading role of the Party survived all the political crises and turnabouts of three decades. There were periods of democratisation and criticism voiced from the highest platforms, of course, but with irresistible force monopolist centralism maintained power, both in the Soviet Union and in the Eastern bloc. In Poland, however, it was destined for a head-on collision with economic reality and rising social discontent.

In 1956, Polish workers rioted to protest against food shortages. In 1968, Polish intellectuals protested against Party censorship and other abridgements of human rights. In 1970, price rises again touched off worker revolt, only this time the government responded with such ferocity that dozens were killed.

In the wake of the 1970 riots, Edward Gierek replaced Wladyslaw

Gomulka as Party leader. Gierek promised dramatic increases in the Polish standard of living, primarily through a massive influx of foreign investment. In the process he destroyed the Polish economy.

Gierek's decision to borrow heavily abroad to finance an expansion of heavy industry was based on an optimistic assumption that new factories, using the best equipment and techniques, would produce goods that would quickly repay the loan. In all, Gierek imported about $10 billion in capital goods and then proceeded to waste them in textbook cases of how not to run an economy.

He sank nearly $1 billion into developing and producing a light tractor at a gigantic new Ursus tractor plant near Warsaw. Unfortunately, it turned out that the company was not licensed to sell its products to the West and they were too expensive to be sold in the East. Even in Poland most farm equipment did not fit the tractor. The result: instead of an expected yearly output of 75,000 tractors, the firm produced 5,000.

Gierek also made a deal with the RCA Corporation and the Corning Glass Works of the United States to build a new colour television factory designed to produce 600,000 sets by 1981. However, due to mismanagement and a shortage of parts, only 50,000 were produced that year. Like a heart transplant in which the system rejects the foreign body, Gierek's Western bought factories simply did not work.

Meanwhile, to keep the people happy, Gierek allowed wages to increase by 40% between 1970 and 1975, compared with a 17% increase between 1960 and 1969. Moreover, he quadrupled imports of grain and fodder, thus allowing the consumption of meat to jump from 132 pounds per person in 1970 to 154 pounds per person in 1980.

This artificial prosperity was sustained by an absurd pricing system. The state paid farmers 10 zlotys for a litre of milk and then sold it for 4 zlotys. Live hogs were bought from farmers at 130 zlotys per kilogram and then sold as butchered pork at 70 zlotys per kilogram. Farmers bought bread and fed it to their livestock because it was cheaper than the wheat it was made of. Towards the end of his rule, Gierek was spending one-third of the Polish national budget on price subsidies.

When the Arab nations raised the price of oil in 1973–74, things came apart. Poland's exports, instead of continuing to rise as planned, began to decline. But rather than re-evaluating and changing policy, Gierek simply began to borrow more to keep going. Poland's foreign debt rose from $4.8 billion in 1974 to $25.5 billion in 1981. This money was owed to 15 Western governments

and 501 Western banks. Just servicing and repaying the loan consumed all of Poland's hard currency export earnings, estimated at
$6.5 billion for 1981. Poland had to run merely to stand still.

When Poland was forced to reduce its borrowing, spare parts
began to run out at its new factories. Things started to go from bad
to worse until by 1981, Polish industry was only running at 60%
capacity. To make matters even worse, poor harvests from 1974 to
1980 devastated Polish agriculture, which Gierek had ignored
anyway in favour of heavy industry.

When Gierek decided to raise prices to ameliorate the situation
in 1976, there were major riots in Radom and at the Ursus tractor
factory. Gierek responded to these with brutal repression
reminiscent of 1970. This time, however, the repression of the riots
led not to another period of resigned apathy but to the formation
of the Committee for Social Self Defence (KOR), which for the first
time linked dissident intellectuals like Jack Kuron with the workers
who later founded Solidarity. Inspired by KOR activists, small
independent trade unions began to sprout in various parts of the
country even though that was illegal. Lech Walesa joined one of
these unions and was arrested.

Dissident intellectuals and workers were joined by Catholic
thinkers and supported by the Catholic hierarchy. In Krakow,
Cardinal Wojtyla emerged as a strong advocate of human rights
and an independent intellectual life. In 1974, the Polish
Communist Party ideologue Andrezej Werblan called the Cardinal
"the only real ideological threat in Poland".[3] Werblan's judgement was given dramatic affirmation in 1978 when Cardinal
Wojtyla became Pope John Paul II.

The Pope's visits to Poland, in 1979 and 1983, have crystallised
the people's resentment against the rulers and strengthened their
resolve. From the moment he knelt to kiss the ground at Warsaw
airport he was wildly cheered by millions of Poles. And although
he never criticised the regime directly, he did not have to. His
meaning was plain enough. "The exclusion of Christ from the
history of man is an act against man", he told an enormous out-
door gathering in Warsaw.[4] With that thinly veiled allusion to an
atheistic government, a deafening roar of approval filled the huge
city square. "The Polish people broke the barrier of fear that day,"
a Polish bishop later recalled. "They were hurling a challenge at
their Marxist rulers."[5]

The spark that ignited Solidarity's "self-limiting revolution" as
Jack Kuron described it, was a government decree that raised the
price of meat in June 1980. Polish workers had been learning from
mistakes made in 1970 and 1976. This time, workers occupied
factories, particularly the Lenin shipyard at Gdansk. Here Lech

Walesa, an unemployed electrician who had been fired eight months earlier for trying to organise an independent trade union took charge. He headed the interfactory strike committee that eventually became the bargaining representative for most of the 500,000 workers, from the Baltic Sea to the coal-mining fields of Silesia, who had joined the strike.

Led by Walesa, the committee set forth a bold series of demands, including the right to form free trade unions and the right to strike. This was something unheard of in Communist countries, and at first the government refused even to discuss the issue. With the rebellion quickly spreading, however, the government was faced with either negotiating or unleashing a massive blood bath. It chose to negotiate. Meeting across a wooden table in the shipyard's conference hall in August 1980, Walesa and his fellow strikers consistently out-manoeuvred the government team.

Meanwhile, the Lenin shipyard became the centre of an extraordinary national movement. Emblazoned with flowers, red and white Polish flags, and portraits of Pope John Paul II, the plant's heavy iron gates came to symbolise that heady mixture of faith, courage and hope that sustained the workers through their defiance of a regime which heretofore had tolerated no dissent, let alone strikes. The world watched, wondering how long the Soviets would let such a demonstration of defiance continue before they sent their tanks in. But Walesa and his fellow strikers stood their ground, and like soldiers before battle made confession and received communion from priests in the open shipyard.

Their firmness and patience won the day. The government finally gave in to virtually all their demands: the right to form free unions; the right to strike; reduced censorship; and access to the state controlled television and radio networks for the unions and the church. At the nationally televised ceremony, where strikers and government representatives alike stood side by side and sang the Polish national anthem, Walesa signed what became known as the Gdansk Agreement with a giant souvenir pen bearing the likeness of John Paul II.

Workers across Poland rushed to join the new union—Solidarity. Soon Walesa and the other ex-strike leaders found themselves at the head of a labour federation of ten million, 90% of the Polish workforce. Over 900,000 Polish Communists left the Party after August 1980, reducing its strength to 2.5 million, only 7% of the country's population. Of the remaining 2.5 million, over a million joined Solidarity without resigning from the Party. The Party was on the verge of collapse. Stanislav Kania, who had replaced Gierek as Party leader in September 1980, did the most sensible thing under the circumstances: he adopted the workers' slogan of

ODONOWA (renewal) in the hope of controlling the new union from the top and limiting its scope. At the same time he cooperated with Solidarity to avoid a possible disastrous confrontation.

After thirty-five years of Stalinism, the challenge of bringing freedom to Poland was an awesome and complicated one. There was an insatiable drive for democracy in Solidarity by a rank and file with no practical experience. Most of the Solidarity activists were young and simultaneously bitter and exuberant: bitter over the Party's economic bankruptcy and moral corruption and exuberant over their new-found strength. As time went on, more and more people who had in one way or another been crushed or maltreated by the regime used Solidarity as a forum to vent their frustration and call for radical reformulation of not just the economy but the government itself. These currents grew stronger as the months went by and the government did not demonstrate the moral will necessary to eradicate the causes of the crisis. Decades of blatant propaganda, ruthless leadership and economic failures had discredited the authorities in the eyes of the public. With a Party shrunken by defections to Solidarity, the majority who were left were die-hard Stalinists and careerists who had fallen into a state of near paralysis. They were unwilling to give in to the demands being made and yet were powerless to assert Party control over the restless masses. "If the government had actually produced a golden egg," gibed Kuron, "people would say it was not golden; second, that it was not an egg; and third that the government had stolen it."[6]

All the while, the leaders of the Kremlin watched with growing concern. Solidarity's very existence was incompatible with the Communist Party's insistence on power monopoly. Moreover, the drive for democracy Solidarity had unleashed had infected the Polish Communist Party, seriously eroding the Leninist and Stalinist doctrine of centralised Party discipline. Finally, Poland's deteriorating economic crisis put a strain on the whole socialist community which was interlocked in COMECON, the East European equivalent to the Common Market. Fearing that this 'Polish disease' might spread to other East European nations, possibly even the Ukraine, the Soviet leaders wanted a return to 'normalcy' at almost any cost.

Emotionally, the Soviets must have wanted to invade Poland on numerous occasions. But they realised the diplomatic and economic consequences could be disastrous. They were embroiled in the results of one invasion already, in Afghanistan. To invade Poland, steeped in a history of anti-Russian feelings and now united in opposing what Stalin had forced on them after the war, would mean a civil war at worst, a bloodbath at the very least.

Such a scenario would further deteriorate already bad relations with the US and Europe; it would antagonise the Third World; and it would put on Soviet shoulders the burden of Poland's bankrupt economy. Therefore, short of invading, the Kremlin exerted all the pressure it could. Kania was summoned to Moscow and lectured at least three times, the East Germans closed their border with Poland for a while, and a constant barrage of propaganda was aimed at the Polish nation from its Warsaw Pact allies denouncing Solidarity and calling for re-establishment of Party control.

In June 1981, the Soviet Central Committee sent Kania a letter that criticised the Polish Communists by name. "We are disturbed by the fact that the offensive by antisocialist enemy forces in Poland threatens the interest of our entire commonwealth and the security of its borders—yes, our common security", the letter read.[7] In early July, Soviet Foreign Minister Andrei Gromyko came to Warsaw himself with yet another admonition against any liberalising tendencies within the Party.

Nevertheless, the influence of Solidarity was too steeped, and at the Party Congress in late July 1981, Party reformers proved strong enough to purge the Central Committee of most of the hard-liners. Only five of the top officials were re-elected, a General Wojciech Jaruzelski among them. Control stayed in the hands of Kania and those trying to hold a moderate line. They allowed an amount of freedom in Poland considered unthinkable even after the Gdansk accords had been signed.

Perhaps the greatest accomplishment of Solidarity was that for the first time since the war it was possible for Poles to speak their minds. Solidarity's national weekly *Solidarnosc* ran a two-part expose on the privileges of the top Party officials that would have shocked the most tolerant censor in any other Communist country. Moreover, a liberal passport law was passed, allowing Poles unprecedented freedom to travel. Many Poles left the country and did not return. Some 33,000 fled to Austria alone. Most of them were enticed to South Africa.

As battles for freedom were being won, the war for bread was being lost. The economic situation continued to deteriorate. Lines in front of stores would begin to form before dawn. Outside food stores the queues would often stretch for fifty metres or more. Waiting for petrol took up to eight or nine hours. Even after all the wait, there was often nothing left to buy, especially meat. Soap was in such short supply that a doctor complained in a weekly newspaper that physicians were unable to wash properly. New mothers were discharged from hospital as soon as possible for fear their babies might contact infection if they stayed longer. Indeed, because of their poor diet, the long waits in the cold, the scarcity of medical and other hygienic supplies, and the anxiety resulting from such deprivation, the Polish people began suffering from an epidemic of viruses.

As the value of currency plummeted, Poles bought almost anything they could find. A barter system began to operate and urban dwellers began travelling to the countryside to obtain goods directly from the farmers.

Something had to give. On 18 October 1981, Kania was ousted and General Jaruzelski, who had been made Premier in February, was elevated to the party leadership. He was thus the head of the Party, the government and the army. In doing this, the Poles violated another cardinal rule of Communist dogma, that civilians must always control the military. But this time the Soviets did not react in dismay. Jaruzelski was a man they could trust. He had been trained by the Soviets and had fought in the Red Army in World War II. As Defence Minister, he controlled the only disciplined and organised institution left in the country—the army.

Jaruzelski appealed for national unity, inviting Solidarity and the church to join with the Party in a 'front of national accord' that would cooperate on economic recovery. On 4 November Jaruzelski met with Walesa and Archbishop Jozef Glemp to begin the process. But the idea did not produce encouraging results. The government insisted that Solidarity support its plan to raise prices but it refused to give the union any concrete guarantees that its rights would be respected. Moreover, the regime refused to consider the types of economic reforms that the Solidarity leaders felt were essential for the recovery of Poland's economy. This basically involved the demand that the government give up its policy of *nomenklatura*, whereby the government chose plant managers not for their skills but for their party loyalty. Solidarity wanted a system of self-management that would allow workers' councils to participate in the selection of managers and in the making of other decisions. Jaruzelski stalled on any agreement, apparently hoping that the worsening economic situation would erode public support for Solidarity and split the union. He even began to talk about going back on the Gdansk accords and curbing the right to strike. This obdurance on the part of the government served to strengthen the radicals within the union, weaken Walesa's moderate position, and hasten the final confrontation.

As the unity talks stalled, a remarkable event occurred which showed the degree to which the monolithic centralism of the Communist Party had eroded. Jaruzelski decided to put more pressure on Solidarity by asking parliament to approve a bill banning strikes during declared emergencies. The parliament refused—stark proof that the Stalinist pyramid had collapsed.

With the economic situation still worsening, Solidarity still remaining defiant, the authority of the Party disintegrating, and the Soviets pressing him to take 'constructive' action, Jaruzelski turned to his soldiers. With army units held in reserve, he used riot police to break up a sit-in of students demanding academic reform at the Fire Fighters' Academy in Warsaw. Then he broadcast on the radio tapes, secretly obtained, of Walesa warning a Solidarity meeting that "the confrontation is unavoidable and will take place". For the first time, Walesa was singled out for public criticism. The army newspaper called him "a great liar and provocateur" who was leading a group of "madmen" striving for "anarchy and chaos".

On 12 December 1981 Solidarity radicals finally gave Jaruzelski the excuse he needed to do what he had been planning. From the start, both the Polish government and the Soviet Union had made it clear that they would not tolerate a challenge to the right of the Communist Party to rule Poland nor any loosening of ties with the USSR. This is exactly what the Radicals voted to do in their last meeting in Gdansk. Overruling pleas from Walesa, they called for a national referendum on the future of the Communist govern-ment in Poland and a re-examination of Poland's military alliance with the Soviet Union. The meeting adjourned at twenty minutes past midnight on 13 December 1981.

By 3.00 am Walesa and most of the union leaders had been arrested and army vehicles were out in force all over Poland. At 6.00 am Jaruzelski announced on the radio that martial law had been imposed. Later he went on television in full military uni-form with the white Polish eagle prominently displayed behind him. The "growing aggressiveness" of Solidarity "extremists" had forced him to take repressive measures "with a broken heart, with bitterness", he told the nation.

The crackdown was harsh. Military authorities rounded up thousands of Solidarity members, dissidents, intellectuals, and some 30 former government officials, including ex-Party Leader Gierek. Tanks encircled factories and mines where Solidarity members had retreated. Soldiers and police forcibly ejected any who resisted, leaving scores dead and hundreds injured. It was clear that Jaruzelski realised his coup could only succeed if he established once again what Stalin had taught the Polish Communist Party, that resistance to the regime was not only futile but also fatal.

But once again the authorities misjudged the people's determination. Walesa managed to smuggle out a directive to all Solidarity members not interned in camps to engage in passive resistance. This took the form of work slow downs, absenteeism, and a general lack of cooperation with the new military authorities. Political dismissals at factories were questioned, intellectuals turned in their party cards, people banded together and refused to sign loyalty oaths, and artists and performers refused to cooperate with the state owned radio and television. It was as if the Polish people were living out the words inscribed on the tomb of their national hero, Marshal Pilsudski: "To be defeated and not surrender, that is victory".

Even the Poles interned in the detention centres—estimated by church authorities at 15,000—managed to organise resistance. Imprisoned activists set up political seminars and study groups to work out plans for rebuilding Poland's independent labour movement, when and if martial law is lifted. The military reacted by sending the most outspoken activists to other camps, but that just offered them new opportunities to organise.

A daily account of a Polish regional strike committee of the first days of martial law was smuggled out to the West. The following are extracts of the Committee's newspaper, "From Day to Day":[8]

> Issue No. 18 (January 15/16): On January 13, a Mass requested by the regional strike committee was celebrated by three priests at Wroclaw Cathedral .... One of the priests delivered a homily about Herod and his atrocities .... Herod's people, he said, have gone through Poland, armed with pistols, seizing from their homes the nation's best sons .... A collection was taken up for families of internees. The baskets overflowed.
>
> ... On January 5 at 10.10 pm a ZOMO (riot police) patrol stopped a tram just before the last stop and beat all the passengers without first checking identity papers or night (curfew) passes.
>
> ... On January 10 at 10.15 pm ZOMO stopped a man in the street and asked for his papers. When he tried to take them from his pocket, he was hit on the back of the head and on the eye with a truncheon. An ambulance took him to hospital.
>
> ... ZOMO people then visited him in hospital and examined him. One of them said: 'Oh, there's hardly any blood. He can't have been beaten properly.' The beaten man had been on his way to work and had a pass. He will probably lose the sight of one eye.
>
> ... On Poznanska Street two soldiers and a ZOMO were disarmed by the people of Wroclaw. They set the soldiers free but the ZOMO man was beaten up.
>
> Issue No. 20 (January 20/21): Pafawag (railway works) was 'pacified' on December 16. This is what happened: at a meeting at noon most of us vote for strike action. At 1 pm we hear tanks

approaching. A ZOMO column arrives on the bridge. Some of the intelligentsia leave the plant after the first appeal to 'citizen workers'. Others of the intelligentsia stay on with the workers.

Barbara Litwiniuk (perhaps a Solidarity activist) has a chance to escape but decides to share the plight of the others and stays. She sings and the workers join in the national anthem, drowning out the voice of the ZOMO officer with the loud-hailer. The production floor vibrates as ZOMO attack in a wedge, grabbing Barbara and threatening the workers. Voices call out: 'Peace, peace'. The national anthem is sung again—never before has it come so much from the heart. A ZOMO officer threatens to use force. There is silence. We are made to return to our respective sections . . . . We cannot believe what is happening.

. . . On December 30, Franciszek Tyszko was returning home from the grocery shop where he is manager on Ruska Street. It appeared that he had had a drink. In front of his own door, he was stopped by a ZOMO patrol and beaten up . . . . He was taken to a drying-out clinic where he was hit twice in the stomach. This burst his intestines.

After many days of great pain he died on January 9 in the Railway Hospital. His family have been warned not to disclose the cause of death.

. . . In primary schools, the militia and the security service question the children—even those in first grade.

Issue No. 21 (January 22/23): Roman Skawinski, lecturer in political and social sciences at the medical school (and a party member), was attacked after appearing before a 'verification committee'. On January 12 he was asked to declare his loyalty to the Party. He replied: 'In order to agree to this loyalty oath I would have to place myself on the side of betrayal, atrocity, falsehood and deprivation.'

Issue No. 22 (January 28): On January 27, ZOMO and the secret police 'pacified' the Municipal Transport Service's three largest depots—on Tromwajowa Street, Slowianska Street and Grabiszynska Street (where Solidarity's Lower Silesian section had been formed). They searched all vehicles and offices. It is not hard to guess they were hunting (Wladyslaw) Frasyniuk (a Solidarity leader). They consoled themselves by removing seven rolls of printing paper. They are tilting at windmills.

. . . Medical personnel who tried to help the miners (at Wujek mine) were beaten by police. The report of the Department of Health in Katowice says: 'During the action in the mines, intervention of the police affected medical personnel who helped injured miners. Five ambulance drivers and four nurses were beaten. Personnel were dragged from the ambulances even though they wore white uniforms. Injuries were inflicted.

'From one ambulance an injured miner was dragged out and was seen being carried to the river ... ZOMO and doctors fought each other for injured miners. ZOMO wanted to kill them .... Ambulances managed to evacuate only seven dead.'

Issue No. 25 (February 24): Fadroma (construction machinery) plant—workers pretend to work. They tell military personnel: 'We are too hungry, we have no energy.'

... At Bialoleka internment camp, the prisoners decorated a snowman to resemble General Jaruzelski, with dark glasses, epaulettes, etc. (The Polish word, *balwan*, can mean both 'snowman' and 'retarded person'). The camp commandant noticed the resemblance and shouted: 'this is Jaruzelski!'

The internees said: 'No, no, it's a snowman!'

'I say it's Jaruzelski!'

'Not so. It's a snowman.'

The commandant then went into his office and consulted someone. He re-emerged, demanding that the snowman be demolished.

The internees cried: 'But this is Jaruzelski!'

'No, no, it's a snowman,' the commandant said and threatened them all with solitary confinement and other sanctions.

One of the internees then approached the snowman, agreed that it was indeed Jaruzelski, removed the cap and epaulettes and with a swift blow chopped off the head.

General Jaruzelski, nevertheless, is well and continues to be in control. He does not think that conditions in Poland are right for lifting the martial law, at least for the moment. He is simultaneously premier of the government, first secretary of the Communist Party, Chairman of the Military Council for National Salvation, and Minister of Defence. Not since Stalin has a single individual in the Soviet bloc combined so many positions into one.

Second to Jaruzelski is Lt. General Florian Siwicki, the Vice-Minister of Defence and a major figure in the Military Council. Siwicki was the commander of the Polish forces during the Warsaw Pact invasion of Czechoslovakia in 1968. The rest of the 21-man military council share backgrounds similar to Jaruzelski and Siwicki: they are between 56 and 60 years old, were trained at Soviet staff colleges, joined the Soviet trained Polish army during World War II, and participated in the liquidation of anti-Communist partisans inside Poland between 1946 and 1948. Another distinguishing feature is that many of them occupied political positions within the military, such as chief political officers at staff training colleges. They are nothing if not politically reliable. Moreover, most of them became senior officers under Gierek. Gierek appointed Jaruzelski and he appointed them. Almost everyone of significance today owes his political career to Jaruzelski.

This has meant the eclipse of the Polish United Workers Party. Several members of the party's Central Committee did not even know about the imposition of martial law until they heard about it on the radio. Civilian politicians were presented with the military takeover as an accomplished fact. Moreover, widespread dismissals and reshuffles of civilian and party personnel were ordered by the military as the party formulas of political dialogue had to give way to the military directive of defending the existing order by enforced measures.

The military coup in Poland also had a dramatic impact on the West, demonstrating with considerable force the inability of the NATO alliance to respond effectively. Indeed, so slow was the American response that for the first time, former Secretary of State Henry Kissinger publicly attacked the Reagan administration. "It took four weeks after martial law was declared," he said, "before the foreign ministers of NATO managed to assemble in council to consider a 'response'." Meanwhile,

> Thousands of Solidarity leaders were shivering in concentration camps; scores of intellectuals had been arrested; strikes had been broken; freedom-loving Poles who looked West saw dithering procrastination, sophisticated justifications for impotence, or rhetoric incapable of rising to serious action. And when the ministers at last met, the alliance expressed regret about Soviet complicity but then responded with a non sequitor—that action should be postponed . . . .

> These arguments reflect an odd coalition of extremist views between those who want to do nothing and those who argue that unless one does everything it is better to do nothing. In a deeper sense, we face a conceptual breakdown. Once the Polish Army was unleashed, it should have been clear that Solidarity, as it had developed, would be crushed unless a decisive reaction by the West imposed the need for a reconsideration.

> All the time-wasting indecision—all the threats of action unless conditions eased—missed the two principal points. First, time was on the Soviet side. The longer martial law lasted, the more likely was the collapse of resistance; conditions would ease visibly because opposition had been smashed. Second, the only chance of saving anything would have been a Western reaction so immediate, so clear, so beyond rhetoric, so strong— and at the same time leaving open a road for negotiation—as to

have given some pause to the Soviet Union and raised some
thought of compromise. The prospects for this were admittedly
slim; but even these prospects vanished completely when the
West carefully rehearsed reasons why nothing should be done
and so tacitly, if unintentionally, colluded with the martial
law.[9]

While Kissinger's charge must be taken seriously, it seems more
accurate to say that NATO did little about Poland simply because
it could find nothing credible to do. As matters presently stand,
NATO has little influence upon what the Soviets do, or cause to
be done, in that zone of Europe given over to their influence by the
Yalta Conference in 1945.

NATO is designed and committed to defending the West, not
the East. The countries actively being threatened by the USSR are
its 'friends' not its enemies. NATO and the US, whatever sanctions they may impose, are marginal to what is happening.

Nevertheless, certain things have changed. Something significant has happened since the last time the Soviets caused one of
its allies to be invaded. The suppression of the Czechoslovakian
'spring' in 1968 seemed to demonstrate the permanence of the
division between East and West in Europe and thus to prove,
however paradoxically, the durability of the post-war balance of
power. The Polish situation, because it is a mass movement, shows
that there is no lasting stability in Eastern Europe. No matter what
the Soviets do, their problems with their 'allies' are only going to
get worse, not better. Their future in Eastern Europe will be one
of recurrent revolts reminiscent of Hungary (1956), Czechoslovakia
(1968) and Poland (1980). Sooner or later, one of their 'allies' will
break bonds. What effect that will have upon the rest of the
Warsaw Pact is open to speculation.

What is certain is that the Soviet policy in Eastern Europe makes
a grotesque caricature of what is supposed to happen in a socialist
state. People are supposed to have faith in the Communist Party
as the 'vanguard' of the working class which serves their interests,
raises their standard of living, and leads the country into a bright
future free of class struggle, exploitation or deprivation. The party
is supposed to be an indispensable force in their nation's destiny.

But in Poland, not only was the Party ruthlessly forced upon the
people, its Stalinist behaviour so alienated the working class it was
supposed to be leading that finally 10 million out of 11 million in
the industrial work force rebelled and joined Solidarity, which,
ironically, was a genuine socialist workers' movement. This so
threatened the Soviets, the established elite in Poland and the
Eastern bloc Communist Parties as a whole, that Solidarity had to
be crushed by force of arms. The fact that the Soviets used Polish

militia as the cat's paw to do the job does not change the colour of repression, for which we are all ultimately responsible.

In the USSR, at least one can say that Stalinism was not imposed from outside. The Communist Party there arose out of the historical experience of the Russian people. No one seriously resists it other than scattered and quickly isolated dissidents. There is no Solidarity movement among Soviet workers, no stirrings of mass opposition, no major uprisings against the Party or the State. The Soviet people may not love their government, but no foreign country imposed it upon them; hence, it has its own legitimacy. The Soviet people brought in Lenin's 'dictatorship of the proletariat' by revolution; they could reject it by revolution. For better or for worse, it is the result of their own choice.

But what is legitimate in the USSR has been imposed in Eastern Europe where it has earned no legitimacy at all. In Poland today, as in Czechoslovakia and Hungary, the existing Communist Parties would be seriously challenged, if not overthrown, were the military forces of the Soviet Union not there to prevent it.

This fragility of Communist governments in Eastern Europe provides a permanent source of insecurity to the USSR itself. In the long term, how Poland works out its destiny may be more threatening to the USSR than anything the US or NATO could do. What security can the Soviets have in the face of the fact that their allies, upon whom Soviet national security intimately depends, prefer the system of the West than the ways of the Soviets?

It is true of course that the Yalta Conference in 1945 handed over Eastern Europe to the USSR. At the time there seemed no credible alternative, particularly since Soviet troops were all over Eastern Europe anyway. The West conceded this division by its attitude to the revolts in Hungary and Czechoslovakia. The Helsinki Declaration in 1975 ratified it, although it coupled recognition of the existing frontiers with agreement that all signatories adhere to basic notions of human rights.

Nothing serious has been done to explore how this division of Europe, now a source of instability for both East and West, might peacefully be changed. What Poland has made clear, however, is that this re-examination of the Yalta accords must take place, particularly in terms of the right of one superpower to crush a small neighbouring state simply because it deems it necessary. Kissinger, in the same article quoted above, is clear about this:

> Poland represents a fundamental challenge to East-West relations not only because of the brutal violation of the Helsinki accords. It does so primarily because of what it tells us about the Soviet perception of security. It is one thing for the Soviet Union to seek to be secure against a hostile military presence in sur-

62 *Know Your Enemy*

rounding countries; it is quite another to equate security with a cordon of vassal states subject to an ultimate Soviet right to impose a totalitarian government on populations that over-whelmingly reject it. The United States can be forthcoming on Soviet strategic concerns; it must resist Moscow's claim to a constant right of intervention. Especially inadmissible is the proposition that the Red Army is the guarantor of the irrevers-ibility of history, the enforcer of the rule that what is Communist is eternal and what is non-Communist is fair game for undermining, or worse.

It is interesting that someone like Kissinger should make a statement condemning 'Moscow's claim to a constant right of intervention'. What happened in Poland does stand in judgement against the Soviet notion that Eastern Europe, somehow, must always serve Soviet interests. But it is not for the Americans to make this charge. They are guilty in more than equal measure for what they have done and are now doing in *their* sphere of influence.

An interesting parallel to the Soviet intervention in Poland can be found in the American intervention in Chile when Salvador Allende, a Marxist, was elected President in free and democratic elections back in 1970. The Americans did not directly invade but, like the Russians in Poland, found a hatchetman in a general who would execute their designs. Incidentally, Kissinger was intimately involved throughout the Allende affair. Kissinger's role not only sheds light on the cynicism of international politics, it also offers a prelude to our discussions concerning the United States and *its* allies. The Russians are not the only threat in the world—either in war or to peace.

Within a week of Allende's election to the Presidency of Chile on 7 September 1970, Augustino Edwards, Chile's richest industria-list, flew to Washington, D.C. He owned banks, a television station, and Chile's largest daily newspaper, the ultra-conservative *El Mercurio*, which had violently opposed Allende during the campaign. Edwards was a board member of International Basic Economic Corporation (IBEC), a multi-faceted company owned by the Rockefeller family with considerable interests in Latin America.

On 14 September, Edwards met with Nelson Rockefeller, his son Rodman Rockefeller (the President of IBEC), and Nancy Maginess, who became Kissinger's wife. Edwards pleaded a very simple case: Allende had fought his campaign on the issues of nationalising the Chilean economy and ending the exploitation of Chile by foreign capital. Both these programmes would seriously threaten America's economic interests and, therefore, political stakes in the country. The US had to intervene in Chile, Edwards urged, preferably before Allende had time to carry out his promises.

The next day, the Chilean businessman met with Donald Kendall, the president of the Pepsi Cola Corporation, also threatened by Allende's victory. As Edwards was a member of the Pepsi Cola board of directors, he felt free to argue his case to Kendall for the overthrow of Allende to protect Pepsi's as well as American economic interests. It was not until he had met with key figures of multinational economic activity that Edwards sat down with America's political leaders. Pepsi President Kendall arranged for him to meet with US Attorney General John Mitchell, a close friend and confidant of President Richard Nixon, and with Kissinger, who was then chief of the US National Security Council. After this meeting, Edwards was taken to meet Richard Helms, Director of the CIA and later US Ambassador to Iran. Finally came the meeting at the White House. "This meeting was arranged because of Edwards's presence in Washington and following Kendall's words to the President concerning Edwards's view of the Chilean situation", CIA Director Helms was later to testify to Congress.[10] Nixon had just received a report form the US Ambassador to Chile, Edward Korry, dated 12 September 1970, that the chances of using the Chilean army to change the situation were 'non-existent'. Nevertheless on 14 September, just after Edwards had met with Rockefeller, a session of the '40 Committee', which Nixon had set up in 1969 to authorise secret operations abroad, was called. Despite its name it only had five members: Kissinger, Helms, Under Secretary of State Joseph Sisco, Under Secretary of Defense William Clements, and General George S. Brown, Chairman of the Joint Chiefs of Staff. After various suggestions were made, including the spending of $250,000 in bribing members of the Chilean Parliament to oppose the ratification of Allende's election, it was decided to await Nixon's decision.

That came the very next day. Helms jotted down a random selection of Nixon's comments: "One chance in ten perhaps, but let's save Chile ... Not concerned by risks implied .... Ten million dollars, more if necessary ... Full time jobs and the best we have ... make their economy groan."[11] The President appeared "hard", noted Helms, who was directed by Nixon to work with certain factions in the Chilean army in preparing a *coup* against Allende. Kissinger called the operation 'Track 2'. It was so secret that only the CIA was to be involved, not the State Department nor the Pentagon. By the end of the meeting, Kendall and Edwards, two directors of an American soft drinks corporation, had succeeded in persuading the American government to overthrow a constitutionally elected government three thousand miles away because it had just won a public mandate to end the tyranny of foreign capital.

The International Telegraph and Telephone Corporation (ITT) was soon called in by the CIA to help with planning. Public acceptance of the need for a coup was essential, so a vast billboard campaign was mounted with pictures of Soviet tanks entering the Chilean capital of Santiago as they had done in Prague, Czechoslovakia in 1968. News stories, bulletins, press releases were generated by the hundreds linking Allende with the Soviet Union in a manner as to conclude that he posed a direct threat to 'democracy and freedom' in the Western Hemisphere.

Edwards' paper *El Mercurio*, a part of this campaign, received $700,000 from the '40 Committee' in 1971 alone. Another $900,000 was given in April 1972. The paper published vituperative attacks on Allende, all but calling for sedition and civil war. A vast press campaign was co-ordinated via CIA connections in Europe and Latin America. More than 700 editorials and articles from *El Mercurio* were syndicated abroad.

With the public relations campaign underway, the CIA attempted the coup in October 1970. It failed. Credit diplomacy then took over, like the one used in Poland in 1982. Within two years the international banks had reduced their credit facilities to Chile from $300 million to $17 million. Direct American investment had fallen from $1 billion in 1969 to less than $100 million in 1972. The Swiss banks played a key role in this strangulation exercise. The International Trade Bank of Geneva, owned by an extremely right wing Chilean family, provided a direct link between the opponents of Allende in Chile and international financiers who were willing to provide covert funds for undermining the regime.

Undaunted, Allende continued to nationalise the Chilean copper mines. This hit Anaconda Corporation and ITT particularly hard. To undermine the Allende administration, top personnel from both these multinationals began working closely with Kissinger's assistant, General Alexander Haig. General Haig was assisted by Peter Peterson, banker, advisor to Nixon and Secretary for Trade. Kissinger and Haig were under constant pressure from President Nixon to produce immediate and definite results, according to a later Senate report. Allende's life and the overthrow of his government of Popular Unity cost the United States taxpayer $11 million.

In 1972, Allende addressed the international community from the rostrum of the United Nations. With great dignity he declared, "I accuse ITT before the conscience of the world of having tried to provoke civil war in my country, which means total disintegration in any land".[12] Allende should have known that the microphones into which he was speaking and the amplification system bearing his appeal had all been manufactured and installed by ITT. Elsewhere, when he tried to rally political support, his audience consisted of ordinary consumers who hired Avis automobiles, lived in Levit houses, bought Oceanic televisions, or stayed in Sheraton hotels, all parts of the ITT empire. It was difficult for many to understand this conflict between buyer and supplier, and most dismissed Allende as paranoid. To them is was like a man ringing them up to say, 'my telephone wire is strangling me'.

Even in Moscow, where Allende finally travelled for support, ITT was already there. The Soviets restated the "unfailing collaboration of the USSR in the just and progressive struggle of the Chilean people against Fascist and imperialist schemings by the great North American monopolies". But just three days prior to Allende's arrival, Brezhnev had signed a ten-year trade agreement with Frank Barnes, Vice-President of ITT. ITT had been in most Communist countries since 1955 and in Moscow since 1968, supplying the Soviet Union with aviation communications systems. Allende asked the USSR for $500 million in hard currency credits. He received $30 million. And the Lenin Peace Prize.

In Washington, ITT created the possibility of Allende's overthrow. In Moscow it exerted the subtle pressure necessary to make that a certainty. In late September 1973 Allende was murdered in a CIA co-ordinated coup. Soon the Chilean military were hunting down the last centres of his Popular Front 'infection' with flamethrowers.

Washington's new man in Chile was General Pinochet. Like his Polish counterpart, Jaruzelski, Pinochet's coup was swift and harsh. Thousands were killed, tens of thousands detained. Also like Jaruzelski, trained by and intimate with his Soviet backers, Pinochet was intimate with his American backers and worked directly with the CIA before, during and after they overthrew Allende. Indeed, Jaruzelski could learn a technique or two from Pinochet.

In recent years Pinochet has developed methods that allow him to maintain his authoritarian control, yet escape the charges of violating human rights. The Lawyers Association for Human Rights, a group associated with the Roman Catholic Church, reports that instead of the usual detention, imprisonment and torture, dissidents in Chile are being done away with through "battles between armed leftists and the security forces", as the Chilean government describes it. Evidence indicates these battles are, in fact, executions.

"In the past," says one of the lawyers of the human rights group, "they made someone disappear, but now they just kill them."[13] If someone disappears or is tortured, it is noted the world over by various human rights groups. But if a person is killed by government forces claiming to "prevent an act of terrorism" then the death is supposedly sanctified by legitimate law.

It is known that at least thirteen people were killed by this new technique in 1981. All of them were alleged to belong to the Movement of the Revolutionary Left. All of them were claimed to have returned from exile to foment 'subversive' activities.

This is not to say that Pinochet has stopped his other methods. Since 1978 alone, over 5,000 people are known to have been picked up and detained without warrant or charge. Pinochet has also established torture centres and practices what he euphemistically calls 'relegation'—the sending of opponents, particularly students, into internal exile in isolated parts of the country.

"Pinochet cries out against his opposition as Communists and anarchists," one of the human rights lawyers says, "but they (the government) are the anarchists. This is not a government of law, but of terror."[14]

Pinochet's government is given full backing by Washington, particularly since Reagan assumed the Presidency, and full support by the CIA. The degree of their involvement in Pinochet's torture centres is not known, but it is well known that the CIA trains South American security forces—including those from Chile—in torture techniques at the International Police Academy in Panama. In return, Pinochet keeps Chile open to ITT and other 'great North American monopolies'.

Pinochet was and is a close friend of Augustino Edwards. He is a former chairman and director of *El Mercurio*, and sat on the board of IBEC with Edwards. Pinochet's Finance Minister, Jorge Cavas, lived in the United States during the Allende years, working for the World Bank. When Pinochet's Foreign Minister, Ismael Huerta, visited the US in October 1973 to justify the coup, he had more than 120 meetings with representatives of American and Canadian banks.

A syndicate composed of First National City Bank, the Irving Trust and the Banker's Trust offered credits of $150 million. The Chase Manhattan, controlled by the Rockefellers, and the Bank of America, formed another syndicate to help the junta. Dow Chemical sent a technical team to Chile to check the condition of its two Santiago factories Allende had nationalised. Dow Chemical was followed by General Motors, General Electric, Textron, Dodge, and General Tire and Rubber Company. Declaring that "true nationalism does not consist in rejecting foreign capital", Pinochet appointed Henry Gardner his public relations man in the

US. Gardner was a vice-president of the Anaconda Corporation—the American interest which exploits the Chilean copper deposits. Pinochet could also count on the support of the influential Council of the Americas, directed by David Rockefeller. It is composed of over 200 multinationals representing 80% of all US investments in Latin America. The Council arranged for the Chilean Minister for the Economy, Fernandez Leniz, to meet 100 directors of its member multinationals at a luncheon in New York in February 1974. By May, Chile had become one of the major buyers of American armaments with expenditures running at nearly $70 million per annum.

Given this inseparable connection between economic interests and political intrigue, one can only wonder at what role the Americans played in the Polish crisis some eight years later in view of the fact that $28 billion of the Polish debt was owed to over 500 Western banks. One also wonders at the collusion there might have been between the US and the USSR. Just as Brezhnev demurred helping Allende take on ITT, it is interesting to note that the Kremlin informed the White House of Jaruzelski's coup three days prior to its happening.

Both superpowers have their spheres of influence which they jealously guard. In both Chile and Poland, the superpowers were confronted by popular movements. They perceived them as risks to their respective influence and called them a threat to their 'national security'. Rather than allowing either the Chileans or the Poles *themselves* to work out their own national destiny, each superpower assumed the right to *dictate* that destiny. Both chose to use a military coup to solve the situation, which resulted in death, detainment and denial of human rights on a massive scale.

What happened in Chile and in Poland is the dictate neither of 'democracy' nor of 'socialism'. The pain and the blood of two sovereign people are the sacrifice demanded by submachine gun politics and made inevitable by their geographic proximity to the two giants.

This raises two fundamental questions. Which superpower should we trust—the one that we do not know to be honest or the one that we know to be dishonest? Of what should we be afraid—the political oppression in the name of 'equality' or the economic exploitation in the name of 'liberty'?

WHAT ABOUT AFGHANISTAN?

In international affairs, things are very seldom what they are seen to be and even less what they are reported to be. Yet, seldom has the gap between reality and rhetoric been quite so great as over the Soviet presence in Afghanistan. It must be said that the Soviet intervention in that country was a blatant violation of the internationally recognised principle of national sovereignty. It must also be said that the sooner this intervention is ended the better. However, the irony of the situation is that the Western response, particularly that of the Americans, has been so sterile and stereotyped that it seems calculated more to perpetuate the Soviet presence in Afghanistan than to end it.

Aided by China, Pakistan and other Western Asian countries, the US has seen to it that on the one hand the United Nations General Assembly continues to condemn Soviet actions (by a vote of 116–23 in the 1981 Session); on the other, the US is making sure that the proposed dialogue betwen Afghanistan and Pakistan under the auspices of the UN Secretary General's Special Representative simply does not get off the ground. At the same time the Americans are also stirring the pot inside Afghanistan itself by giving limited assistance to the Afghan rebels. One way of giving this aid is by paying Egypt for its old Soviet military hardware and having it slipped into Afghanistan via Pakistan. But Pakistan, which has its own agenda of securing massive supplies

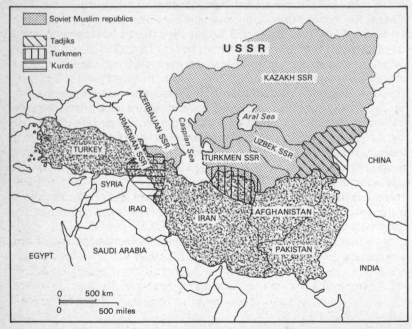

The Arc of Crisis; Upsurge of Islamic Fundamentalism threatening the Soviet Union (*Source:* The Soviet Superpower, *Heinemann Educ.*)

of US weapons without unduly alarming the Soviets, is not prepared to act as an overt conduit for military aid to the rebels. American strategy seems designed to get just enough weapons to the rebels to keep the Afghan pot boiling. The objective appears to be creating a Russian Vietnam. By keeping the Russians embroiled in a war they cannot win, the US has an ever-ready example of Soviet global 'expansionism' behind which it can expand its own influence and presence throughout the Indian ocean area.

While it is important to be clear in condemning the Soviets for their intervention in Afghanistan, it is also important to be equally clear about the manipulation of the situation by the US to legitimate a continued arms build up in the area instead of seeking to create peace.

The basic error of the US and Western European assessment was that the Soviets had invaded Afghanistan as part of a sinister grand design to grab the oil fields of the Persian Gulf. Whether this was a genuine misreading of the situation or a calculated propaganda smokescreen is unclear. What matters is that the US and NATO assessment is erroneous. Any policies built on such a premise can only be faulty. The Russians did not march into Afghanistan for offensive reasons. They acted defensively and for political reasons in the face of a situation that had left them no other option.

The narrative is rather long and complex. In order to understand it, we must begin in July 1973 when President Mohammed Daud staged a coup and overthrew his cousin, King Zahir Shah. This coup upset an equilibrium which had existed in Afghanistan since the nineteenth century.

Traditionally, the monarchy had been the only focus of authority in Afghanistan and the primary instrument of unity in a society riddled by deep and complex tribal, ethnic and religious divisions. The Afghan monarchy had also managed to maintain a policy of non-alignment. In return the Soviet Union left the Afghans alone to live their lives under their king. Moscow did nothing to push Afghanistan towards its brand of socialism. The Soviets took little interest in the communist party of Afghanistan, called the People's Democratic Party in Afghanistan (PDPA). All this was generally accepted by the US and NATO as only fair.

Daud's coup upset an applecart that basically had been trundling along since 1917. He created a vacuum from which Afghanistan was not to recover. His regime was corrupt and cruel, breeding discontent and uncertainty. The more insecure he felt the more rash Daud became until Afghanistan found itself embroiled in the high stakes of the cold war.

The year 1973 was an important year in other respects besides Daud's coup. It marked the Yom Kippur War between Israel and the Arabs; the first-ever oil embargo; the rise of Arab financial and petroleum power and the consequent emergence of Islamic fundamentalism. It was at this point that the most dazzling and dangerous actor entered the stage: His Imperial Majesty Shah Mohammed Reza Pahlavi of Iran, Aryamehar, King of Kings, etc.

The Shah had been cast by the United States in the role of gendarme in the Middle East. His script called for him to maintain the flow of oil to the West through the Persian Gulf. Flush with the sudden rise in oil wealth, the Shah also found himself the recipient of all the sophisticated weaponry which he could use or could not use but wanted anyway. Iran offered a parking place for American weapons at the time of withdrawal from Vietnam.

The Shah proceeded to launch a determined bid to oust Soviet influence in the region. This was done in part to keep the area safe for the Western oil corporations, in part to recreate a modern version of the Persian empire. (Remember the Persepolis celebrations when President Carter was wined and dined by moonlight midst the ruins of the ancient capital of Persia?) Part of the Shah's strategy was to draw Afghanistan into a Western oriented but Iranian dominated security and economic alliance. He suggested a 'common market' extending from Iran to Malaysia with Iranians playing the role of Senior Partner.

For his own reasons, Daud responded affirmatively. He quickly signed a $2 billion economic agreement with the Shah. Daud also accepted the Shah's offer of crack squads of SAVAK, the Shah's secret police, to help him 'root out communist influence' from the Afghan civil and military sevices.

This understandably alarmed the Soviets. The US might have saved the situation by persuading the Shah to get off his high horse, at least as far as Afghanistan was concerned. But in those heady days, everything seemed to be going well for the Americans—diplomatic relations had been established with China which had begun to seek anti-hegemony agreements in the Far East; the Soviets had been expelled from Egypt; and the Shah had become the Troubleshooter-in-Chief for the United States in the Middle East.

By 1975, Daud's alliance with the Parcham faction of the PDPA, which had initially supported him, broke down. Khalq, the other major communist faction, had opposed him from the beginning. In September 1975, Daud dismissed 40 Soviet trained officers of the armed forces at the Shah's *diktat*.

The Soviet Union naturally reacted to all this. Having left the rival Parcham and Khalq factions of the PDPA to squabble amongst themselves during the monarchy, the Soviets now began concerted efforts to reunite them. The ideological and social differences between the pragmatic Parcham, led by Babrak Karmal, and the more doctrinaire Khalq, headed by Hafizullah Amin, were deep. Consequently, it took until May 1977 to get the rival factions to agree to unite. The Communist Party of India lent a helping hand in this process. The PDPA was unified under the leadership of Noor Mohammed Taraki, a compromise candidate between Karmal and Amin.

By this time both the Shah and Daud stepped up their anti-communist intrigue. The SAVAK had the run of the capital city, Kabul. Traditionally, Afghan military officers had been trained in the Soviet Union. Daud curtailed this and made training arrangements with Egypt and India. Daud also went to the extent of saying that Iran's new economic and military power had changed the geopolitical situation in the region. "Our historical relations with Iran were unpleasant," he stated, "but we must adapt to new realities."[1]

All this was music to many an exalted ear in Tehran and Washington. But more seasoned observers became deeply alarmed. The British ambassador in Kabul, an old Afghan hand, warned of trouble in the event Daud joined the Washington-Tehran axis.

By March 1978, Daud signed an agreement with Pakistan at the Shah's instance, and set off to Egypt and Saudi Arabia. The Shah planned to visit Afghanistan in June and fix a meeting between Daud and President Carter in Washington.

All this was not to be. A sudden showdown developed between Daud and the reunified communists on 17 April 1978. The confrontation was touched off when the highly respected Parcham leader, Akbar Kaiber, was brutally murdered. Evidence pointed to Daud's staunchly anti-Soviet Prime Minister, Abdul Qadir Nuristani, who had just promulgated a one-party constitution. Nuristani had promised to 'finish off' all Afghan communists.

The reaction to Kaiber's murder was sharp. Thousands of his supporters took to the streets. Daud ordered a general crackdown. But in spite of the SAVAK training, or perhaps because of it, his police units made a mess of things. Amin's arrest, for instance, was delayed for so long that before he was hauled off to prison he was able to set in motion the coup that eliminated Daud and brought a Marxist-Leninist government to power.

No one has suggested that the Soviets either engineered or even encouraged a coup. They, like everyone else—particularly the CIA and SAVAK—were taken by surprise. In Soviet reckoning, the PDPA was in no position to exercise power. How right this assessment was, was borne out in the following year. In any case the sequence of events was so bizarre and Daud's reflexes so clumsy that the April 28 coup has been nicknamed the 'comic coup'. This coup 'could only have háppened in Afghanistan or in a Neil Simon comedy', wrote Louis Duprée, perhaps the greatest authority on Afghanistan in the West.[2] It was clearly not a carefully calculated Soviet move on the international chessboard.

All the grief that the Russians have had to face subsequently in Afghanistan and the shadow that this has caused over the region ranging from Iran to India, to say nothing about the world situation in general, has been really the result of the April 1978 coup, which came well before the PDPA was ready to assume power, took place clumsily, and left a lot of loose ends which were not easy to clear up. Nevertheless, once the coup had succeeded, the Soviets could only hail it as a 'great victory for world socialism' and offer full support for the Taraki government.

The social base of the new communist rulers was narrow. The rivalries between the Parcham and Khalq factions were acute. Their policies of speedy reforms alienated public sympathy. Moreover, real power in the government soon passed to Amin, who was inclined to be extremist in his economic and social policies and antagonistic to Moscow's friends in the Khalq faction.

Amin proceeded to give the Soviets cause for concern almost in direct proportion to the increase in his power. It was not merely that he consistently ignored Soviet advice; it was more that Amin considered himself an Afghan version of Stalin who was going to force an impoverished and illiterate agrarian society into the twentieth century by any means. However, while Stalin could unleash a reign of terror, Amin was soon wallowing in a rising tide of public disenchantment and was faced with open revolt. The arrogance of his cohorts and the pace of their over ambitious reforms exacerbated the situation further.

Russian patience with Amin broke when Amin, like Daud before him, began keeping much too close a contact with the Americans. Amin had been educated at Columbia University in New York. Amin was also very close to Adolph Dubs, the US ambassador to Afghanistan from the time of the April 1978 coup until January 1979, when Dubs was killed in Kabul under mysterious circumstances. During these months, Amin and Dubs met no fewer than 14 times. Amin was determined, according to Dubs, to maintain 'discreet links' with the US as 'insurance' against increasing Soviet pressure.

By September 1979, this rift between Amin and the Soviets was so complete that the Soviets decided to get rid of him. But their instrument for doing so, President Taraki, bungled things so badly that when the shooting was over it was Taraki who lay dead, not Amin.

After the 'wrong man' got killed, a bizarre situation arose. Amin now assumed complete control. He was anti-Russian but as head of a Marxist-Leninist government he was entitled to all possible Soviet support. And he was getting it, too, for without it he would have been unable to cope with the rising opposition created by his policies.

The Soviets were down but not out. Learning from their mistakes, or, more accurately, *over-reacting* from their mismanagement when they tried to get rid of Amin the first time, they tried again in December 1979. This time they not only had Amin killed along with his entire family, to be replaced by Karmal, but they also invaded the country with a total of 85,000 troops to ensure that from then on things went their way.

The Soviet invasion of Afghanistan marked the first time since 1945 when Soviet troops had moved beyond the boundaries of the Warsaw Pact countries in hostile action. In doing so they violated the 1945 United Nations Charter, the 1955 Bandung Declaration and the 1975 Helsinki Agreement principle on the inviolability of national frontiers. Moscow's claim that its actions had been in response to a request for help from the Kabul government was rejected by the UN by 104 to 18 votes and by 35 Muslim nations in Islamabad, Pakistan, in February 1980.

Since then, things have gone from bad to worse. An already unpopular regime now has the backing of foreign troops. To a country as fiercely nationalistic as Afghanistan, this is like waving a red flag at a bull. They fought the British attempt to colonise them in the eighteenth and nineteenth centuries and won. There seems little doubt that they will fight now till they drive the Russian troops back across the border. Whatever mistakes the Soviets made before their invasion, the biggest miscalculation was that they could reverse the already far advanced disintegration of the ruling regime.

The Afghan army dwindled from 85,000 in 1978 to 20,000 by early 1983. As a result the government had to rely on press gangs to enforce the mandatory service laws. Unannounced road blocks and sweeps through various parts of cities and towns rounded up males ranging in age from 15 to 50. They were then 'processed' to see if they were 'eligible' for the draft.

The Soviets are also plagued by the continuing feuds between the Parcham and Khalq factions. The numerically superior Khalqis are struggling to regain some of the power they lost when the Soviets installed Karmal and the Parchamis at the time of the invasion. The Parchamis seek to have the Khalqis purged but the Soviets, mindful of Khalq strength in the military, continue to seek a reconciliation. They have insisted that leading Khalqis be kept in top positions. However, internecine fighting is not likely to abate. In view of the deteriorating security situation and obvious failure of party and government policies, mutual recriminations can only increase.

There are indications that the Khalqis, in their anger at the Soviets and the Parchamis, are cooperating with the Mujahiddin, the Afghan rebels. Numbering well over 100,000, and receiving overwhelming public support and just enough arms, the rebels had fought both the Soviet troops and the Afghan army to a standstill by 1982. There have been reports of their incursions into the Soviet Union. Like the US in Vietnam, the Soviets and the Afghan army maintain control of the main cities and the road links between them but little else. The rebels control the countryside.

An indication of Soviet desperation in Afghanistan can be seen in its willingness to use chemical warfare techniques. Each of the five Soviet divisions which rolled across the border in December 1979 and January 1980 was equipped to engage in chemical warfare. Within three weeks of their arrival in Afghanistan, refugees streaming into Pakistan were telling of horrific experiences with multi-coloured gases. Nerve gases, however, are colourless and odourless. Moreover, there has not been produced any direct physical or pathological evidence to substantiate these stories. What *is* substantiated though by history is that the British invading armies used phosgene and mustard gases against resisting forces in the Afghan Campaign of 1919. No doubt, the Russians have read this chapter of history.

In any event, this state of affairs suits US designs down to a tee. Senator Birch Bayh, who was chairman of the committee that approved the CIA plan to arm the Afghan rebels through Pakistan, has clearly indicated that the US has restricted its aid so as not to "raise the conflict to the level of conventional warfare. . . or provide so much assistance that the Soviets would pour troops in".[3]

Meanwhile, the US has been proclaiming loudly that it was the Soviet intervention in Afghanistan that 'destroyed' detente. The truth, however, is that detente had broken down long before intervention in Afghanistan was even a gleam in any Soviet Marshal's eye. Before the Soviet invasion on 24 December 1979, the SALT II treaty, signed by Carter and Brezhnev, had been torpedoed in the US Congress by a resurgent right wing of military planners and legislators when the Americans had decided to build the MX missile system. Henry Kissinger had lectured NATO about the need to step up its defences against the 'Soviet threat' and the decision had been made to deploy the cruise and Pershing II missiles in Europe.

On the Eastern front, China had been given most-favoured

trading nation status with the EEC, something which the USSR has constantly been denied. Both the US and the EEC were opening military dialogue with the People's Republic, and the Chinese, with American help and collaboration, were setting up surveillance posts on the Sino-Soviet frontier. The Soviets had airlifted Cuban troops into Angola. But here again, Cuban troops moved into the area after South Africa had done so, with US backing. Not before.

The Persian Gulf has frequently been represented by the US as the 'jugular vein' of the Western economy due to the heavy Western reliance on Gulf oil. The Soviet military presence in Afghanistan is cited as proof of its design to make a beeline for the oil fields in the area. This explanation has been given credibility by the classic vision of the Russian bear stalking towards warm water ports. There were also CIA reports released around the time of the Soviet intervention indicating that by 1985 the Russians would have to import 3.5 million barrels of oil per day.

Secretary of Defense Weinberger announced as late as March 1981 that the Persian Gulf "is and will be the fulcrum of contention for the forseeable future. The Soviet Union will almost certainly become a net energy importer. This, coupled with their economic necessity for eventual access to the Gulf oil basin, is their long-range objective of denying access to oil by the West".[4]

The US countered this 'aggressive design' of the USSR by mobilising a 100,000 strong Rapid Deployment Force (RDF) in the Indian Ocean; attempting to establish a military presence in the Persian Gulf; extending NATO influence into Gulf politics; and risking the Camp David peace process by priority considerations of the 'security' of Saudi Arabia. However, by May 1981, the CIA was forced to abandon its claims that oil is the core reason for the Russian invasion of Afghanistan. Afghanistan has no oil. Soviet oil production is, in fact, rising and not declining. The USSR produced 12.1 million barrels of oil every day during 1980. That makes it the world's largest producer—bigger than Saudi Arabia and the United States. The Russians have been and remain net exporters of oil. The estimates of newly charted Siberian deposits indicate that the Soviet Union may have as much oil as the rest of the world put together. Prevailing conditions, as discussed later on, show that the Soviets cannot afford to have any designs of controlling Gulf oil.

What this means is that "we should at least allow for the fact that the Soviets are not desperate for petroleum", says Marshal Goldman, associate director of Russian Research Center at Harvard. "So far we have been conducting our foreign policy on a worst-case scenario. The estimates that have been governing

policy have been proven wrong so far. It doesn't mean that the
Soviets are now benevolent in the Middle East, but those who
think they must go into the Middle East for oil are wrong."[5]

So why did the Soviets invade? The evidence indicates that it
was mainly due to the machinations of the Shah and the CIA
which altered Afghanistan's long held policy of non-alignment. In
the 1980s, the Soviets refused to be confronted by a pro-American
regime on their Southern border even as in the 1960s the
Americans had refused to accept a pro-Soviet regime in Cuba. The
American invasion of Cuba did not succeed. The Soviet invasion
of Afghanistan, at least initially, did.

The second reason for their intervention is that the coup that
overthrew Daud in 1978 brought in a Marxist-Leninist government. Despite its immaturity and repressive policies, as well as its
inability to win popular support, the Soviets felt compelled, for
ideological reasons, to back the regime. The worse the situation got
the more they felt compelled to give aid, even to Amin who was
anti-Soviet. The Soviet military high command and Soviet intelligence had both argued against military intervention. Both felt it
was a no-win situation, militarily and politically. Nevertheless, the
momentum of support for their sinking Afghan ship was such that
the Kremlin overruled the military and KGB advice. Their move
was not offensive in intent but a defensive response to an
unacceptable challenge to strategic Soviet interests in an area of
vital concern.

An all-party committee of the British House of Commons
concluded:

> The Soviet Union did not go into Afghanistan earlier because
> the Afghan regimes prior to 1978 had been stable, even though
> not Marxist. Once a Communist regime had been established,
> the USSR had the double incentive of ideological commitment
> to the maintenance of Communist gains, in line with the
> Brezhnev doctrine, plus the desire to restore stability on its
> borders.[6]

To point this out is not to deny that the Soviets have proven
themselves to be ham-handed and ideologically rigid from the
beginning. They were compelled by events to make one mistake
after another. Yet these mistakes were not a part of some grand
design to grab the Gulf oil fields. Having made this series of
mistakes which has embroiled the Soviets in a 'Vietnam' situation
in Afghanistan, they are not about to embark on the dissolution of
the socialist empire by controlling Gulf oil, although the Americans
fear so. They know that if they began controlling Gulf oil, Western
Europe will become one of their dependencies and, in time, be the

cause of dilution of Moscow's authority. The criticism of the Russians is not so much that they intervened in Afghanistan when they did, but that they were foolish enough to put themselves in a situation where such an intervention became perceived necessity.

Ironically, this is the same position in which President Reagan placed the US with regard to El Salvador. Like the Soviets, he perceived a threat to America's national security from the south; and like them he over-reacted by force of arms without realising that the consequences of his actions would result in only embroiling the US further in a no-win situation. What must be remembered about the American experience in El Salvador is that it is not unique. The Soviet invasion of Afghanistan has a long history. So does the American road to El Salvador.

It began in the nineteenth century. In 1823, President Monroe declared that any European interference in the affairs of the newly formed Latin American republics would be considered an 'unfriendly act' by the United States of America. This declaration became known to the world as the 'Monroe Doctrine'. It established, among other things, the 'right' of the US to 'protect' Latin America from 'foreign intervention'.

During the nineteenth century the defensive paternalism of the Monroe Doctrine was coupled with another key term in American history: 'manifest destiny'. The United States developed the popular myth that it had been destined for a special historical mission: namely, to carry democracy, capitalism and the Christian faith westwards across North America to the shores of the Pacific Ocean and, later, throughout the Western Hemisphere. Westward expansion was completed by the end of the nineteenth century; the last 'frontier' area was officially closed in 1912. Realising America's 'manifest destiny' to stretch from 'sea to shining sea' was only accomplished by decimating the native Indian populations and annexing over half of Mexico to create the states of Texas, New Mexico and California.

In the mid-nineteenth century, the US began seriously to implement its Monroe Doctrine by challenging British power in Central America and the Caribbean. At the time, Britain dominated the region with its naval power and in addition to its Colonies in the West Indies, controlled part of the Atlantic coast of the Central American isthmus, including British Honduras, now Belize, and eastern Nicaragua.

As the US became a Pacific as well as an Atlantic power, its desire for a cheap route linking the two oceans came into conflict with Britain's desire to control such a route. Both countries began to eye Nicaragua as a possible site. In 1850, the Clayton-Bulmer treaty was signed, whereby neither country was to hold exclusive control over the Nicaraguan route. In 1867, however, the US abrogated the 1850 treaty, and signed a separate agreement with Nicaragua, which granted the US exclusive rights of transit across that country.

In 1890, following the publication of an influential book which suggested that sea power was the key to greatness, the US built its first battleship. Its westward expansion was virtually complete. It now had a larger population than any other single European country. With unrivalled steel, coal and iron production, the giant monopoly firms that dominated the American economy during the late nineteenth century began to look beyond American shores for raw materials and markets in which to invest their surplus capital. The United States was ready for an empire.

Senator Albert Jeremiah Beveridge reflected the popular mood when he wrote that American factories

> are making more than the American people can use .... Fate has written our policy .... The trade of the world must now be ours. And we shall get it, as our Mother England has told us how .... We will cover the ocean with our merchant marine. We will build a navy to the measure of our greatness. Great colonies, governing themselves, flying our flag, and trading with us, will grow about our ports of trade. Our institutions will follow .... and American law, American order, American civilization and the American flag will plant themselves on shores hitherto bloody and benighted by those agents of God henceforth made beautiful and bright.[7]

The shores nearest to the United States and those most likely to be granted the privileges offered by Senator Beveridge were in Central America and the Caribbean—America's 'backyard'.

Cuba was offered the first opportunity. Unfortunately, Cuba was still a Spanish colony, and the Spanish refused to sell it to the Americans. By the 1880s, US capital was heavily involved in the Cuban economy, particularly in the sugar industry. "It makes the water come to my mouth when I think of the State of Cuba as one in our family", wrote an American financier in 1895.[8]

In 1898, the Americans finally decided to rescue Cuba from the tyranny of Spain. The Spanish American War ensued, during which the US declared it had 'liberated' Cuba. It also invaded Puerto Rico and bought the Philippines for $20 million. Guam and Puerto Rico were later ceded to the US by Spain as 'spoils of war'.

Although Cuba was not formally annexed, it was occupied by US troops from 1898 to 1902. US troops only withdrew when Cuba adopted the Platt Amendment to its constitution. This gave the US the right to intervene in Cuban affairs and to establish military bases on the island, including the one *still* in US possession at Guantanamo Bay. The US manipulated Cuban political and economic life for American benefit until 1959. The US sent troops to occupy the island from 1906 to 1909, again in 1912, and from 1917 to 1923.

Cuba offers a model of American imperialism. Without formally reducing its status to that of a colony, the US managed to secure the economic and political domination it wanted by a combination of ruthless economic manipulation and the use of force when 'necessary'. This enabled the US to boast of its anti-colonial traditions while making sure Cuba remained secure for American companies. America's neo-colonialism was diplomatically called 'sphere of influence'.

The US had a more difficult time explaining the status of Puerto Rico, which it had defined in 1901 as a "non-incorporated territory which belongs to, but is not a part of the United States". An editorial in the *New York Times* in 1898 justified this anomaly in the context of the anti-colonial image of the US:

> There can be no question of the wisdom of taking and holding Puerto Rico without any reference to a policy of expansion. We need it as a station in the great American archipelago misnamed the West Indies, and Providence has decreed that it shall be ours as a recompense for smiting the last withering clutch of Spain from the domain which Columbus brought to light and the fairest part of which has long been our heritage.[9]

Theodore Roosevelt had been the American hero of the Spanish-American War. When he became President in 1901, he stressed the strategic importance of the Caribbean to US interests and frequently expressed his impatience with the Central American governments which threatened these interests. Roosevelt's aggressive use of power—characterised by invasions, threats and treaties signed at gunpoint—came to set the pattern for later US policies and actions. His 'big stick' policy, backed by an attitude which maintained that the Anglo-Saxons of America were singled out to help backward races unable to govern themselves, were expressed in his famous 1904 Roosevelt Corollary to the Monroe Doctrine:

> Chronic wrongdoing or any impotence which results in a general loosening of the ties of civilized society, may in America, as elsewhere, ultimately require intervention by some civilized nation, and in the Western Hemisphere the adherence of the United States to the Monroe Doctrine may force the

United States, however reluctantly, in flagrant cases of such wrong doing or impotence, to the exercize of an international police power.

The first target of this Corollary was the Isthmus of Panama. The Americans decided that it was in the economic and military interests of the US to build a trans-oceanic link which would cut the cost of US trade with Latin America as well as facilitate trade between the east coast of America and US interests in the Orient. Direct control of a canal along with US military bases already established in Cuba and Puerto Rico would also enable the US to defend its military and economic interests against the Europeans still in the area, Britain, France, the Netherlands and Denmark.

The fact that the Isthmus of Panama belongs to Colombia was of no concern to Roosevelt. The Americans encouraged and financed a Panamanian independence movement. When it came to power in 1903, the new government of Panama immediately signed a treaty with the US, giving the US the right to build a canal and lease the land in perpetuity. In return the US agreed to guarantee Panama's independence and to assume the maintenance of 'public order'. US troops were sent into Panama in 1908, 1912 and 1918 to discharge these guarantees.

The experiences of Cuba, Puerto Rico and Panama have been shared by most of the other Central American nations. The following is a partial list of US interventions in the area:

1823	Monroe Doctrine pronounced
1835	Clayton–Bulmer Treaty
1898	Spanish-American War
1898–1902	US troops occupy Cuba
1901	US acquires Puerto Rico
1903	Panama becomes independent from Colombia
1905	US marines land at Puerto Cortes, Honduras
1906–1909	US troops occupy Cuba
1908	US troops sent to Panama
1909	US-backed overthrow of Zelaya in Nicaragua
1910	US troops land in Honduras
1912	US troops sent to Panama
1912	US troops occupy Cuba
1912	US troops briefly occupy Puerto Cortes, Honduras
1912–25	US marines occupy Nicaragua
1914	Panama Canal is completed
1914–34	US marines occupy Haiti
1916–24	US marines occupy Dominican Republic
1917–23	US marines occupy Cuba
1918	US troops sent to Panama
1919	US marines occupy Honduras' ports

1926–33	US marines occupy Nicaragua and set up National Guard under Somoza
1924	US marines land in Honduras
1932	US warship stand by during El Salvador *matanza*
1954	CIA-backed invasion of Guatemala
1961	Abortive CIA-backed Bay of Pigs invasion of Cuba
1964	Bornham defeats Japan in Guyanese elections following CIA destabilisation campaign
1965	US marines invade Dominican Republic
1966	The first death squads appear in Guatemala with US complicity and CIA training—they are responsible for 20,000 deaths from 1966–76
1981	US advisors sent to El Salvador

These interventions in Central America are matched in equal measures by US interventions in South America. Chile, as discussed earlier, was only one such example. Bolivia, Argentina, Paraguay, Equador, Brazil are some of the other countries which have experienced similar interventions.

Numerous interventions have allowed the US to build up an impressive collection of weapons and techniques to maintain and promote US interests. These have ranged from economic blockades and sanctions, to clandestine 'destabilising' operations—including assassinations of 'unfriendly' political leaders—to the use of surrogate troops (indirect military intervention), to the threat of force ('gunboat diplomacy'), to direct military intervention, according to the exigencies of the situation. Although the US does not use all these methods in each instance, none of them have been abandoned.

The humiliations which many countries in the Caribbean and Central America were to receive stemmed from the fact that while colonies, their economies had been incorporated into the world market as exporters of one single crop. The wealth from this crop, originally based on slave labour, promoted the capital wealth of Britain, France, Holland or the US, as the case may be, but it devastated the colonial economies themselves. Barbados, the Leeward Islands, Trinidad and Tobago, Guadaloupe, Puerto Rico, Haiti, the Dominican Republic, Jamaica, Cuba and Guyana, all are essentially dependent on their crop of cane. In Central America the crops are coffee and bananas. So dependent did these countries become on single crops, that they have been referred to as 'banana republics'.

The United Fruit Company offers a case in point. Its penetration of Central America began in the late nineteenth century with its construction of railroads and port facilities. The company came to

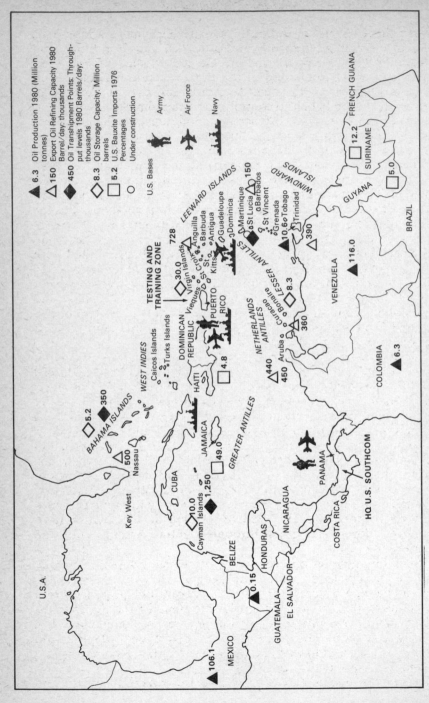

Strategic Resources in the Caribbean (*Source:* Under the Eagle © *Latin Amer. Bur*)

Legend:

▲ 6.3   Oil Production 1980 (Million tonnes)

△ 150   Export Oil Refining Capacity 1980 Barrel/ day: thousands

◆ 450   Oil Transhipment Points: Through-put levels 1980 Barrels/day: thousands

◇ 8.3   Oil Storage Capacity: Million barrels

☐ 5.2   U.S. Bauxite Imports 1976 Percentages

○   Under construction

U.S. Bases

    Army

    Air Force

    Navy

U.S.A.

Key West

MEXICO ▲ 106.1

BELIZE

GUATEMALA ▲ 0.15

EL SALVADOR

HONDURAS

NICARAGUA

COSTA RICA

PANAMA

HQ U.S. SOUTHCOM

CUBA

Cayman Islands ◇ 10.0

JAMAICA ☐ 49.0   ◆ 1.250

GREATER ANTILLES

BAHAMA ISLANDS ◇ 5.2   ◆ 350

Nassau △ 500

WEST INDIES

Caicos Islands

Turks Islands

HAITI

DOMINICAN REPUBLIC ☐ 4.8

PUERTO RICO

Vieques

Virgin Islands △ 30.0

St. Croix

TESTING AND TRAINING ZONE

LEEWARD ISLANDS

Anguilla

Barbuda

St. Kitts △ 728

Antigua

Guadeloupe

Dominica

Martinique

St Lucia ◆ 150

Barbados

St Vincent

Grenada

Tobago ▲ 10.5

Trinidad △ 390

WINDWARD ISLANDS

LESSER ANTILLES

Bonaire ◇ 8.3

Curaçao △ 360

Aruba ◆ 440   ◆ 450

NETHERLANDS ANTILLES

VENEZUELA ▲ 116.0

COLOMBIA ▲ 6.3

GUYANA

SURINAME ☐ 12.2

FRENCH GUIANA

☐ 5.0

BRAZIL

own, either directly or indirectly, Guatemala's only Atlantic port, the major railroad network in Costa Rica and Honduras, and nearly 900 miles of railroad in Guatemala and El Salvador. Although at the beginning of the present century, United Fruit signed contracts with local landlords for the production of bananas, it soon began to control production directly. Eventually, United Fruit owned 400,000 acres in Honduras and 500,000 acres of the most fertile land in Guatemala. It also established an immense network of plantations in Costa Rica, Nicaragua and Panama as well as in Cuba, Jamaica and the Dominican Republic.

The company's plantations were directly linked to the US market. They made little or no contribution to the local economies. The railroads that United Fruit built linked the plantations with the ports, leaving the rest of the country without any system of transportation. The wages paid to the workers were minimal. Almost all of it was spent in company owned shops. United Fruit itself enjoyed a variety of tax exemptions and profit remittances. In Guatemala, for instance, its contract with the government gave it unlimited use of the country's best land for 25 to 99 years, and exemption from stamp, port and import duties. In Honduras, United Fruit acquired over 175,000 acres of prime land without payment of a single dollar.

Despite their interest being solely economic, the impact of United Fruit and other such corporations has been to wreak social and political havoc. They have manipulated the political situation to sustain their economic privileges. Moreover, they have let competition between themselves spill over into local politics. In Honduras, competition between United Fruit and Cuyamel Fruit Company actually provoked a civil war in 1923. In Guatemala and Costa Rica, the banana and coffee corporations have played a key role in the selection of every President, and throughout Central America they are allied with their arch-conservative landlords and the militaries, who receive their own advantage from the presence of these corporations. The incidents of Chile detailed earlier, have occurred dozens of times through Central America and the Caribbean.

Such attempts by one country to dominate others are usually called 'imperialism'. Not surprisingly, the US portrays its intentions and actions otherwise. American foreign policy has a vocabulary all its own, consciously side-stepping the use of terms that would even hint at aggression or imperial domination, and taking refuge in abstract formulae, stereotyped phrases and idealistic cliches. Phrases like 'Monroe Doctrine', 'no entangling alliances', 'open door', 'good neighbor policy', 'Truman doctrine', 'Eisenhower doctrine', strew the pages of American history but throw little light on the dynamics of American foreign policy. Repetition of these abstractions and other generalities produces an emotional reflex which assumes that American diplomacy is 'different', purer, morally better than the diplomacy of other powers. It is only more subtle.

The US did not indulge in the costly military and political colonialism characteristic of the European powers. It saw that real power lay in controlling the commodities which make life and society possible: food, drink, property, labour, industry and most importantly money, which under the capitalist system is the ultimate referent. The USA colonises Latin America economically, only using its military and political force when deemed 'necessary'.

Particularly since World War II US economic interests have been increasingly supported by the CIA and by military and economic aid. This has been embodied in the Military Assistance Advisory Groups (MAAG) which administer the Military Assistance Programme (MAP) and the Foreign Military Sales Programme (FMS). MAAG works very closely with the armed forces of local governments in developing and assessing the country's military requirements, evaluating particular requests for assistance, advising and training local forces to use the aid provided, and screening and recommending the local candidates proposed for military training in the US. All agreements must conform with policies laid down by Washington, and MAAG can by-pass the local US embassy and communicate directly with CIA headquarters in Washington as well as with the Pentagon, when expedient.

The emphasis given by US military and economic aid is upon internal security against subversion rather than training for war against external enemies, as is the case for NATO. The military doctrine and preparedness in NATO is for conflict against the USSR. The Latin American officers trained at the International Police Academy in the US and the War College in Panama are oriented to combat internal enemies. In Latin America, the ultimate power to secure the survival of the nation, traditionally accepted when there is war with an external enemy, is seized by the military and directed *within* the nation. Since war is and has been taken as allowing no compromise because survival itself is at stake, the military in most Latin American nations have taken over the civil governments. Thus the national government becomes a military dictatorship both in theory and in practice.

Apart from an outright civil war, this internal war is a war of words, internal policies and social attitudes rather than merely a question of bombers, missiles and tanks. The military lays down what ideas are the right ones, and defines civil liberties and national priorities. The war waged within the countries is essentially an ideological warfare. The military juntas work hand-in-hand with the CIA, MAAG and the multinational corporations to allow 'capitalism' to flourish. All enemies of this system are 'communists'. The human rights violations tolerated in wars with external enemies have become everyday occurrences in Latin America, where the internal war is omnipresent, unremitting and unceasing. Both external and internal wars exhibit the same violence; the same reliance on spying and reporting; the same abridgements of due process of law; the same repression of any ideas not in consonance with the government. The system being fostered in Latin America by the US is one that precludes mutual tolerance, genuine understanding, or any humanistic interpretation of politics. It is simply a celebration of power, power over people. As Pinochet of Chile put it in his textbook *Geopolitica*:

> National power is the power wielded by the State in organizing social life in the broadest sense of the term, and this includes organizing the people with a view to controlling the country and the population living within its boundaries, in order to implement the will of the State in an essentially dynamic fashion.[10]

The collusion between brutal violence perpetrated by the military juntas and economic exploitation of national resources by the US has been most vividly revealed by the civil war in El Salvador. The illumination provided by world media has enabled people to look behind the veil of US rhetoric to examine the reality of US intervention.

Although most people only awoke to the crisis in El Salvador in 1980, when a full scale civil war had erupted, the roots of the problem go back to the international coffee boom of the late nineteenth century. In 1881, under US and European pressure, the government of El Salvador abolished all communal forms of land tenure, thus paving the way for the wholesale expulsion of the peasants from their land and the consolidation of vast estates in the hands of the coffee magnates.

The result of this economic exploitation was to condemn the mass majority of El Salvador to extreme poverty while a small elite enjoyed the wealth. So deep rooted was this division that even a century later, in 1980, an estimated 84% of the rural population earned an annual income of less than $225 per person. On the other hand, 2% of the population, dominated by 14 large families, owned 60% of the land and received 35% of the national income. This oligarchy, which works in league with the US multinational corporations, dominates the officer corps of the military as well as El Salvador's political life. They have created or destroyed virtually every government that has held office since independence from Spain.

In 1932, peasants turned out in a street demonstration to demand changes. The military, with US backing, massacred 30,000 of them. After 1932, the oligarchy ruled through the military that usually controlled the Presidency and the Ministries of Defence, Interior and Labour, while the oligarchy's representatives have controlled economic affairs.

The rich families and the military together institutionalised repression and brutality. The main instrument for this was the military itself, many of the officers of which were trained in the US. There are also a number of police agencies. The National Guard was given free rein to fight 'communism' and had garrisons throughout the country, often described as independent fiefdoms. It worked in direct association with the CIA. The usual 'rule of thumb' was that new equipment was channelled to the Salvadorean army, while the Police and the National Guard were trained to use less barbaric methods. "The idea is that if a guy is standing with a protest sign, you don't have to cut him down with a machine gun," a US official explained, "you just gas him."

During the 1960s, political parties linked with the trade union movement and the Catholic Church once again began to demand reform. By 1972, their candidate managed to win the presidential elections. But the army, still controlled by the 14 families, annulled the victory. Armed forces and death squads directly employed by the families started to assassinate those campaigning for reform and for democracy.

Following this repression, a group of reform-minded officers who supported a return to constitutional rule tried to stage a coup. US reaction was swift, as Dr Fabio Castillo, former President of the National University of El Salvador, recounts:

> At about 8 o'clock in the morning, the headquarters of the insurgents agreed to receive the US military attaché who arrived in order to intervene on behalf of the military faction of (the) overthrown government which, at that moment, was at the international airport, ready to flee the country. At 11 am unmarked planes flying in from unknown bases started to bomb the civilian population and the positions held by the insurgents. The bombardments were intense and bloody and lasted until 5 pm. During the raid rockets and missiles were used of a type not available to the army of El Salvador. While this happened Guatemalan troops penetrated into Salvadorean territory after crossing the eastern border, and units from Nicaragua appeared

in San Miguel in the east of the country .... A few days after the Constitutionalists' insurrection had been smashed, officers of that movement declared that they had been able to observe the participation of US personnel using the US Embassy's communications for the purpose of co-ordinating the operations of the armies of Guatemala, Nicaragua and Honduras across the so-called *Consejo Centroamericano de Defensa*, CONDECA (Central American Defence Council).[11]

The United States then provided the new President, Colonel Arturo Armando Molina, at the time travelling in Taiwan, with a US air force jet to rush back to El Salvador.

The United States' intervention in 1972 was to prove disastrous. On the one hand, the army felt no restraint in launching a bloody wave of repression against the leftist opposition, and on the other, the 1972 electoral fraud signalled the demise of the reformist centre. The vacuum thus created gave rise to armed opposition. A guerrilla army began to take shape in the countryside.

The Americans backed Molina because he promised them and the ruling families 'structural capitalist modernization within the framework of national security'. Molina revitalised ORDEN, set up in 1967 by the CIA and the Salvadorean National Board. At the same time, the army stepped up its repression against the peasants, trade unionists and students.

On 29 November 1974, for instance, more than 60 soldiers and members of ORDEN entered the rural hamlet of La Cayetana in San Vicente province. A priest, who came to the scene later, reported:

> ... I saw the plaza covered with people's hair. The National Guard had cut off their hair with machetes, taking part of the skin with it .... The National Guard arrived in Cayetana with 60 machine guns, tear gas, a cannon .... When the farmers came, they grabbed their machine guns and sprayed the workers with gunfire .... (A) wife was able to reach her husband, grabbing him by the leg. The bullet hit him and she was bathed in blood ..... Those they killed, they cut their faces in pieces and chopped up the bodies with machetes. If you like, I will show you where they buried the brains.[12]

Such actions only increased the people's revolt against the regime swelling the ranks of the guerrilla 'Army of Deliverance'.

In fraudulent elections of 1977, characterised by mounting political violence by the army and security forces, Molina was ousted. In 1979 there was another coup, which only lasted six weeks. Another junta came to power and then another, each with fewer civilians and reformers than the previous one.

Meanwhile, two things occurred which dramatically changed the situation. The first was the increasing strength and popular support for the guerrilla army; and the second was the revolution in Nicaragua. The overthrow of the Samoza regime by Sandinista guerrillas renewed Washington's resolve to avoid the establishment of a second 'socialist' regime in Central America.

El Salvador was now caught between an irresistible force and an immovable object. The irresistible force was the guerrilla army of the countryside determined to battle to the end to rid El Salvador of the repression it has endured so long. The immovable object was the determination of the US to end the spread of 'communism' in its 'backyard'.

Thomas O. Enders, assistant Secretary of State for Inter-American affairs, put the issue thus:

> The decisive battle for Central America is underway in El Salvador .... If El Salvador is captured by a violent minority, who in Central America would not live in fear? How long would it be before strategic US interests—the canal, sea lanes, oil supplies—were at stake?[13]

This rationale failed to convince very many people. Congressman Gerry Studds asked: "Who has run El Salvador for the entire century if it hasn't been a violent minority? The Salvadorean junta is a violent minority".[14]

Nevertheless, the United States firmly backed the ruling junta. The Reagan administration announced its intention to "draw the line" at "communist subversion" in El Salvador. In February 1981, the State Department published a White Paper entitled "Communist Interference in El Salvador". It argued that "the insurgency in El Salvador had been progressively transformed into a textbook case of indirect armed aggression by communist power".[15] Documents were produced which the State Department claimed proved that Cuba was channelling arms from Ethiopia, Vietnam, East Germany, various Arab countries and the USSR to guerrillas via Nicaragua. Within days the US National Security Council announced plans to provide the junta with $25 million in additional military aid and another $40 million in economic assistance and aid.

Close examination of the White Paper revealed that the most important documents were fraudulent. They were attributed to guerrilla leaders who did not write them. Moreover, the conclusion drawn in the White Paper cannot be supported by the documents at all. This led the *Wall Street Journal* to conclude that "A close reading of the White Paper indicates ... that its authors probably were making a determined effort to create a 'selling' document, no matter how slim the background material".[16]

It is true that the liberation movement in El Salvador is Marxist. But it became Marxist, not out of a passionate devotion to Soviet dogma or communist principles, but because Marxism offered the only salvation from the economic exploitation and political repression enforced upon the people by a ruling elite backed by the United States. They are only 'communists' because they are fighting against the present 'capitalist' regime. As Jose Napolean Duarte put it to the *Los Angeles Times* in an interview in 1979, before he became El Salvador's President: "They (the military) have been told for 50 years to kill Communists; and anyone who disagrees with the government is a Communist. So that is all they know—to kill."[17] And kill they do. It is estimated that between the 1979 coup that brought Duarte to power and the end of 1981, 32,000 Salvadorean people were killed as a result of political violence.

In March 1980, repression escalated to an unprecedented level. Mutilated and tortured corpses began to appear daily throughout the country. One of the victims was Archbishop Romero who was shot by a hired assassin while taking Mass on 23 March 1980. Archbishop Romero had not only been concerned with the immediate issue of the repression, he also took a strong stand on the question of socio-economic injustice. He supported the right of the people to resist oppression. On 18 February 1980 he gave a homily in which he said: "For our Church, the political aspect of faith finds its boundaries in the world of the poor . . . . Depending on how the poor people are faring, the Church will support this or that political project from its specific position as a Church."[18] In a press interview on 7 March 1980, not long before his death, he stated:

> . . . given the present situation in the country. I believe more than ever in the popular organizations. I believe in the true necessity for the Salvadorean people to organize themselves because I believe they are the social forces which are going to advance, which are going to pressure, which are going to achieve a society with a genuine social justice and freedom.[19]

During the week Romero was assassinated, the Legal Aid office of San Salvador's Archbishopric reported that 798 other people were killed, 681 of them peasants. Also during March, President Duarte put in a request for $300 million in more aid. Reagan not only sent more aid but sent six US 'advisors' as well to El Salvador to help coordinate US-junta links and the training of the El Salvador army. The US also engaged other Latin American countries, Argentina, Honduras and Guatemala in particular, to aid the junta. "The United States is not going to allow a military triumph of the guerrillas," Thomas Enders told the Nicaraguan Minister o Foreign Affairs, Miguel D'Escoto, "It has the means and the desire to do so, irrespective of the political cost."[20]

On 24 February 1982, President Reagan made Enders' private remark formal executive policy. In a speech to the Organization of American States he asserted that the civil war in El Salvador came down to simple "communist subversion".

> Guerrillas armed and supported by and through Cuba are attempting to impose a Marxist-Leninist dictatorship on the people of El Salvador as part of a large imperialistic plan . . . .
> If we do not act promptly and decisively in defense of freedom, new Cubas will arise from the ruins of today's conflict. I believe free and peaceful development of our hemisphere requires us to help governments confronted with aggression from outside their borders to defend themselves . . . . Let our friends and our adversaries understand that we will do whatever is prudent and necessary to ensure the peace and security of the Caribbean area.[21]

What Reagan meant by acting 'decisively in defense of freedom' quickly became apparent. The US began conducting secret negotiations with a number of Latin American countries that could add to the number of military facilities available for use in "regional emergencies". The US currently maintains a large naval and air base at Guantanamo Bay on the south-eastern tip of Cuba. The Army's Southern Command—with land, air and naval facilities—is located in Panama. In Congressional testimony on 2 March 1982, within a week of Reagan's speech, Secretary Weinberger stated:

> We have discussions under way, basically of a classified nature, that would enable us to add to the number of facilities that we see in the future we may sometimes need. Obviously, they are proceeding on a completely negotiated basis between sovereign countries. I think there is a full appreciation in a number of those areas of the importance of having facilities of this kind that can serve our mutual benefit.[22]

The Pentagon asked for $21 milion in the 1983 military budget for "airfield improvements in the western Caribbean area". Although the Defense Department declined to say which countries would be involved, the State Department was more forthcoming. Spokesperson Dean E. Fischer stated:

> We are talking specifically in this instance about Colombia and Honduras.
> In any agreement we would reach for airfield construction, we would seek permission for use of the improved airfield by US aircraft on training, search and rescue and relief flights, and for such other activities as agreed upon by the two countries.[23]

Mr Fischer said that the decision to seek base rights in Colombia and Honduras was part of the Reagan administration's overall policy to improve economic, social and security conditions in the so-called Caribbean basin. Honduras and Colombia have expressed 'concern' about Cuban activities in the area; Honduras has been particularly 'worried' because of its borders with Nicaragua and El Salvador, he said.

When asked if it was contemplated that the Rapid Deployment Force, which is being developed primarily for the Middle East, might be used in the Caribbean, Mr Fischer said, "We do not envision the use of such facilities for rapid deployment forces, but I can't anticipate all future contingencies".

There was no explanation from the Pentagon or the State Department on the military need for new facilities in the western Caribbean. But a State Department official said that if the facilities were secured it would be as much a 'psychological advantage' as anything else, to demonstrate US backing to the countries there, particularly El Salvador.

Adm. Thomas B. Hayward, chief of naval operations, told a House Armed Services subcommittee that the Pentagon was studying options for using Navy and Marine forces to protect US interests in Central America and the Caribbean.

> The Joint Chiefs of Staff have been examining anew the numerous options considered feasible in support of our continued interest in Central America and the Caribbean. Our commitments require us to present increasingly a counterweight to Castro's expanding support of Central American and Caribbean insurgents, as well as his continued appetite for opportunism in Africa.[24]

The President also authorised covert operations against Nicaragua. He directed the CIA to begin building and funding a paramilitary force of up to 500 Latin Americans who would operate out of commando camps spread along the Nicaraguan-Honduran border.

The CIA plan would attempt to destroy vital targets in Nicaragua, such as bridges and power plants in an effort to disrupt transportation, communication and the economy. It would also divert Nicaraguan attention away from aiding the revolutionary army in El Salvador.

Operating with a $19 million budget from CIA funds, the commando unit would take orders from Washington. Reagan administration officals said that its size would be increased 'if necessary' by another commando unit of up to 1,000 troops the CIA is helping to train in Argentina.

Reagan's belligerence caused alarm throughout Latin America, even among US diplomats. Many were concerned that the US position was being based on wishful thinking rather than objective reality. As a US diplomat in San Salvador put it:

> In order to justify policy you make propaganda and interpret facts to justify a position. That's fine. Now the question is, are we making policy on the basis of our own propaganda? Is the information tainted by our own view?[25]

The answer, as this diplomat and some others came to conclude, is, 'Yes, absolutely'.

Having elevated El Salvador from a postage-stamp country to a battleground of the cold war, Reagan has narrowed his options. The US finds itself in El Salvador in a position similar to that of the Soviets in Afghanistan. In both cases, the superpower in question has dug itself in, supporting a regime that can hold on to its authority only by increasing violent repression of the people while maintaining a client relationship with a foreign government. This further alienates the people. They turn to the only alternative available—the guerrillas. "It's a replay of the Vietnam debate," a congressional aide said. "You have the phenomenon where some people are starting at a fairly early stage to say we're going to get over committed, we're not on the side of the angels. The other side may be raising the stakes, but if we're going to counter by also raising the stakes, we're just going to get further and further involved in support of a regime that we have no business supporting."[26]

It has often been said that those who do not know history are condemned to repeat it. As public and congressional opposition to his policy on El Salvador mounted, the connection between El Salvador and Vietnam became increasingly clear. Among the few who seemed not to see the connection was the President.

At a news conference on 17 February 1982, Mr Reagan was asked if he could assure the public that the United States would not be drawn deeper into the El Salvador conflict as it had in Vietnam. In reply, the President gave his personal recollections of history, which seemed to clash with what really happened.[27]

Mr Reagan said, "North and South Vietnam had been, previous to colonization, two separate countries." He said that at the 1954 Geneva conference, provisions had been made that "these two countries could by a vote of all their people decide together whether they wanted to be one country or not." He said that Ho Chi Minh, the Vietnamese Communist leader, "refused to participate in such an election".

The President said that US military advisers were then sent to South Vietnam to work in civilian clothing and without weapons, until they were attacked with "pipe bombs". Ultimately Mr Reagan said, former President John F. Kennedy authorized the "sending of a division of Marines".

Nearly all of these statements are either wrong or open to challenge.

When not artificially divided by Chinese or French colonialists, Vietnam has often been politically united. One of the most recent unifications was achieved by the Emperor Gia Long in 1802.

It was the French who administratively divided Vietnam into not two but three units. However, even under French rule, the country was reunified under Emperor Bao Dai in 1950, and the United States gave that entity diplomatic recognition in the same year.

The Geneva accords of 1954, which ended French rule in Indochina, provided for a temporary partition of Vietnam at about the 17th parallel and called for national elections in 1956. Neither the new government of South Vietnam nor the United States signed the accords, but Washington did undertake not to undermine the agreement.

The Saigon government under President Ngo Dinh Diem refused to participate in the proposed elections or even to participate in discussions on how such elections could be held. North Vietnamese President Ho Chi Minh was willing to stand for election and complained when such balloting did not occur.

In the mid-1950s, a US Military Assistance Advisory Group, in uniform, trained nine South Vietnamese divisions. As the civil war in the South grew in intensity, Kennedy, in late 1961, authorized 'combat support' of Vietnamese forces. Armed helicopter units, US fighter pilots flying with Vietnamese co-pilots and an eventual total of 19,000 combat advisers were soon in the country.

However, Kennedy did not send US ground combat units to Vietnam. President Lyndon B. Johnson sent a Marine Brigade there in March 1965, followed by the Third Marine Division and the 173rd Airborne Brigade.

Mr Reagan also seemed to misunderstand legislation on congressional 'oversight' of covert intelligence operations. He said "there's a law by which things of this kind have to be cleared with congressional committees before anything is done". In fact, the Intelligence Oversight Act of 1980 provides that the select intelligence committees of the Senate and the House should only be *informed* of covert intelligence operations, although the president may in some circumstances delay notification until after the operation is completed. The committees do not have, and have not sought, authority to veto such actions.

At another point in the news conference, when asked by a reporter if there were plans to destabilize the Nicaraguan government, Mr Reagan seemed to confuse Nicaragua and El Salvador.

"Well, no, we're supporting them," he said. Then realizing that the question was about Nicaragua, which the United States has called 'an ally' of Cuba, he cried out "wait a minute, wait a minute, I'm sorry, I was thinking of El Salvador. Here again, this is something upon which the national security interest—I just, I will not comment."

DO THE RUSSIANS WANT TO RULE THE WORLD?

Whatever the realities, the people in the West are frightened of Soviet actions in areas like Eastern Europe and Afghanistan. When that is coupled with Soviet support for revolutionary movements from Vietnam to Central America, people suspect that the Soviets are trying to implement a masterplan for world domination. The US and the West are seen as trying to protect the *status quo*, the Soviets as attempting to disrupt it, generally by subterfuge and violence. The Soviet policy is seen as being pro-Russian, pro-Soviet. They see themselves as the vanguard of the world's socialist movement. By contrast, the Western and American policy has largely been anti-Russian, anti-Soviet rather than being pro-West, pro-American. Although the West has sought expansion of economic interests, it has been caught in a negative mesh on political and ideological levels. On balance, the Soviet manoeuvring on the international chessboard often emerges as more positive than that of the West. They seem to be taking the initiative while the West is continually put on the defensive.

Because the Soviet state is a totalitarian system, it can employ a long term strategy. Before Andropov, the Soviets essentially have had only four rulers: Lenin, Stalin, Khrushchev and Brezhnev. What is possible, therefore, is the continuity of pressure over a long period of time in the attempt to transform any given situation into conformity with Marxist-Leninist ideology as defined by Soviet national interests.

Western democracies do not have the same advantage. During Brezhnev's single term there were five US Presidents, five British Prime Ministers, and four West German Chancellors. Electoral policies being what they are, it is well-nigh impossible to articulate, much less implement, a long term strategy. Democratic systems are by nature inclined to short term solutions in which practicality, not ideology, is the watchword. The one question that needs to be answered is 'What do I have to do to get elected?' Expediency governs political thinking. The dominance of the multinational corporations in the West has exacerbated this tendency. These corporations are governed by profit motive, not by concern for social welfare or the national good. They thus further direct Western thinking towards immediate results/profits/electoral successes rather than the imperative of thinking in long term strategies. 'What is good for General Motors is good for the United States'. On the international level, however, these corporations are not only capable but also willing to pervert the national good as well as the legitimate political process for their own long term economic gains. The events in Chile and El Salvador are only two examples among many.

This basic difference between the USSR and the West gives the USSR a distinct advantage. It goes a long way towards explaining why it is that despite the overwhelming superiority of the West in economic, scientific and technological terms, the USSR has managed in less than seventy years to emerge from Czarist obscurity to challenge the United States as the world's other superpower. This new found status underscores the fact that the USSR has over the years consistently outmanoeuvred the US and its allies in the areas of international politics.

Indeed, it can be said that because of its military, economic and scientific inferiority, the USSR had *had* to outmanoeuvre its rivals *politically* in order to survive. This political manoeuvering has taken the form of espionage, infiltrations, setting up of communist cells, and agitating especially in the trade unions and university campuses—in short, doing all those things necessary to destabilise target countries in order to generate the 'revolutionary situation' that will benefit the communist groups involved. This type of subterfuge and underhand manipulation of the levers of mass control have caused great alarm amongst those who wish to protect the democratic and capitalist systems from the encroachments that the totalitarianism of the USSR represents. This alarm is only deepened when the Soviets proclaim the 'inevitability' of world socialism.

Soviet international strategy, from Lenin onwards, has been based on the willingness to accept political risks despite relative military-strategic inferiority. They have proved themselves masters of the technique of creating a *fait accompli* which defies their adversaries to 'undo what has been done'. Moreover, while the Soviets have never been able to impose their will on the West, they have successfully *deterred* a Western counteraction on numerous occasions. Hungary 1956, Czechoslovakia 1968, Afghanistan 1979, and Poland 1981 are only a few examples.

In Soviet perceptions, the use of force and the acceptance of political risks are subject primarily to criteria of *expediency*, not legitimacy or morality. If Soviet military or political strength can 'objectively' serve to further Soviet state interests and thus, by

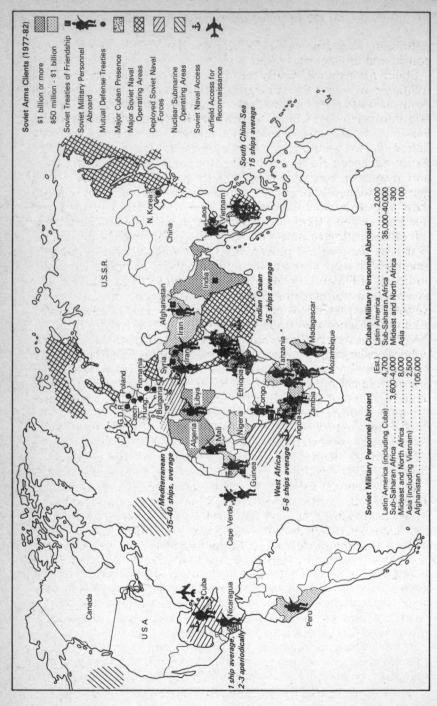

Soviet Arms Clients (1977-82)

- $1 billion or more
- $50 million - $1 billion
- Soviet Treaties of Friendship
- Soviet Military Personnel Abroad
- Mutual Defense Treaties
- Major Cuban Presence
- Major Soviet Naval Operating Areas
- Deployed Soviet Naval Forces
- Nuclear Submarine Operating Areas
- Soviet Naval Access
- Airfield Access for Reconnaissance

South China Sea 15 ships average

Indian Ocean 25 ships average

Mediterranean 35-40 ships, average

West Africa — 5-8 ships average

1 ship average, 2-3 aperiodically

U.S.S.R.

China

N. Korea

Laos

Vietnam

India

Afghanistan

Iran

Iraq

Syria

Poland

Romania

G.D.R.

Czech.

Hung.

Bulgaria

Libya

Algeria

Mali

Nigeria

Guinea

Cape Verde

Ethiopia

Congo

Tanzania

Zambia

Angola

Mozambique

Madagascar

Canada

U S A

Cuba

Nicaragua

Peru

Soviet Military Personnel Abroad

	(Est.)
Latin America (including Cuba)	4,700
Sub-Saharan Africa	3,600-4,000
Mideast and North Africa	8,000
Asia (including Vietnam)	2,500
Afghanistan	105,000

Cuban Military Personnel Abroad

Latin America	2,000
Sub-Saharan Africa	35,000-40,000
Mideast and North Africa	300
Asia	100

Soviet Global Power (*Source: Soviet Military Power: U.S. Government*) definition, strengthen world socialism, the acceptance of risks is considered as 'legitimate and just'.

Stalin, for instance, clearly recognised the political significance of military power and the strategic advantages of advancing the Red Army as far as possible into Eastern Europe, into Iran in the south, and into north-east China, Manchuria, Korea and Sakhalin in the Far East. In the last case, Soviet military offensives were only halted *after* the announcement of Japanese capitulation. As the Red Army advanced there were recurring conflicts over saving lives and resources versus making speedy military advances. Soviet generals frequently urged the minimising of losses. Stalin ordered them ahead to maximise territorial gain. The result has been that history received a tremendous kick from the Russian military boot.

It is interesting to note that while the US emerged from World War II as the *strongest* power, the USSR was the only country to emerge with *more territory*. It acquired Latvia, Estonia, Lithuania, and parts of Finland, Poland, Romania, China and Japan. With the exception of Iran and the Soviet occupation zone in Austria, the Red Army never retreated, even after the war was over. Soviet military presence was translated into Soviet political control.

Khrushchev carried forward the Stalinist technique of accepting political risks despite relative military-economic inferiority. Only Khrushchev included nuclear sabre rattling to the repertoire of Soviet political options. In fact, Khrushchev has been the only Soviet leader to threaten the use of nuclear weapons in a particular situation. During the Suez Crisis of 1957, he warned both the British and the French that they—as well as the Middle East—were within range of Soviet missiles. Again in both the Berlin crisis of 1960 and the Cuban missile crisis of 1962, Khrushchev tried to use Russia's newly developed nuclear strength to political advantage.

These attempts did not succeed, and Khrushchev was soon deposed by Brezhnev and Kosygin. What had become clear to the Soviet leadership was that the discrepancy between claims and capabilities, between doctrine and power could not be used to any advantage at the nuclear level. In the first place, the USSR was no match for the USA. When Kennedy and Khrushchev had come eyeball to eyeball over Cuba, it was Khrushchev who blinked. Secondly, the Soviets realised that at the nuclear level the only *real* options were to risk either global suicide or retreat. Khrushchev had wisely chosen the second option although he had to suffer humiliation before the world.

Marshal M.V. Zakharov, then Soviet Chief of Staff, summarised this critique of Khrushchev by saying that "subjectivism is dangerous in any activity ... particularly in military affairs which deal with problems of the country's defence".[1] This applied especially to those who claimed "strategic far-sightedness" but lacked "rudimentary knowledge of military strategy". Zakharov warned against over-emphasis on the nuclear weapon, stating that it was only "one weapon, and at that an untried one". Reliance on the nuclear weapon, he said, should not be turned into a "fetish".

Rather than use their nuclear strength *offensively*, therefore, the circle around Brezhnev realised that nuclear weapons could only be used *defensively*, that is, in the strategy of deterrence-through-denial described earlier. They realised back in the 1960s what the Americans have yet to realise, that nuclear war cannot be used for political advantage. The Soviets, therefore, began to seek parity and disarmament in nuclear weapons with the West, while attempting to regain the political initiative particularly in the Third World. A *defensive* strategy in the nuclear field combined with an *offensive* strategy in the political field came together. This was the cornerstone of the Soviet policy of *detente*.

For the Soviets, detente was a tactic, not a strategy. It was a means to an end, not the end itself. After the completion of the necessary buffer zones in the late Stalinist years and during the years of Khrushchev, combined with the lessons they had learnt from his mistakes, the Soviets now sought to cooperate with the West in economic and technological areas while keeping the ideological struggle alive. "Peaceful coexistence does not extend to the ideological struggle", Brezhnev said at the June 1969 meeting of communist parties in Moscow.[2] Before his departure to the US in 1973, he made it clear that "the class struggle of the two systems ... in the sphere of economics, politics, and ... ideology will be continued .... But we shall ensure that this inevitable struggle is transferred to a channel which does not threaten wars, dangerous conflicts and an uncontrolled arms race".[3]

The American leaders understood this view of detente. In 1974, Secretary of State Kissinger stated:

> Detente is not rooted in agreement of values: it becomes above all necessary because each side recognizes that the other is a potential adversary in a nuclear war. To us, detente is a process of managing relations with a potentially hostile country in order to preserve peace while maintaining our vital interests.[4]

Nixon and Brezhnev understood each other. Detente was the balancing of coexistence while maintaining one's 'vital interests'. For the Soviets, this meant above all catching up with the United States in nuclear capabilities. This can be seen in the *quantitative* leaps from the deployment of 200 land-based intercontinental missiles in 1964 to 800 in 1968 to actual numerical superiority over the US during SALT I with 1,530 missiles. The USSR also sought to catch up in the field of submarine-launched ballistic missiles. In *qualitative* terms also, the Soviets sought parity. New types of missiles were deployed. The multiple independent re-entry vehicle (MIRV) was introduced, and the manoeuvrable independent re-entry vehicle (MARV) was developed. All these developments came some years behind the US, of course, but during the period of detente, the Russians did attain rough quantitative and qualitative parity with US nuclear forces. This is not to say they had actually caught up with and could match the US system for system. Our examination in later sections will demonstrate that in most categories of comparison the US has a comfortable lead over the USSR. Rough 'parity' only means that the two superpowers, between them, can destroy our world many times over. Since it is the first and the first time alone that matters, the capacity to kill beyond the first time has no strategic meaning.

Perhaps the experience of Tamerlane after the general massacre of Delhi ordered by him is a case in point. An old fakir told him "your will is as sharp as the edge of a sword which has put everybody to death, but if your desire for blood be not satiated, give these corpses life so that you can kill them again".

The Soviets have also challenged US superiority at sea, although the Soviets match US naval power even less than US nuclear power. The US navy dominates all the major oceans of the world with nuclear powered fleets of aircraft carriers, submarines and warships. The Soviets have only managed to establish a mere *presence* in these oceans. Yet coming from a position in 1945 where they had virtually no navy at all, this is quite an achievement. As with their attainment of nuclear parity, this presence of Soviet vessels on the high seas is considered by them as defensive, at least vis-a-vis the US. It has been pointed out by US Commander Herrick, who observes that "the complete lack of (Soviet) strike carrier forces constitutes a fundamental qualitative difference that necessitates resorting to the defensive in naval strategy".[5]

As the USSR established itself as a global power, it often acted offensively in that area of conflict in which it had always excelled, *political agitation*, particularly in the Third World. In the late fifties and the early sixties when the West was pouring money into India's rural electrification programme, the People's Publishing House was distributing free copies of the Koran and the Mahabharata printed in Moscow. But only to those households which had been connected. The people enjoying the blessings of this new luxury, electricity, which illuminated their holy books in the dark, invariably said "these Russians are great people!".

America's debacle in Indo-China resulted in the collapse of the South-East Asia Treaty Organisation (SEATO) in September 1975.

This treaty had been initiated by the US during the Cold War as part of its 'containment' policy towards the USSR. After SEATO disintegrated, southern Asian nations had to make some sort of accommodation with Moscow. Moreover, with their alliance with the newly independent Vietnam, the Soviets had a south-east Asian counterweight against China. As the Chinese had played the US card against the Soviets, so the Soviets played the Vietnamese card against China. On 29 June 1978, Vietnam became a full member of COMECON and on 3 November 1979 signed a treaty of friendship and cooperation with the USSR. Moscow did not control Vietnam, however, and had to support Hanoi both when Vietnam invaded Kampuchea in December 1978 and when Vietnam provoked a Chinese attack in February 1979. Through all this, Vietnam was careful not to hand over to the Soviets the huge ex-American military base at Cam Ranh Bay. The Vietnamese have had enough of foreign domination.

Africa also was a target of Soviet political manoeuvring. In 1974, Soviet opportunities were increased by the collapse of the Portuguese empire, the fall of Emperor Haile Selassie of Ethiopia, and the establishment of radical regimes in Benin, Somalia and

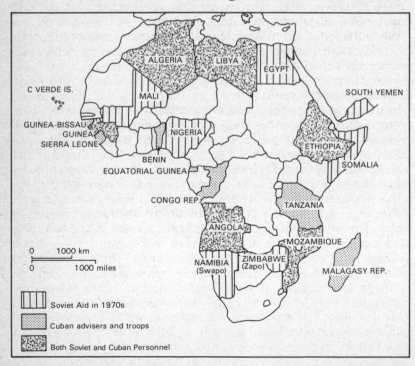

The Soviet Involvement in Africa
(*Source:* The Soviet Superpower, *Heinemann Educ.*)

Madagascar. It was in Africa, in particular, that the Soviet naval strength, weak though it was as compared to that of the Americans, could be brought to bear. The USSR had the airlift and sealift capabilities to deliver and supply the Cuban troops in Africa.

Joint Soviet-Cuban operations in Africa began in Angola in 1975. The Americans had been in Angola prior to the Soviets and the Cubans, pouring materials and money into their particular groups in the civil war. Then the South Africans invaded in order to further tip the scales in favour of the pro-Western factions. At this point the Soviets took action. In October 1975, 28 Soviet ships and 22 Soviet air freighters brought arms, Soviet technicians, and 13,000 Cuban troops to the assistance of the Marxist faction of Agostino Neto. Neto went on to win and set up a socialist state. By 1980, 20,000 Cuban troops were engaged with the Angolan army in fighting guerrillas still being armed and supported by the US and South Africa. Despite this Soviet and Cuban aid, however, Angola refused to give the USSR the naval facilities it requested. Guinea also refused to give the Soviets naval facilities, in spite of Soviet and Cuban aid. The Soviet-Cuban presence, whether in combat or in training, has also occurred in Mozambique, Tanzania, Ethiopia, Libya, Algeria, Guinea-Bissau, Sierra Leone, Benin, Equatorial Guinea and the Congo Republic.

While the initial aid to Angola was a necessary counterweight to US and South African intervention, much of the Soviet-Cuban activity since then does not seem to have an ideological rationale. In the Horn of Africa, for instance, the Russians have been downright opportunistic.

In the early 1970s, the USSR acquired naval facilities at Berbera on the Somali coast. This allowed the Soviet navy to maintain a presence in the Red Sea, Persian Gulf and Indian Ocean. The USSR equipped and trained the 20,000 strong Somali army but when Somalia attacked Ethiopia in 1977, the Soviets responded to Ethiopian pleas for help and airlifted 20,000 Cuban troops into Ethiopia. For a while, until President Siad Barre of Somalia threw the Soviets and Cuban troops out of his country, the USSR enjoyed the novel experience of aiding, training and equipping both sides in the same war—a tactical lesson they had learnt from the history of the British Empire. The Somalis were defeated in 1978. Cuban and Soviet advisers then helped Ethiopian President Haile Mengistu against the Eritrean separatists in north-east Ethiopia who had previously been receiving aid from the USSR.

What has struck people in the West as particularly alarming about Soviet activity in the Third World has been that the Soviets have largely given military aid. Unable to match the economic aid of the West and with no surplus food or industrial supplies, the

Soviets have had little to give other countries except weapons. This inspired Chinese Premier Chou En-lai to ask: "What has happened to the first socialist country in the world? It's become nothing but an armaments dealer."[6] This state of affairs has been capitalised upon by the US, prompting Kissinger to remark "All the Russians can give you is arms; we Americans can give you peace."[7] While US arms sales are vastly more than the Soviets, the Russians have seemed more sinister because while the US can afford to give bombs as well as butter, the Soviets can only afford to supply bullets.

Soviet international diplomacy has been hampered in other ways. A considerable proportion of Soviet aid is directed towards Islamic countries where Soviet atheism is found to be jarring. Additionally while English is an international language, thanks to British colonialism in the last two centuries, few speak Russian outside the USSR, particularly in the Third World. The Soviets have frequently been beset by linguistic and cultural problems.

All this has contributed to the image of the 'Ugly Russian'. The Soviets have broken out of the US network of bases and alliances. They have established themselves as a global power, acting at times opportunistically. But they, too, have had their share of disasters. They have been thrown out of numerous countries. They have little to give their client states except a few weapons and an unlimited supply of ideology.

Indonesia, a major Soviet client in the 1960s, broke ties with the Soviets in 1965 after the failure of a communist led coup. Over 500,000 died in the resulting bloodbath.

Egypt received over $4 billion in Soviet military aid during the 1960s and early 1970s. After the Yom Kippur War in 1973, President Sadat abruptly threw the Russians out and turned to the US and NATO for weapons. In 1979–82, Soviet arms previously supplied to Egypt turned up in Afghanistan in the hands of the rebels fighting the Soviet forces.

Mozambique, recipient of Soviet arms since 1975, rejected Soviet requests for a naval base and turned to the US and NATO for military and economic aid. The Sudan broke all relations with the USSR in 1977, expelling all Soviet military advisors, after receiving Soviet support for years.

China has been the USSR's most important foreign policy failure. They had a falling-out in the 1960s, and Soviet technicians were abruptly withdrawn. Among other forms of aid, the Soviets had supplied China with information on how to construct nuclear weapons. These two communist giants now glare at each other with nuclear missiles over a tense border.

Even in Europe, the most important area of Soviet concern,

things have gone badly. Despite Soviet attempts to consolidate Eastern Europe, Yugoslavia, Albania and Romania have managed to evade the WTO net. Hungary 1956, Czechoslovakia 1968, Poland 1981, do not bode well for the area the Soviets do control. There has also been a major recession in pro-Soviet communist movements in the West. The Cominform, which Stalin set up in 1947 to unite all communists in European countries, east and west, has broken up. This indicates a serious setback in the Soviet strategy of using political agitation to attain objectives. Unable to agree with Soviet actions in Hungary, Czechoslovakia, Afghanistan and Poland, most communist parties in the West of Europe have rejected the supremacy of Soviet leadership and moved in the direction of 'Eurocommunism'. The Italian Communist Party even endorses a critical commitment to NATO.

As if this is not bad enough, many of the countries in the Soviet bloc are in heavy debt to Western banks, particularly Poland and Romania. All Soviet bloc countries, including the USSR, are dependent on Western technology and now, even food. The Soviets depend on the American mid-west for their grain and IBM for their computers. Not a good omen for a nation wanting to rule the world, is it?

The Cold War picture most Westerners have of Soviet political agitators and the Red Army relentlessly pursuing the goal of world domination must be seriously reframed if not completely discarded. Despite a foreign policy that seems robust and grabs the initiative, the Soviets have met with far more foreign policy reverses than successes over the last three decades. They are proving inept at controlling their 'allies' in the Warsaw Pact. They have lost control over the communist parties in the NATO countries. They blundered into Afghanistan and do not know how to get out. They have been thrown out of, or denied facilities in, most of the Third World countries they have tried to influence. While they have established a sea and air power that can now link their forces worldwide, this capability has not served them particularly well, much less presenting a threat to the US.

In fact, if one looks closely, one discerns a genuine hesitance and insecurity in Soviet behaviour. With the important exception of the Cuban missile crisis in 1962 when Khrushchev beat his shoe in the UN and tried to pull a nuclear bluff on President Kennedy that brought the world perhaps the closest it has ever come to nuclear war, Soviet leaders have by-and-large acted cautiously and have pulled back when seriously challenged. Soviet advances in the military-technical field, notably in the armaments race, have only been in *general terms*. They have not linked their nuclear capabilities to specific contingencies or automatic obligations, except in the instance of the Suez crisis, thus leaving plenty of room for ambiguity. This is an important factor in keeping tensions under control. Their escalations in the arms race have occurred when the *actual dangers* of military conflict involving the two superpowers *were least*, and most of their forays into Africa and the Middle East occurred during the era of detente.

The US, on the other hand, has in fact used nuclear weapons twice and has threatened to use them at least nineteen known times. To give just a few examples: Eisenhower threatened to use them during the Korean war; Kennedy threatened to use them during the Cuban missile crisis; Nixon threatened to use them in Vietnam and actually put all US nuclear forces on alert during the Middle East war in 1973; and Carter threatened to use them during the Iranian crisis.

Since 1945, there have been 125 violent conflicts between nations; 95% of these have occurred in the developing world. In most cases, foreign troops were used. The US and NATO have accounted for 79% of these foreign interventions; other developing nations for 15%; the USSR and the WTO for 6%, according to World Military and Social Expenditures, 1981. Moreover, while the Soviets, emphasising the Middle East and Africa, trained some 40,000 military personnel between 1955 and 1980, the US trained more than 400,000 during this period, mostly in Latin America and the Far East. Approximately 75% of those trained by the superpowers came from nations run by military juntas. Finally, while the two US corporations, General Electric and Westinghouse, control 70% of the world nuclear reactor market and US and Western European countries are involved in selling nuclear technology to nearly 50 countries worldwide, thus enabling the recipient countries to develop nuclear weapons, Soviet nuclear exports have been limited to its WTO allies, Finland and India.

US strategy since the 1960s has been to encircle the USSR with a string of alliances: in the Pacific joining the US fleets and bases with South Korea, Japan, China, Philippines, New Zealand and Australia; in the Indian Ocean, joining the US rapid deployment force with Australia, Somalia, Kenya, Pakistan, Saudi Arabia and South Africa; dominating the Mediterranean with the US Mediterranean fleet and the alliance with Egypt, Israel, Turkey and Greece; in Europe, holding together the member nations of the NATO in an anti-Soviet coalition; and on the Western Hemisphere, using whatever force necessary to keep the area immune from Soviet influence. The common link between all these 'theatres' is over 2,000 US bases around the world backed up by the conventional and nuclear strength of the US Armed Forces.

What is important to note about US power, however, is that

although it has used its troops numerous times in overseas interventions, has threatened to use nuclear weapons in numerous specific instances, controls the major oceans and dominates the world's arms and nuclear technology trade, its strength is eroding. Its overwhelming nuclear strength has not proved to be very much use in the turbulence of every-day politics.

The US suffered a crushing defeat in the Indo-China war, for instance, after pouring in hundreds of billions of dollars, over 500,000 troops, and using extensive chemical warfare techniques. In Iran also, the Americans suffered ignominious defeat. The Shah had been the best weapons customer the US had, receiving nearly $1 billion in military aid. His secret police, SAVAK, were trained by and worked closely with the CIA. Yet he was toppled by revolutionaries armed with 300,000 US weapons looted from government armouries. As if that was not bad enough, youthful militants stormed the US embassy and took nearly the entire staff as hostages. President Carter did little besides wring his hands, although he finally tried a helicopter rescue attempt that ended up in flames in the desert.

Closer to home, the US backed President Samoza of Nicaragua, giving him $24 million in military aid and training his army and secret police. Samoza was overthrown by the Sandinista rebels in 1979, who installed a socialist government with links to Cuba, the USSR and Eastern Europe. A similar dynamic seems to be at present emerging in El Salvador.

US foreign policy, particularly since the Second World War, is giving eloquent, if not tragic, testimony to what is perhaps the oldest lesson in history: the futility, frequently the fatality, of foreign interference to maintain a government in power which is unwanted or hated by its own people. The Soviets have not yet learnt this truth either.

Like the USSR, the United States seems to be losing its grip, even over its friends. It was mentioned earlier that democracies generally do not articulate long-term strategies or seem able to discern consequences much beyond immediate profit or the next election. Nowhere is this more true than in the United States, where this tendency has been accentuated by the fact that the US is geographically cut off from most of its allies and all of its enemies.

In 1950, the US ambassador to the USSR, George Kennan, made an entry in his diary:

> Never before has there been such utter confusion in the public mind with respect to US foreign policy. The President doesn't understand it; the Congress doesn't understand it; nor does the public, nor does the press. They all wander around in a

labyrinth of ignorance and error and conjecture, in which truth
is intermingled with fiction at a hundred points, in which
unjustified assumptions have attained the validity of premises,
and in which there is no recognized and authoritative theory to
hold on to.[8]

American ignorance at the close of the Second World War was
matched only by its arrogance. Its economic and military strength
was unmatched. It was the sole possessor of the atomic bomb. The
tragedy of the last four decades is that American strength did not
diminish American ignorance nor humble its pride.

It remains the only major country in the world that has never had
a political Labour movement or Social Democratic party
participating directly in its national government. The American
electorate is apathetic. Since 1964, each successive President has
been elected by a declining proportion of the eligible electorate.
When Ronald Reagan was elected in 1980, 50% of those eligible did
not vote.

The average American seems driven much more by the desire to
have more and better consumer goods than by the desire to use
strength wisely. Citizens learn little of European or Third World
affairs either at school, or through newspapers, radio, or television. Americans, even in the last quarter of the twentieth century
essentially remain what they have always been—isolationists.

It is this combination of an internal sense of isolationism,
ignorance of world affairs and misplaced pride, which is the single
greatest factor in the decline of US power. The Soviets have played
no part in the creation of this combination. At most they have
benefited by exploiting US weaknesses already there. In the past
two decades, the US economy has entered a long decline in
relation to its competitors, particularly Japan, West Germany and
France. The cultural and diplomatic authority of the US has also
been sliding downwards.

This became particularly clear when President Reagan sent a
cheerful message to world political and economic leaders meeting
at the European Management Forum in Davos, Switzerland in
early February 1982. "Our values and principles have never failed
us when we have lived up to them," Reagan said in a colour movie
presentation. "Think back over the past 35 years. They have been
remarkable years of peace, prosperity and progress."[9]

Former British Prime Minister Edward Heath responded by
asking why, if everything had been so rosy and progress so
'remarkable', Reagan now seemed determined to change
everything. Everything was *not* well, charged Heath:

> The edifice of international cooperation, built up by the West for
> over 30 years, is disintegrating. In the Atlantic alliance, we have

become disunited as rarely before in our response to crises, particularly those arising in the Middle East, Poland, Afghanistan and other regions of the Third World.[10]

The NATO reaction to the Soviet invasion of Afghanistan might be understood, he said, for it came as a surprise. But NATO consulted about Poland for a year and a half and "yet failed dismally to provide any unified response to this action".

Heath went on to call the monetarist policies of Britain and the US a "disaster". He said we live in an 'interest rate society' where excess funds seek out high interest rates, not new investment outlets. He concluded with a prediction:

Unless Europe takes speedy action to insulate itself effectively from the American policy of large budget deficits and high interest rates, it will be condemned indefinitely slavishly to follow US monetary policy. This will leave most European governments with no option but to tighten fiscal policy sharply. Yet the most inevitable result of such fiscal cutbacks is to endanger expenditure on defence and security—ironically the foremost priorities of the very governments which have helped to bring about this situation.[11]

Besides economic problems with its allies, the US is also beset with diplomatic ones. Ever since the Second World War, American Presidents and Cabinet secretaries have talked mainly about either more defence or more war. Yet talk of war sounds much different to the people in Germany, who know they are the front line, than to the public in the US, not all of whom could even find Germany on the map. It is somehow different to hear Europeans talk about cruise missiles in Vienna where highway signs to Budapest are as commonplace as signs to Newark are for Manhattan taxi drivers, than to hear such talk in the US where more cruise missiles merely mean more business for America.

The US talks so much about weapons and its plans to use them that many Europeans are becoming convinced that this is all Americans have in mind. This has caused resentment and fear. In the little town of Burghfield, England, for instance, near where the Americans wish to deploy some of their cruise missiles, an action committee was formed to fight plans to house the 800 US service people, who are supposed to accompany the missiles. This is only a small example, but similar anti-American feeling and actions are becoming evident all over Western Europe, particularly in West Germany, giving rise to a tide of hostility towards the US.

The Sunday Times of London said in an editorial on 1 February 1982 that this anti-American feeling was due to two factors:

One is a generalized fear that superpowers have fallen apart and lost control of events. The other is a specific fear that President Reagan's administration is determined to challenge the Soviet Union to an arms race which cannot but raise tension and increase the danger of war.

As one Dutch politician put it:

We expect the Russians to do things like those they have done in Poland and Afghanistan, and we condemn them. But we don't expect the United States, which we have always respected, to behave in the aggressive way that Mr Reagan is behaving, so many of us feel hurt and disappointed.[12]

Egon Bahr, a leading member of the West German Social Democratic Party, stated in an interview that "The Reagan administration's foreign policy balance sheet is ... uniquely negative. All along the line, and to all their friends, things look worse than they did at the end of 1980."[13] He added: "If by some devilish trick Moscow had placed an agent in a top Washington job and given him this task, it is doubtful whether he would have been so successful."

The tragedy is that American belligerence is the inevitable consequence of political ineptness and economic decline. The more US military superiority and global economic control has been challenged, not only by the USSR, but also by Third World countries, Japan and even members of NATO, the more the US has relied on the threat of its nuclear arsenal to protect its 'vital interests'. Beginning from its policy of mutual assured destruction (MAD) in the 1950s when it threatened to blow up the world before relinquishing control, it has now articulated an even more insidious nuclear strategy by which US 'vital interests' can be maintained: the notion of being able to fight 'limited' nuclear wars in particular 'theatres' of the world where US interests are seriously threatened. The Soviets may indeed harbour the secret dream of attaining world dominance one day. But it is the US which in fact *has* world dominance and has given every intention to resorting to nuclear war before relinquishing global control.

While the Soviets present a threat in *political* terms, because of their incessant ideological warfare and agitation, it is the Americans who are the threat in *nuclear* terms. The US is seeking to compensate for its loss of real influence by using the muscle of its nuclear superiority. It has yet to learn what the Soviets apparently learned after Khrushchev's mistakes, that nuclear strength cannot be translated into political advantage.

Both superpowers seem, at best, to muddle along from one crisis to another, winning here, losing there, taking advantage of a situation here, being taken advantage of there. As the Russian experience in Afghanistan indicates, mistakes are the norm, particularly in the Third World, where after centuries of colonialism, the people want neither the neo-colonialism of the US and Western European multinationals or the rigid orthodoxy of Marxist-Leninism.

What is even more important than either Soviet intentions or American threats is the fact that world control by any single nation is a thing of the past. It belongs to that chapter of world history called 'Imperialism and Colonialism' in which European powers spread out around the world to conquer it, colonise it, exploit it. Britain built the largest empire in recorded history during the eighteenth and nineteenth centuries. There was a time when the sun never set on the Union Jack. While some have suggested that this is because God did not trust the British in the dark, perhaps it is also true that the ease with which the Europeans colonised the rest of the world was due to the comparative weakness of the people colonised. The Third World, as we know it today, had no industry or modern weaponry; there was not a developed sense of nationhood, particularly in Africa; and there was not the realisation of what was happening until it was too late.

The twentieth century has seen a dramatic change. Britain is now the 'poor man' of Europe. The Arabs, once colonised, now control the world oil production. African countries have been established and white supremacy has been successfully challenged in every section of the continent except South Africa. China, once carved up by the Europeans and Americans and put to sleep by the British with Indian opium, is an awakening giant. Vietnam successfully fought first the French colonialists and then the American military and has kept the Soviets at bay. In Latin America, Brazil and Argentina are on the verge of possessing nuclear weapons. In 1982, Argentina challenged the British sovereignty over the Falkland Islands.

Soviet and American power will inevitably decline in the face of nationalism, non-alignment, and the economic and military competition that arises from independence. The USSR's chance of supplanting the US is minimal, if not non-existent. At most, both superpowers will retain their alliances in Europe, although for how long is an open question. Outside this sphere it will be independence and competition, not more colonialism that will be the watchword. Increasingly, nations will be banding together in blocs for mutual strength and security: the Common Market, the COMENCOM, the Organisation of Petroleum Exporting Countries (OPEC), the Organisation of African Unity, Organisation of American States, the 77 Group, etc. The Soviet and the American 'blocs' are only two among many.

If there is any new movement that can and should bring the

world together it is that of internationalism. Colonialism, hegemony—whether from the East or the West—has now passed. The agency of the United Nations, imperfect as it is, must increasingly be seen as the arena in which disputes must be taken, the discussions held, and solutions worked out. Given the enormous nuclear arsenals of the Americans, Russians, British, French and Chinese today and others tomorrow; the increased strength of the Third World; and growing equality between states, history leaves only two choices for the human race:

Unity or Annihilation.

3 Nuclear Balance

The NATO decision to deploy nearly 600 American Cruise and Pershing II missiles beginning in 1983 has caused the greatest storm of protest since the early 1960s. The magnitude of the public outcry against their deployment belies their size. The Cruise missiles are really nothing more than small pilotless jet airplanes programmed to traverse a prescribed route and then explode into their targets. Moreover, while many missiles soar into outer space and travel at incredible speeds, the Cruise is rather slow and is limited to operating in the lower atmosphere where it can ingest enough air to mix with its fuel for combustion. The Cruise missiles are also small. About twenty feet in length, they are propelled by a fanjet engine only thirty inches long by twelve inches wide, weighing a mere 126 pounds.

Then why all the fuss?

First, the Cruise missiles are remarkably versatile. They can be launched from airplanes, from the ground, from surface ships, and from submarines under the sea. They also have an extremely sophisticated navigational system. The system consists of an autopilot controlled by an inertial guidance platform, which in turn is updated periodically by a sensor system called TERCOM (terrain contour matching). With TERCOM, a Cruise missile can skim along the ground so low that radar detection is virtually impossible and continue on course by comparing the terrain below it with a map of the target route stored in its computer. When it must deviate from its course due to an obstacle, a correctional signal is sent to the guidance package which orders corrective manoeuvres. This self-correcting device is designed to enable each missile to hit its target with deadly accuracy. The explosive capacity of each missile is equivalent to 200,000 tons of TNT—$16\frac{1}{2}$ times more than the Hiroshima bomb. Finally, Cruise is the first missile system to be virtually undetectable by the enemy. Up until now, Soviet and US satellites could photograph the 'enemy' missile silos and therefore be sure of their positions. Submarines can be tracked;

airplanes monitored; and warships counted. The Cruise missile, however, cannot be satisfactorily tracked or monitored or counted.

The initial reason for the deployment of the Cruise and Pershing II missiles was that they were necessary to counter the Soviet deployment of SS–20s. This was made clear in the NATO communiqué concerning the Cruise and Pershing II decision in December 1979. In a speech entitled "The Challenge for NATO in the 1980s", the US Permanent Representative to the North Atlantic Council, W. Tapley Bennett, stated:

> ... it is clear for those who will see that for twenty years the only long-range nuclear missiles in Europe have been Soviet; it is clear that the modernization of that Soviet force of SS–4 and SS–5 missiles with newer, mobile, MIRVED SS–20 missiles began prior to the NATO decision to modernize its forces with the deployment of Cruise missiles and Pershing Two; and it is clear that the size of the agreed NATO program is less than the size of the force the Soviets already have deployed. Moreover, the Soviets are continuing to expand their ... force rapidly, with some 220 SS–20s now deployed, representing 660 warheads, which cover all of Europe with lethal danger.[1]

Although widely disseminated, this rationale did not convince the European public. Tens of thousands of people demonstrated all over Europe. The message was clear; no Cruise missiles, no Pershing IIs. Why this upsurge of public opposition to what has officially been claimed as a protection of NATO populations? Did the people know something that officials did not?

The SS–20 is a medium-range nuclear missile capable of hitting any European target. It is a modernisation of the old SS–4s and SS–5s which the Soviet Union deployed against NATO in the early 1960s. Each SS–20 missile carries three warheads. These new warheads are in fact smaller than the SS–4s and SS–5s but their increased precision gives them about the same destructive power. Moreover, while NATO decries the fact that the SS–20s can hit targets anywhere in Europe, the SS–4s and SS–5s have been able to do this for 20 years. So nothing is really new about the vulnerability of targets in Europe.

What is interesting is that if one looks at the official record of NATO pronouncements, the 'threat' of the SS–20s did not really begin to loom large until the Cruise missile contracts were being signed between the Boeing Aerospace Corporation and the US Defense Department, signalling that the missiles were shortly to roll off the assembly lines.

Former Italian General and Allied Supreme Vice-Commander in Europe for Nuclear Affairs Nino Pasti, has chronicled the official statements of NATO referring to the 'threat' of the SS–20s.[2] He points out that the NATO military analysts and high command have known about them for years without raising any alarm. The final communique of the Atlantic Council on 8 December 1976, for example, did not even mention the Soviet theatre weapons (meaning weapons capable of hitting NATO targets). The final communique of the NATO Defence Planning Committee on the same day merely referred to the 'expected' deployment of the SS–20s. Again on 11 May 1977, the communique of the Atlantic Council made no mention of the SS–20s. In fact, the communique of the NATO Ministerial Guidance of 18 May 1977 stated that "it is in the conventional field ... where the growth of Warsaw Pact capability is most pronounced. In particular the Warsaw Pact ground forces have the capability to stage a major offensive in Europe without reinforcement".[3]

The communique of the Atlantic Council on 9 December 1977 again made no mention of the SS–20s. What concerned the Defence Planning Committee was the 'build-up' of conventional forces. In presenting the US defence budget for 1978, US Secretary of Defense, Donald Rumsfeld, expressed confidence in the existing NATO nuclear deterrent: "Theatre-wide strike forces," he said, "include US and allied nuclear armed tactical aircraft (for the US primarily Air Force F111, F4, Navy A6 and A7), US and FRG (Federal Republic of Germany) Pershing, UK (United Kingdom) Polaris, SLBM (Submarine Launch Ballistic Missile) and bombers and some US Poseidon SLBM warheads. These forces can execute pre-planned and selective strikes against a variety of targets in the theater in support of both limited and theater-wide operations."[4]

For almost all of 1978, no concern about the SS–20s was expressed by either NATO or the US. It was on 6 December 1978 that the Defence Planning Committee raised concern, and then not against the SS–20s as such but about the possibility that they might be transformed into intercontinental missiles of the SS–16 variety. Because the SS–4s and SS–5s could already cover Europe, there was no cause for alarm as far as Europe was concerned.

The Nuclear Planning Group communique of 25 May 1979 is the critical one, according to General Pasti. It states that the ministers took note of the SS–20 missiles and that their examination of a modernisation of the long-term capability of NATO mandated that it maintain and update the nuclear theatre forces "without increasing dependence on the nuclear weapons or prejudicing long-term defence improvements in conventional forces".[5] No decision was taken at this stage regarding the possible updating of long-range theatre components. "The Ministers emphasised that consideration of a modernisation effort would need to take full account of arms control possibilities". Pasti points out three important things about this communique: first, the non-dramatic nature of the SS–20 and hence the need for further studies; second, the concern about not increasing the role of nuclear forces; and thirdly, the concern about arms control.

But the Cruise missile makes arms control impossible, a point conceded even by the US National Security Council in April 1977, when it stated that the Cruise missile "raises complex issues due to its relatively small size, mission flexibility and its compatibility with different kinds of launch platforms .... Verification of arms control limitation with Tomahawk (the US name for the Cruise missile) is a difficult problem ... missile range, for example, is difficult to verify because range can be extended through non-detectable changes in flight profile or payload fuel rations."[6]

The Nuclear Planning Group on 25 April 1979 and The Atlantic Council on 31 May 1979 again stressed the importance of arms control. In October President Brezhnev agreed publicly to the importance of negotiations and withdrew 20,000 troops and 1,000 tanks from East Germany as a gesture of good faith. Despite this, the US put enormous pressure on NATO to accept the Cruise and Pershing II missiles. On 12 December 1979, NATO agreed to do this. This complete turnabout came in only a few months.

Public opinion exploded into such an outcry that by March 1980, the Pentagon began to have second thoughts. It publicly floated the idea of not deploying Cruise missiles in Britain, Holland, Belgium, West Germany and Italy in 1983 but rather stationing them on submarines. This might be necessary, the Pentagon reasoned, "to avoid embarrassing political discussions" in Britain, Holland and Belgium.[7]

Under the weight of the "embarrassing political discussions" which the Pentagon was hoping to avoid, the official rationale for wanting the Cruise and Pershing II missiles ceased to emphasise the "threat" of the SS–20s. One increasingly heard an indictment against the Soviet Union for not having proposed arms control negotiations before building the SS–20 missile. To have any moratorium on weapons would lock a Soviet "advantage" in place. Thus the Cruise missiles were needed to keep "parity".

Again, General Pasti is helpful. Having been an integral part of the NATO command structure, he was in a position to know. "This accusation," he says, "is absolutely false and turns the truth upside down."[8] He points out that at the press conference in Vladivostock on 24 November 1974, after Presidents Ford and Brezhnev signed the agreement limiting strategic nuclear weapons (the nuclear weapons the US and USSR reserve exclusively for each other), Secretary of State Henry Kissinger said "As you know, the Soviet Union has maintained that the forward based systems (theatre nuclear weapons aimed at Europe) should be included in the total, and this was one of the big obstacles to an agreement previously. The progress that has been made in recent months is that the Soviet Union gradually gave up asking for compensation for the FBS (forward based systems), partly because (they) are not suitable for a significant attack on the Soviet Union".[9] The facts, therefore, are that it was the *US*, not the USSR, which rejected talks on limiting missiles aimed at Europe. The USSR only gave up its insistence for including the forward based systems in the negotiations after it was assured that NATO would not deploy any missiles capable of hitting Russian territory. Both the Cruise and Pershing II are strategic weapons from the Soviet perspective. They are capable of hitting Russian territory.

By June 1981, public disbelief in the official statements had reached the point where NATO was forced to change its rationale again. European governments started emphasising the *arms control* potential of the Cruise missiles. Arguments about the 'threat' of SS–20s and about the Soviets not asking for negotiations before were minimised. The new thrust stressed that the NATO decision to adopt the Cruise and Pershing II missiles offered the only way to convince Moscow to reduce the number of its SS–20's.

This shift of emphasis, however, which in Europe was felt to be essential to stem the rising tide of public opinion, brought about a major divergence of thought with the Reagan administration. Some US officials were privately caustic about what they saw as a European temptation to pursue arms control uncritically. Over-emphasis on arms control, they warned, might create unrealistic public expectations and make NATO's military policy too dependent on negotiations with the Soviet Union.

German Chancellor Helmut Schmidt publicly unveiled his 'zero-option' proposal at this time, calling for the West not to deploy the Cruise and Pershing IIs, if the Soviets would not deploy their SS–20s. US strategists responded by saying such a proposal was remote and probably undesirable. Secretary of State Haig called the idea 'preposterous'.[10]

The Americans acknowledged that both military security (deploying the Cruise and Pershing IIs)—and disarmament diplomacy (more talks on arms control)—were part of the original 12 December 1979 NATO decision. But they insisted that each track of the plan be implemented by a separate NATO committee and each committee be chaired by a Reagan administration official. This made sure that arms control discussions were kept separate from the deployment programme; they were *not* to be a substitute. "We have a deployment schedule", said a US official, "which is not related to disarmament talks."[11]

The American insistence on keeping the deployment of the new missiles separate from negotiations with the Russians is perhaps the single greatest reason for the upsurge of public opposition. Despite the rhetoric about NATO asking the US to deploy them, people have sensed that the reality is the other way around. Chancellor Schmidt said as much on 17 January 1982. He told a rally of his Social Democratic Party in Bavaria that the US would station its Cruise and Pershing II missiles in West Germany even if Bonn disagreed.[12] As one of the victorious allies of World War II, said Schmidt, the US was entitled to equip its forces in West Germany with whatever arms it chose. Indeed, fearing that the Cruise and Pershing IIs might not be ready for their 1983 deployment, the Pentagon, in the Fall of 1981, decided to begin production even before their development and testing programmes were completed.

Pentagon officials said that this 'concurrency program'—producing the missile while simultaneously testing to see if it works—was necessary because any delay would increase Western European opposition to their deployment. "The program does have risks in it in the context of how much concurrency has been accepted", Deputy Under-secretary of Defense James Wade told the House Appropriations Subcommittee on Defense in a closed meeting in September 1981.[13] But the US was determined to push the programme in this faster-than-normal manner, he said, because of "a commitment to our allies" made in December 1979.

At the time the 'commitment' was made, neither system was expected to be ready by December 1983. The Pershing II had a December 1984 target date. Because of this, the Pentagon announced in March 1982 that the Pershing II would only have undergone two of its planned 28 test flights before production began. However, in June 1982, the Pentagon announced that even these two tests were delayed. Production began nevertheless, prompting one Congressional defence expert to say: "The Pershing is so bound up in NATO politics and arms control negotiations that we could end up deploying a system that doesn't work."[14]

The ground-launched Cruise missile, planned for deployment in May 1983, is already two years behind schedule due to technical difficulties the US Air Force has had with its computer system. "The problems we have run into have been in the development of the software for the computer", Major General R. D. Russ testified to the House Appropriations Subcommittee on Defense.[15] "I think maybe we were a little ambitious when we started." Nevertheless, "we need to proceed at the pace that we are going".

What underlies this crash programme to get the Cruise and

Pershing II missiles deployed in Europe is a fundamental change in US strategic policy. Pentagon thinking is shifting away from the theories of the 1970s, which were dominated by why the United States might have to fight and with what means. Now the emphasis is on how a 'limited' war would be fought and what environments might be encountered, whether the deserts of the Middle East, the jungles of Africa, or the pine forests of Germany.

"The old scenarios that envisaged a rapid escalation of any war into a strategic nuclear combat no longer appear as valid as they did 20 years ago", a senior Pentagon official has said.[16] Presidential Directive 59, enunciating the policy of 'limited' nuclear war, reflects this thinking.

US strategy seems to be evolving towards a nuclear *war fighting* capability similar to that of the Soviet Union, with one important difference. While the Soviet strategy is based on *denial*, US strategy is increasingly based on the notion of *first strike attack in a 'limited' nuclear war*. Deploying Cruise and Pershing II missiles in Europe would allow the US to unleash a first strike against the USSR in that particular 'theatre', with the intention of keeping the conflict 'limited' to Europe.

While on one side of the Atlantic the Americans were worrying about production problems and how to implement the strategy of 'limited' nuclear wars, on the other side NATO officials were worried about how to stem the rising tide of public opposition. "Theoretically," said one European official, "there is no risk of one process skewing the other (arms control negotiations getting in the way of deployment); but, politically, there could be problems in practice."[17]

Just how big these "problems in practice" were was demonstrated in the autumn of 1981, when several million people marched in demonstrations all over Europe, East and West, protesting against the NATO plans as well as against the Soviet deployment of the SS–20s. Public distrust of American motives was heightened with President Reagan's now famous statement that "you could have the exchange of tactical nuclear weapons ... without bringing either of the major powers to pushing the button".[18] Reagan seemed to confirm a statement made several years ago by US Admiral LaRoque, that "we fought World War I in Europe, we fought World War II in Europe, and if you dummies let us, we'll fight World War III in Europe".[19]

Now clearly on the defensive the Americans had to do something, particularly when President Brezhnev responded to Reagan's gaffe by again denouncing the American notion of 'limited' nuclear war as "insidious". "If nuclear war breaks out," he said, "whether in Europe or in any other place, it would

Europe caught in the Nuclear Crossfire (*Jim Borgman © King Features*)

inevitably and unavoidably assume a world wide character."[20] As for Europe, he declared, "maybe somebody really hopes that it will be possible to confine nuclear war to the territory, and considers it to be an acceptable variant for himself. Needless to say, such a variant hardly suits the Europeans. To them it would be death, a catastrophe, that would lead to the destruction of entire nations and their many centuries old civilization."

Stung by the Russian reply and by the fact that Brezhnev was about to embark on a state visit to West Germany, where public opposition to the Cruise and Pershing II missiles was so strong that Chancellor Schmidt had threatened to resign if opposition in his own party did not stop, the Americans had to do something to demonstrate they were not really warmongers. They had to come up with a proposal, said one West German diplomat, that "must be simple and dramatic, so there is no way that Moscow can escape public blame if the talks fail. Otherwise, it will be politically difficult for us to implement the other half of the (NATO) decision."[21]

Coming up with a proposal that would catch public attention, probably fail, but in such a way that could easily be blamed on the

Russians without disrupting deployment of the Cruise and
Pershing IIs might have daunted lesser men, but President Reagan
rose to the occasion. On 25 November 1981, in a virtuoso
performance broadcast live to an estimated 200 million people
world-wide, he offered to the Russians a "four-point agenda for
peace". First, he said, the US would be willing to cancel the
deployment of the 108 Pershing IIs and 464 ground-launched
Cruise missiles if the Soviets would dismantle the 600 or so SS–20,
SS–4 and SS–5 intermediate range missiles it now has in place.
This was Schmidt's 'zero-option' proposal, rejected by the
Americans in June. Second, Reagan called for a new round of talks
on strategic nuclear weapons, aiming not merely at setting limits
on both the Soviet and American arsenals, but at actually *reducing*
them. The President had a new acronym for this. Rather than
SALT—Strategic Arms Limitation Talks—we should have START—
Strategic Arms Reduction Talks. Thirdly, Reagan asked for a
shrinking of conventional forces in Europe—"equality at lower
levels" for both NATO and the Warsaw Pact. It was hardly
necessary, he said, for the Soviet Union to maintain in East
Germany a garrison larger than the entire Allied force that stormed
the Normandy beaches on D–Day 1944. Finally, the President
urged the Soviets to accept a European plan for advance
notification of military manoeuvres anywhere between the Atlantic
Ocean and the Ural Mountains in Russia, traditionally the eastern
boundary of Europe.

The President's words were chosen carefully. He even avoided
the words 'theatre nuclear forces', which conjure up for Europeans
an image of Europe as an atomic wasteland while the Americans
sit smugly untouched on the other side of the Atlantic. It was also
brilliantly timed, completely upstaging Brezhnev on the eve of his
visit to West Germany. As one British official gloated, Reagan
"completely spiked (the Russian's) guns".[22] Its net effect was to
"put the Soviets on the defensive, precisely where they ought to
be" said US Senate Minority Leader Robert Byrd.[23]

The Soviet reaction was predictable. The Soviet news agency
Tass dismissed it as "propaganda". A Soviet television commen-
tator added that "to an absolutely ignorant people, these suggestions would appear logical and even promising, but in reality they
are sheer demagoguery".[24]

The European peace movement reacted with scepticism. "The
proposal is a rather obvious piece of political gamesmanship," said
Msgr. Bruce Kent, General Secretary of the British Campaign for
Nuclear Disarmament.[25] "It is designed to confuse well-meaning
people in Europe and make them think that Reagan is doing the
right thing." By proposing reductions he knew the Russians

wouldn't accept, some argued, Reagan was hoping to simultaneously defuse public opposition and then take advantage of the changed public attitudes to deploy the Pershing II and Cruise missiles anyway.

At base, Reagan's 'peace offensive' boils down to Schmidt's 'zero-option' proposal, that NATO not deploy the Cruise and Pershing IIs in exchange for the Soviets dismantling their existing SS–20s, SS–4s and SS–5s. In essence it asks the Russians to get rid of what they *already have* in exchange for the US not deploying what they *do not have*, yet.

Several things need to be understood about this 'zero option' proposal. The first is why the Soviets rejected it. Most importantly, the Cruise and Pershing II missiles strike at that place in the Russian psyche where the Russians feel the most vulnerable. The 7,000 tactical nuclear weapons currently in the NATO stockpile are only capable of hitting the western republics of the USSR—the Ukraine, Byelorussia and the Baltic States. The Russians are used to having these territories invaded and traded. But to strike Russia itself, as Cruise and Pershing IIs could do, intensifies Russian fears. This is what Napoleon and Hitler did.

The Soviets further point out that Reagan did not say the US would stop *manufacturing* the Cruise or Pershing II missiles. Indeed, virtually simultaneously with the President's speech, the first Cruise missile was rolled off the production line at ceremonies at the Boeing Aerospace plant in Kent, Washington. Along with the General Dynamics Corporation, Boeing is producing thousands of Cruise missiles. When Defense Secretary Weinberger unveiled the Defense Guidance of the Reagan administration in May 1982, the Cruise missiles were seen to be an integral part of US strategic capabilities for 1982–84. The US Air Force intends to buy 3,418 air-launched missiles; the US Navy intends to buy 1,200 sea launched missiles; and the US Army is studying the feasibility of putting chemical warheads on ground-launched Cruise missiles. Even these preliminary figures indicate why the Soviets are so concerned about this prolific new weapon. Cruise missiles aboard US bombers, fighter aircraft, surface ships and submarines around the world, perhaps tipped with chemical warheads, would be able to attack the USSR from so many directions that defence against them will be well-nigh impossible.

The final objection of the Soviets is more to the heart of the matter. The Americans, they said, wanted something for nothing: removal of existing Soviet missiles in exchange for the promise not to deploy new American ones. Moreover, for the Soviets to get rid of all their intermediate range missiles would leave the Americans with their entire arsenal of 'forward based systems' in

The European Nuclear Balance from Two Points of View
(© *The Guardian* 3 Nov. 1981)

Europe—including medium range bombers, fighter bombers and missile-launching submarines. Reagan did not even mention these in his proposal. Also excluded were the independent British and French nuclear forces outside NATO. If all these were to be included, the Russians argued, there would exist rough parity between the forces of Western and Eastern Europe. The West has 986 systems; the East has 975. For Reagan to charge the Russians with a 6-to-1 nuclear advantage over the West, therefore, could only be achieved by excluding 80% of what the Americans have and by excluding totally what the British and the French have.

The wide divergence between what the Americans said and what the Russians said during 1981 can be seen in the diagrams on page 121.

At base, the wide divergence between the two sides comes down to what each side means by 'strategic' nuclear arsenals and 'theatre' nuclear forces. The British and French, for instance, refuse to be involved in the talks between the Russians and the Americans because they argue that their fleets are 'strategic' ones. The Geneva negotiations are about 'theatre' forces. Also excluded are the 400 nuclear missiles in the US Poseidon submarine fleet permanently assigned to NATO. Although part of NATO's nuclear arsenal, they were counted as 'strategic' in the SALT II talks and therefore could legitimately be excluded from any discussions about 'theatre' nuclear weapons. All very confusing.

What does 'strategic' as opposed to 'theatre' mean? Basically, they are American terms, used by the Pentagon to categorise different levels of nuclear warfare and different reaches of nuclear weapons. For the US, with two vast oceans to its East and West, 'strategic' weapons refer to those that can be used between continents over the North Pole. It usually refers to the weapons the US and the USSR reserve for any inter-continental missile exchange. From a US perspective, nuclear weapons that would be used 'just' in Europe are termed 'theatre' weapons. For the Pentagon, Europe is one of the many 'theatres' in which war could break out and 'limited' nuclear exchanges could take place. But the USSR is partly *in* Europe. What are termed by the US as 'theatre' weapons, therefore, are regarded by the Soviets as 'strategic' threats. The Cruise and Pershing II's can hit the Russian homeland.

Then there are the 'independent' nuclear forces of the British and the French, which are considered as strategic by them but as 'theatre' by the Americans. The Soviets point out that while the US, Britain and France only have one nuclear enemy, i.e. the Soviet Union, the Soviets have four—i.e. the US, the UK, France and China. For the Soviets, therefore, what is important is the *aggregate of forces* on each side, taking what the total arsenal is between the US, Britain and France and then comparing this amount to what the Soviets possess. When this is done, the Soviets say, there is rough parity of nuclear forces in Europe, the Chinese factor remaining indeterminate.

However, the Americans, NATO and France want to limit the discussion to the specific *category* of 'intermediate range nuclear missiles'. This is the basis of the 'zero-option' proposal. We are being told that a Soviet 'threat' in this category needs to be countered if NATO is to keep an adequate 'deterrent'.

In order to make an informed decision about this, what must be fully explored are the nuclear arsenals at the disposal of NATO and the WTO. Is it in fact true that the Soviet Union has a nuclear superiority over NATO, such that the Cruise and Pershing II missiles need to be deployed?

DO THE SOVIETS HAVE NUCLEAR SUPERIORITY OVER NATO?

The British Ministry of Defence brochure on the Cruise missiles states that:

> For many years NATO has had medium-range nuclear forces which can reach Russia from Europe (but not from the United States). These are the UK Vulcan bomber and the US F111 bomber. But there are less than 250 of these aircraft and they are becoming more vulnerable as the Russians improve their weapons. The Vulcans will have to be phased out over the next few years.
>
> The Russians already have nearly 400 similar aircraft and over 500 medium-range nuclear missiles, which are already being modernised. In particular their new mobile SS–20 has three separate warheads and greater range and accuracy than older missiles. The swing-wing backfire bomber can fly supersonically at low level to attack Britain.[1]

We are told that it is because of this overwhelming Soviet superiority that the Cruise missiles are needed. Is that a fact?

In order to answer this question, it is necessary to recall that the United States was the first of the two superpowers to deploy 'tactical' nuclear weapons in Europe. By 1960, it had deployed over 2,500 warheads in various NATO countries, particularly in Britain and West Germany.

The Soviet Union reacted to this escalation of the nuclear arms race with alarm. It was one thing to have warheads aimed at the Soviet Union that could be launched from the United States. The Soviets could threaten the US homeland in return. But by deploying nuclear weapons in Europe, the United States brought possible disaster for the Soviets on to their doorstep. In 1962, the Soviets tried to jeopardise the US in the same way through deploying short-range missiles in Cuba. President Kennedy threatened to go to nuclear war before allowing the Soviets to do to the Americans what the Americans were doing to the Soviets. Because of overwhelming US strength, both nuclear and conventional, Khrushchev backed down. By the mid-1960s, the US had deployed 7,000 warheads in Europe aimed at Eastern Europe and the USSR. The total number of US tactical nuclear warheads was put at 22,000 in 1975, with the following locations.

Europe	7,000
Atlantic	1,000
Asia	1,700
Pacific	1,500
USA	10,800

The secondary nuclear powers, Britain and France, add about 2,000 warheads to the US total of 22,000.

The Soviets responded to this US build-up by deploying, among others, their SS–4s and SS–5 missiles. Located in the Soviet Union, the SS–4 and SS–5 missiles could hit any target in Western Europe. While not being able to place the US in double jeopardy, the Soviets could now devastate the European allies of the US. The SS–20s, which the Soviet Union is currently producing, are essentially replacements for the SS–4 and SS–5 missiles. Altogether, it is estimated that the USSR has some 4,400 warheads aimed at Western Europe. Soviet missiles have a longer range than most NATO missiles because Soviet missiles are deployed in the USSR, not in Eastern Europe. There is a great deal of uncertainty as to how many of the Warsaw Pact tactical aircraft are actually capable of carrying nuclear weapons. To assert that the Soviets have nuclear superiority over NATO is to distort the truth.

Dr Mary Kaldor has done research indicating that this claim is less than the whole truth.[2] She points out that these NATO figures leave out all land-based missiles with a range less than 600 miles; they leave out the US Poseidon missiles assigned to the NATO command; they leave out the British Polaris missiles; and they leave out the French land and sea-based missiles.

The London based International Institute for Strategic Studies (IISS) also gives the Soviets an advantage over NATO in long and medium-range nuclear systems.[3] It, too, leaves out NATO's Lance missiles and the French Pluton missiles, presumably because their range is less than the 100 miles the IISS has set for qualifying in the 'medium-range' category. In estimating how many warheads will actually get to their targets, the IISS also assumes that Soviet aircraft have both a higher survivability and deeper penetration ability than NATO aircraft. With different assumptions the balance could easily be tipped the other way.

The Real Military Balance
Long, medium and short range nuclear systems in the European theatre

Warsaw Pact Systems	Warheads	Nato Systems	Warheads
Long-range		**Long-range**	
105 SS-4/5 RBM	315	45 Poseidon SLBM	400
435 SS-4/51/MRBM	435	64 Polaris SLBM	192
60 SS-N-6 SLBM	60	80 French M-20 SLBM	80
30 Backfire bomber	120	57 Vulcan bomber	114
177 Badger/Blinder bomber	354	33 Mirage IVA bomber	33
		109 F-4 fighter bomber	109
		78 F-111 E/F bomber	156
		10 A-6E carrier-based aircraft	20
		20 A-7E '' '' ''	40
		6 Etendard IVM '' ''	12
Medium-range		**Medium-range**	
487 SS-12/Scud B SRBM	487	180 Pershing 1A SRBM	180
9 SS-N-4 SLBM	9	90 Lance SRBM	90
54 Fencer fighter bomber	108	32 Pluton SRBM	32
161 Fitter '' ''	161	30 Buccaneer bomber	60
260 Flogger '' ''	260	40 Jaguar fighter bomber	40
200 Fienbed ''	200	15 Mirage 111E '' ''	15
		95 F-104 '' ''	95
Total long & medium-range 1978	2509	**Total long & medium-range** 984	1668
Short-range None currently available to hit W. European targets since approx. 3,500 short-range nuclear weapons are kept in USSR		**Short-range** Various systems of 16 types including artillery, mines, missiles and aircraft	6000
Total long, medium & short-range	2509	**Total long, medium & short-range**	7668

Key:
IRBM = Intermediate Range Missile
MRBM = Medium Range Missile
SLBM = Submarine-launched Ballistic Missile
SRBM = Short Range Ballistic Missile

Sources: Long and medium range figures taken from *The Military Balance 1980-81*, taking into account assumed utilization rates but not serviceability, except for Poseidon, Polaris, Lance and Pluton; *SALT and the NATO Allies*, US Senate, Committee on Foreign Relations Staff Report, Washington DC, October 1979; Ulrich Albrecht, Alain Joxe and Mary Kaldor 'Gegen den Alarmismus' in Studiengruppe *Militarpolitik Aufrüsten um Abjurüsten?*, Rowohlt, Hamburg, September 1980.

A further inadequacy in the figures indicating a Soviet nuclear superiority over NATO can be seen in the exclusion of the RAF Buccaneer aircraft. None of these are included in the 'long-range theatre nuclear force' category because the RAF claims they do not have sufficient range. Yet these aircraft not only have sufficient range, they are specifically targeted on Soviet cities and military and industrial installations.

From their base in East Anglia, the Buccaneers are to attack targets on the Baltic coastal strip of the USSR including the cities of Riga, Tallin and Kaliningrad. The Buccaneers which are stationed in Jaarbruch, West Germany, would attack targets in western central Russia, including cities like Lvov.

When the Buccaneers are added to the list, the Ministry of Defence claim of a Soviet superiority in long-range aircraft with nuclear capability disappears. Yet when confronted by this fact about the Buccaneer, an MoD spokesperson would only say "I can't really talk about what its actual role would be".[4]

When the numbers game is over, and the Western, that is to say the NATO, the US, the British and the French capabilities are counted together, there are 9,200 tactical nuclear warheads deployed in Europe. The Soviet Union can muster only 4,400. The Western lead is accounted for by inclusion of nearly 6,000 *short-range* nuclear weapons, which the IISS and British MoD omit. NATO possesses 300 nuclear demolition mines, a host of M–109 and M–110 howitzers armed with 3,000 rounds of nuclear shells; 320 short range Honest John nuclear missiles; 700 Nike Hercules nuclear air-defence missiles; and various other short-range aircraft with nuclear capability. In the *intermediate range*, the Soviet Union does have a slight advantage of numbers but not of capability. The 1,650 Soviet launchers have only 2,250 warheads available for delivery while the 1,470 launchers in the Western arsenal have 3,150 warheads for delivery.

Correctly interpreted, these facts and figures show very clearly that while the Russian bear might look more ferocious, particularly when viewed from the 'intermediate' range, the American eagle is in fact more deadly. The question that needs to be asked is not whether NATO needs the Cruise and Pershing IIs. It clearly does not. The greater question is whether it is American deadliness that prompts the Russians to constantly increase their ferocity.

DO THE SOVIETS HAVE BIGGER AND BETTER BOMBS?

For better or worse, it is those who think the worst about the Soviet Union who are in power in the West and dictate policy. The most

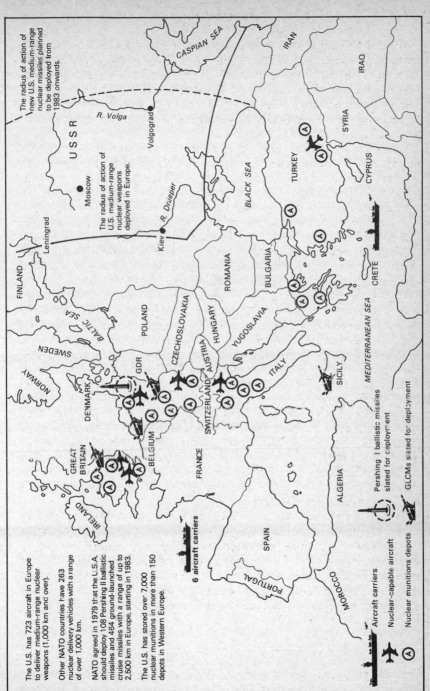

The U.S. has 723 aircraft in Europe to deliver medium-range nuclear weapons (1,000 km and over).

Other NATO countries have 263 nuclear delivery vehicles with a range of over 1,000 km.

NATO agreed in 1979 that the U.S.A. should deploy 108 Pershing II ballistic missiles and 464 ground-launched cruise missiles with a range of up to 2,500 km in Europe, starting in 1983.

The U.S. has stored over 7,000 nuclear munitions in more than 150 depots in Western Europe.

The radius of action of new U.S. medium-range nuclear missiles planned to be deployed from 1983 onwards.

The radius of action of U.S. medium-range nuclear weapons deployed in Europe.

Pershing I ballistic missiles slated for deployment

GLCMs slated for deployment

Aircraft carriers

Nuclear-capable aircraft

Nuclear munitions depots

6 aircraft carriers

The Soviet Version of U.S. medium range Nuclear Weapons Systems in Europe. (*Source:* Whence the Threat to Peace) common indicator they use to gauge the 'growing Soviet threat' is that of the Soviet superiority in the area of nuclear *throw-weight* and *equivalent megatonnage* (EMT). Throw-weight refers to the overall weight of the top stage of a nuclear missile—the warhead, the guidance system and re-entry vehicle; that is, throw-weight essentially measures how *big* the bomb is. Equivalent megatonnage (EMT) has to do with how big a *blast* the bomb makes when it explodes. It is claimed that the Soviets lead the West in both these areas: they not only have *bigger* bombs but also *more powerful* bombs.

Paul Nitze, named by President Reagan in 1981 to head the US delegation to the Geneva talks on arms control with the Russians, considers throw-weight and EMT to be the single most important ingredient in measuring the capability to destroy targets. A Soviet superiority in this area, he argues, will cause them to use their nuclear weapons more easily and to engage in more coercive policies generally.[1] To meet this challenge, Nitze urges the US and NATO to 'batten down the hatches' and deploy a vast array of new weapons. If we do not take up the challenge, he warns, the Soviets will be encouraged to launch a nuclear strike first, knowing that their remaining arsenal will be bigger than the American one.

Nitze's argument deserves close scrutiny. In the first place, his assertion that after an initial 'limited' exchange of nuclear weapons the Soviets will have the military advantage is not necessarily well-founded. Does he know what kind of an 'initial exchange' would take place? How has he determined the character of that exchange? Why does he assume that it is the USSR that will strike first? After all, the Soviets have never used nuclear weapons in combat; nor do they have an official policy of first strike. The Soviets have constantly reiterated that they will never use nuclear weapons first; but if attacked, they will respond with everything they have got. In fact, at the 1981 General Session of the United Nations, Soviet Foreign Minister Gromyko submitted a proposal that all countries possessing nuclear weapons agree that they would not be the first to use nuclear weapons. Such a statement, he said, would lower tensions between the weapon states and would ease growing public fears about the probability of a nuclear war. The US and Britain refused to agree. In the 1982 Special Session on Disarmament, the Soviet Union declared *unilaterally* that it would never be the country to use nuclear weapons first. Again, the US and Britain refused to make similar pronouncements; indeed, they stressed that the doctrine of first strike would remain in force for the NATO alliance.

Secondly, Nitze seems to be trying to fit the Soviets into the US mould by assuming that they finely calibrate strategic nuclear conflicts as the Americans do; that they see political and military advantages in less than all-out nuclear exchanges; and that they see the feasibility of 'limited' nuclear wars. All these are American assumptions. The Rand Corporation has articulated for the Pentagon 44 different categories of warfare, beginning from minor city disturbances to that category which calls for the total destruction of the world. Below total nuclear war are the categories of 'limited' engagements, where only a part of the planet would be devastated, and then there are the 'counterforce' strikes which would be 'surgical' in the sense that only specific targets such as missile silos, airfields or ports would be nuclear bombed. The Soviets have constantly asserted that there cannot be such fine calibrations in the event of any nuclear war.

These notions are purely American and relatively new even there. They have only come to public notice within the last few years. In 1975, US Secretary of Defense Schlesinger spoke of the possibility of a "limited" nuclear exchange in which the US would shoot between ten and forty warheads into Eastern Europe "within a short time span, a few tens of minutes ... to change the perceptions of the Warsaw Pact leaders and create a situation conducive to negotiations". If this failed to bring results, the US also had a plan which calls for shooting all 30,000 of its nuclear warheads. This is termed 'wargasm' in Pentagon slang.

In 1977, General Alexander Haig, Supreme Commander of NATO, ran the first computer scenario of a 'limited' nuclear war in Europe as part of the NATO war games that year. His scenario called for 'counterforce strikes' against 19 East European targets: five in East Germany, five in Bulgaria, three in Poland, three in Hungary, and three in Czechoslovakia. After these salvos, he and the US President were to get on the 'hot line' to Moscow and see if the Soviets were willing to negotiate.

Can you imagine what the British response would be if 'just' London, Manchester or Glasgow were to be wiped out or 'just' Greenham Common, Molesworth, Mildenhall, Windscale and Dounraey were 'counterforced' out of existence? Given how they reacted in the Falklands crisis of 1982, would the Prime Minister and the military chiefs be ready to negotiate, knowing that they had in their remaining nuclear arsenal more than enough warheads to wipe out the enemy? Of course not. The British would retaliate, perhaps initially knocking out 'only' 19 enemy targets in return. That is how wars are started. But in the confusion of dozens, perhaps hundreds, of Hiroshima type situations happening virtually simultaneously all over Europe, can anyone reasonably expect any exchange to stay 'limited'? Does anyone really think the Soviets would stand back and let 19 cities of their allies, on whom their own defence rests, be attacked without hitting back? And would they be content to sustain damage to themselves without bringing the Americans in? And what would happen if the Soviets and Americans began nuclear exchanges? With Europe in ashes, radioactive fallout encircling the globe, would either side give in until all their weapons were exhausted? This is what 'wargasm' is all about.

The notion of 'limited' nuclear war does not make any sense whatsoever. Even at the level of computer scenarios, once the above questions were factored in, every single 'limited' nuclear war game conducted by NATO has resulted in the complete destruction of that 'theatre', meaning Europe. General Bernard Rogers, who replaced General Haig at NATO, states that "the use of theater nuclear weapons would in fact escalate to the strategic level, (meaning between the Russians and the Americans), and very quickly".[2] Soviet military doctrine and official policy also reflect the same conclusion. Once strategic deterrence fails, there will be no middle or limited level to what follows. No rules. No morality. No respite. As President Brezhnev said, "If nuclear war breaks out, whether in Europe or any other place, it would inevitably and unavoidably assume a world wide character".[3]

US attempts to categorise and legalise nuclear exchanges into neat slots by "ascribing to the Soviet Union intentions and readiness to wage 'limited strategic war' are doomed to fail", says Soviet strategist G. A. Trofimenko.[4] In any "test of strength, the Soviet Union will not act in accordance with American "rules" ... but in accordance with its own military doctrine—with the aim of fully smashing any aggressor".

The third point that needs to be raised about Nitze's argument is to ask the question, whether the Soviet intent of "fully smashing any aggressor" is better served by having bigger and more powerful bombs. Aside from the question of who will strike first and how, we must explore whether more *throw-weight* and *equivalent megatonnage* has any real meaning.

In 1980, the US began to install Mark–12A warheads on 300 of its Minuteman III intercontinental missiles. This installation adds a mere 35 pounds to the throw-weight of the missile, yet the new warhead releases *twice* the destructive power as the old warheads—335 kilotons as opposed to 170 kilotons. The US will be getting twice the blast with only a 2% increase in throw-weight.

The Soviet SS–18 intercontinental missile has twice the throw-weight of the planned MX missile which the US is proposing to build—16,000 pounds to 8,000 pounds. Despite this, both missiles contain 10 warheads and while the SS–18s have a higher explosive yield, the MXs will enjoy higher reliability and accuracy, thus making them more deadly than the SS–18s. While the SS–18s carry 10 warheads of 600 kilotons each, they are only accurate to within 200 metres and have only an 81% probability of actually hitting the target. The US MX, on the other hand, while having 10 warheads of only 335 kilotons, can get within 100 metres of its target with 97% accuracy. The conclusion from this comparison is obvious: the United States has lighter missiles but they are more deadly.

This is due to the fact that in the 1960s, the US Defense Department made a conscious and deliberate choice to emphasise accuracy more than throw-weight. The strategy Secretary of Defense McNamara developed called for a 'flexible options response' rather than massive retaliation. This made military installations and industrial sites, rather than cities, the targets. Pinpoint accuracy was therefore needed, and defence laboratories developed weapons of such accuracy that the Cruise missile, for instance, is designed to hit within 30 metres of its target, this after travelling hundreds if not thousands of miles. These accurate weapons are characteristically called 'Post Box Bombs'. The new more accurate missiles meant that the old missiles with gigantic throw-weights had become obsolete.

Throw-weight comparisons are dishonest, misleading and dangerous because neither the US nor Britain nor NATO need comparatively heavy throw-weight to perform their strategic missions. It is interesting to note that those who continually complain about the SS–18 being the only 'heavy' missile in either arsenal do not argue, not even Nitze, that the US or NATO should also have one. More than any other argument, the one concerning throw-weight can most clearly be seen to be a device to whip up anti-Soviet hysteria amongst people who do not have the knowledge of high technology at their command. Nevertheless, this point *must* be understood, because it forms the cornerstone of President Reagan's START proposals made during the summer of 1982.

A fallback from the throw-weight argument is that of *equivalent megatonnage* or explosive yield. Explosive yield measures the actual amount of damage each weapon can cause. The Soviets have more explosive yield to their missiles than either the US or NATO, it is claimed. Charts portraying the Soviet nuclear arsenal as being vastly larger than the American one are common in the Western press.

This is true, but contrary to being a sign of ominous import, it is a sign of Soviet deficiency. This is because a weapon's effective power of destruction is not proportional to its explosive yield. When a bomb explodes, its effects burst in all three dimensions, whereas the earth's surface has only two. Thus, as the explosive yield increases, the area of damage expands by only two-thirds of explosive yield. If the yield is increased by one megaton the damage increases by the square root of the explosive yield. Therefore, while ten one-megaton bombs are equal to ten equivalent megatons, one ten-megaton bomb only equals 3.16 equivalent megatons. To say that the Soviets have more explosive yield, and not to adjust their megatonnage to account for the above differentials between explosive yield and the potential damage, is to distort the truth.

Besides only giving half the scientific truth, this argument about the Soviet's explosive yield also obscures the strategic reality of the US superiority in missile accuracy, perhaps the most important single indicator of who's 'ahead' in the nuclear arms race.

What increased accuracy means in terms of explosive yield is that by making the warhead twice as accurate the effect is to make the bomb eight times as effective. Put another way, if the distance by which the warhead misses the target is cut by half, say from 100 metres to 50 metres, then the warhead need be only one eighth as powerful to inflict the same damage.

An example may help clarify these formulae. The US Minuteman II missile has a one-megaton warhead and is accurate to within .3 miles of its target. The Minuteman III missiles not having Mark–12A warheads are only 170 kilotons (.17 megatons) in explosive yield but are accurate to within .2 miles. Moreover, each Minuteman III is designed to carry three warheads, which increases their lethality even more. The net effect is that the US, while reducing the equivalent megatonnage by 40% has succeeded in doubling its 'hard-target kill capability'. Because the Soviet missiles are not so accurate, they must have higher explosive yields and equivalent megatonnage to inflict the same damage. Yet in a counterforce or 'limited' nuclear war where the aim is to attack specific targets, it is accuracy which counts; therefore, the higher explosive yield of Soviet missiles is an indication that they are lagging behind, not forging ahead of NATO and the US.

Another constant theme of those who, like Nitze, warn us of Soviet aggression is that the USSR has more *strategic delivery vehicles*; that is, more missile launchers and bombers than does NATO or the US. The USSR has 1,398 intercontinental missile launchers; the US has 1,054. The USSR has 947 submarine launched missile tubes, the US has 656. The USSR has 156 heavy bombers, the US 348. All told the USSR has 2,501 delivery vehicles, while the US has 2,124. This means that they can simultaneously launch more missiles than the US can. Is this important?

Having more missile launchers was significant until the advent of the Multiple Independent Re-entry Vehicle (MIRV), which allows each missile to carry multiple warheads. While the USSR

Playing the Numbers Game

On April 2nd, 1982, the New York Times published a graph to illustrate relative nuclear strengths of the United States and the Soviet Union. On quick reading, the illustration suggests a clear superiority of the Soviet Union in marine-launched ballistic missiles. The more pertinent numbers of nuclear *warheads* were given in the notorious small print and remained unillustrated.

United States vs. the Soviet Union in Strategic Weapons
Numbers of weapons in each category, with totals for land, sea and air power at right.

THE UNITED STATES

576 submarine-launched ballistic missiles. These have 4,750 deliverable warheads, carried on 36 nuclear powered missile subs. Eight Ohio class submarines, each to carry 25 Trident missiles, are being built, one is now on sea trials.

450 Minuteman II Intercontinental Ballistic Missiles. Each carries a single warhead.

550 Minuteman III ICBMs. Each carries three MIRV warheads, 300 of which will be retrofitted with MK12A improved warhead.

52 (operational) Titan liquid-fueled single-warhead ICBMs. These will be dismantled soon.

Bombers. 316 B-52s. **60** medium-range FB-III bombers.

On order: 100 MX missiles, with another **100** likely to be ordered.

Submarine-launched ballistic missiles
(with 4,750 warheads) : **576**

ICBMs: **1,000**
(with 2,100 warheads)

Bombers: **150**

THE SOVIET UNION

989 submarine-launched ballistic missiles. These are carried in 84 subs, with 1,900 deliverable warheads.

Intercontinental ballistic missiles. 1,398 missiles (figures may vary slightly during missile conversion programs), carrying approximately 5,500 deliverable warheads. Of these the most important are 308 SS 18 heavy missiles, each carrying 8 or 10 MIRV warheads; 300 SS 19 missiles, each carrying 6 warheads, and 150 SS 17s, mostly carrying 4 each.

Long-range bombers. 150 planes.

Submarine-launched ballistic
missiles: (with 1,900 warheads) **989**

ICBMs: **1,398**
(with 5,500 warheads)

Bombers: **150**

The following figure restores these omissions by illustrating the small print. It thereby rounds out the picture, and may keep a busy President from getting the wrong ideas about Soviet superiority.

Number of Warheads

	Vulnerable (ICBMs)	Not Vulnerable (Submarine based)
UNITED STATES	2100	4750
SOVIET UNION	5500	1900

Playing the Numbers Game: The top figure suggests a clear superiority for the Soviet Union by setting the crucial numbers in small type (*New York Times*). The lower figure give a true position (*Bull. Atom. Sci.*)

can launch more missiles, the US can deliver more *warheads*. It is
the warheads which count. The US can launch 3,200 warheads at
any given time from its submarines alone. The Soviet capability is
limited to 150. Because submarines are practically invulnerable,
this means that in 'secure retaliatory capability'—Nitze's chief
concern—the United States is twenty times better off than the
Soviet Union. When the submarine forces are combined with the
land and airbased strategic forces, the US has 9,400 warheads. The
Soviet Union is expected to have 7,000 by 1985. Furthermore, 55%
of the US nuclear submarines are combat ready at all times. 33%
of all US bombers are on constant alert. This compares with 15%
of Russian nuclear submarines; and none of their bombers.

Again the question: Are Russian bombs bigger and better? It is
true that the Soviet Union does have bigger bombs. Soviet bombs
also yield bigger explosions. Moreover, the Soviets have more
strategic delivery vehicles. But these facts do not indicate strength,
they reveal weakness. What counts is not the *size* of the blast but
whether the warhead will actually *hit* the target. In this area the US
is years ahead of the USSR. Being more accurate, US warheads do
not have to have as much explosive power to destroy their target.
Not only does the US have more *accurate* warheads, it also has *more*
warheads than the USSR. US submarines and bombers are kept in
a *higher state of combat readiness*. Being bigger does not mean better.
Ask Goliath.

DO THEY HAVE BETTER CIVIL DEFENCE?

A major emphasis in the current nuclear debate is the need for
massive expenditures in civil defence. The argument made is that
the Soviets are protecting their people and so the West should do
the same. So pervasive is the assumption that the Soviets have an
enormous civil defence programme that it is assumed as a fact by
many. The Soviet civil defence programme is so well developed
that the Soviets could easily strike a crippling first blow and suffer
only 2–10% of its population dead—5–25 million people—when
NATO and/or the US retaliated, asserts retired Director of USAF
Intelligence, General George Keegan.[1] The former Director of the
US Defence Intelligence Agency, General Daniel Graham,
describes a likely scenario:

> The Soviets evacuate their cities and hunker down. Then they
> move against NATO or Yugoslavia or China or the Middle East
> with superior conventional forces. The United States is faced
> with the demand to stay out or risk nuclear exchange in which
> 100 million Americans would die, as opposed to 10 million
> Russians.[2]

Where does the assertion of an enormous Soviet civil defence programme come from? Believe it or not, it comes mostly from reading Soviet civil defence manuals. They are impressive. They record that the general population has been trained in civil defence since 1955; the programme is taught for a total of 52 hours in the second, fifth, and ninth grades; some 16–20 million school children participate in civil defence exercises every year as part of a nation-wide war games programme. There is a 20-hour compulsory course for adults that is repeated annually; there is a network of special training facilities that offer programmes of two-to-three-day-long comprehensive exercises; and the mass media are engaged in continuous civil defence propaganda and instruction. Because their people are so well prepared, it is claimed, they can evacuate their urban populations in something like 72 hours.

Civil defence plays an important part in the Soviet notion of 'war preparedness'. As discussed earlier, the Soviet nuclear strategy relies on an effective war fighting capability rather than any notion of mutual assured destruction. Soviet policy makers are pre-occupied with the lessons of World War II, which has meant primarily an obsession with the fear of invasion. Soviet post war thinking has been influenced by a 'Barbarosa Complex' (the code name of the German surprise atttack in June 1941) almost to the same degree that the US has been influenced by a 'Munich Complex' (an intense fear that appeasement can only lead to disaster). The result has been the Soviet missile build-up in the early 1960s and the call for the Soviet people to be in a state of 'constant readiness'. "We do not want to find ourselves in the position in which we were in 1941", states Soviet Marshal Malinovsky.[3] "This time we shall not allow the imperialists to catch us unawares." With China to the east, rapidly gaining the capacity to target most of the important Soviet cities, the Soviets are doubly paranoid of a nuclear attack. They are particularly concerned with the whole US notion of 'limited' nuclear war in which 'selective targeting' and 'counterforce' attacks could occur. "Improvement of Soviet civil defence and an increase in its effectiveness constitute one more major obstacle in the way of the unleashing of a new world war by the imperialists", says Soviet military analyst Milovidov.[4]

Civil defence also helps to maintain internal order; it is an ideal way of imparting to the public a sense of participation in any war effort; and it brings home to people in their every-day lives that the Communist Party watches over and is doing the best it can to protect the Soviet people.

The question is, are Soviet civil defence preparations any better than they are in the West?

According to a CIA document, *Soviet Civil Defense*, the Soviets have never even staged an evacuation drill in any of their major cities; nor have they evacuated completely even a small town.[5] Former CIA Director Stansfield Turner has testified in Congress that he sees "little evidence today of serious efforts at mass indoctrination of the population" on civil defence matters.[6] Leon Goure, who wrote the book, *War Survival in Soviet Strategy: USSR Civil Defense*, asserts that even with an adequate civil defence programme, the apathy of the Soviet public would pose major problems.[7] The Soviet people just do not believe in the efficacy of civil defence against nuclear attack. A popular joke reflects this tendency of the Soviet people: 'Question: What do you do in the event of a nuclear attack? Answer: Cover yourself with a sheet and crawl slowly towards the graveyard. Question: Why slowly? Answer: So you don't cause panic.' In Russian, 'civil defence' translates as 'grazhdanskaya oboruna'. In referring to civil defence the Soviets combine the first two letter of both words to call it 'grob'. Grob in Russian means coffin.

The shortcomings of the Soviet civil defence programme are so apparent to the Soviet military leaders that the Civil Defence Chief Marshal Aleksander Altunin has complained that even 'high level' civil defence trainings were done only

> after a delay, and at times at a low methodological level. Many people assembled for such sessions and were led through the various points of a demonstration exercise, but the trainees did not receive what was most necessary. The practical portion was poorly organised and in a stereotyped manner.[8]

Leon Goure points out that there is a bureaucratic indifference to civil defence in the USSR and that the Party and Politburo leaders are more than aware of the Russian talent to avoid unpleasant jobs; of complete indifference towards civil defence preparation by professionals; of the factory managers who deliberately schedule civil defence exercises during peak work hours and then 'because we're so busy' cancel them; and, perhaps most importantly, of the limited funds available to be spent on civil defence preparation.[9]

Even if the Soviets had adequate procedures, however, an evacuation in the USSR would be much more difficult than in Europe or the US because the transport in the Soviet Union is much poorer. Even assuming a well co-ordinated evacuation of Soviet cities with access to all motor and rail transport available, 20 million people would still have to walk. Plans call for these people to walk for a day and then build 'expedient shelters', although there is little information on how the materials for these shelters —shovels, bricks, cinder-blocks, sheet metal, boards and timber—would be obtained. Without these 'expedient shelters', even someone such as Thomas K. Jones, Deputy Under-Secretary of Defense for Strategic Theater Nuclear Forces who talks about a 'credible' Soviet civil defence programme, admits that at least 70 million Soviets would perish, although he adds that this is ''only about 27 per cent of the Soviet total population".[10] Since the hospitals, the fire-fighting centres and the homes would be left behind in the cities, which presumably would also be bombed, millions more would die, particularly if it were winter.

It is often asserted as fact that the Soviets have 'hardened' their industries so that they can withstand nuclear attack. According to a CIA report, however, ''little evidence exists that would suggest a comprehensive programme for hardening economic installations .... Overall, the measures the Soviets have taken to protect their economy would not prevent massive damage from an attack designed to destroy Soviet economic facilities".[11] Moreover, a US Congressional study, *Civil Preparedness Review*, which investigated the possibility of 'hardening' US industries, found that many simply cannot be protected.[12] These include power plants, oil refineries, steelmaking facilities, chemical storage areas, trucks and tractor factories and repair and spare parts facilities.

Soviet defence manuals state that a steel-reinforced industrial plant can be disabled with blast pressures equalling 3 to 6 pounds per square inch. Bomb shelters can withstand a pressure of up to 17 pounds per square inch. Under normal circumstances such 're-inforcement' is considered adequate. In nuclear terms it is negligible. A warhead exploding with the force of 100,000 tons of TNT (100 kilotons) *two miles* from the site would cause disabling damage. The Soviets calculate:

> It is impossible to make buildings less vulnerable to shock wave without radical structural changes that involve considerable technical difficulties and cost .... It is impossible to guarantee building survival in a damage area even by somewhat increasing the strength of individual structures and their components.[13]

Another point often raised concerning Soviet civil defence is that they are 'dispersing' their industry, i.e. spreading their industrial base throughout the country. It is true that laws have been passed in the USSR to disperse industry; there have also been laws to limit population concentration in cities. These laws have had little effect. Dispersal of industry has taken place, mostly to sites east of the Urals. However, this trend is because of economic necessity as much as for military preparedness, for the western part of the USSR is undergoing a depletion of resources. Soviet economic planning has called for a massive exploration and exploitation of Siberia as a result.

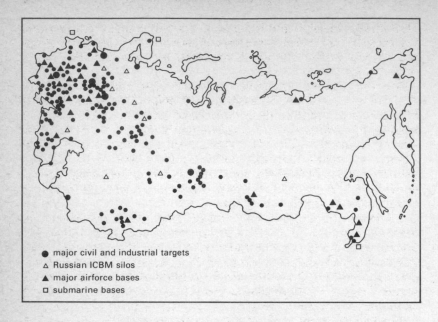

○ major civil and industrial targets
△ Russian ICBM silos
▲ major airforce bases
□ submarine bases

Soviet Targets for a U.S. Nuclear Attack, according to Western sources.

Despite this official effort, not much has happened. New industries continue to be built in European Russia and new machinery continues to be installed in existing plants. The latest Five Year Plan allocates 60% of its capital investment for the modernisation of existing plants. In fact, it lays a greater emphasis on renovation rather than on new construction. Construction patterns for many industries are becoming more dense, not more dispersed. This is not surprising, given Soviet economic and political thinking, which has always stressed centralisation, collectivisation, specialisation, and concentration.

The centralisation of the Soviet economy is demonstrated by statistics. Twenty-five cities contain virtually all of the chemical plants; 60% of all Soviet national steel is produced in 25 plants; only five power plants produce most of the electricity for the Central and Volga regions where 59 million people live; the Soviet Union has only 34 major petroleum and 8 copper refineries; there are only six turbine generator factories, three of which are in Leningrad and one in Kharkov; seven cities are the base of most Soviet engineering; almost all transmission equipment for the powerplants in Siberia is produced in four cities—Moscow,

Leningrad, Kharkov and Riga; there are only 8 major shipbuilding facilities, 16 major heavy machine plants and 15 major agricultural machine factories, almost all of which are based in the largest Soviet cities.

So concentrated is Soviet industry that the US office of Technology Assessment asserts that *only three Minuteman III intercontinental missiles (9 warheads) and seven Poseidon submarine missiles (63 warheads) could devastate nearly 75% of Soviet industrial refining capacity.*[14] The US Arms Control and Disarmament Agency estimates that 150 plants produce 50% of the USSR's primary metals, petroleum, chemicals, synthetic rubber and power generators.[15] *A mere six Poseidon submarine missiles (54 warheads) would suffice to demolish this capacity.*

T.K.Jones argues that using submarine launched missiles would 'only' destroy 3% of Soviet territory. However, what Jones does not mention is the fact that the top 200 Soviet cities total less than 0.25% of Soviet land area. So even if the Soviets managed to blast away the entire US nuclear strategic force with the exception of seven Poseidon submarines, less than one-third of the US submarines normally on-station, the US could still not only pulverise every one of the 229 Soviet cities over 100,000, and a lot of the countryside in between, it could destroy nearly two-thirds of the entire Soviet industrial base in the process. This is what overkill is all about. *Less than 1% of the US nuclear arsenal can totally devastate the USSR.*

For anyone to think that Soviet, or any other, civil defence can withstand this amount of kill power, is to believe in a fantasy. Civil defence in the face of nuclear war is like arranging deck chairs on the sinking Titanic.

The NATO governments generally accepted this view during the 1960s and 1970s. It was realised that no matter how much was spent on it, civil defence would have only marginal effects on the chances of surviving a nuclear attack. Lord Carver, former Chief of the British High Command, went so far as to state that if nuclear war comes, it will be better not to survive. The living will envy the dead.

Nevertheless, 1980 marked a definite turning point in NATO attitudes towards civil defence. Civil defence preparations are not only being given credibility but are actively being pursued by NATO governments, particularly Britain and the US.

What is alarming about this new wave of enthusiasm is that it marks the first time that civil defence is being viewed as an integral part of a nuclear *attack* strategy. For all that is said about Soviet civil defence, it is generally agreed that it is seen in defensive terms by Soviet strategists. It forms an integral part of their notion of deterrence-through-denial.

Similar views about civil defence prevailed in the West until just recently. Nuclear war was understood to be total, if fought at all, and therefore civil defence was recognised as being ineffectual. The civil defence programmes undertaken were more the symptom of helplessness than efforts at credibility. Now civil defence is increasingly being viewed as an essential component of a 'limited' nuclear exchange strategy.

Viewing civil defence as part of an offensive nuclear war strategy is the inevitable result of change in the nuclear doctrine from that of mutual assured destruction to that of counterforce. It directly reflects a change from nuclear deterrence to nuclear first strike.

But more than a doctrinal shift is involved in the new perceptions of civil defence. The new generation of 'tactical' nuclear weapons which are accurate enough for first strike precision embody the tacit assumption that 'theatre' nuclear wars can be fought *and* won. This necessitates the persuasion of the public that not only is nuclear war less horrible than formerly believed, but that nuclear exchanges, like conventional forces, are an acceptable part of today's world. To that end NATO now argues that 'limited' nuclear war is possible and can be made bearable by simple and inexpensive measures of civil defence.

''This attempt by Western governments to lull populations into entirely false views of the most obscene technology in the history of man can quite properly be regarded as a gross, wicked and even insane deception'', write Anthony Tucker and Dr John Gleisner in their book *Crucible of Despair: The Effects of Nuclear War*.[16] These words have been given stark fulfilment by the governments of Britain and the United States in particular.

Beginning in 1979, the British Home Office inundated the country with 'Protect and Survive' pamphlets which called upon homeowners to whitewash their windows against the thermal heat of a nuclear explosion and put sandbags against the doors to protect against the blast. The basic message of the brochure was that a nuclear war would be, at worst, a nuisance, and that all would be well if one went indoors, wrapped one's head in a jacket (behind the sandbags, of course) and did not come out until the BBC gave the all clear signal.

The government knew it was lying to the public. The Faculty of Community Medicine of the Royal College of Physicians drew up a statement, ''Health Care Planning in Relation to Nuclear War'', which pointed out that the health issues surrounding nuclear war were so serious that full public discussion was essential.[17]

The report argued that it would be irresponsible not to have a contingency plan after a nuclear attack, since it is "impossible to exclude the possibility that there would be survivors". However, it suggested that there may not be much point in planning for the

The Ministry of Disinformation: various positions adopted by the British Government on the issue of Nuclear War (© *Richard Willson*)

aftermath of an attack involving some 200 megatons designed to destroy Britain's urban centres (77% of the British population live in cities). It would also be pointless to plan for an attack involving a 1000 megaton attack designed to eliminate Britain's retaliatory capability because few people, if any, would survive.

Therefore, plans for an 'effective' civil defence must assume a very small, limited attack of 'only' one megaton per city. Effective plans must also assume that Britain would be given three to four weeks' warning before the attack actually came. Even under these circumstances, the report stated that civil defence could only make 'a very small contribution indeed to mitigating the suffering.'

The report estimated that a one megaton bomb on Birmingham would kill 400,000 to 700,000 people outright. A similar bomb on London would mean up to a million casualties; would kill or incapacitate half of the city's doctors; and would destroy half of the city's 60,000 hospital beds. Each surviving doctor would have to treat up to 900 seriously injured people without the facilities to do so. "It is out of the question that the immediate casualties of a nuclear attack could be medically treated in any presently understood sense of that term", the report stated.

(More recently, the British Medical Association in its well researched document expressed similar doubts on the efficacy of any defence against a nuclear attack and confirmed human helplessness in the face of such an eventuality.)

Assuming that there were surviving patients and doctors, and assuming that they could overcome the lack of transport, services and supplies, it would take each doctor 17 days to treat his patients. This care would be complicated by the fact that doctors would not be able to attend their patients "without exposing themselves to possibly lethal levels of radiation. Indeed, doctors might be instructed not to do so."

Admission to hospitals might well have to be "limited to those casualties assessed as likely to be alive after seven days, and requiring no more than limited surgical procedures. People suffering only from radiation would not be admitted, as there is no specific treatment for radiation injury."

The report also covered the important issue of mercy killings after a nuclear attack. "In addition to those killed immediately, there will be large numbers of people so severely injured by blast or heat that their death within hours or days is wholly unavoidable. It has been suggested that it would not be useful to divert over-taxed medical and nursing resources to them, but traditions within these professions might complicate the difficult decision not to treat them." The report called for a "generally agreed resolution of this dilemma. If it is decided that very seriously injured people should not be treated, then the usual strictures against euthanasia become less defensible. It may need to be decided to identify inevitably moribund individuals and dispatch them quickly—a task perhaps better assigned to military or police personnel rather than medical, although the selection of individuals for such treatment may call for some medical judgement. Decisions on these issues require full public discussion and democratic decision."

The report also dealt with casualties where death is not inevitable but major permanent disability is unavoidable. "Depending on the scale of the attack and its likely consequences, it may be decided that it would be undesirable to devote medical and nursing attention to them." If casualties were incurred on the predicted scale of up to a million in a major city, it would probably be necessary to restrict medical treatment to either a small proportion of selected cases or to certain sections of the city, the other areas being cordoned off and left.

As to the effectiveness of fallout shelters, the report estimated that a staggering £300,000 million would be necessary to even "modify" the scale of death and injury. It seems clear, however, that "the necessary expenditure is not being incurred. The emphasis in present civil defence is on provision for the maintenance of law and order .... The plain facts are that such shelters are not being provided and would be very difficult to provide at short notice. It seems best to conclude that civil defence measures are unlikely to effect any significant reduction of the scale of casualties."

The report concluded: "We are convinced that medical and health service plans for responding to the situation following a nuclear attack should be widely publicised. There is no security need for secrecy, since there is no way in which the medical plans could help any enemy."

The report was never published. The doctors who wrote it were told by Department of Health officials that Government ministers would be "singularly displeased" if publication went ahead.

What was really behind government 'home defence' plans was the development of the police state structures necessary to deal with domestic order. A private Home Office "Training Manual" stated that the first objective of civil defence planning was to "maintain the internal security of the United Kingdom"; only second came the task of "mitigating the effects of a nuclear attack"; and third came the "recovery". The text noted:[18]

The overall threat can be divided into the following:
a) internal threat (sabotage, subversion and possibly *adverse public reaction to government policies*)
b) conventional attack
c) nuclear attack

The document characterized British "dissident groups" and anyone arranging strikes or anti-war demonstrations as having already thrown in their lot with the "enemy". Civil defence militia would be empowered to arrest any critics of government policy; the police or army would be asked to move against anyone who "obstructed" the NATO build-up to war. According to another document, the Police Manual of Home Defence, the actual organizing of "the detention or restriction of movement of subversive or potentially subversive people" would be the task of MI5 (Military Intelligence) and police officers.

As to who "subversives" are, the Training Manual stated that there are certain dissident extremist groups "which are known to be in sympathy with our potential enemies and which can be expected to react against the good of the nation in times of tension". These people would attempt "to weaken the national will and ability to fight" by "fomenting strikes in key industries, promoting anti-war demonstrations to turn the populace against the government and disruptive activities connected with war preparations".

The overall aim of the civil defence preparations was to establish an 'integrated' government control system with a Central Office of Information co-ordinating the news media. The chief information co-ordinator and censor would be the Prime Minister's Press Secretary.

The response of the British Campaign for Nuclear Disarmament to all this was to publish "Protest and Survive", written by Edward Thompson. The response of 152 counties and local communities to the Thatcher programme was to declare themselves 'nuclear free zones'. In the process, the whole of Wales became officially 'nuclear free', setting an example for Europe. The response of over 3,000 doctors, asked by the Government to participate in emergency planning procedures, was to form the Medical Campaign Against Nuclear Weapons in order to inform the public that civil defence in the face of a nuclear war was utterly useless. "We are simply trying to focus people's minds on the enormity of nuclear arms", said Miss C. Ryle, National Organiser of the Medical Campaign. "You can't call them weapons. It sounds too sane. They are instruments of mass genocide against which doctors can do very little—except try to stop them ever being used."[19]

So effective was the reaction of the British peace movement to government plans that the then Home Secretary, Lord Whitelaw, had to cancel the national civil defence exercise 'Hard Rock', which was to have been held in September/October 1982 in conjunction with NATO war games. Only 34 out of 54 local authorities had agreed to take part.

The civil defence programme in the United States is not only as facile as the British 'Protect and Survive' programme, but enormously more expensive.

A new US government civil defence manual states: "Victory in a nuclear war will belong to the country that recovers first."[20] To demonstrate how explicitly he believes in this claim, President Reagan announced in April 1982 that he planned to spend $4.2 billion on civil defence between 1983 and 1988. This marks the largest civil defence programme in the history of the human race.

On paper, the US civil defence programme rivals that of the USSR. Government officials claim that the US has 230 million identified shelter spaces. Altogether, almost 5,000 communities containing 91% of the US population are said to participate in a 'comprehensive national warning and communications system'. We are told plans for sheltering over 85% of the population have been made. There are 180,000 radiological monitoring systems nationwide and 925 completely operational as well as 1,100 substantially complete 'emergency operating centers'. And there are 72,000 full time civil defence staffers, many of them military, who not only co-ordinate the US civil defence planning but run two civil defence staff colleges in Obeney, Maryland, and Battle Creek, Michigan.

Reagan's plan would revamp the existing programme. It focuses on 'crisis relocation' to evacuate probable target areas and on contingency plans for resuming 'normal operations' after a nuclear attack. The assumption made is that the Federal Emergency Management Agency (FEMA) would have a week to move Americans from 380 'high-risk areas' to an unspecified number of 'host areas'. The high risk areas include 61 'counterforce targets' such as missile bases, strategic bomber bases, nuclear submarine ports and nuclear power plants, and the 319 cities with populations over 50,000.

Reagan's programme envisions construction of blast shelters for key industrial workers who would remain in high risk areas during a nuclear 'crisis'. There are also plans for unspecified protection of 'key defense and population relocation support industries'. The Reagan programme claims to be able to save 80% of the American people. Its evacuation plans, like most other policies of the Reagan administration, have been painstakingly constructed. For example, the evacuation plan for Washington D.C. requires people driving cars with odd-numbered licence plates to wait patiently for those with even-numbered licence plates to leave the city. The inhabitants of Minneapolis have been directed to seek emergency shelter across the river in St. Paul. The inhabitants of St. Paul have been told to seek shelter in Minneapolis.

The President has also directed the Postal Service to issue postage-free 'emergency change-of-address-cards'. The Postal Service has also been directed that, in the event of a nuclear holocaust, it must suspend registered and first class mail; continue to accept personal letters not exceeding 8 ounces; and ensure that mail ordered destroyed to prevent it from falling into enemy hands 'will NOT be opened and examined'.

If the Postmaster General is unfortunately vapourized, it is clearly laid down that his or her duties will pass first to the Deputy Postmaster, and then down the line until they fall to five surviving regional administrators. This quintet will assume the burden of ensuring that enemy alien registration forms are properly distributed before hostilities begin and, once the warheads start falling, that post arriving from devastated cities will be screened for radiological contamination.

As a concession to disaster areas, postcards will be accepted without stamps.

The Department of Housing and Urban Development has formulated a procedure for requisitioning houses 'whose owners have disappeared'. The Department of Agriculture has prepared a food rationing plan to distribute, among other things, six eggs and four pounds of cereal to each surviving American each week after the nuclear war.

The Reagan plan also hopes to provide for an equally ambitious method of saving the economy. Under existing plans, the twelve Federal Reserve banks maintain emergency quarters underground. Records are updated every day. According to Reagan's National Plan for Emergency Preparedness, the system will try to clear all cheques—'including those drawn on destroyed banks'. However, just in case, the Federal Reserve Bank's main relocation centre in a hillside bunker in Culpepper, Virginia, is stocked with a large stockpile of currency. Credit cards will also be honoured, Reagan advises. Evacuees should not leave home without them. T. K.

Jones, the principal enthusiast for Reagan's civil defence plans, told a *Los Angeles Times* interviewer how Americans might survive a nuclear attack: "Dig a hole, cover it with a couple of doors, and then throw three feet of dirt on top. Everyone's going to make it if there are enough shovels to go around."[21]

Not surprisingly, the Reagan plan has met with widespread cynicism. "Civil defense is a cruel and dangerous hoax that encourages the false notion that nuclear war is ... tolerable and perhaps even winnable," said Senator Alan Cranston.[22] Marin County supervisor Barbara Boxer was more direct. After the Board voted not to participate in Reagan's programme, she said, "the bottom line is that there's no way we can evacuate skeletons".[23]

A congressional panel looking into the civil defence plan for Washington, D.C., discovered that there were no provisions for evacuating members of Congress, among others, in the event of an attack. "Whether the public might be better served by the evacuation of Congress in the event of attack is, I suppose, a highly debatable proposition", said Rep. Stan Parris, a Republican from Virginia.[24] However, he did venture to ask whether members of Congress qualified as "critical workers". "We have not really identified members of Congress as critical workers at the present time", replied Richard Bottoroff, the District of Columbia's Director of Emergency Preparedness. He added, however, "We know that they are, of course."

The Congressional panel questioned how a planned contingent of 179,000 residents of the city could get beyond the outskirts of the metropolitan area, where masses of suburban dwellers would also be trying to leave, and reach the Shenandoah Valley, 130 miles away. The panel pointed out that the principal facilities in the valley now consist of one hotel and a golf course. It also noted that the charts and pamphlets prepared by the city's civil defence staff estimate that even under the most optimistic of scenarios upwards of 20% of the city residents would not get out.

Rep. Parris questioned the present plan to use city buses for the evacuation of city residents without cars. The plan calls for drivers to make three round trips to the distant shelter in a period of as much as a week, presuming that a warning of a nuclear attack would come that far in advance. "The world is not like that", Rep. Parris said. "Can you really imagine the typical Metro bus driver taking his wife and family on the first trip, we can assume, then being talked into leaving them and making two more round trips back when a nuclear holocaust is coming?"[25]

The 20,000 member strong Physicians for Social Responsibility (PSR) responded to the Reagan programme by pointing out that no civil defence scheme can possibly come to grips with the staggering medical impact of even a 'limited' nuclear strike, to say nothing about a war in which 'only' 50 million Americans were killed. The most successful evacuation programme would still have to cope with *millions* of burn and radiation victims, deprived of hospitals left behind in the devastated cities. Epidemics would strike in the post-attack environment of decaying flesh and polluted water while the drug companies and medical supply houses would be lying in ruins. Such is the reality of nuclear war. Dr. Helen Caldicott, President of PSR, denounced as an 'illusion' and 'hoax' the idea that medical care could be provided for relocated populations.[26] Indeed, in the aftermath of a nuclear holocaust, the few surviving Americans might find that their government's best civil defence plan was its 130,000 pound stock of opium to help them face the darkness at the end of the long tunnel.

DOES THE UNITED STATES HAVE A 'WINDOW OF VULNERABILITY' THAT IS OPEN TO SOVIET ATTACK?

On 2 October 1981, when the Reagan administration unveiled its six-year $180 billion modernisation programme for strategic nuclear forces, an astonishing new factor was introduced—the 'Mobile Window of Vulnerability' (MWV). "A window of vulnerability is opening", warned the President, "one that would jeopardize not just our hopes for serious productive arms negotiations, but our hopes for peace and freedom."[1]

What exactly is a 'window of vulnerability'? Some Pentagon analysts have claimed that Soviet intercontinental missiles are becoming so accurate that Soviet leaders will soon be able to order a 'knock-out blow' against the 1,000 American land-based missiles. The Soviets could then call on the US President to surrender or face the obliteration of US cities in a second strike attack. At that point the US President would have only two choices. If he ordered a counter attack from US bombers and submarines, it would be mutual obliteration. Or else, he could surrender.

To prevent such an eventuality, President Carter ordered the production of a mobile MX missile system to replace the Titan and Minuteman missiles which are currently deployed in fixed missile silos. The MX, however, was not to have a fixed location. The US Air Force planned to put each of the 300 MX missiles, when ready, in underground tunnels from six to twenty miles long, so as to be able to move about the missiles in the tunnels. This mobility would make it impossible for the Soviets to know the precise locations of the US land based systems.

Having absorbed this idea, people were puzzled when President Reagan announced that he was ordering from 36 to 100 of the MX missiles to be deployed, not according to the Air Force missile-shell-game-in-the-desert idea, but in reconstructed Titan and Minuteman silos, which are in fixed locations. Greatly confused by this, a reporter asked the President at his 2 October 1981 press conference: "Mr President, exactly when is the 'window of vulnerability'? We heard yesterday the suggestion that it exists now. Earlier this morning a defense official indicated that it was not until '84 or '87. Are we facing it right now?"[2]

The President seemed bewildered by the question. He responded, "I think in some areas, we are, yes." As an example he cited the long-standing "imbalance of forces in the Western front—in the NATO line, we are vastly outdistanced there". And then, in an apparent off-the-cuff assessment, the President added, "Right now they (the Soviets) have a superiority at sea". But one could not understand what any of this had to do with silo vulnerability.

Another reporter asked: "Mr President, if there is or will be a 'window of vulnerability', why is the MX any less vulnerable if it's in silos, the location of which the Soviets presumably already know, unless we were going to launch on their attack (sort of a mutual first strike)?" Reagan responded by noting that while the Soviets could improve "their accuracy, their power, and their ability" to attack the new superhardened silos in which he intends to deploy MX beginning in 1986, it would "take them some time to do that and they would have to devote a decided effort to doing that".

One must assume that the President of United States knows what he is talking about. His remark indicates either a revision in the estimation of the timing of the Soviet threat to the American land-based system or the subordination of facts about Soviet capability to the political, economic and bureaucratic momentum of weapons production in the US. If one assumes that Reagan does *not* know what he is talking about, then a third alternative emerges—namely, that the notion of a 'window of vulnerability' is a hoax, and neither the President nor anyone else in the Administration can offer a legitimate rationale to justify either the 'window' or the 'vulnerability' or the 'mobile window of vulnerability'. The President is offering to close that 'window' to remove the 'vulnerability'.

The whole notion of a 'window of vulnerability' is a myth, according to Prof. J. Edward Anderson, Professor of Mechanical Engineering and Director of the Industrial Engineering Division of the University of Minnesota. He should know. While the President was busy making movies, Prof. Anderson invented and developed the Long-range Ballistic Missile Guidance System capable of making corrections during mid-flight; he also led the development of the Inertial Reference System for Polaris submarines; and he directed the advanced development of Solar Probe spacecraft.

In a paper entitled "The Probability of Destruction of a Missile Silo",[3] he has calculated that even if the Soviet missiles are as accurate as the CIA and President Reagan claim (within 300 feet of the target), and assuming that the Soviets simultaneously attacked all 1,000 of the US land-based missiles, at least 108 of these would survive. Remembering that each US missile has multiple warheads, one hundred and eight Minuteman III missiles mean 324 warheads left. If the MX missiles were to be deployed in the Minuteman III silos, then the US would still be left with between 1,008 and 1,504 warheads, each with an explosive yield of 200 kilotons—the Hiroshima bomb was 12 kilotons—with which to counterattack. This does not include the other two parts of the US strategic 'triad'—bombers and submarines, comprising 76% of entire US strategic arsenal.

If a more reasonable margin of error is assumed, namely that the Soviet missiles would only get to within 600 feet of their target, then 606 missiles would remain intact. This would leave the US with between 1,824 and 8,484 warheads to launch a counter-attack depending on whether there were Minuteman III or MX missiles in the silos.

For the Soviets to achieve the 90% accuracy that would 'only' leave 108 silos intact, would require first a force capable of launching such an attack and second, the conducting of tests to make sure such accuracy was certain. In the first place, the Soviets have only deployed about half the force necessary on paper to launch a countersilo first strike. Secondly, they have never fired a missile over the North Pole, the route ballistic missiles would have to traverse if they were aimed by one superpower at the other. The only basis upon which either the Soviets or the Americans could undertake such a launch would be large scale computer calculations.

It is unlikely that the Russians have gravitational field maps to the necessary accuracy over North America, or the Americans over the USSR. Mid-course correction devices are equally unreliable, argues Professor Anderson. Star tracking is insufficiently precise and navigational satellites depend on microwave transmissions between the satellite and the warhead that could be jammed in various ways. Moreover, terminal guidance systems, which allow the missiles to check their position against maps of the ground such as are used in Cruise missiles, would not work in ballistic missiles. They travel too fast, re-entering the earth's atmosphere at 16,000 miles per hour. At this speed the warhead is enveloped in an ionised shock layer which cannot be penetrated by the optical or infra-red frequencies needed for it to discern its position relative to the ground. Slowing down the missile creates even more problems.

Professor Anderson goes so far as to cast doubt on the certainty of all the weapons working in the first place. Temperature fluctuations, humidity, chemical changes, and vibrations all can upset the delicate systems which make a missile operate and a warhead explode. "Laboratory accuracy under field conditions is required", he says, adding that "dignatories have been gathered on a number of occasions to witness a Minuteman firing, only to be disappointed that nothing happened when the key was turned". Professor Anderson, a scientist, concludes,

> Intercontinental ballistic missiles are, and will, remain city busters not silo busters. In the mad scenario of the nuclear age, they are useful for deterrence of war, not for war fighting against hardened military targets.

Anderson is not alone in his assessment. In a speech on 22 March 1976, then Secretary of State Kissinger, a diplomat, stated:

> Indeed neither side has even tested the launching of more than a few missiles at a time; neither side has ever fired them in a north-south direction as they would have to do in wartime. Yet initiation of an all-out surprise attack would depend on substantial confidence that thousands of re-entry vehicles launched in carefully coordinated attacks—from land, sea and air—would knock out all their targets thousands of miles away, with a timing and reliability exactly as predicted, before the other side launches any forces to pre-empt or retaliate and with such effectiveness that retaliation would not produce unacceptable damage. Any miscalculation or technical failure would mean national catastrophe. Assertions that one side is 'ahead' by the margins now under discussion pale in significance when an attack would depend on decisions based on such massive uncertainties and risks.[4]

Accurately assessing reality as it really is, however, is not the forté of either the President, the Pentagon or the CIA. They are much more concerned with 'worst-case scenarios'. This involves heaping upon the Soviets *now* capabilities they *might* or *might not* obtain some time in the future, and assuming they *want* to pursue such a capability even if in fact they *do not*. Therefore, the President and the Pentagon insist that a 'window of vulnerability' *does* exist and that only the new MX system can close that 'window'.

While Reagan is to be credited with discarding Carter's plan of a mobile MX system in underground silos, he has gone from the absurd to the illogical in suggesting that the MX now be deployed in hardened silos. He made a mockery of the whole 'mobile window of vulnerability' strategy. This paradox alienated even his own right-wing supporters.

In October 1981, Secretary of Defense Weinberger testified before the Senate Armed Services Committee about Reagan's new proposal.[5] Democratic Senator Exon of Nebraska, considered to be a hawk, came right to the point:

> I came here two and a half years ago and I was not convinced at that time ... that we needed or could afford an MX system. Since that time I have been barraged as a member of this Committee with testimony from previous administrations, with testimony from the highest officials of our defense establishment, from innumerable closed door sessions with the CIA, that lead me to believe that indeed there was a window of vulnerability that likely we could not have a chance of closing unless we went to the MPS–MX. Do you believe I was misled by all these gentlemen?

"I don't think you were misled", Weinberger replied, "but I think it is inevitable that there will be different viewpoints". In President Reagan's view, Weinberger explained, the Carter administration's proposal "is not a survivable system worth the investment that is required for it .... It uses up the resources that would be available for other systems".

Senator Gordon Humphrey told Weinberger how "unsettling" it was for him "in the space of ten months to hear completely contradictory testimony from the most respected and expert defense officials on the basing mode ...".

Humphrey did not have to go far to find yet another contradictory opinion. Accompanying Weinberger at the witness table was General Jones, chairman of the Joint Chiefs of Staff. "In my own view," Jones testified, "I considered the MX in a very survivable mode to be extremely important to the security of the nation. I remain to be convinced that there is a survivable mode other than MPS (mobile positioned systems)." If forced to choose, for budget reasons, between the B–1 bomber, the Advanced Technology ("Stealth") bomber, and the MX, "I would put MX last under the current program slice," Jones testified.

All things considered, Jones said, "readiness still continues to be my No. 1 concern. If there was a major reduction in (budget) authority, I would take a look at the B–1, but it would not be one of the first things I would look at. I would protect most items of readiness before almost anything". Jones testified that he put "first priority on Command, Control and Communications"(C–3) noting that the Joint Chiefs of Staff "endorsed" the Reagan programme to build a 'C–3' system which can survive a nuclear attack.

Despite Secretary Weinberger's claims to the contrary, it is clear that the Air Force, to which Gen. Jones belongs, and probably a majority of the Joint Chiefs, consider that the new MX plan takes lesser priority than conventional force readiness, strategic command and control improvements, and a new bomber. Apparently, the professional military—*when forced to choose*—is not as concerned with the 'window of vulnerability' as the President or his Secretary of Defense.

As one analyst put it, "Force exchange charts are the tarot cards of the strategic priesthood, and the Reagan administration has suddenly shuffled the deck". Former Secretary of Defense James Schlesinger put it more bluntly. "It was," he said, "a decision to punt."

In fairness to Reagan, it should be said that placing the MX missiles in existing silos was to be only a first stage. In 1984, three other options were to be considered: continuous airborne patrol; an anti-ballistic missile defence around the silos; and/or deployment of the MX missiles 'in survivable locations deep underground'. Weinberger has also suggested basing the MX in tunnels drilled into the south side of mesas in the desert of the south west, where they would presumably be immune from Soviet missiles shot over the North Pole.

Congressional hawks, however, relentlessly attacked Weinberger for such an incredible about-face. Senators Exon and Levin reminded Weinberger of the views he had expressed during his confirmation hearing nine months earlier:

I would feel that simply putting it into existing silos would not answer two or three of the concerns that I have: namely, that the location of these are (sic) well known and are not hardened sufficiently, nor could they be of strategic value to count as a strategic improvement of our forces.

Weinberger tried to explain that he had been discounting the value of further silo hardening as a *permanent* remedy for the vulnerability of land-based missiles, but that it was indeed valuable as a temporary measure. "I think they can be hardened to give added strength for a few years."

"How many years?" Senator Nunn wanted to know. "Three or four," Weinberger replied, adding that the silos could be hardened before the MX missile becomes available in "1985 or 1986". And when would hardening no longer be effective, Nunn wanted to know. "We are estimating 1987 or 1988". So by the Reagan administration's own reckoning, the MX in Titan silos would be survivable for at most three years and possibly only one.

Weinberger was then asked about the cost of the programme. He did not know. And, wisely, he was not willing to make a guess. A study released by the Rand Corporation gives an idea. Deploying MX missiles in 565 superhardened silos would cost at least $25.4 billion or about $45 million per silo at 1981 prices. This means that US taxpayers could be forced to pay as much as $4.5 million *per day* for the protection of a mere 3.5% of America's strategic arsenal. This is a lot of money for a reinforced concrete hole in the ground with a giant shock absorber useful only for a period of one-to-three-years.

Perhaps this is what General Jones had in mind when he said to the committee: "It is still to be determined whether it is a cost-effective time tradeoff." Former Secretary of Defense Harold Brown was not quite so diplomatic. "Hardening doesn't buy much," he said, "if your hardened shelter is in the middle of a crater (created by the exploding Soviet warhead)."

Brown's point was not missed by the Committee. They brought to Weinberger's attention the fact that just a few days previously the Pentagon had released a glossy booklet, *Soviet Military Power*, which contained the statement that the Soviet SS–18 missiles "are capable of destroying any known fixed target with high probability". Since Weinberger had written the Introduction to the booklet, the Senators queried the statement. At first Weinberger replied that the statements in the booklet represented "mixtures of projections and current capabilities". But Senator Cohen pressed the point, asking whether the phrase, "any known fixed silos" included hardened silos. "Not immediately," Weinberger answered. "Within a few years. We don't know the month or the date, but not immediately . . . . I guess my trouble is that I am not able to fix the date when the strengthened Soviet capability will be deployed."

No such doubts about the extent of Soviet countersilo capabilities seemed to bother Senator Henry Jackson, who has been raising the alarm about the Minuteman's impending vulnerability since the early 1970s.

> I am only using the Administration's position, which I share, about the vulnerability of our land-based system. Once you agree with that assumption, which I do, then the only response that you can give is that you have hardened it against every thing but a direct hit. But their ability to make direct hits, based on the Administration's own assumptions as to accuracy on a saturation (that is, multiple warhead attack), basis, means to me, at least, that this system is not survivable as proposed.

Jackson is right. If one agrees with all the assumptions of the Minuteman vulnerability scenario, then clearly, deployment of an even more lucrative target such as the MX in silos amounts to little more than a strange exercise in psychic self-flagellation. That is why the hawks are up in arms over this aspect of the Reagan proposal.

To his credit, Weinberger spared the senators a repetition of his previous minuet over the timing and extent of the infamous 'window', and faced squarely the issue raised by Senator Jackson:

> We have reached the conclusion that there isn't any ground-based system that is survivable, and therefore we are studying a number of things that we hope we can add to that .... Meanwhile, we can't stand still. *We can't take the MX as it comes off the production line and put it in the warehouse because we don't have an MPS (Mobile Positioning System) system finished.* Therefore, we do the very best we can to get all the additional strength we can as quickly as we can get it. (emphasis added)

Weinberger had finally got to the point. The MX missile is being produced. Full stop. The first MX missiles are slated to come off the production line in 1986. Because the MPS will not be ready in time, the decision Reagan made was to put them in existing silos even though it meant negating the very rationale used to produce the weapon. The production and deployment of weapons have become ends in themselves, serving no larger purpose than to satisfy the US Administration's lust for more destructive strength 'as quickly as we can get it'.

This became particularly clear on 11 February 1982 when after the mental gymnastics of Weinberger defending the siting of the MXs in hardened silos, the Administration decided to throw the whole idea out of the window. However, less than a month later the Pentagon had decided to deploy the first 40 of its MX missiles in existing, unhardened silos scattered through Wyoming, Nebraska and Colorado. But there was now a new twist: the Pentagon planned to construct as many as 14 additional silos around each silo containing an MX missile, in order to 'deceptively base' the weapon. Each MX would be housed in a transportable cannister. Eventually, officials said, an anti-ballistic missile defence may be built to protect the MX installations. This move could destroy the current Anti-Ballistic Missile Treaty between the US and the USSR while at the same time severely damaging chances for future arms control. Under the existing ABM treaty, the US can erect such a defence system only at its missile base in Grand Forks, North Dakota.

This new plan was a rehash of the Carter plan Reagan had already rejected. It unleashed another storm of controversy. On 24

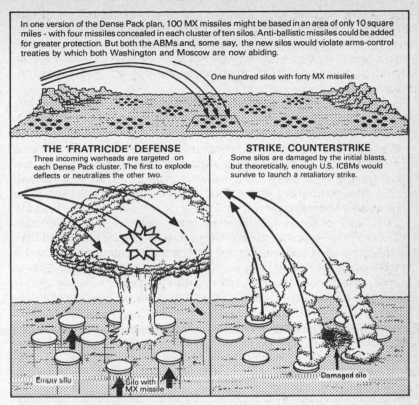

In one version of the Dense Pack plan, 100 MX missiles might be based in an area of only 10 square miles - with four missiles concealed in each cluster of ten silos. Anti-ballistic missiles could be added for greater protection. But both the ABMs and, some say, the new silos would violate arms-control treaties by which both Washington and Moscow are now abiding.

One hundred silos with forty MX missiles

THE 'FRATRICIDE' DEFENSE
Three incoming warheads are targeted on each Dense Pack cluster. The first to explode deflects or neutralizes the other two.

STRIKE, COUNTERSTRIKE
Some silos are damaged by the initial blasts, but theoretically, enough U.S. ICBMs would survive to launch a retaliatory strike.

Empty silo   Silo with MX missile   Damaged silo

Dense Pack plan for the MX Missile System.

March 1982, the Congress finally had had enough. The Senate Arms Services subcommittee voted unanimously to stop the MX missile in its tracks. Subcommittee chairman John W. Warner stated that the action was "a bipartisan effort to redirect and strengthen the President's strategic program". He charged that Pentagon testimony about putting MX missiles in Minutemen holes just did not add up "so we took the bit in our teeth" and delayed production.[6]

Undaunted, the Pentagon came up with still another plan. In April 1982, the Air Force unveiled the 'MX Deceptive Dense Pack Basing Concept'. Dense Pack, as the name implies, involves bunching MX missiles in fairly tight formations. Each missile would have 10 vertical capsules it could go into, spaced 600 metres apart. The combination of one missile and 10 capsules is called a pack. Only when a missile was taken out for maintenance would it be slipped into another capsule covertly. Twenty packs, meaning a total of 20 missiles and 200 capsules, is what the Air Force calls an 'array'. An array would require less than 52 square kilometres storage space.

This represents a strategic rationale for the MX that is completely the opposite of the original, that is having them so far apart and so mobile that a first strike against them would be impossible. The new reasoning went like this: the first Soviet warhead to come down on the Pack will not only destroy its target but will also blow up the other Soviet warheads flying behind it. This is known as 'fratricide'. Thus some of the US MX missiles would survive.

The only trouble is that no one is sure whether fratricide would really occur. The Russians just might be able to figure out a way of removing the 'fratricide' factor by making all their warheads flying into the MX Dense Pack explode simultaneously, thus wiping out everything.

The irony of it all was that the production of the missile was coming along "smashing well", as one Air Force officer put it. "It's a highly successful development program," he said, "surprisingly trouble-free, on schedule, on cost and with no surprises."[7] There are, however, two little surprises. One, there is no place to deploy them. And two, there is no earthly strategic doctrine to justify their existence.

Strategic doctrine or not, the President was determined to have his missiles. He created a blue ribbon commission, headed by retired Air Force Lt. General Brent Scowcroft, to make a 'final' recommendation. In May 1983, after several months of deliberation, the commission announced its conclusion: the US should deploy 100 of the MX's in existing Minuteman silos and develop a new small 'Midgetman' missile with a single warhead.

In making these recommendations, the Scowcroft Commission conceded that the vulnerability of America's land based missiles to Soviet attack is not an 'urgent problem', particularly since the other two components of the US strategic triad—the nuclear bombers and nuclear submarines—are more than sufficient to destroy the Soviet Union. However, the commission felt compelled to endorse the new missile system anyway for 'political' reasons. Within hours of the public annnouncement of the commission's findings, Reagan went on the air and agreed with everything it said. Within weeks, Congress had authorised full funding. It voted for the MX system only days after the House of Representatives voted for a nuclear freeze.

There is no doubt that the United States does have a window of vulnerability. The doubts are about where it is. Nobody knows whether it opens upon the US land based missiles or resides in the space between the White House, the Pentagon and the Capital dome.

4 Conventional Strength

ARE THE RUSSIANS STRONGER THAN WE ARE?

According to the Pentagon booklet, *Soviet Military Power*, Soviet Ground Forces total 1,825,000 soldiers under arms. They are deployed in 180 divisions of varying degrees of combat readiness. Of these, 71% are motorised rifle divisions, and 4% are airborne.

Seventy-nine percent of Soviet Ground Forces are stationed inside the borders of the USSR; 16% are stationed in East Germany, Poland, Czechoslovakia and Hungary; 3% are stationed in Mongolia; 2% are engaged in combat in Afghanistan.

The Soviet High Command deploys conventional forces in four groupings: against NATO in the West; against China in the East; towards the Middle East in the South; and a strategic reserve.

Soviet Air Forces comprise 880 long range and 4,800 short range bombers and fighters. Their air defence forces include 2,500 interceptors and 10,000 surface-to-air-missile launchers. All of these are kept within the borders of the USSR and the WTO except those now in Afghanistan. Soviet reconnaissance aircraft also operate from Vietnam, Ethiopia, Angola and Cuba.

Soviet Naval Forces include 1,297 surface warships, 377 submarines, and 755 auxiliary ships. Soviet Naval Aviation numbers 1,440 airplanes. Ground, air and sea forces combined, the Soviet military strength is 3,673,000 soldiers.

Military Balance 1981–1982, a publication of the IISS, gives the total number of Warsaw Pact forces at 4,788,000. The NATO forces number 4,771,759. However, when the 504,030 soldiers in the French armed forces are added to the NATO figures, the Soviet Union and its allies are outnumbered by 443,789 soldiers in their Western Sector alone.

Yet, this is not the whole story. What neither *Military Balance* nor NATO analysts seem to take into account is the fact that 75% of Soviet territory is in Asia facing an armed force of 4,750,000 Chinese. If Chinese, NATO and French forces are put together, the Soviet Union and its allies are outnumbered by 4,237,789 soldiers. This disparity is in excess of total Soviet strength.

Tables like the one below, common in the Western press, indicate that in virtually every military category the Soviets lead the West:

The Balance of Ready Forces in the Eastern Atlantic

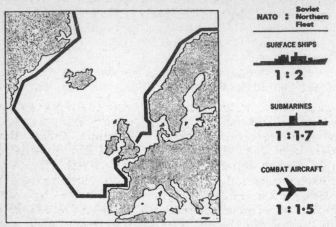

NATO :	Soviet Northern Fleet
SURFACE SHIPS	
	1 : 2
SUBMARINES	
	1 : 1·7
COMBAT AIRCRAFT	
	1 : 1·5

This illustration makes the Soviet military forces seem superior by confining the comparisons to limited geographical areas.
(*Brit. Defence White Paper. 1976*)

The Military Balance on NATO'S Central Front (ready forces)

	NATO	Warsaw Pact	NATO: Warsaw Pact
TOTAL SOLDIERS			1:1·3
SOLDIERS IN FIGHTING UNITS			1:1·4
MAIN BATTLE TANKS			1:2·7
FIELD GUNS			1:2·5
TACTICAL AIRCRAFT			1:2·3

This illustration makes the Soviet military forces seem superior by omitting tactical nuclear weapons, anti-tank weapons, etc. (where NATO has an overwhelming lead). (*Brit. Defence White Paper, 1976*)

It is useful to consider the numbers in another way. The Warsaw Treaty Organisation consists of 7 nations: the USSR, Bulgaria, Czechoslovakia, Hungary, Poland, Romania and East Germany. NATO numbers 15: the USA, Canada, Belgium, Britain, Denmark, West Germany, Greece, Iceland, Italy, Luxembourg, Netherlands, Norway, Portugal, Spain and Turkey. If one adds France, still closely aligned with NATO, sharing the same anti-Soviet foreign policy, the seven nations in the WTO are faced with 16 nations in their Western sector alone.

As for the Soviet superiority in tanks, the former US Secretary of Defense Harold Brown, noted:

> I am of course aware that we estimate the Soviets as having more than 45,000 tanks while the United States has only 10,000 but while we recognise the Soviet armour threat, that raw comparison does not convince me of the military Soviet superiority in Central Europe or make it advisable for the United States to bring another 35,000 tanks. Our allies happen to have tanks as well as anti-tank launchers—of which we and our allies have already acquired more than 17,000—and more than 40,000 anti-tank missiles are also relevant to stopping tanks. It is most unlikely, in any event, that the Soviets could bring these tanks to bear against the United States and its allies.[1]

Number comparisons are not an accurate measure of strength. They yield biased results depending on who's counting and, particularly, why. What does matter is quality and experience, as former US Admiral Gene LaRoque points out in the following interview.[2]

> The United States Navy today has 550,000 men. The Soviet Navy has 450,000 men; that is, the United States has 100,000 more men than the Soviets. In addition, the United States has a Coast Guard; the Soviet Union does not. The United States also has 185,000 marines; the Soviet Union has 16,000 marines. The United States has more marines than all the countries in the world put together, including the Soviet Union. The United States Navy has about 3,000 active aircraft. The Soviet Union has 1,500 active aircraft. The United States Navy is younger than the Soviet Navy when you compare the age of all our ships and all the Soviet ships. Our Navy is more modern and physically younger by actual measure of years of operation. We have 44 naval bases around the world. The Soviet Union has six major naval bases and no naval bases outside of its territory. None. And of the six naval bases the Soviets have, four of them freeze up in winter. In one of them you have to pass under a Turkish bridge in order to get into the Mediterranean; that is the naval

base in Sevastopol in the Black Sea. So the whole fleet in the Black Sea must pass under the bridge that connects European and Asian Turkey. The Soviet Union has a hundred fewer submarines today than it had ten years ago.

Q. What types of submarines are they?

A. Soviet submarines are more modern than they were ten years ago; and so are ours. And our anti-submarine capabilities are more modern too. The Soviet Union has 75 nuclear attack submarines—the kind that attack ships. The United States has the same number. The United States is building, has funded, and actually has under construction 25 new nuclear attack submarines.

Q. How does your analysis conform with that statement by Senator Henry Jackson: 'The state of our defenses and especially projections of our preparedness in the immediate future has reached crisis proportions'. He notes that the Soviets lead us in tanks by five to one, in artillery pieces by two-to-three to one, in attack submarines by 3.5 to one, in ground force divisions by ten to one, in medium bombers by eleven to one, and in air defence systems by 278 to one.

A. Let me respond to this in reverse order. First, it is true that the Soviet Union has tremendous air defense capability. The Soviets are very fearful of an attack by the United States and by Germany, and they have a far greater defense capability against air attack than we do. As a matter of fact, we've practically dismantled our air defence capabilities because we recognise we cannot defend the United States against a missile attack and there is no need to arm ourselves with thousands of expensive air defense missiles in trying to defend ourselves against the few aircraft that could mount an attack on us. By the same token, the Soviet Union has chosen to go ahead and provide this huge air defense capability. You can take any one selective group and point out certain areas where the Soviets are in a relatively better position. Let's take the case of attack submarines. Yes, the Soviet Union has more attack submarines than the United States but many of them are old-fashioned diesel vessels which today are of very little significance when compared to the nuclear attack submarines. Ten or fifteen years ago the United States stopped building diesel submarines because they were old-fashioned at that time. And we have put our emphasis on building modern, effective, nuclear attack submarines that can go around the world totally submerged.

Q. So you're saying that when you start measuring things in terms of numbers rather than effectiveness, you can be misled.

A. Yes, easily. It's very important to look well into the numbers. Many of the Soviet submarines, for example, also are very short-range. They have to stay in their own coastal waters. Again, theirs is a defensive navy. The Soviets have almost no logistics capability.

Q. Is the Persian Gulf within their range?

A. It would be very difficult for the Soviets to maintain more than a couple of ships, say five or six, in the Arabian Sea. It's 10,000 miles away from the Soviet Union by water just as it's 10,000 miles away for us. But the United States has successfully been able to maintain a large naval force in the Arabian Sea ... because of our tremendous logistics capability and because we have a major naval and airforce base at Diego Garcia in the middle of the Indian Ocean, with repair-ships present. We have

Military Resources of NATO, Warsaw Pact and China

	NATO	Warsaw Pact	People's Republic of China
Population	554,800,000	365,700,000	900,000,000
GNP	$3,367 billion	$1,240 billion	$309 billion
Military spending	$175 billion	$139 billion	$23–28 billion
Military manpower	4,900,000	4,850,000	4,300,000
Strategic nuclear weapons	9,400	4,500	200?
Tactical nuclear weapons	22,000?	15,000?	N.A.
Tanks	25,250+	59,000	9,000
Anti-tank missiles	200,000	N.A.	N.A.
Other armoured vehicles	48,000+	62,000+	3,500
Heavy Artillery	11,400+	22,600+	20,000
Combat aircraft	8,900+	10,400	5,900
Helicopters	12,300	4,550	350
Major surface warships	522	247	22
Attack submarines (all types)	211	239	66

Note: The figures presented in these tables are the latest available. They may vary slightly from year to year, being long term in incidence, comparisons between them would not substantially change until disarmament reduces them. (The US Defense Department estimates of Warsaw Pact manpower include 750,000 uniformed civilian personnel making the total Warsaw Pact manpower 5.6 million.)
Source: US Department of Defense.

also had, for the past thirty years, a naval force of three to five ships, under a US Navy admiral, based physically in the Persian Gulf at Bahrain. Most people aren't even aware of the fact that we've had this base. And I think it is significant that the US Navy base in Bahrain did not prevent the Soviets from going into Afghanistan. It did not prevent the Iranians from capturing our hostages. On top of that, all the new ships we have sent to the Arabian Sea adjacent to the Persian Gulf—20 ships, 2 aircraft carriers, 200 hot planes, 200 hydrogen bombs on our navy ships—did not prevent the Russians from going into Afghanistan. Those ships were there in the Arabian Sea but they were not deterrent to either Iran or the Soviet Union.

Are the Soviets stronger than we are? No. The fifteen countries in the NATO alliance outnumber the members of the Warsaw Treaty Organisation. The Soviet Union is also outnumbered by China. Combining Chinese and NATO strength puts the Soviet Union and its allies at a distinct disadvantage both numerically and strategically. Moreover, while the Soviets do outnumber the West in certain categories of weapons, such as tanks, the quality and efficiency of the NATO weapons more than make up for any numerical superiority.

DO THE SOVIETS OUTSPEND THE WEST?

Many experts claim that the USSR spends a lot more on both its defence and strategic nuclear forces than does the US. It is also claimed that the rate of growth in Soviet military spending is substantially higher than for either the US or the NATO Alliance.

The CIA estimates that in 1979 alone, the USSR spent $150 for every $100 spent by the US.[1] When President Reagan presented his new economic plan to Congress in 1981 he claimed that "since 1979, the Soviet Union has invested $300 billion more in its military forces than we have .... To allow this imbalance to continue is a threat to our national security".

Reagan based his figures on a CIA report, "Soviet and U.S. Defense Activities 1970–1979: A Dollar Cost Comparison". The CIA conclusions were obtained by examining the Soviet military establishment and then calculating how much it would cost the US Administration *in US dollars* to build the same thing *in the US*. That is to say, how much it would cost the US to deploy the same number of troops, the same number of planes, the same number of weapons systems, and the same research and development as the Soviet Union.

On the face of it, this method may seem 'reasonable'. But discrepancies arise in such areas as wages. Soviet soldiers are drafted and paid a mere four roubles a week (about $8.00); yet the CIA estimate pays each one of the 3,673,000 soldiers in the Soviet military $288 per week; that is the salary of US soldiers, who are paid on a par with US industrial workers. Paying Soviet soldiers US wages adds up to $70 billion a year. As US pay scales have gone up and US inflation continues to rise, the American estimates of the Soviet defence budget 'rise' accordingly. This is such a glaring discrepancy that in a little publicised document, *A Dollar Cost Comparison of Soviet and US Defense Activities 1966–1976*, the CIA itself admitted that "If all personnel costs were removed from both sides, US outlays exceed the estimated dollar costs of Soviet defense activities by about 10% over the period 1966–1976 as a whole".

The CIA also converts the US expenditure into roubles and compares it with the Soviet military. It manages to get the Soviet spending 25% more than the US. But again there is less in this conclusion than meets the eye. The US and NATO economies are capitalistic 'free market' economies with prices and wages dependent largely on market forces. The USSR, and WTO, in contrast, are socialist 'command' economies in which market forces are determined by government policies fixing wages and prices. Comparing the two systems is like comparing apples and radishes. This fact had led Rand Corporation, a Pentagon think tank, to conclude that "the administered nature of Soviet prices make them deficient tools for analysis of real costs".[2]

Perhaps the most balanced appraisal of a US–USSR defence spending comparison comes from the Stockholm International Peace Research Institute (SIPRI).[3] It asserts that while the US does in fact outspend the USSR, there is a rough parity between them. What is important to note about this parity, however, is that while the US and NATO defence spending is virtually all directed at the Soviet Union, the Soviets do not spend all their money for preparation only against the US and NATO. About 35% of the Soviet military expenditures are used to deploy about 40% of Soviet forces along the Chinese border and elsewhere. On this note it is worth mentioning that the highest of all estimates for Soviet military spending come not from the CIA or NATO but from the *Peking Review*.

In terms of the *rate of growth* for Soviet military spending from year to year, SIPRI is again rather revealing. It concludes that if the growth rate for Soviet spending is calculated by the same method as that of the US, the Soviet figures show a growth rate of between 1 and 2% per year.

This 1–2% figure is important in light of a decision made by the NATO Foreign Ministers on 12 May 1981 to increase NATO defence expenditures by 3% in real terms. This decision was made after US Secretary of Defense, Weinberger, using CIA data, warned his colleagues that the USSR was spending 12% of its national wealth on military preparations, twice the NATO amount, and that the Soviets had been maintaining a 4–5% growth rate in their defence spending, again twice the NATO rate. He warned, "the current and prospective leaders of the Soviet Union may be impelled by their lack of success in other fields to turn to the one field where they have confidence and capability—stark military power and military threats".[4] The NATO Foreign Ministers did not feel the need to check the veracity of Secretary Weinberger's CIA sources. Either because of fear or of surrounding political realities they acquiesced and voted unanimously for a NATO military spending growth rate of 3% a year. After the meeting, Admiral Falls of Canada, Chairman of the NATO military committee, stated: "The alliance nations will, all of them, do what they have to to assist the United States. When it is needed I'm sure that other nations, and I include France, will assist in whatever way is needed at the time".[5]

The NATO Alliance has been consistently outspending the USSR and its East European allies over the past twenty five years. This is the conclusion of the US Arms Control and Disarmament Agency which points out that between 1970 and 1979 NATO outspent the WTO by over $200 billion, $1,946.6 billion against $1,739.6 billion.

An analysis of total NATO and WTO military spending shows

NATO vs Warsaw Pact Military Spending
(in billions of 1979 dollars)

Year	NATO	Warsaw Pact	NATO advantage
1970	$201.8	$149.5	$52.3
1971	192.8	153.7	39.1
1972	195.6	159.4	36.2
1973	190.9	166.7	24.2
1974	193.9	173.4	20.5
1975	190.5	178.6	11.9
1976	186.6	186.2	.4
1977	193.5	186.8	6.7
1978	195.4	190.7	4.7
1979	205.6	194.6	11.0
	1,946.6	1,739.6	207.0

Source: "World Military Expenditures and Arms Transfers 1969–1978," U.S. Arms Control and Disarmament Agency. 1979 figures from former Secretary of Defense Harold Brown's January 1981 final report to Congress.

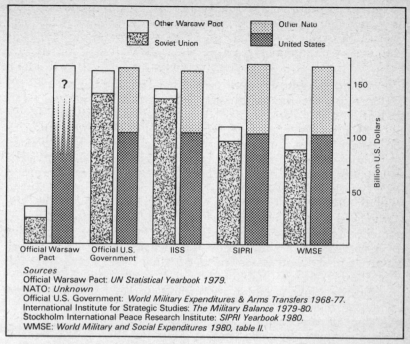

Five Views of Military Expenditures of the Major Alliances, 1977.

that NATO spent $207 billion more than WTO betwen 1970 and 1979. The table above gives the figures.

The next table gives the various military expenditures of the US, USSR, WTO and NATO, as estimated both officially and by neutral organisations:

Does the Soviet Union outspend the West? No it does not. The facts are that the US and NATO outspend the USSR and its Warsaw Pact allies and have been doing so consistently since the 1960s. Moreover, while the USSR has had a 1–2% increase in its military spending from year-to-year, NATO and the US have pledged themselves to a 3% increase. Claims to the contrary, such as CIA data, are based on faulty computation such as attempting to price the Soviet military in US dollars and paying each Soviet soldier according to US pay scales.

WILL THE SOVIETS INVADE?

Notwithstanding the fact that the Soviet Union is out-spent, out-gunned, out-numbered and surrounded by different groupings of hostile powers, many people nevertheless continue to believe that given half a chance, the Soviets would invade Western Europe.

There is no evidence available that indicates that the Soviets either want a war or plan to invade. This is not because they are peaceloving. Whenever opportunities have arisen they have seized control—from the annexation of Estonia, Latvia and Lithuania and the partition of Poland in 1939, to domination of Eastern Europe since 1945, to the invasion of Afghanistan in 1979. Unlike the US, the Soviet Union during this century alone has experienced devastation twice, during the two world wars. It has invaded neighbouring countries to counter a direct geographical threat to Soviet land. It is equally true that with increased unrest in the Eastern block and with resistance growing in Afghanistan, the USSR is finding it increasingly difficult to control the sphere of influence it already has. It is not likely that the Russian rulers want to create still more difficulties for themselves by taking over countries far beyond Soviet borders. They have their hands full with Kabul, Prague, Budapest, and Warsaw. It is difficult to imagine that they would want to add Rome, Paris, Bonn and London to their list.

Indeed, if any country has learnt the lesson that fellow communists are not to be trusted any more than the 'capitalist' West, it is the USSR. Most Soviets have a clear understanding of the cost of hegemony, particularly after the experience with China's hostility and the unrest within the Warsaw Pact. To be a fellow communist does not imply friendship.

Further, the Soviets are aware that they cannot afford many more Cubas—Cuba costs the USSR over $6 million per day. Learning from this, they refer to other client states such as Ethiopia, South Yemen and Angola as countries with a 'socialist orientation', thus releasing themselves from both burdensome military and financial obligations. On the other hand, the Soviet Union also realises that the continued existence of Western Europe is to its own advantage as a source of both high technology and trade. The Soviets must be credited with at least rudimentary awareness of limits of power. The fact is that the USSR has so many enemies surrounding it that an invasion of NATO is simply a losing proposition. The Soviet Union is by necessity on the *defensive* in foreign policy terms.

This can be seen by simply examining the extent, or lack of it, of Soviet influence around the world. The Center for Defense Information in the United States, in a 1980 study of Soviet influence in 155 countries around the world, concludes that history since World War II "does not support perceptions of consistent Soviet advances and devastating US setbacks". Of the 155 countries in the world the USSR has significant influence in only 19. Setbacks in China, Indonesia, Egypt, India and Iraq dwarf marginal advances the Soviets have made in other countries. Soviet influence can be seen to have peaked in 1958 with the launching of Sputnik, and it has been waning ever since. Not even other communist countries follow its dictates without question. In 1979, anti-Soviet countries spent $265 billion on their military preparedness as against the Soviets' and their allies' $175 billion. Anti-Soviet countries have 9,500,000 military personnel compared to 4,800,000 for the Soviets. And anti-Soviet navies have 445 major surface ships while the USSR and its allies have only 235.

In fact, if the 78 countries around the world which have some degree of political or military power are divided into pro-Soviet or pro-West sentiments, and then given power ratings according to demographic, geographic, economic, and military factors, pro-Western governments have a total power rating of 1800 as opposed to 556 for those which are pro-Soviet. Admiral LaRoque puts the matter clearly:[1]

> The Soviets are in six little relatively unimportant countries today. They're in Angola, Mozambique, Ethiopia, Cuba, Afghanistan and South Yemen, none of which is important, and all of which cost the Soviet Union money and resources every day. Then, take a look at the Soviet Union over the last thirty years and look at the places they've been kicked out of. They've been kicked out of Indonesia, the sixth largest nation in the world, kicked out of China, kicked out of Egypt, and kicked out of Somalia where they had the only naval base outside of the Soviet Union. *I think our fear of the Soviets is based on lack of information and total absence of factual data.* If you look at the success of the Soviets as imperialists, they are flops. They are not strong around the world. They have not had a major naval exercise in the last five years, while we conduct them with NATO two or three times a year .... I just can't get excited about the Soviet military threat. Now, I am concerned about the Soviets' desire to spread communism around the world. I am angry with the Soviets and their treatment of their people within their own country. But the way to deal with those problems is not through building more nuclear weapons or more tanks or more aircraft or going to war. We're going to have to learn to compete with the Russians in non-military ways, as we compete with other countries of the world. And, we're going to have to learn to live with the Russians, or some day we and the Russians are going to die at about the same time.

But what if the Soviet Union *did* invade? Although Thatcher and Reagan fantasise about life under the Russians being one big concentration camp reminiscent of George Orwell's *1984*, the reality of life in Eastern Europe indicates otherwise. It is true that there has been an assault on human rights, there has been censorship, there has been a bureaucratic elite that seeks to crush all opposition, but all these facts are also true to a greater or lesser extent in the NATO countries and in the US, although methods vary. Moreover, despite Soviet control, there have been strikes and uprisings and the continued attempt on the part of the common people in Eastern Europe and Afghanistan to regain control over their lives. Poland is the latest example of how fragile Soviet control really is.

This last point is of fundamental importance. What NATO and the US are constantly reiterating is that 'it is better to be dead than red', i.e. it is preferable to experience nuclear annihilation on both sides than to experience or even risk a Soviet takeover. Thus NATO has its 9,000 tactical nuclear weapons, Britain and France their own nuclear 'deterrence', and the US has its 10,000 strategic warheads. Could anyone seriously suggest that we drop nuclear bombs on Warsaw to get rid of the Russians?

Occupation by the Russian armed forces is not pleasant. Is there any occupation which is? However, occupation is not death either. It involves forms of oppression and exploitation against which people can and do fight back. That is why if one asks the most courageous of the dissidents in Russia and Eastern Europe whether they would swap their present oppression for nuclear annihilation, their answer would be an emphatic 'no'. If one is dead, one cannot do anything. Not even fight back. The hope of creating a future much better than the present essentially requires the continuity of life.

5 Star Wars

DO THE SOVIETS HAVE 'KILLER SATELLITES'?

In 1977, General George Keegan, the retired chief of US Air Force intelligence, revealed in the trade journal *Aviation Week and Space Technology*, that the USSR would have developed by the early 1980s the ultimate anti-ballistic weapon system—a 'charged-particle-beam' device that would be able to wipe out the entire missile force of the US and its NATO allies. This weapon would enable the USSR to execute not only a conventional force invasion of Europe but a simultaneous nuclear first strike against the US, or at least threaten to do so. If NATO or the US retaliated with a nuclear strike the Soviets would have the assured capacity to shoot the missiles out of the sky.

It is of course true that the USSR is conducting research in and development on the military applications of charged-particle physics. The US also is working in this area. After General Keegan's 'warning' this research has been accelerated. However, experts familiar with what both countries are doing assert that both efforts have thus far been fruitless, and that to speak of a 'Soviet threat' in this area is either naïve or a deception.

Using charged-particle-beams for weapons imposes an enormous challenge. Such a system would have to include long-range sensors to both detect and track incoming warheads; it would have to be able to discriminate between decoys; it would have to be able to generate a beam, point and track that beam on a missile which would be a MARV, meaning designed to alter its trajectory to *avoid* detection, and then shoot the beam without dissipation through the earth's atmosphere, adjusting to the earth's electromagnetic field, gravity and other forces; finally, the system would have to be able to detect and measure near misses, correct for them, and then fire again. And it would have to do this against hundreds, perhaps thousands (the US has 30,000 nuclear weapons, the Soviets 20,000) of warheads zooming down at speeds of five miles per *second*. If this charged-particle-beam system was mounted on space platforms in order to hit the missiles before they had unloaded their multiple warheads, it would have to be supplied continuously with enormous amounts of energy—several power plant's worth for each of them. Further, its orbit would have to be such that it was in the right place at the right time when the missiles were launched. Such positioning would be difficult against American ICBMs and virtually impossible against nuclear submarines, Cruise missiles or nuclear bombers. It has been calculated by two physicists, John Parmentola and Kosta Tsipis of the Massachusetts Institute of Technology, that to take care of the American arsenal alone, the Soviets would have to have at least 150 beam-platforms orbiting in outer space.[1]

Even if such a programme were put into effect, simple counter measures could nullify it. The charged-particle-beam satellite itself could be destroyed or damaged; the communication links between the weapon and ground control could be jammed; US or NATO missiles could shoot out 'chaff'—aluminium shreddings which show up on radar—to confuse the system; missiles could even shoot out a layer of air to disperse the beam before it struck, if it ever got that close.

So large are the problems of any such system that former Secretary of Defense Brown, a trained physicist, discounts claims that the Soviets are developing a "threat" in this field. "The laws of physics,' he says, 'are the same in the United States and the Soviet Union."[2]

The USSR is asserted to have a 'lead' in other areas besides that of high-energy particle beam weapons. As early as the 1960s, NATO and US military analysts were also reporting a Soviet 'lead' in the realm of *satellite warfare*. The warning was that the Soviets would have an anti-satellite capability by 1963. As is usually the case, the facts were otherwise. The Soviets did not even begin to *test* such devices until October 1968, in a series that continued until December 1971. A second series of tests began in February 1976, and is still going on. All of these tests have involved co-orbital intercepts, which consist of shooting a target satellite into orbit and then launching an interceptor satellite to track it down. It is estimated that there have been about a dozen and a half tests of this system, with various degrees of success. All the tests have been carried out with satellites in low orbit and have been so limited that the target satellite can be identified as such even before the 'killer-satellite' has been launched. Because of this, it would be a relatively easy thing to track the killer-satellite and destroy it before it reaches its target. Even if the Soviet killer-satellites could avoid the identification problem, however, they would still be ineffectual against US and NATO communications and early warning satellites because these are kept far beyond where the current Soviet tests are being run. The Soviets have not demonstrated any direct-ascent intercepts as was thought in 1975 when a US early-warning satellite was blinded for four hours. After loud claims about this being due to a Soviet 'breakthrough' in the field, it was officially, though very quietly, admitted that the blinding had been due to large natural gas fires.

While crying 'wolf' about Soviet capabilities, the US has been unobtrusively building up its own anti-satellite programme. While always referring to Soviet interceptor satellites as 'killer-satellites', the Pentagon calls its own SAINTS, an acronym for satellite interceptors. By 1961, a half-scale prototype of SAINT was already under construction with intercept tests scheduled for 1962. In February 1962, the Pentagon ordered a complete censorship of any information of the US programme.

It is known, however, that in 1963, Secretary of Defense McNamara directed the Army to conduct anti-satellite tests in Kwajalein Atoll, at the western end of the US Pacific Missile range. The Navy got into the field in 1964 in their 'Early Spring' programme, during which they used modified Polaris missiles launched from submarines to spray a screen of metal pellets in front of satellites. In 1966, the US Air Force used special thrust-augmented Thor missiles with nuclear warheads in anti-satellite tests. This resulted in an operational anti-satellite system based on Johnston Island in the Pacific. Despite the fact that using nuclear weapons in space is a violation of the Outer Space Treaty signed by the US and the USSR, these missiles were kept in readiness until 1975. Since then they have been 'deactivated' but can be reassembled 'if necessary'.

So complete has been the news blackout on the US satellite programme that even the name of the single largest military space programme was kept a secret until just recently. That programme is the National Reconnaissance Office (NRO). Its $2 billion plus budget per year is said to be buried in US Air Force allocations. Working with the top defence contractors such as Lockheed and Hughes, the NRO builds and flies the most sophisticated spy satellites in the world.

Such satellites collect electronic data from around the world for intelligence processing. Of particular interest, of course, are the Soviet radio signals that control missiles and spacecraft operations, telegraph, telephone and other types of data transmissions, photographs of military installations, even measurements of water temperatures in the oceans, useful in anti-submarine warfare. Some US satellites detect nuclear explosions; others constantly monitor all Soviet military movements for surprise attack. A third type carries 70% of all US military and diplomatic communications, including the famous Washington-Moscow hot line.

Satellite-linked sensors and communications nets are known by the acronym C–3I, for 'Command, Control, Communications and Intelligence'. C–3I advocates, such as the US Air Force, claim that satellites enable the US to conduct world-wide battles which would be fought under a centralised comand maintained in some remote location, perhaps even outside the US but directly linked to the C–3I satellites in outer space.

These satellites would give instant intelligence on the entire Soviet military deployment; would guide missiles launched from deeply submerged and hidden US submarines to hit targets inside the USSR with deadly accuracy; would detect any Soviet retaliation; would synchronise the 'appropriate' US second strike. Use of the US Fleet Satellite Communications system would even enable US forces to virtually destroy the Soviet undersea ballistic missile fleet. According to Joel S. Wit, a US naval analyst, the system could co-ordinate land based computers with US attack submarines with such speed and accuracy that up to 90% of Soviet ships could be destroyed before the Soviet counter-strike, particularly since the USSR keeps a high percentage of its fleets clustered in ports.[3]

An integral part of the US Fleet Satellite Communications system is a constellation of eighteen navigating 'stars' in the form of satellites which have been specifically established to give unprecedented accuracy to US nuclear missiles. Called the Navstar Global Positioning System, it offers the US its latest in first-strike capability, assuring that any warhead it directs will be able to hit within ten metres of the target, thus giving Pentagon strategists confidence that they would be able to hit and crack Soviet missile silos and therefore destroy their missiles before they can be launched in retaliation. According to Lieutenant General Richard Henry, commander of the Air Force Space and Missile Systems Organization, the Navstar is 'so staggering that the strategic and tactical doctrine of our fighting forces will be rewritten'.[4]

Four Navstar test satellites are in orbit already, at a cost of $24,000,000 apiece. Like the twenty-four operational satellites that are to follow during the 1980s, they orbit at 10,900 feet and carry atomic clocks which the Air Force claims are accurate to within one second in 30,000 years. The cost of each clock: $200,000.

Although Navstar has serious implications for carrying the nuclear arms spiral into space, then US Secretary of Defense Harold Brown, claimed that the US effort is legitimised because the Russians are carrying out such satellite research as well, particularly in the area of killer satellites, which are capable of destroying other satellites while in space orbit.[5] Such killer satellites, said Brown, "pose a threat to all satellites" used by the US. With Navstar, however, the US has emerged "comfortably ahead" in this dimension of the US–USSR competition.

This "advantage" carries grave risks, says Wit, particularly in a world balanced on the razor's edge of nuclear terror:

> complete target information on enemy submarines would probably be available at the outbreak of hostilities .... Russian commanders might then be confronted with the dilemma of having to use their nuclear weapons or lose them while the hostilities were still non-nuclear.[6]

The tendency for a relatively minor conflict to escalate into a 'pre-emptive nuclear strike' by either side, bringing nuclear war to the world, is significantly increased because of satellites.

Despite this, the US continues to spend enormous amounts on military space research; approximately $60 billion has been spent since 1960. By 1982, the US was simultaneously deploying 40 to 50 active military satellites in space, worth some $5 to $10 billion. They orbit amongst some 4,500 other human-made space objects, both active and inactive, which are identitifed and tracked by the US Space Detection and Tracking system.

ARE THEY AHEAD IN THE SPACE RACE?

The Soviets do have a solid track record in space exploration, and if numbers alone were the criterion for superiority, the Soviets would definitely have it. They spend 2% of their gross national product on space, compared with 0.20% in the US. The Soviets lifted the first human into orbit, Yuri Gagarin, in 1961. Since then they have sent 50 cosmonauts on a total of 46 missions, compared with 45 American astronauts on 33 missions. In 1981 alone, the Soviets launched 8 spacecraft against only one for the US.

The Soviets have been operating with a different strategy than the US. They have emphasised space endurance. Their cosmonauts have logged over five and a half years in space while the Americans have only logged two and a quarter years. The cosmonauts Leonid Popor and Valery Ryumin hold the space record: 185 consecutive days in space. Since 1977, they have used these long stays in space to construct a space station, Salyut–6, where cosmonauts live and work. Current plans are to enlarge Salyut in a twelve person space house.

US officials have reacted to the Salyut space station with characteristic alarm. "We expect a large, permanent, manned orbital (Soviet) space complex to be operational by about 1990", the Pentagon research director Richard DeLaver told the House Armed Services Committee in February 1982.[1] This would give the Soviets the capability of effectively attacking "ground, sea and air targets from space".

Gen. B. L. Davis, commander of the Strategic Air Command,

had told the committee the day before in public session that unless
the United States prepared to operate in space, "the Soviets will
eventually be able to deny us use of space as a support medium
and use it as a high ground to launch attacks on US targets".[2]

"If they should achieve superiority in space, they could well
attain a decisive war-winning edge", he said.

From Salyut, cosmonauts have developed an astronomic
telescope camera and an earth observation camera which were
both then transferred to a spy satellite. Salyut also has a furnace
which is used to forge new metal alloys that are vital for
reconnaissance hardware, and the cosmonauts are perfecting the
Soviet early-warning and navigational-tracking systems necessary
to monitor US military movements and warn of a US nuclear first
strike attack.

Salyut has also been used for non-military purposes. It
photographs the earth to find forests, gas deposits and fisheries.
It made an aerial inventory of the world's wheat crop in 1979, the
year the Soviet harvest was short. The cosmonauts have also
grown gallium arsenide crystals which can be used to make
computer components which are faster than silicon chips; they
have also developed other alloys impossible to create on earth
where gravity prevents materials of different densities from
amalgamating with one another.

Yet there are two drawbacks to the Soviet strategy. First, unless
they can find a cheaper way of getting to and from the Salyut space
station, their progress will remain slow and very much dependent
on their earth-bound socialist economics. Currently they use an
expensive Progress rocket to get cosmonauts up to Salyut which is
only good for one trip. Secondly, human minds and bodies do not
seem to be adjusting to long stays in space. Muscles atrophy in
spite of daily exercise, the heart changes its pattern of contractions;
and bones lose up to 0.50% of their calcium each month because
gravity is required to build new deposits. There is also the
psychological problem of long isolation without company.

Rather than endurance, the US has emphasised short stays to do
specific jobs, such as landing a person on the moon. It has just
completed a space shuttle which is designed to zip in and out of
orbit for short stays. Its maiden voyage in 1981 was performed with
near perfection, and American officials announced the US was in
space to stay.

Although the space shuttle is touted as an economic breakthrough, since it can be reused up to 100 times, and for a variety
of commercial and scientific endeavours, its primary purpose is to
increase America's military dominance in space.

From the beginning, the shuttle programme was a joint
civilian-military venture but as things got nearer to completion the

military took over more and more control of the National Aeronautic and Space Administration (NASA) which was building the shuttle. So pervasive is the military control of NASA that Kosta Tsipis, a physicist at the Massachusetts Institute of Technology, has warned that "NASA may become a mere bus driver for the Defense Department".³ The Pentagon admits its interest. Lt. General Daniel O. Graham, former head of the Defense Intelligence Agency, states categorically that "eventually, we will have a very significant part of our military capability in space. The shuttle helps bring that day closer".⁴

By 1984, the Pentagon intends to operate its own space shuttle from Vandenburg Air Force Base in California. From that site, satellites can reach polar orbit from where they can monitor most of the globe. In 1986, the Defense Department intends to open its own Mission Control Centre near Colorado Springs, where it can direct its own shuttle and satellite flights. All this will cost money, and Reagan and the Pentagon are more than ready to provide it. In 1982 alone, the Pentagon planned to spend $8.8 billion, $3 billion of which is hidden in classified programmes. The US has been in space for 23 years but sees in the shuttle the opportunity to jump into the commanding seat. According to Lt. General Graham, "The shuttle will not open up a new contest but put us ahead in one already going on".

The shuttle will allow the Pentagon to put satellites into orbit far more frequently and cheaply than the Soviets can. It will also allow for greater accuracy and reliability than has been possible up till now for either side; and it will allow for transporting bigger and more sophisticated military hardware than could be put in space by rockets.

Most importantly, the space shuttle will allow the US an unparallelled opportunity to develop new weapons and defence systems. In 1983, for instance, the US launched an experimental sensor, code-named 'Teal Ruby', designed both to pick up infrared radiation emitted by strategic bombers and to detect any Soviet satellites camouflaged as space debris. In 1985, in a project code-named 'Talan Gold', the shuttle will test an aiming weapon essential for space laser warfare. Because of the shuttle, the Pentagon expects to have orbiting laser weapons by 1990.

The shuttle is also important for the development of the hunter-killer satellite, a satellite designed to pull up next to enemy satellites and explode. The shuttle's likeliest role in this area would be akin to a minelayer—seeding the skies with automated hunter-killers and then quickly ducking away and returning to earth for replenishment.

Although competition between them is fierce and the US maintains a clear lead, there have been four treaties signed between the US and USSR which limit the militarisation of space. The first one was the 1963 Partial Test Ban Treaty which prohibited nuclear explosions in the atmosphere or in outer space. In 1967, the Treaty of Principles Governing the Activities of States in Exploration and Use of Outer Space was ratified by both sides, prohibiting the deployment of either nuclear weapons or other weapons of mass destruction in outer space. It also prohibited weapons from being placed on the moon or other celestial bodies. But it did not prohibit the testing of non-nuclear interceptors and their weapons.

Then in 1972, the Anti Ballistic Missile Treaty was signed which pledged both the US and the USSR not to interfere with each other's reconnaissance satellites. This treaty is closely linked with the Convention of the International Telecommunications Union, to which both the US and the USSR belong, which bans radio frequency interference, such as destroying or disabling a communications satellite. Also important is Article II of the 1971 US–Soviet Accident Measures Agreements which requires immediate notification in the event of interference with the other side's early warning system. Finally, the 1974 Agreement on the Prevention of Nuclear War obligates both signatories to abstain from satellite interference if such interference poses a risk of war.

What has not been covered by treaty law is a ban on the testing or deployment of conventional anti-satellite weapons, and that is what the race just described is all about.

In June 1982, Secretary of Defense Weinberger announced that an anti-satellite system was an "essential ingredient" of President Reagan's programme to "revitalize" the US nuclear deterrent.[5] Weinberger stated that the US "should acquire the capability to negate, as well as disrupt, hostile space systems".

Although Weinberger refused to give details, it is known that the Air Force has been developing a system in which an F–15 fighter would launch a 'miniature homing vehicle' powered by a two-stage rocket to fire it into orbit. Once in orbit, the homing vehicle would seek out and destroy a Soviet satellite.

For now, the Reagan administration has decided not to negotiate an agreement prohibiting the use of anti-satellite weapons with the Soviet Union despite a public announcement by Soviet President Andropov that the USSR was willing to sign such an agreement. Rather, the US 'will actively support an integrated space defense capability including surveillance, command, control and communications, and anti-satellite segments,' said Weinberger. The US Air Force has been directed to 'identify concepts defining an enduring strategic war fighting anti-satellite system' and to deploy such a system by 1987.

6 Human Rights

ISN'T THE USSR JUST ONE BIG GULAG ARCHIPELAGO?

An honest examination of the Soviet threat in military terms compels one to conclude that if it does exist, it is largely overblown. In virtually every category of comparison, it is the US and its allies which maintain a strategic and technical superiority, not the Soviet Union as is made out.

When confronted with facts, most people will accept, even if grudgingly, the Western lead. Most realise that in the final analysis the West has economic, technical, scientific and military superiority over any other power bloc in the world. The might of the United States in particular is so awesome that few seriously doubt its ability to inflict unacceptable damage upon any other nation. Moreover, since Russia has never attacked the West, there is not a historically conditioned fear of the Russian military. The Soviet Union has always been regarded as unconquerable because of its enormous size—one sixth of the entire land mass of the planet. It is this size which also makes the Soviet Union openly vulnerable. Moreover, it has always been known for the number of soldiers it boasts but never for their competence or efficiency.

And yet the mass majority of the Western public will insist that the Russian threat is not only real but so pressing that only the possession of continually improving nuclear weapons keeps them from unleashing their tyranny on the West. What people fear about Russia is not the Red Army, but the *red system* which it inflicts on areas under its control. It is a system that above all is symbolised by a deprivation of human rights. In the West, the idea of individual freedom to speak, write, believe, travel and work as one wishes is considered to be fundamental to our societal structure. Individual freedom is essential if either capitalism or democracy are to function. There are of course numerous and important violations of these freedoms; nevertheless, these freedoms are considered, in certain senses, to be 'inalienable' to all. In Russia this does not appear to be the case. Ever since 1917, one has heard of purges, mass executions, slave camps, brutal

repression of the individual's rights and a denial of any alternative
to either Marxism-Leninism as an economic system or the 'dictatorship of the proletariat' as a political structure. Although the system
had been enunciated in the greatest interests of the greatest
number of people, it has degenerated into a cult of personality. The
name of Stalin raises the spectre of the Gulag Archipelago and an
entire nation cringing under the ruthless oppression of a tyrant
assisted by his secret police. In Eastern Europe, where Soviet
control is enforced by the presence of the Red Army, one sees
virtually the same thing: a society of greyness dominated by a
simple monolithic party which has centralised all authority into the
hands of a selected party elite. All opposition is eliminated.

It is the prospect of this oppression spreading to the West that
fills people with such dread that they acquiesce to the theory of
better dead than red. It is the oppression in the Soviet system,
therefore, not Soviet military power alone that people ultimately
fear. It is the Soviet's consistent denial of human rights to their
own people and their usurping of the rights of the people in
Eastern Europe that is the essence of the 'Russian threat'. Most
would agree with Rosa Luxemburg's statement that "the remedy
invented by Lenin and Trotsky, the general suppression of
democracy, is worse than the evil it was supposed to cure".[1]
Therefore the spectre of an invading Red Army bringing with it a
Party that will suppress all democratic values, motivates the
common people to support any defence, even a nuclear one, to
protect human freedom.

Cases of Human Rights Violations

In its new constitution promulgated in October 1977, the Soviet
Government "fully guarantees and ensures" the practical
implementation of all principles 'concerning human rights'. Article
34 of the Constitution proclaims that all citizens of the USSR are
equal before the law "without distinction as to origin, social or
property status, race or nationality, sex, education, language,
attitude to religion, type and nature of occupation, domicile or
other status". The text of this article repeats virtually verbatim the
proclamation of non-discrimination in Article 26 of the 1966 International Covenant on Civil and Political Rights. The Soviet Constitution deviates from the International Covenant by not prohibiting
discrimination on grounds of "political or other opinion". But it
goes on to guarantee "equal rights of the citizens of the USSR in
all fields of economic, political, social and cultural life".

The Soviet Constitution as read is probably the most liberal
constitution in the world. It guarantees protection to every Soviet

citizen. Unfortunately, there is nothing in the Soviet Union to protect the Constitution. The society is dominated by one party, the Communist Party of the Soviet Union (CPSU); one economic and political philosophy, Marxism-Leninism; and one historical goal, the establishment of communism. Competing parties, different economic and political theories, or alternative futures are considered 'anti-Soviet'. To argue for them, even privately, is a codified criminal offence.

Participants in virtually all strains of dissent in the Soviet Union have been tried and sentenced to imprisonment either for "anti-Soviet agitation and propaganda" or for "dissemination of fabrications known to be false which defame the Soviet state and social system". Persons active in disseminating information about human rights violations in the USSR have consistently faced such charges. Since it is official dictat that human rights violations do not exist in the Soviet Union, any such information is labelled as 'slanderous'. It is also official dictat that there is no discrimination between the fifteen republics and the 130 ethnic nationalities that make up the Union of Soviet Socialist Republics. Therefore, members of minority nationalities who criticise the official policy or advocate greater autonomy or cultural rights have been accused of 'sowing enmity' amongst the peoples of the Soviet Union or showing 'anti-Soviet intent' by advocating 'bourgeois nationalist' views which could weaken the Soviet system. In recent years, Estonians, Latvians, Lithuanians, Georgians, Armenians, Crimean Tartars, Moldavians, and, most frequently, Ukranians, have been tried on such charges and variously sentenced even to execution. A notable exception to this has been the Soviet Jews who have been imprisoned after applying to emigrate. Jews are usually warned about possible prosecution for 'anti-Soviet' activity but are invariably tried on non-political charges, like refusing to serve in the armed forces.

The following cases, documented by Amnesty International,[2] illustrate what literally *millions* of Soviet citizens have been forced to go through because they dared to question the state.

In 1974, a group of mostly young Russian orthodox believers established a seminar to discuss religious and philosophical questions in Moscow. Officials told the seminar that to discuss such things was 'anti-Soviet' but the group carried on. In July 1976 a member of the group, Alexander Argentov, 25, was forcibly confined to a Moscow psychiatric hospital. In September another member, Edward Fedotov, was also confined to a psychiatric hospital. Both men were detained for some two months and released. The group still persisted and eventually took on the title "Christian Seminar on Problems of Religious Rebirth". In 1978 it began to produce a journal called "The Community". In late 1978 two other group members, Alexander Kuzkin and Sergei Yermolayev were detained. Kuzkin was confined to a psychiatric hospital while Yermolayev was charged with 'hooliganism' and detained. After two months in jail, Yermolayev was sent to the Serbsky Institute of Forensic Psychiatry for examination. In November 1978, the group leader, Alexander Ogorodnikov, was tried for 'parasitism', and sentenced to one year in prison. Another group member, Alexander Pushkin, was confined to a psychiatric hospital in the spring of 1979.

In 1976, after her visit to the US Embassy for advice regarding an application to emigrate, Tatyana Shatolov was forcibly confined to a psychiatric hospital for four months. Her son Vasily was then arrested and sentenced to two years' imprisonment for refusing to respond to the draft. Finally, the husband Nikolai was arrested in August 1977. The official indictment against him alleged that he "had written and mailed (a letter) to the General Secretary of the Central Committee of the Communist Party of the Soviet Union, Comrade Brezhnev, which contained slanderous fabrications known to be false which defamed the Soviet State and social system". Shatalov admitted sending the letters but defended himself by saying that he had no intention of slander; rather, he merely sought to point out to Comrade Brezhnev that human rights are systematically violated in the USSR and that his family was being victimised by such violations. Rejecting his defence, the court sentenced Shatalov to 18 months in prison.

In 1978, a personal letter from a Byelorussian worker, Yergeny Bozinnikov, was intercepted by the authorities. She was sentenced to three years' imprisonment for the 'dissemination' of 'anti-Soviet slander'.

Balys Gajavkas was released from prison in Lithuania in 1973 after serving 25 years' imprisonment for 'counter-revolutionary activity'. He had participated in the resistance movement in 1939 when the USSR annexed Lithuania under the terms of the Molotov-Ribbintrop agreement with Hitler. After his release, Gajavskas was active in trying to help other prisoners and their families. He was re-arrested in 1978 for 'storing anti-Soviet literature', principally Alexander Solzhenitsyn's book *The Gulag Archipelago* and literature relating to the Lithuanian partisan movement of the 1940s and 1950s. He was also charged with 'anti-Soviet intent' because the prosecutor asserted that Gajavskas knew this material would be published abroad and used there 'for anti-Soviet agitation and propaganda'. In April 1978, Gajavskas was sentenced to 10 years' imprisonment and 5 years' internal exile.

The final example is that of Vladimir and Maria Slepak, arrested ostensibly for 'hooliganism' in Moscow on 21 June and 26 July 1978. Vladimir Slepak had been trying since 1970 to emigrate. The following is the official charge brought against them:

Maria Isaakovna Slepak committed malicious hooliganism, that is, premeditated actions rudely disrupting public order and showing open disregard for the public, of a particularly impertinent nature, namely: on 11 June 1978 at about 4 pm she and Vladimir Semyonivich Slepak, motivated by hooliganism, hung out on the balcony of their flat, No. 77 at No. 15 Gorky Street, overlooking a street in the centre of Moscow, several sheets with the inscription 'Let us go to our son in Israel' and notwithstanding repeated requests by policemen and officials of the Housing Allocation Bureau to cease her activities, she continued to demonstrate, holding in her hands a sheet with the inscription 'let us go to our son in Israel', accompanying her actions of a prolonged and persistent nature with threatening gestures, shouts of anti-Soviet content and spitting, and by these actions attracting a large crowd on both sides of Gorky Street, as well as in the street itself, causing a temporary interruption of the normal function of public transport, serious disruption of order in the street and disturbance of citizens, i.e. she committed the crime stipulated in Article 206, part 2 of the Russian Criminal Code.

Vladimir Slepak was sentenced to 5 years' internal exile. Maria Slepak was sentenced to 3 years' imprisonment suspended for 5 years.

The list is virtually endless. However, official censorship and secrecy regarding penal practices and the threat of arrest of those who speak out about political imprisonment make it difficult to make an accurate count. What does seem clear is that Amnesty International has not heard of a *single* person being acquitted after having been charged with political or religious offences.

Inmates of the Soviet penal institutions are subjected to a regime of chronic hunger, inadequate medical care and often dangerous compulsory labour. Inmates of psychiatric hospitals are deprived of virtually every right that would enable them to protect themselves against medical maltreatment.

Evaluating such consistent and pervasive violation of human rights is well-nigh impossible, particularly since it is such a highly emotive issue for so many. That human rights violations exist in the Soviet Union is beyond dispute. What needs to be explored, however, are the *historical roots* of the present situation in order to discern whether human rights violations in the USSR are something deliberately intended by the Soviets or something generated by the peculiarities of the Russian history.

The Russian Past in the Soviet Present

In his story *Hadji Murad*, Leo Tolstoy portrays Czar Nicholas I ordering the punishment of a Polish student who had attacked and slightly wounded his professor:

> He took the report and in his large handwriting he wrote on its margin with three orthographical mistakes:
> "Diserves deth but thank God, we have no cpitle punishment, and it is not for me to introduce it. Make him run the gauntlet of a thousand men twelve times"—Nicholas.
> He signed, adding his unnaturally huge flourish. Nicholas knew that twelve thousand strokes with the regulation rods were not only certain death with torture, but were a superfluous cruelty for five thousand strikes were sufficient to kill the strongest man. But it pleased him to be ruthlessly cruel and it also pleased him to think that we have abolished capital punishment in Russia.

A contemporary of Tolstoy, Russian historian Nikolai Karamzin, observed that despite the ruthlessness of their leaders, Russians have gloried in the very thing foreigners criticised them for—blind and boundless devotion to the will of the monarch, even when in his most insane flights he trampled underfoot all the laws of justice and humanity.

Six centuries of authoritarian rule from Ivan the Great and Ivan the Terrible forward have made the Russian people monarchists in their bones long before Lenin or Stalin arrived on the scene. There is no heritage of common law with its habeas corpus, no historical well-established traditions of public political debate, no panoply of institutions designed to disperse power and buttress the individual against the state.

Under the czars, Russians had an authoritarian state. Under the commissars, they have a totalitarian one. The leaders and the people have the same authoritarian frame of mind. Andropov and the simple people of the Soviet Union both think alike—might is right. That is all. This is not a question of ideology. It is simply a question of conditioning. The person on the street and the leader in the Kremlin, both have been conditioned by the same social forces. Even Solzhenitsyn is no different. He wants change. But even he does not want democracy. He wants to go from the totalitarian state of the present back to an authoritarian monarch and church of the past.

So much has been inherited from the past that an ordinary Soviet citizen takes for granted elements of political despotism that are instantly an affront to a Westerner. History has conditioned Russians differently. The cruel tyrannny of Stalin was prefigured by the bloody reign of Ivan the Terrible in the 16th century and the iron rule of Nicholas I in the 19th century. Peter the Great, celebrated for opening Russia to the West and introducing a more modern army and state administration, is less well known abroad for having also improved the efficiency of authoritarian controls, some of which survive today. It was Peter who set up the political police administration and who officially instituted censorship and the practice of issuing internal passports to keep Russians from travelling away from their permanent homes without special permission.

Czars were not different in their treatment of political dissenters either. Peter had his own son, Alexis, tried and sentenced to death for passive opposition of his 'reforms'. By some accounts, he killed Alexis with his own hands.

Nicholas I was the personal censor of Pushkin. Count Leo Tolstoy, like dissident writers today, smuggled some of his controversial writing to the West for publication. Dostoyevsky was banished to Siberia. The Soviet practice of putting dissidents in mental hospitals has its precedent in the famous case of Pytor Chaadayev, an eminent early nineteenth century scientist and thinker who was officially branded insane for an essay that condemned Russia as backward and advocated Westernisation and Catholicism as a panacea. The Revolution has certainly altered many things, but the historical parallels are powerful.

Whether under the czars or the commissars, Russians have traditionally had a deeply ingrained fear of anarchy and the centrifugal forces that tug at the unity and stability of their vast state, which covers one-sixth of the land mass of our planet. Absolutism is inevitable under such circumstances.

It is important to bear in mind that the Soviet Union is both in Europe and in Asia. The traditional boundary betwen them is the Ural Mountains. But the Urals are low, easily penetrated and are more for the convenience of geographers rather than sociologists. In fact, Russia has always been a land with two frontiers: the Orient, and the Occident. It has fought off and assimilated invasions from both China and Germany. It has attracted the culture of both India and France.

It was during the formative period of the land of Rus that it was conquered by the Mongol hordes of Genghis Khan, who subjugated the Russians between the 13th and 16th centuries. This permanently engraved upon the Russian psyche the mark of oriental despotism. Its rulers, both Czarist and Soviet, have ruled in that Oriental manner ever since.

On the other hand, Peter the Great sought to open Russia up to the influence of the West during the 18th century. He brought in Dutch, French, German and Italian masters to build his palaces and paint his icons. He ordered Russian men to shave their beards and Russian women to adopt the clothing styles of the French. With Western architecture, painting and styles came Western ideas of democracy and individual rights, particularly after the French Revolution in 1789. Many of the Russian officers who helped defeat Napolean when he invaded Russia in 1812 were executed later by the Czar because they sought to promulgate and implement Napoleon's ideas of 'liberty, equality, fraternity'.

The basic polarity of Russian history has been the despotism of its rulers on the one hand, and the intense commitment to freedom on the other. These have been symbolised by the czars and now commissars and the dissidents. What is both the tragedy and beauty of the Russian people is that they have seemingly remained content to allow this polarity to play itself out. Unlike Western Europeans and even nations in the Orient which have opted increasingly for a government elected by adult suffrage which guarantees basic human rights, the Russians have retained an authoritarian government, counter-balanced by the passion and heroism of the dissidents. The contradiction between Stalin and Solzhenitsn amply indicate the expanse of Russian history.

A State Besieged

The year 1917 found all of Europe and the United States in the grip of the First World War. Beginning in 1914, the Entente countries—Britain, France and Russia, joined later by the US, Japan and Italy—fought the quadripartite alliance of Germany, Austro-Hungary, Turkey and Bulgaria. The war was not to end until Autumn 1918.

In March 1917, with fighting raging along the entire Russian-German front, the Czar suddenly abdicated. The Czars had ruled Russia for centuries and the vacuum left by the abdication of Czar Nicholas II was enormous. In normal times this vacuum could have been filled by careful planning and strong leadership. But his abdication in the middle of war, when unity, discipline, and strong leadership are most essential, left the country in chaos and the army demoralised and confused.

A Provisional Government, headed first by a Prince Lvov and then by Kerensky, tried to fill the vacuum. It was composed of constitutional monarchists, social democrats and social revolutionaries, all of whom were well-meaning liberals seeking to create a representative democracy. None of them had any actual experience in running a country, let alone providing leadership during a time when the people were demanding not democracy but peace, not voting rights but bread, and not a constitution but land.

In effect, the Provisional Government changed nothing. The armies still fought at the German front, invariably suffering defeat. The bureaucratic machine still churned out orders which were largely ignored. The aristocracy continued to luxuriate in their palaces. The Provisional Government had neither a popular mandate nor national support. It simply carried on the old system, like a chicken running around the yard with its head cut off. No one knew how to change direction. The result was that power fell into the streets.

A Soviet, or council of workers and soldiers, was set up in Petrograd (later renamed Leningrad). Its leaders were moderate Socialists, anxious to do nothing illegal, who were critically supportive of the Provisional Government. When the first Bolsheviks, including Stalin, returned from Siberia where they had been exiled by the Czar, they, too supported the Provisional Government and gave patriotic support to the war.

Only Lenin, far away in Switzerland, realised the revolutionary potential of what was happening. He believed that a socialist revolution was possible, not only in Russia but in all of Europe. If the Russian people withdrew from the war, the workers of every belligerent country would do likewise. There would be general revolution and the establishment of international socialism. This was the keynote of Lenin's policy: world revolution out of the ashes of the First World War.

However, with the war still raging, it was difficult to get back to Russia. After being refused permission to cross France, Lenin struck a bargain with the German General Staff and, accompanied by some 30 other Russian revolutionaries, travelled across Germany in a sealed train. Once back in Petrograd, he went directly to the Bolshevik headquarters and urged that they prepare for a second revolution (the first one being considered to be the abdication of the Czar). Lenin's proposal was defeated by twelve votes to one, Lenin's being the one. He laughed at his defeat, saying: "The Russian people are a hundred times more revolutionary than we are."[3]

In July 1917, Kerensky ordered a new offensive against the Germans. It ended in catastrophe, sparking off enormous street demonstrations in Petrograd demanding an end to the war and 'All Power to the Soviets'. Kerensky reacted by arresting many of the Bolshevik leaders, including Trotsky. Lenin went into hiding in a nearby village and then in Finland. The Petrograd Soviet, which had occupied a splendid hall in the centre of the city was relegated to the Smolny Institute, formerly a suburban high school for daughters of the nobility.

Kerensky decided to smash the Bolsheviks once and for all and encouraged a former czarist General Kornilov to march on Petrograd to 'restore order'. Belatedly, he discovered that Kornilov intended to destroy the Provisional Government as well as the Soviets. Kerensky now appealed to the workers of Petrograd to 'save' the revolution. The Bolsheviks were released from prison. Trotsky became President of the Petrograd Soviet. A Military Revolutionary Committee under his direction organised the Red Guards. They were equipped by the Provisional Government. The Red Guards and Provisional Government troops stopped Kornilov with a minimum of fighting.

The Bolsheviks now had a majority on the Petrograd Soviet and on many others, including Moscow. They controlled the Red Guards. But with Lenin far away, they seemed at a loss for direction.

On 28 September 1917, the Bolshevik central committee met in Petrograd. Lenin, still in Finland, sent his famous "Letter from Afar", urging that "we should at once begin to plan the practical details of a second revolution". The central committee, including Trotsky, Stalin, Zinoviev and Bukharin, were horrified and resolved unanimously to destroy every copy of Lenin's letter. One copy survived by chance.

Weeks passed, during which the political situation in Russia went from bad to worse. The country was literally disintegrating. In the Don region, something like a Cossack Republic had been established. The Kuban declared itself an independent Cossack state. Elsewhere, in the Ukraine, in Finland, Poland, Byelorussia, other nationalist movements gathered strength. The local governments, controlled by the propertied classes, claimed autonomy and refused to obey orders from Petrograd. At Helsingfors, the Finnish Senate declined to loan money to the Provisional Government, declared Finland autonomous, and demanded the withdrawal of Russian troops. The Ukranians extended their borders until they included all the richest agricultural lands of South Russia, as far as the Urals, and began the formation of a national army. They hinted at a separate peace with Germany. Siberia and the Caucasus demanded separate constituent assemblies. In all these areas there were increasingly bitter struggles between the propertied classes and local authorities and the local Soviets of workers and peasants.

The Provisional Government was powerless to react. Conditions were daily more chaotic. Soldiers deserted the front and began to move by the hundreds of thousands in vast aimless tides toward their homes. The peasants themselves, tired of waiting for land, exasperated by the repressive measures of the Government and encouraged by the Soviets, burned manor-houses and massacred landlords. Widespread strikes and lock-outs convulsed Moscow, Odessa and the coal mines of the Don. Transport was stopped; the army was routed; and the cities were rendered breadless.

When the Provisional Government responded to the crisis at all it always supported the interests of the propertied classes. Cossacks were dispersed to 'restore order' among the peasants and break the strikes. The Soviets of various cities were attacked. The old regime military officers demanded that harsh measures be adopted to restore discipline in the Army and Navy. Government actions only exacerbated the people's anger; every refusal to act raised their contempt.

It was in this situation that Lenin, just returned from Finland and still in hiding in a suburb of Petrograd, demanded again that the Bolsheviks seize power. On 23 October 1917, the central committee agreed by ten votes to two.

The two dissenters in the central committee, Zinoviev and Kamenev, did not limit their opposition to a seizure of power to private discussions. They published an attack on Lenin in a non-Bolshevik paper. Kerensky was thus alerted. On 5 November the Provisional Government resolved to deliver the first blow by arresting the Bolshevik leaders and closing down their press. That night a detachment of soldiers occupied the offices of *Pravda*, the Bolshevik paper.

At 11.00 am on 6 November, the Bolshevik central committee, thinking in defensive terms, decided that armed resistance to Kerensky should begin early next morning. Trotsky and Lenin huddled together in the Smolny Institute making final preparations. At 2.00 am on 7 November 1917 Trotsky pulled out his watch and said, "It is begun". Lenin said, "From being on the run to supreme power—that's too much. It makes me dizzy", and he made the sign of the cross.[4] Then the two men lay down together on the hard office floor, covered themselves with a blanket, and waited for the news they hoped would change the face of the world.

The Revolutionary Military Committee had planned a desperate resistance to the expected onslaught of the Provisional Government. But there was no onslaught. Kerensky fled Petrograd, protected by the American embassy. The other members of his government dithered in the Winter Palace until they were arrested by Red Guards who filtered in through the kitchen entrance and took the Palace without a struggle. Such was the end of old Russia.

Most of Petrograd either did not know or paid little attention to what had happened. The stores and banks remained open; the trams and buses kept running; and the theatres and restaurants were crowded. Most of those 'in the know' expected Lenin and Trotsky's *putsch* to blow over in a couple of days and the government to return to 'normal'. It did not.

Lenin was the man of the hour. He was a strange popular leader: on the one hand, colourless, humourless and detached; on the other, possessing such acuity of intellect that he dwarfed all rivals. To the common people, he had that rare ability of explaining profound ideas in simple ways. Moreover, Lenin had the insight to realise that a Russia at war, in chaos, and facing starvation in many quarters, needed a strong leader with a clear programme; it did not need a 'provisional government' that spoke of 'democracy' but merely continued the policies and oppressions of the czarist order. Lenin intuited that the Russian people wanted no further experiments in 'bourgeois democracy'. They would follow whosoever would give them bread, land and peace. This was the programme for Lenin's 'dictatorship of the proletariat'.

Lenin's first executive action as chairman of the Council of People's Commissars was to sue for peace. He signed a peace treaty with Germany called the Brest–Litovsk Treaty. The terms of the treaty were onerous for Russia: it gave up vast expanses of territory to Germany: the Baltic regions, the Ukraine and Byelorussia. The new Bolshevik government was also required to pay enormous reparations; and it had to agree to unfavourable commercial agreements. But all this was worth getting Russia out of the war and allowing time to consolidate the new Socialist order.

With a declaration of peace came land reform. Although the Bolsheviks had never worked out a coherent programme for land redistribution, Lenin was astute enough to recognise that reforms were what the people wanted. He told the thousands of soldiers on the fronts to go home and reclaim the land. The soldiers, most of whom were peasants, did just that, in most cases overthrowing the local landlords in the process. The landlords and the well-to-do fled to join the armies, led by former czarist generals, which dominated large parts of Southern Russia. These armies came to be known as the 'White armies', as distinct from the 'Red army' of the Soviets.

This was one of Lenin's most brilliant tactics. The peasantry of Russia, together with crafts people and artisans accounted for 70% of the population. However, the social structure was so unbalanced that 50,000 landowners owned as much land as 10.5 million peasant families. By encouraging the soldiers and peasants to reclaim the land, Lenin forced the mass majority of Russians to side with the Bolsheviks against the Whites, who not only sought to restore the land to its 'rightful' owners but had supported the continuation of the war against Germany. Elsewhere the same thing happened. The common soldiers, the peasants and the industrial workers supported the Soviets by a vast majority. The officers, the middle class, the Church hierarchy, the financiers, the wealthy peasants and the aristocracy all were on the side of the now deposed Provisional Government. In numerous towns and cities these threatened classes organised Committees for Salvation of Country and Revolution, arming for civil war. Yet these classes had neither adequate funds nor the numbers of soldiers necessary to win a civil war. They thus turned to foreign governments for material and military assistance.

This was more than forthcoming. Because it was still fighting the First World War, the Austro-German coalition was eager for even more Russian territories than had been conceded by the Treaty of Brest–Litovsk. Russia's western provinces were rich in coal, oil, ores and grain. The allies, on the other hand, especially Britain, France, the United States, and Japan, had their own reasons for fearing Lenin's revolution. They saw his socialist revolution as a direct threat to their capitalist economies at home and their imperialistic policies in the colonies.

The Marxist revolution in Russia marked the first time in modern history that a country broke away from the capitalist world economy, which had been growing and expanding since the Industrial Revolution. In colonising most of the Third World, the US, Britain and Western Europe had succeeded in bringing almost the entire planet into one laissez-faire economic system. One of Lenin's first economic acts was to nationalise foreign holdings in Soviet Russia and cancel the foreign debts incurred by pre-revolutionary governments to the West. With Russia's defection, one sixth of the planet was 'liberated' from the capitalist economy. This determination was given political weight when Lenin withdrew Soviet Russia from World War I. In so doing, Soviet Russia ceased to be an ally with the US, Britain and France, in the war against the German bloc. Lenin made it clear that the Socialist Path of his revolution would not be amenable to external economic or political control. He also condemned the colonial and imperialistic policies of Western Europe and the US, declaring that socialist Russia would befriend any other country which, like Russia, sought to break away from the capitalist economy dominated by the US, Britain and Germany.

In recent years, we have become accustomed to revolutions in countries which result in the nationalisation of foreign ownings and the enunciation of a new political path, whether it be non-aligned or socialist. But in 1917, Russia shocked the world by nationalising all foreign holdings and articulating a new political tradition.

On 23 November 1927, the military attaches of the Allied nations presented a note to Lenin, in which he was solemnly warned not to "violate the conditions of the treaties concluded between the Powers of the Entente".[5] The note went on to say that if a separate armistice with Germany were concluded, that act "would result in the most serious consequences" to Russia. Lenin disregarded this threat. The allies reacted by drawing up a plan to aid the counter revolutionary forces and White armies. France was to secure the overthrow of Soviet power in the Ukraine, the Crimea and Bessarabia; Britain was to do the same in the north, on the Don and Kuban river basins, and in the Caucasus; and the United States and Japan were to deal with Siberia and the Far East.

US President Woodrow Wilson proposed in 1918 that the allies tear from Russia the Ukraine, the Caucasus, Central Asia and the Baltic area. Siberia could then become a US–Japanese 'sphere of influence'.

This intervention into Soviet affairs and onto Soviet territory began without a declaration of War. In fact, the allies stated that they wished 'to defend' Russia from 'the German danger'. In March 1918, British, American and French forces landed in Murmansk, on the north west coast of Russia, and quickly occupied it and the neighbouring area of Archangel. By June, the number of allied troops increased to 10,000 and were placed under the command of British General F.C. Poole. In dislodging Red Army units the British resorted to the use of mustard and phosgene gas.

The rationale offered by the US government for landing troops in north Russia was given by Senator Claude A. Swanson. He stated: "The port of Vladivostok and this port of Archangel are the two most important ports and were in considerable danger at the time of the Russian collapse. Germany was trying to get both."[6] Apparently, Swanson confused Vladivostok with Murmansk. Vladivostok is a port on the Pacific coast of Russia, thousands of miles from the German front. Geographic niceties aside, the US government went so far as to assert that the Bolsheviks were 'German agents'. Edgar Sisson, an official representative of the US, even produced documents 'proving' that Bolshevism was an 'arm of Berlin'. Known as the 'Sisson documents', President Woodrow Wilson ordered them to be published in September 1918.

In January 1919, the *Washington Post* came out against a 'Germanised Russia'. The newspaper stated categorically that 'the extermination of the Bolsheviki is a necessity of life to free men and free nations'.[7] Between November 1917 and November 1919, the *New York Times* reported no less than ninety-one times that the collapse of Lenin's government was 'inevitable'.

The American-Russian Chamber of Commerce fully supported US intervention in order to make Russia 'safe for democracy'. "Without any question," it argued, "Russia will present at the termination of the war, the largest and most favourable field for the extension of American business of any foreign country."[8] In September 1918, the executive committee of the Chamber of Commerce urged that a "civil-economic mission" be added to the US military forces in order to consolidate economically those portions of Russia conquered militarily.[9] A book, *A Message to the American People*, by Catherine Breshkovsky, was published in 1919 and given wide circulation. In plain terms, it declared "Americans, come to Russia! Do not hesitate to invest your capital, and right on the spot convert our raw materials into all kinds of products."[10] All this, of course, was to be done after the overthrow of Lenin.

Besides intervening in Murmansk and Archangel, the Soviet Far East was also occupied. Before the end of 1917, the US cruiser Brooklyn, the Japanese cruisers Iwashi and Asahi, and the British cruiser Suffolk appeared in Vladivostok harbour. No immediate action was taken because a decision could not be reached as to who would land troops first. This question was resolved at a conference of prime ministers and foreign ministers of France, Britain, and Italy that met in London in March 1918. They proposed that Japan send in troops first but that the US also take an active role. On 4 April 1918, Japanese troops landed in Vladivostok. A British landing party went ashore the same day. When the Soviet government protested, the British replied that their sole purpose was "to protect the security and property of foreign citizens in the area". Japan proceeded to assist the White detachments which were operating in the Transbaikal and Primorye areas around Vladivostok. In August, an American Expeditionary Force, under the command of General Graves, and new British, French, and Italian units landed in Vladivostok.

Because of these foreign interventions, the Whites in the area were able to overthrow Soviet power and establish a 'government of autonomous Siberia' centred in Vladivostok.

Simultaneous with intervention on the Soviet northern and eastern borders, the allies intervened in the Volga and Ural regions of central Russia. The Czechoslovak Legion, formed in Russia from former Austro-German prisoners of war, with Allied help, aided the Whites in the area to overthrow Soviet control.

The British were also active in the southern areas of the Soviet Union, in the North Caucasus, Transcaucasia and Turkestan.

Forming an alliance with Terek Cossacks, British troops entered
Azerbaijan and Baku in August 1918 after aiding in the overthrow
of Soviet power in Transcaspia in July.

The Austro-German coalition also took advantage of Russia's
weakened position. In March 1918, they moved a 300,000 strong
army into the Ukraine; by May virtually the whole republic was
occupied. They also made incursions into the Transcaucasus, the
Don region and the Crimea, supporting the former czarist
Generals Krasnov and Mamantov, who incited the Don Cossacks
against Soviet power. The Austro-German army also established
its role over the captured territory in Byelorussia and the Baltic
area.

What is clear from the interventions into the Soviet Union in 1918
is that while the Austro-Germans and the Allies were still *fighting*
each other in Western Europe, they were certainly *united* in their
intentions against Soviet power in Russia.

Rather than withdrawing from the First World War and work on
his revolutionary programme,therefore, Lenin, in July 1918, was
forced to conclude that "whether we like it or not, the question
stands as follows: we are at war, and on the outcome of that war
hangs the fate of the revolution".[11]

The situation was indeed serious. The country's richest
areas—the Ukraine, the Urals, Siberia, the Don, the Kuban—were
occupied by the enemy, both foreign and domestic. Land still
under Soviet control was besieged. Factories ground to a halt;
transport stopped; the Cities were without adequate fuel; and
there was not enough bread, meat, sugar or other necessities.

On 29 July 1918, Lenin directed that all resources be mobilised
for the defence of the country. Under the slogan 'Everything for
the Front, Everything for Victory over the Enemy', the Soviet
government took measures to turn the country into a united armed
camp which it has remained ever since. The Council of Defence
was formed. It accelerated the reorientation of the country's
economy towards military needs. The Supreme Economic Council
nationalised all large and middle scale industry and subjected
production and distribution of goods to centralised management.
Free commerce was replaced by state distribution of foodstuffs,
and industrial goods were all rationed. In order to feed the army
and workers, a 'surplus appropriation' system was enacted,
whereby farmers were required to surrender their foodstuffs at a
fixed price. The Soviet government also introduced labour
conscription for the entire adult population under the slogan: 'He
who does not work neither shall he eat.' Leagues of young
peasants and workers, initially numbering some 22,000 members,
were organised to help in the war effort. This became known as the
Young Communist League (the Komsomol).

This mobilisation of the Soviet people to repel the foreign intervention and the White armies supported by them has been known in Soviet history as War Communism. The whole society was mobilised to support the Red Army which numbered only 300,000 in the summer of 1918. This number was tripled by October, mostly due to the universal conscription decreed in July. By the End of 1918, the Red Army numbered over one million, and deployed twelve field armies and 42 rifle and 3 cavalry divisions.

Lenin singled out the Volga and Ural areas as the decisive fronts. In occupying these, the enemy had cut off Soviet controlled land from Russia's most important grain growing regions. Beginning there, then moving to the southern front of the Don, the Lower Volga and the North Caucasus, the Red Army slowly pushed the invaders and the White armies away.

By the end of 1918, Soviet Russia's international position had changed substantially. The First World War had ended and a revolution had occurred in Germany. Russia quickly annulled the Treaty of Brest-Litovsk when the Austro-German occupation collapsed and regained the Ukraine and Byelorussia. Soviet backed regimes were also set up in the former Russian provinces of Estonia, Latvia and Lithuania. (The Baltic states had been ceded to Russia by Sweden in 1710.)

The defeat of the Austro-German bloc permitted the Allies to step up their interventions, particularly in the north, south and east. In Siberia, for instance, the American government supplied White troops with 200,000 rifles, 220,000 shells and numerous other types of guns and machine guns. Britain provided an additional 100,000 rifles and France gave 50,000,000 francs per month. Despite this assistance, the Red Army advanced successfully and by early 1919 had regained Ufa, Birsk, Orenburg, Uralsk and other important cities in the southern Urals, which once again put them in direct contact with Turkestan.

The mood in the US by this time was combative. Talk of a 'state of war' between Russia and the US was heard frequently on Capitol Hill. On 14 January 1919, Senator Charles Thomas of Colorado asserted that the "Bolsheviki long ago declared war against us " by nationalising US holdings in Russia and cancelling Russia's foreign debts. "Russia," he stated, "is the center from which all Governments are being attacked."[12] Senator Porter J. MacCumber of North Dakota proposed on 14 February 1919 that the President increase the American army in Russia to 500,000 men in order to "liberate" the Russian people "from the assassins who now hold them in subjection".[13]

Voices of calm were also heard. Senator Hiram Johnson of California introduced a resolution in which he pointed out that a "state of war" existed between the US and Russia without official sanction of Congress. He demanded that the Secretary of State provide the Senate, "if not incompatible with the public interest", all of the information on the basis of which the American government had sent troops to Russia.[14] On 7 January 1919, Senator Robert LaFollette of Wisconsin declared that "the Congress and the country ought to know why we are making war upon the Russian People".[15] Two days later Senator William Borah of Idaho warned the President: 'If we ever go into Russia to set up a government by force we will leave millions of our boys in nameless graves, bankrupt our Treasury, and in the end come out something as Napoleon did'. He spoke out in the spirit of peaceful coexistence: "I take the position that the Russian people have the same right to establish a socialistic state as we have to establish a Republic."[16]

Despite these words of wisdom, President Wilson joined with the British, French and Japanese in escalating the conflict against Soviet Russia. In March 1919, the Allies and White armies mounted a six-front offensive that aimed at driving Lenin from power. Soviet control was eliminated from the Baltic states. The Red Army was badly beaten in Siberia where large numbers of American, British, French and Japanese troops backed a 200,000 strong White army under General Kolchak.

Lenin's directive to meet this offensive was to obtain a numerical superiority in the east without withdrawing troops from the south. Up till then there was as yet no united Socialist state. Each Soviet republic had its own armed forces. There was no joint military command and no common system of supplies. On Lenin's directive, a unified military command was established in July 1919. This united command plus a Red Army of more than 4.5 million was enough to gain victory in the Urals, Siberia, the Ukraine, the North Caucasus and Central Asia by the end of 1919. The Allies and the White armies were driven from territories inhabited by more than 50 million people.

The last campaign began in 1920. The Poles were driven from Kiev; Soviet power was regained in Turkestan and Transcaucasia; Armenia and Georgia were liberated; and finally, the territories in the Far East were regained. However, the Baltic States were not recovered.

As each republic was rid of the White and foreign armies, the Soviets unified it with the Russian Republic. On 30 September 1920 a treaty was signed with Azerbaijan; on 28 December 1920 with the Ukraine; on 16 January 1921 with Byelorussia; and on 21 May 1921 with Georgia. Thus did the Union of Soviet Socialist Republics begin to emerge.

"The experience of the Soviet Republic which has suffered the armed invasion of all the powerful imperialist countries", said Lenin, "demonstrates that no revolution is worth anything unless it can defend itself."[17] Altogether 8 million Soviet people died during these years of foreign intervention and civil war; 50,000 of them members of the Communist Party.

The US interventionist army in Russia had amounted to 17,000 troops—5,000 in the northwest Russia and 12,000 in the Far East. Although this force did not engage in any major battles with the Red Army, skirmishes had left 244 Americans killed and 305 wounded in the northern sector alone, according to US casualty figures. The US force, like its British, French, German, Polish and Japanese counterparts, had contributed to the effort to overthrow Soviet state primarily by supplying, advising, and directing the White armies. General William Graves, the US Commander in Siberia, had kept the railroads of Siberia open only to the Whites and had allowed the Red Cross only to help the counter-revolutionaries. In his memoirs Graves wrote: "without the support of foreign troops, I doubt if Kolchak or his Government ever possessed sufficient strength to exercise sovereign powers."[18] American aid alone to the White armies amounted to over $4 billion at that time.

The US, Britain and France also put in motion an active diplomatic effort against the Soviet Union. Through their combined efforts the Versailles Peace Conference became the headquarters of the interventionists and White Guards. Herbert Hoover characterised the "Russian question" as "among the worst problems before the Peace Conference".[19] On 22 January 1919, President Wilson put forward a plan for summoning a conference of all the governments that had military forces in Russia to discuss conditions for a cessation of hostilities. When the representatives of the White Army defeated the plan, President Wilson and British Prime Minister Lloyd George dispatched William Bullitt to Moscow with the task of sounding out Soviet conditions for peace. The American envoy was received personally by Lenin, and a draft of Soviet-American peace proposal was soon agreed upon. However, when Bullitt returned to Paris, neither the American President nor the British Prime Minister would see him to discuss the peace proposal.

The Senate Foreign Relations Committee investigated this diplomatic about-face in September 1919. When Senator Warren Harding asked "why the Soviet proposal was not given favourable consideration", Bullitt replied:

> Kolchak made a 100–mile advance, and immediately the entire press of Paris was roaring and screaming on the subject, announcing that Kolchak would be in Moscow within two

weeks; and therefore everyone in Paris, including, I regret to
say, members of the American commission, began to grow very
lukewarm about peace in Russia, because they thought Kolchak
would arrive in Moscow and wipe out the Soviet
Government.[20]

Kolchak never made it to Moscow, but the US government's
wish that he did has never dissipated. Kolchak's idea of a united
and indivisible Russia, dominated by the old order and closely
aligned with the capitalist world economy was what President
Wilson meant by 'Russian democracy'.

The complete defeat of the White Army and the consolidation of
Soviet power in almost the entire territory of the former Russian
empire meant the total collapse of Wilson's Russian policy. The US
removed the last of its troops from Russian soil in 1920. On 7 July
1920, the State Department announced the removal of restrictions
on trade with Russia in non-military goods. It made it clear,
however, that this did not constitute 'political recognition' of 'any
Russian authority' and that any individuals and corporations who
traded with Russia 'will do so on their own responsibility and at
their own risk.'[21]

It was Secretary of State Bainbridge Colby who charted the
course that the US was to follow in its relations with the Soviets
for the next thirteen years. Formulated when the Polish-Soviet war
was at its height, the 'Colby note', as it was called, was the most
expressive and fundamental State Department document during
the period of non-recognition of Soviet Russia. The idea of Russia's
territorial integrity occupied an important place in the note.
Secretary Colby agreed with the British and the Japanese that
southern Finland, Polish speaking parts of the Ukraine and
Byelorussia and Armenia (where the US still hoped to establish a
sphere of influence) should be excluded from a united Russia. But
Washington did not want Russia divided further. Colby disapproved of the programme of the Supreme Council of the Allies
which favoured independence for Estonia, Lithuania, Latvia and
the Caucasus. His public statements to the contrary, President
Wilson privately opposed separating the Baltic States from Russia.
He expressed the opinion that these republics would eventually be
reincorporated into Russian territory. The US only recognised
these states as independent in 1922 when it became clear that the
other allies were adamant in excluding them from a united Russia
and that the Soviet government was unwilling to engage in the
military measures necessary to regain these territories. The Colby
note also disapproved of the activities of Japan, which still had part
of the Russian Far East under military control.

This position favouring a united Russia did not stem from any altruism on Wilson or Colby's part. The British empire and the emerging Japanese empire sought a weak Russia in which they could establish spheres of influence, the British in the North-West and Middle East, the Japanese in the Far East. American strategy sought a united Russia as a counterweight between the British and Japanese empires. Ideally, the US Government would have wanted a strong united Russia, economically reliant on US goods and capital. Consequently, the Colby note stated the US did not want the Japanese or any other power coming forward with plans to further cut into Russian territory.

Despite this policy favouring Russian territorial integrity, the Colby note was decidedly hostile to the *government* currently in place in Russia. In Colby's estimate, "the existing regime in Russia is based upon the negation of every principle of honor and good faith, and every usage and convention, underlying the whole structure of international law; the negation, in short, of every principle upon which it is possible to base harmonious and trustful relations, whether of nations or of individuals".[22] He ascribed to the Bolsheviks the belief that the very existence of Soviet power in Russia was dependent on the overthrow of the governments "in all other great civilized nations, including the United States". "The diplomatic service of the Bolshevist Government," warned the secretary of state, "would become a channel for intrigues and the propaganda of revolt against the institutions and the laws of countries, with which it was at peace, which would be an abuse of friendship to which enlightened governments cannot subject themselves."

Because of this, Colby argued that the US should not extend diplomatic recognition to the new Soviet government. On 21 February 1923, Senator Henry Cabot Lodge gave the following arguments against recognition: the Soviet government wanted, he said, "to overthrow all capitalist governments", did not honour its agreements, and violated "the unalterable principle of private property".[23]

For some years the US government held out official recognition as a carrot to entice the Soviet government to liberalise its economic programme. The Soviets were unreceptive, arguing that normal diplomatic relations could only make sense under the principle of equality between the two countries. From the beginning, the Soviet government expressed the willingness to recognise and trade with the United States.

During the late 1920s, trade between the two countries began to increase, despite the fact that the US still refused to establish diplomatic relations. In 1927–28 agreements were even signed for technological cooperation in planning and constructing large industrial units in the USSR. Soon after, about 150 US firms sent their representatives to the Soviet Union.

However, when the Great Depression hit in 1929, the Soviet Union was once again enemy No.1. Crusaders for "Russian freedom" came out against "forced labour" in the USSR and against the practice of Soviet "dumping" on the US market. The press was full of exhortations to "fight the Red trade menace".[24]

In 1930, anti-Communist sentiment was revived largely through the efforts of Congressman Hamilton Fish. Like Senator McCarthy was to do in the 1950s, Fish blamed the misfortunes plaguing the US on the Soviet Union and the US Communist Party. On 28 February 1930, Fish castigated the 'liberals and progressives' for their sympathy with the 'Soviet dictatorship'.[25] He was ap- plauded by the House of Representatives when he proposed an investigation of the activities of the Communists in the US. Two months later, the police commissioner of New York, Grover Whalen, following the tradition established by President Wilson in fabricating the 'Sisson documents', published falsified evidence purporting to 'prove' that the Soviet foreign trade organisation Amtorg and the Soviet Information Bureau in Washington were emissaries from the Comintern to the Communist Party of the US and that the latter was preparing to overthrow the lawful government of the United States. Responding to this 'evidence', the US House of Representatives created a committee headed by Fish, to investigate 'Communist activity' in the US. Shortly after the creation of the committee, Whalen's documents were shown to be counterfeit, a fact which even Fish acknowledged.

The impasse between the US and the USSR was finally broken by President Roosevelt. Like President Nixon was to do in 1978 when he enunciated the policy of detente with the Soviet Union and opened the door to China, Roosevelt realised that trying to ignore the reality of Soviet power or to conspire towards its elimination was counterproductive. The government that controlled one sixth of the land mass of the planet had to be recognised. In November 1933, diplomatic relations between the USA and USSR were established and ambassadors exchanged.

However, the hostility of the industrial democracies toward Lenin's revolution left a heavy toll. The Bolsheviks had come to power promising to end Russia's participation in World War I and begin a programme of national renewal. Instead, they were immediately besieged on all sides as the greatest powers on earth—the Americans, the British, the French, the Germans and the Japanese—sought their demise and overthrow. Combining military, economic and diplomatic pressure, these nations first aided the internal enemies of the revolution until they were defeated and then levied external force to compel the Soviet Government to submit. It did not. The revolution prevailed, a fact finally recognised by the US in 1933.

But because it was born besieged and never allowed the freedom to build in peace, the Socialist revolution in Russia became a revolution perverted. It was perverted by the exigencies of maintaining itself on a permanent war footing. The revolution which began with the slogan 'Peace, Land, Bread' was soon appealing to the people, 'Everything for the Front. Everything for Victory.' Lenin's revolution had sought to establish itself by ending war. It was forced to shape itself by waging war. Thus Lenin's vision of workers socialism was replaced by war communism.

The war communism that was forced on the new republic left a permanent stamp on the Soviet psyche. Lenin put the matter most clearly in stating to the Soviet people that "if you are determined to carry this to its logical conclusion, you must understand that you will have to contend against the onslaught of the exploiters of the whole world. If you are ready to offer resistance and to make further sacrifices in order to hold out in the struggle, you are a revolutionary; if not, you will be crushed".[26]

Wars may be fought to gain liberty, but peace is required to nurture the seeds of liberty into flowers of freedom. The Soviet Union, since the day it came into being, has not been permitted to know that peace. After the Wars of Intervention and the economic and diplomatic siege of the 1920s, came the rise of fascism in the 1930s and World War II. After the Second World War came the Cold War, poisoned by the nuclear arms race. In this atmosphere, human rights in the Soviet Union suffered a stillbirth.

The Great Purge

The combination of war communism and Lenin's notion of the 'dictatorship of the proletariat' destroyed any democratic tendency within the Communist Party. The Party Secretariat transferred Party officials for political reasons, and Party committees were transformed into appointed bodies. In effect, power was taken from party cadres and the masses of people and handed over to the manipulators of the Party machine. The question in czarist Russia was 'Who will be the next czar?'. The answer to that was determined by heredity. In Soviet Russia the question became 'Who will rule the Soviet people?'. The answer was 'The one who wins the faction fight for Party Leadership'. In the former the person had to be born of the nobility and survive the palace intrigue. In the latter, the man had to work his way into the Party elite and then survive the political intrigue. The one who ensured that this was so was to become the most feared, the most hated, and yet the most powerful Soviet administrator, Josef Visarionovitch Jugashville, known to the world merely as Stalin.

As general secretary of the only legal party in the USSR, Stalin was at the hub of the Soviet wheel. When Lenin died in 1924, Stalin quickly showed himself a master of using the intricate patronage system to build support, out-manoeuvre rivals and pack the various party and government committees with enough loyal followers to ensure his will prevailed. This, combined with his exceptional intelligence, political acuity, attention to detail, immense capacity for work and utter ruthlessness produced perhaps the most total dictatorship in modern times, spanning a quarter of a century, from 1928 until Stalin's death in 1953.

Stalin's dictatorship was characterised by the purges he used at regular intervals to remove enemies, real or imagined, as well as their families, from the party, the government, the armed forces, and the society at large. His Great Purge came in the 1930s. In 1933–34 over a million members were expelled from the Party; many were imprisoned, tortured and executed. Of the 1,961 delegates to the 1934 Party Congress, 1,108 were arrested. They vanished from public life. Between 1936–38, 70% of the Central Committee were arrested on charges of sabotage or treason and executed. In the purge of 1937–38, three of the five Soviet field marshals, 57 of the 85 corps commanders, and 110 of the 195 divisional commanders were shot. By 1938, all members of Lenin's Politburo were either executed or exiled, and an estimated 8 million people had been sent to concentration camps.

What characterised Stalin's Great Purge were four things: first its immense scale, in which millions died and every Soviet citizen feared for his or her life; second, the extraordinary methods used, in particular the confessional trials where the victims publicly denounced themselves for treason; thirdly, its secrecy—apart from the public trials and a few announcements concerning executions, nothing was ever officially said about any part of the whole vast operation; and fourth, its rationale, which never seemed to change. The Soviet people were given a clear and consistent story of the purges, which, because of their experiences in the Wars of Intervention, seemed almost credible. A vast conspiracy, it was said, led by disgraced members of the Party leadership, had penetrated every part of Soviet life. Working in consort with the intelligence services of Germany, Poland, Britain, Japan and the United States, these people—whoever was on trial at the time—were seeking to restore capitalism; to defeat the USSR in the war; to assassinate the Soviet leadership; and to sabotage every phase of national life from mines to the ministries. This conspiracy had been uncovered, its leader had confessed, and they had been fairly tried and justly punished to the complete satisfaction of the Soviet people. Those not executed were sent to perform 'corrective labour' by which society would redeem them.

It has been argued that Stalin's purges had a positive aspect. David Lane, for instance, asserts that the purges

> ... had integrative effects for the society as a whole .... Rapid and violent social and political upheavals require both the destruction of the values of the *ancien regime* and their replacement with a new value system otherwise society may disintegrate.
>
> The purges and terror isolated and frightened men and broke down old values; at the same time, for those who did not wish to be purged or terrorized, they acted as mechanisms through which they could affirm their loyalty to the new order.[27]

Stalin himself saw his actions in a more historical context. In a speech in 1932 he said:

> The history of Old Russia consisted, among other things, of being beaten continuously for her backwardness. The Mongol khans beat her. The Turkish beys beat her. The Swedish feudal lords beat her. The Polish–Lithuanian landlords beat her. The Anglo–French capitalists beat her. All beat her because of her backwardness .... Do you want for our Socialist fatherland to be beaten and lose its independence? If you don't want this, you should in the shortest time liquidate its backwardness .... We lag behind the advanced countries by 50 to 100 years. We must make up this distance in ten years. Either we do this or they will crush us.[28]

Stalin did in fact have something to worry about; it was less than ten years later that the Nazis invaded. Nevertheless, it is also true that Stalin's permanent wave of terror kept the whole bureaucracy in such a state of flux that it was unable to form the compact and efficient body necessary to complete the industrialisation Stalin sought. What is more, although he may have desired to liquidate just the leaders of potential treason, meaning those few thousand party officials who in the past had been associated with his rivals, the mechanics of terror Stalin set in motion soon acquired a momentum of their own. The more Stalin killed the more suspicious he became. His passion for revenge was not merely atrocious, it was vulgar. He made the wives and children of his victims suffer, for no one was allowed to curse him, even in private. The Soviet Union had been born besieged from without. Under Stalin, the Soviet Union came under siege from within.

The Molotov–Ribbentrop Treaty of 1939

In Moscow, on 15 August 1942, Churchill asked Stalin how he had come to sign a pact with Hitler in 1939. Churchill later recalled:

> Stalin replied that he thought England must be bluffing; he knew we had only two divisions we could mobilise at once, and he thought we must know how bad the French Army was and what little reliance could be placed on it. He could not imagine we should enter the war with such weakness. On the other hand, he said he knew Germany was certain ultimately to attack Russia. He was not ready to withstand that attack; by attacking Poland with Germany he could make more ground, ground was equal to time, and he would consequently have a longer time to get ready.[29]

Whether or not this is true is still being hotly debated amongst historians. Some are inclined to accept Stalin's explanation, pointing out that he tried very hard in the years before 1939 to secure treaties with Britain and France against the Nazis. Only when Britain and France refused did he finally come to terms with Hitler in an attempt to put as much territory between Russia and the German frontier as possible. Even Churchill himself was later to regret the refusal of the British and the French to come to terms with Stalin. "There can ... be no doubt, even in the afterlight," he wrote in his book *The Gathering Storm*, "that Britain and France should have accepted the Russian offer .... The alliance of Britain, France and Russia would have struck deep alarm into the heart of Germany in 1939, and no one can prove that war might not even then have been averted."[30]

Soviet historian Dr. Oleg Rzheshevsky asserts that while the British and French were stalling the Soviets about signing an anti-Nazi pact, they were in secret negotiating with Hitler to conclude a 'Pact of Four', including Britain, France, Germany and Italy.[31] If this failed, Britain was negotiating to form an Anglo-German alliance. British negotiators made it clear that if a deal could be struck, Britain would end talks with the USSR, abandon the defence of Poland, and even sacrifice the interests of France.

Dr. Rzheshevsky also argues that part of the Anglo-Franco-German negotiations included plans to deliver a united blow against the USSR as they had done in the Wars of Intervention. Britain and France would attack from the north and south; Germany through Poland to the Soviet heartland.

Other historians argue that Stalin and Hitler had a natural affinity with each other and that while on the one hand he sought an alliance that would keep Germany at bay, Stalin was also interested in forming a Soviet-German alliance whereby the USSR could dominate Eastern Europe. Their Pact in 1939 should be seen in this light because it essentially bundled up Europe between them.

From the earliest days of the Nazi Party many of its members had entertained a respect, frequently reciprocated, for what they regarded as the sincerity and ultimately similar aims of the Communists. Both parties were opposed to the old capitalist order; both were highly centralised and hierarchical; both laid great stress on the use of propaganda; both used violence against their enemies and intimidated anyone who opposed them; and both engaged in the personality cult of their leaders, Hitler and Stalin.

Early Nazi membership was frequently recruited from the German Communist Party. A high proportion of the Nazi SA (the Brownshirts) came from the Communists. Ernst Rohm, the SA leader, welcomed them for both their fanaticism and willingness to use violence, nicknaming Communist recruits 'beefsteaks'—brown without, red within.[32] The flow worked the other way as well. In 1923 Hitler is reported to have said that 'either we act now or our SA people will go over to the Communists'.[33]

Although this competition between the Nazis and Communists led to intense conflict, Hitler himself remained ambivalent about them, even while persecuting them after gaining power. In 1934 he declared:

> It is not Germany that will turn Bolshevist, but Bolshevism that will become a part of National Socialism .... Besides, there is more than binds us to Bolshevism than separates us from it. There is, above all, genuine revolutionary feeling which is alive everywhere in Russia except where there are Jewish Marxists. I have always made allowance for this circumstance, and given orders that former Communists are to be admitted to the party at once. The *petit bourgeois* Social Democrat and the trade union boss will never make a National Socialist, but the Communist always will.[34]

Lenin had allowed Germany to conduct secret military manoeuvres on Soviet soil, in violation of the Treaty of Versailles. Stalin had approved of secret military co-operation between the USSR and Germany as soon as Hitler took over power. His brother-in-law, Pavel Allivyer, was the Soviet military representative in Berlin until 1933. Even after Hitler's brutal suppression of the Communists after the Reichstag fire in 1934, Soviet diplomats such as Krestinsky, Molotov and Litvinov continued to reassure the Germans of Soviet goodwill.

"There is no reason why Fascist Germany and Soviet Russia should not get on together, inasmuch as the Soviet Union and

Fascist Italy are good friends," wrote Stalin's chief spokesman on German affairs, Karl Redek, in July 1934.[35] Writing a fortnight after Hitler's Blood Purge, Redek expressed his belief that one day the SA would prove to be a 'reserve' of future Communists. Indeed, German strength and Nazi ruthlessness were more impressive to Stalin than any other considerations. "We must come to terms with a superior power like Nazi Germany", Stalin told his police chief Yezhov in 1937.[36]

In the 1930s, Nazi strength certainly was impressive. In Spain, the Fascists were defeating the Stalinist backed Republican forces; the Japanese were penetrating further into China; and every one of Hitler's moves left the Western powers in greater disarray.

Stalin's policy seemed to be two-pronged. Soviet diplomacy sought to reach agreement with Britain and France to take resolute measures to contain Nazi expansionism. It joined the League of Nations in 1934, entered into diplomatic relations with the US, and advocated any measures, even military intervention, to preserve the integrity of Czechoslovakia against Nazi encroachments.

At the time of the Munich settlement in 1938, when the British and the French again rejected Soviet offers for a united front against Hitler and seemed to have, in fact, come to terms with the Nazis, the Soviets were left isolated and frightened. Undoubtedly discussions about a British-French-German attack on the USSR such as Rzheshevsky described, did take place. Therefore, Stalin renewed his efforts to come to terms with the Nazis.

With both sides seeking detente with him, Hitler was in a position to choose. As his own war plans called for attacking the West before the USSR, it made strategic sense to make peace with Stalin, at least for as long as it took to occupy Western Europe. On 23 August 1939, less than a week before Hitler attacked Poland, German Foreign Minister Ribbentrop and Soviet Foreign Minister Molotov signed a Non-Agression Pact which bound the signatories to observe peaceful relations for ten years and, which, unless abrogated ealier, was to be extended for an additional five years—i.e. until 1954.

A Secret Additional Protocol arranged for the demarcation of Eastern Europe between them. Parts of Poland, Finland, Estonia, Latvia and Bessarabia (part of Romania) were to go to the Soviets; Lithuania and most of Poland were to go to the Germans. A small 'independent' Polish state was to be left centred around Warsaw.

Stalin soon had misgivings about having Germans as far east as Lithuania. On 25 September 1939 he sent Molotov back into negotiations. He proposed that all of Poland be divided, giving Germany all the territory up to the Curzon Line (the line marking the eastern frontier of ethnic Poland proposed by the British in

1919). In exchange, the Soviets would take Lithuania. A Treaty was signed to this effect on 29 September.

If Stalin's reason for signing these agreements was to buy time to fortify the USSR against the expected Nazi attack, he certainly did little to substantiate the claim. When the Nazis invaded some eighteen months later, virtually nothing had been done in the way of fortifications, defensive lines or military airfields in the land gained by the Pact. What he *did* do was to begin a series of elaborate purges and deportations, involving hundreds of thousands of people in each of the 'liberated' territories. These operations were meticulously planned and carried out, and they lasted right up until the Nazis invaded in June 1941.

Recent research by George Watson of Cambridge University indicates that the Soviet secret police, the NKVD, and the Nazi Gestapo had begun close collaboration across their new frontier in 1939.[37] The Non-Aggression Pact stipulated that the secret police forces of the two occupying powers were to co-operate. Less than six months after the signing of the Pact an extended conference was held between the Gestapo and the NKVD in the former Polish city of Crakow. A former member of the Polish underground, T. Bor-Komorowski, has recorded that in March 1940 his unit heard that an "NKVD mission had come to Crakow to work out with the Gestapo the methods they were jointly to adopt against Polish military organizations".[38] He recalls that "the NKVD methods for combating our underground were greatly admired by the Gestapo, and it was suggested that they should be adopted in the German zone". The British government was aware that the Soviets were handing over to the Nazis vast numbers of Poles to be used for forced labour.

By early 1940, the Soviets has already conducted at least one mass slaughter of the Poles. About 15,000 captured Polish officers who refused to collaborate were tied with *Russian* ropes and shot in the back of the head with *German* bullets at Katyn. This first mass slaying and the Crakow conference happening at about the same time is a strange coincidence, especially since the massacre at Katyn reveals striking similarities with later Nazi massacres. Although the Soviets argued after the war that German bullets show that the crime had been perpetrated by the Nazis, it is well known that German bullets were used by the NKVD and that German munitions were reaching the USSR from Germany long before the Stalin-Hitler Pact.

The International Commission that examined the site in April 1943, found eight mass graves, each 6-11 feet deep, with bodies lying face downwards, hands tied behind the back and around the neck. The bodies were piled in layers of ten to twelve; each one of them had been shot in the back of the neck at such an angle that the bullet emerged from the top of the head. One report from a villager asserts that the Polish officers were forced to lie down on top of their dead and dying comrades before themselves being shot.

The SS massacre of about 5,000 Jews in the Ukraine in October 1942 used essentially the same method, although here the victims were naked and unbound and the instrument of killing was a submachine gun. The technique of the mass grave and the angle of the bullets, however, were similar.

This technique originated with the Soviets. Stalin's method of executing the old Bolsheviks after the show trials of the 1930s was to shoot them in the back of the neck, not the heart. Additionally, mass executions were widely understood to be the Stalinist way several years before the first known Nazi one. Sidney and Beatrice Webb had already described it in their 1935 book, *Soviet Communism*, in a chapter uncompromisingly called "The Liquidation of the Landlord and the Capitalist". It is estimated that Stalin killed 14,000,000 Kulaks (rich peasants).

The method of deportation, particularly the technique of packed railroad cars, was also a Soviet idea later adapted by the Nazis. A decree of the Soviet Presidium in September 1941 even speaks of 'resettlement'—a euphemism much favoured by the Nazis also.

The concentration/extermination camps were also of Soviet origin. They were first conceived by Lenin in 1918. The first such camp started functioning near Archangel in North Russia in 1921. The camp was built on the site of an old monastery. The description of prison life in the 1950s recounted by Solzhenitsyn in *The Gulag Archipelago*—barbed wire, search lights, guard dogs, work gangs, summary executions, and constant debilitation of prisoners from the weather and guards alike—all had striking similarities with the Nazi camps.

Soviet exterminations were characterised by exposure, disease, starvation, and shooting. Nazi exterminations were characterised by exposure, disease, starvation and shooting. And gas. First used for incurables in 1939, the use of the gas chamber seems to be the only original contribution the Nazis made to the process of mass extermination.

When the Nazis finally attacked the USSR in June 1941, they met the only enemy they ever fought who was equally ruthless. Of all theatres of war, the Russian-German front was the most ferocious and atrocious. Stalin and Hitler were simply too much alike.

Operation Barbarosa

On 22 June 1941, the Soviet Union was invaded once again. Only this time it was an attack unprecedented in the history of warfare.

Codenamed 'Operation Barbarosa' by Hitler himself, it involved a 5 million strong invasion force of 190 divisions, 4,000 tanks, 5,000 planes, 47,000 guns and mortars, and more than 200 combatant and auxiliary ships.

"It is a struggle for destruction", Hitler told his generals. "In the East ruthlessness itself is a good thing for the future".[39] The "Instructions on the Treatment of Political Commissars", issued on 6 June 1941, just prior to the invasion, were clear: "Kill every Russian, every Soviet person, do not hesitate if it is an old man or a woman, a little girl or a little boy who stands before you. Kill, and by this act you will save yourself from death, provide for the future of your family and become famous for all time."[40]

Soviet losses before the Nazi onslaught were staggering. Material losses amounted to about 25% of total Soviet property. More than 6 million homes, 70,000 villages and 1,700 towns and cities were razed to the ground. In the village of Ola, for instance, the Nazis herded the 1,758 inhabitants, including 950 children, into several barns, and burnt them alive. The Nazis went on to leave 25 million homeless. They blew up 31,850 industrial plants, 65,000 kilometres of railway and 36,000 communication establishments; 16,000 locomotives and 428,000 railway cars were either destroyed or taken to Germany. They plundered and destroyed 96,000 collective farms, 1,876 state farms, 2,890 machine and tractor stations, 40,000 hospitals, 84,000 schools, 427 museums and 43,000 public libraries. The territory which sheltered 40% of the Soviet population and 60% of its industry was left desolate.

According to the plans of Hitler's strategists, Germany was to proceed, already in the autumn of 1941, to conquer Iran, Iraq, Egypt, the Suez Canal area, and then India, where Nazi forces were to join Japanese troops. Hitler hoped to draw Spain and Portugal into the war on the side of the Axis powers, capture Gibraltar, cut Britain off from its sources of raw materials, and then embark on a siege of Britain itself.

Directive No. 32 of the Nazi High Command testifies that after the rout of the USSR and the solution of the "British problem", the Nazis intended, in alliance with Japan, to "do away with the influence of the Anglo-Saxons in North America". This was to be done by landing large amphibious forces from bases in Greenland, Iceland, the Azores and Brazil on the east coast of North America, and from the Aleutian and Haiwaiian islands on the West coast. Hitler's generals believed that the key positions necessary for carrying out world conquest would be provided by defeating the USSR.

Hitler expected to conquer Russia in six months. "You have only to kick in the door," he declared, "and the whole rotten structure will come crashing down."[41] The ground literally burned under the feet of the advancing Nazis. The Soviets practiced a 'scorched earth' policy as they retreated, hoping to deprive the Nazis of food. The Nazis destroyed the rest.

Hitler ordered his generals to take Moscow at any price. In an offensive codenamed "Typhoon", the Germans flung about 2 million troops, 1,700 tanks and assault guns, more than 14,000 pieces of ordnance and mortars, and about 1,400 aircraft toward the capital of the USSR, while simultaneously driving north towards Leningrad and southeast toward Stalingrad and the Volga river basin. "Moscow", Hitler directed, "must be encircled in such a way that not a single Russian soldier, not a single inhabitant—man, woman or child—can leave it. Any attempt to escape must be stopped by force."[42]

Like Napoleon before him, however, Hitler was unprepared for the Russian winter. On 8 December 1941, he was forced to issue Directive No. 39 which ordered the Nazi forces to retrench due to the "early and cold winter on the Eastern front and the difficulties it caused in the delivery of supplies". Hitler had also miscalculated the resilience of Stalin and the patriotism of the Soviet people when their homeland was invaded yet again. Using all the mechanisms of War Communism begun by Lenin, Stalin redirected Soviet industry east of the Ural mountains and mobilised the entire economy on a war footing. Simultaneously, tens of thousands of people formed underground partisan units in the occupied territories of the Ukraine, Byelorussia, Latvia, Lithuania, Estonia, Moldavia and Eastern Russia. They harrassed the Germans ceaselessly, cutting communication lines, sabotaging depots and equipment, and holding up supplies.

The combination of the Russian winter, the manner in which Stalin retooled and redirected the economy, and the patriotism of the Soviet people, whether fighting from behind enemy lines as partisans or attacking the Nazis from the east, was enough to stop the Nazi *blitzkrieg*. By March 1942, the Nazis had lost over 1 million soldiers, and the advance on Moscow was dead. This defeat at the Battle of Moscow was the first one suffered by the Nazis in the Second World War. It destroyed the myth of the invincibility of the Nazi war machine and made the first crack on the morale of the so called invincible Nazi soldiers.

It was on Soviet soil, too, that the fortunes of war changed. This occurred at the Battle of Stalingrad from 17 July 1942 to 2 February 1943. It took place over an area of 100,000 square kilometres and involved more than 2 million soldiers. After heroic efforts on both sides, the Nazis were defeated, losing more than 800,000 soldiers. The Romanian and Italian armies assisting the Nazis were routed. The initiative now passed to the side of the allies. As Churchill said

of the Battle of Stalingrad, it marked "the beginning of the end".
Resistance movements gained momentum in France, Italy, Poland,
Czechoslovakia and other countries occupied by the Nazis.
Relations between the fascist-bloc countries became strained, and
Japan and Turkey decided to reject Hitler's demand that they enter
into the war against the USSR.

Other major battles were fought between the Nazis and the Red
Army. If the Battle of Moscow gave them their first defeat, and the
Battle of Stalingrad took away their strategic initiative, the Battle
of Kursk, fought in the summer of 1943, brought the Nazis to the
brink of disaster, for it smashed the most carefully planned Nazi
counter attack of the war. Even after the D-Day invasion of France
by the British and American forces, the Nazis still concentrated
most of their troops on the Eastern front. The siege of Leningrad,
for instance, lasted 900 days from the summer of 1941 until 14
January 1944, when Soviet troops finally broke through. Even as
late as 3 April 1945 an appeal to Nazi troops issued by the Nazi
leadership said that "the war will be decided in the east, not in the
west".

There were basically five fronts during the Second World War:
the North African, the Italian, the West European, the
Nazi-Russian and the American-Japanese. None of these fronts
involved such massive numbers of troops or materials as did the
Nazi-Russian front. An average of 75% of the Nazi divisions and
a majority of the forces of its allies operated against the USSR. In
fighting the Russians, the Nazis lost 507 divisions and their allies
lost another 100. They lost 167,000 guns, 48,000 tanks, 77,000
aircraft, and over 7.5 million people.

Against the British and Americans, the Nazis and their allies lost
176 divisions, and 2.5 million soldiers. American casualties came to
500,000. British casualties numbered 270,000. The Soviets lost 20
million, and had 30 million wounded: 25% of their entire
population.

Stalin's Legacy
The tragedy of the post-war situation was that peace was not at
hand. Externally, the US quickly assumed global dominance. Its
economy and homeland had been untouched by the war; it was in
sole possession of the atomic bomb; and it saw the USSR as its only
real competitor, even though the gross national product of the
USSR was only 30% of the US in 1948 and the Soviet people and
army were exhausted. The US refused Stalin's request for a $6
billion loan and ended Lend-Lease in August 1945. Unlike the
recipients of America's Marshall Plan, which was to pour some $26
billion into rebuilding Europe and Japan, the USSR had to finance

its own economic recovery from its own resources in the face of growing US power and hostility.

Internally, Stalin reimposed his dictatorial control over the entire state and the purges began again. Whole nations were deported to the east because of supposed 'collective treachery'. The Party Secretary for Moldavia Leonid Brezhnev, for instance, shouldered the responsibilty for the imprisonment, deportation, or execution of over one-sixth of the native Moldavians, some 500,000 people. They were replaced by 250,000 Russians deported from the east.

Stalin turned Lavrenti Beria's secret police loose upon the country. His slave labour establishments included logging camps in Siberia, canal construction products in the tundra, building the Moscow metro and research laboratories, and numerous other work and prison colonies. Thousands were sent to join the millions already in these prison camps, known to the world as the 'Gulag Archipelago'. Moreover, demobilised soldiers were directed to work far from their homes, on the principle that they would be less inclined to speak to strangers about the material glories of Hungary or Germany they had seen during the war. Stalin's revenge was also exacted upon the 3 million Soviet prisoners of war and people forced by the Nazis to work in the German industrial plants who returned to the USSR after the war. Although not to blame for having contact with foreigners, they were either executed or imprisoned.

In the summer of 1946, Stalin set in motion the *Zhdanovschina*, which was a campaign against alien influences upon Russian cultural and scientific life. The hunt was on for 'cultural saboteurs', who turned out often to be 'rootless cosmopolitans' or Jews. Ultra-nationalism was required in all Soviet art; 'kowtowing before the West' became a crime.

Once again the USSR came under siege from within, as Stalin executed, deported or imprisoned people by the millions. His regime was a brutal one from the time he consolidated absolute power in 1928 until he died in 1953. When his body was placed on public view in the Kremlin a few days after his death, the crowds rioted and scores were trampled to death in the snow.

Although many historians seek to understand how the Communist Party produced Stalin, the real question seems to be how the Party *survived* him. Stalin was denounced by the new Party Leader, Nikita Khrushchev, at the Twentieth Party Congress in 1956. For a time there was a lessening of the weight of state control. Alexander Solzhenitsyn's *One Day in the Life of Ivan Denisovitch* was openly published, and Andrei Sakharov was inspired to write: "Our country has started along the path of cleansing itself from the filth of Stalinism." He quoted Chekhov's

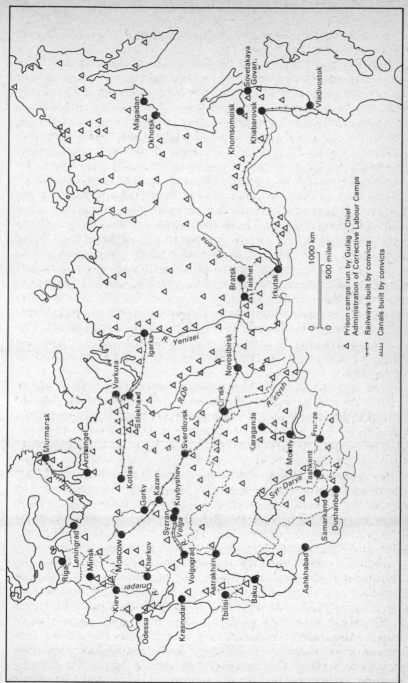

Soviet Prison Camps run by GULAG – Chief Administration of Corrective Labour Camps – and railways and canals built by the convicts. (*Source: The Soviet Superpower: Heinemann Educ.*)

famous line: "Drop by drop we are squeezing the slave out of ourselves."

This freedom and the euphoria did not last. Khrushchev quickly clamped down and religious persecution continued. When Leonid Brezhnev overthrew Khrushchev in 1964, he not only continued the policy of repression but added a new emphasis: the use of psychiatric hospitals for incarcerating political prisoners. Under Stalin's regime psychiatric hospitals had been used, but not frequently. Indeed, they were often used by sympathetic psychiatrists as a way of giving refuge to prisoners who otherwise would have been criminally prosecuted. Under Brezhnev, however, even this loophole was closed. Dissidents such as Vladimir Bukovsky were subjected to cruel and inhuman abuse at the hands of psychiatrists under the directive of Brezhnev and his KGB chief Andropov. When Brezhnev died in 1982 and Andropov assumed command, he gave no indication of changing the policies he and Brezhnev had developed. Instead, dissidents such as Roy Medvedev and Anatoli Scharantsky were subjected to increased repression.

What appears to be happening in the Soviet Union today is a refinement in the methods of social control. Now in full command, with opposition eliminated, only the gentlest of reminders of what has been are necessary for the Party to maintain its grip on Soviet society. Now, dissenters are considered not so much 'enemies of the State' but as 'mentally disturbed', for who in their 'right mind' would dissent against a Party as powerful and all-pervasive as the Communist Party of the Soviet Union?

This being said, it is important also to stress that the regime today has come a long way from its Stalinist past. The Stalinist era of the Gulag Archipelago consumed upwards of *twenty* million people. Amnesty International estimates that 10,000 are today incarcerated in the 'Gulag' for political or religious beliefs. It has documented evidence for 700. Moreover, while brutality, hard labour, long prison sentences, psychiatric abuse, and systematic starvation are known to occur in the Soviet prison system, the mass executions and cruder forms of torture known under Stalin are no longer used. Under Brezhnev, particularly in his later years, state and Party control lessened considerably and one heard increasing amounts of internal criticism and emphasis on personal motivation and initiative. The Party, personified by Brezhnev, was seen more and more as a repressive old uncle rather than a rigid and cruel dictator.

The fact that there are only 700 known political prisoners as opposed to millions is indicative of the security felt by the ruling regime in the Soviet Union. Despite the fact that the USSR has been besieged by the West since its revolution in 1917 and underwent the Stalinist terror from within until 1953, the Soviet people and the Communist Party itself have adapted and slowly, ever so slowly, continued the work of the socialist revolution first envisioned by Marx and Lenin. In the process, ironically, certain human rights have been attained in the USSR not enjoyed by many peoples in the capitalist camp.

In capitalism, *individual* rights are seen as central, social responsibility as secondary. Competition between individuals is fundamental for laissez-faire capitalism to function. Without that freedom, capitalism could not exist. The individual freedoms considered important are the right to own property; the right to make profits; the right to travel freely; the right to speak openly; the right to participate in a pluralistic government, i.e. a representative democracy; the right to a free press.

What is often missed by those who champion human rights in the West is that these notions of individual rights, *because they are so bound up with the capitalist economic system* , would change if the economic system changed. Under a socialist economy there are different emphases as to what are human rights. In the USSR one is allowed to own *personal* property, i.e. one's clothes, one's house, one's car, etc., but not *private* property, i.e. owning property which one uses for profit. There is no private production of goods. The notion so fundamental in the West of personal *profit* is anathema in the USSR. The emphasis is rather on the right to work and the right to be supported by the community throughout one's life.

This notion of human rights may sound strange to someone used to hearing depressing news about unemployment figures and the new rates for insurance premiums. Under capitalism, there is a right to compete. Those who do not compete successfully are either underemployed or unemployed. By keeping a percentage of the work force unemployed, the successful competitors, i.e. the owners of the factories, etc., can keep wages down and those workers who do have jobs under tighter control. Workers must fight for higher wages and benefits by forming unions and going out on strike if necessary. The battle between the workers and the capital owners and the competition between the different capitalists forms the bedrock of our 'free market economy'. There are winners and losers. The 'winners' get the capital to buy as many of the goods being produced as they want. This is defined as 'the good life'. For the losers: 'tough luck, work harder'. Because competition and personal initiative are the watch words, many services such as education, hospital care, old-age pensions, various insurance policies and child care must be paid for by the individuals who want them. If one cannot pay, one goes without.

There are no 'rights' to these services; there is only the right to compete with others to earn the capital to buy the services.

The constitution of the USSR states that every person in the USSR has the *inalienable right* to a job, to an education, to housing, to medical care, to state care for children; in short, to many of those things considered a privilege in a capitalist economy. Unemployment does not exist; there are, in fact, too few workers for the jobs available. Each family is guaranteed a home, the rent and utilities for which come to less than 5% of a wage earner's salary. Medical facilities, educational establishments, childcare centres are free, or virtually so. Public transportation is inexpensive and available to all. The idea of a 'rainy day' against which the Westerns ensure themselves is alien to Soviet citizens. They expect and receive full support from the nation in matters of health, education and retirement.

This is not to say that all the workers are happy with their jobs; nor that the housing provided is totally adequate; nor that the system is efficient. There are inadequacies and deprivations all around. Consumer goods are scarce; economic planning is appalling; bureaucratic incompetence seems to reign supreme. However, the point remains that in the USSR, where *social responsibility* is given highest priority and individual freedom secondary consideration, things are considered to be rights (like jobs) which under a capitalist economy are considered privileges, and vice versa.

Therefore, in any discussion of human rights violations in the USSR, it is necessary to bear in mind that much of what someone raised in a capitalist system would call 'violations' of human rights in the USSR are merely projections into Soviet society of what would be considered to be violations in a capitalist society. The Soviets do the same thing. They decry 'violations' of human rights in the West because millions are jobless, thousands are homeless, and childcare, education and medical care are not free for all. From a socialist perspective, these are human rights violations. But from a capitalist perspective, they are just the 'way it is'.

The distinctions between capitalist and socialist notions of human rights aside, the more fundamental question of *oppression* still needs to be considered. Whatever the economic system, to enslave, oppress and manipulate the citizenry by force of arms is a violation of human rights by *all standards*. This is recognised by both East and West.

The oppression of the Soviet government has been and continues to be appalling. Even after explaining the historical reasons for this, namely, the fact that they have suffered a permanent state of encirclement and war since 1917, what cannot be accepted is that tens of millions have been imprisoned and have died because of the ruthlessness of the Bolsheviks. The testimony of Solzhenitsyn and the recent events in Poland give ample witness to the oppressiveness of the Soviet system. In the USSR, the 'socialist state' has only been attained with the sacrifice of individual freedom. The fact that Sweden, Denmark and Britain under the Labour governments, for example, could evolve socialism without oppression, seriously indicts the last 60 years of Communist rule in the Soviet Union.

What needs to be kept clear about this oppression is that many human rights violations in the USSR are not so much because of 'communism' as because of the heritage of Russian history. For instance, the existence of the 'Gulag Archipelago' was not begun by the Bolshevik overlords to enslave the Soviet people, as many might think. Prison camps in Siberia were a standard part of the Czarist order. The Soviets inherited and refined a system already in place. The notion of exile, internal or external, is not new either. Many decry Soviet rule for sending Sakharov to internal exile and Bukovsky and Solzenitsyn into external exile. But Lenin was both internally and externally exiled by the Czar.

What is indictable about the human rights situation in the USSR is not that the Soviets have deprived people of rights they once had but that the Soviets have *never developed* the notions of the individual freedom of free speech, free religion, free press, free travel, or free political expression, into a meaningful part of Soviet life.

It is important to remember here that in the industrial democracies of Europe, the *ancien regimes* were replaced by a philosophical, political and economic perspective that emphasised individual freedom. The French Revolution, for instance, replaced the oppression of the monarchy and the Catholic church with the notions of 'Liberty, Equality, Fraternity'. The American Revolution overthrew British colonial rule and replaced the king with a constitution containing a Bill of Rights. In Britain, Germany, Holland, Belgium, Scandinavia and Eastern Europe, a similar pattern occurred: the power of the monarchy and the church was either overthrown or circumscribed to allow individual freedom and a participatory pluralistic democracy to flourish. It was an uneven process, one that took different forms in different countries, but nevertheless which began for the first time in modern history to actively experiment with democratic government and the notion of human equality.

This process did not occur in Russia. The czar held virtually absolute power until 1917. The Russian Orthodox Church likewise. When they were overthrown, the czar was replaced by the

Commissar, the Church was supplanted by the Party. Before 1917 there was 'one czar, one church, one nation'. Under Soviet rule there has been 'One Party, one dogma, one nation'. Psychologically, therefore, the Russian people never made the transition from despotism to democracy. The Russian Revolution changed the form of despotism; it did not alter its content. This is not to say that there was no revolution in the Soviet Union. There was. While the October Revolution of 1917 maintained a totalitarian system, it changed the *class* which was dominant, thereby following the pattern of previous revolutions. Other social revolutions have also ended up in a totalitarian way. The French Revolution overthrew the king and a new class, the bourgeoisie, replaced the aristocracy as the dominant class. Nevertheless, after the reign of 'virtue and terror' in which no one was safe from the guillotine, it was Napoleon who took charge and consolidated the revolution. Kings before him had been crowned by bishops and popes, indicating the close connection between church and state and the belief both institutions shared in the divine right of kings. The French Revolution deposed the tyranny of both church and king and vanquished the notion of 'divine right'. Napoleon crowned himself, symbolising that his roots were from the common people and that he did not need the church. But he was still king. Indeed, he was called 'Emperor'.

The Russian Revolution overthrew the tyranny of the czar, aristocracy and church. The new class in power was that of the proletariat. After the chaos and excesses of the Civil War, there was the need to consolidate the revolution. This period of revolution is called 'thermidor' after the month in which Napoleon took power. When it came in Russia it brought in Joseph Stalin who became the most powerful and brutal 'emperor' since Czar Ivan the Terrible.

The cries of the dissidents, now as they were under the czars, are all the more passionate because they represent the yearnings of a people who must still give historical content to the word 'democracy'. To have a job, a free education, free medical and child care is to have *security*. This the Soviet people have in ways the capitalist West has yet to attain. This right to security is a fundamental one, without which a society decays from its own failure to take care of its vulnerable elements. However, what the Soviet people have yet to develop is the *right to individual freedom*. Lenin replaced the despotism of the czar with the 'dictatorship of the proletariat', thereby fulfilling his promise of peace, land and bread. But man shall not live by bread alone; we shall also live for freedom.

HOW SHOULD THE WEST RESPOND?

The fact that the Soviet Union has been placed under a state of siege by the United States and its allies since 1917 has made the development of the pursuit of freedom virtually impossible. In war, truth and freedom are the first casualties. The *external* pressures on the USSR, therefore, are as much responsible for the violations of human rights that have occurred as has been the unfortunate marriage of Czarism and Marxism *inside* the USSR.

To heighten hostilities will only worsen an already bad situation. How does one respond to a paranoic? Should one *increase* the pressures on that person? Or should one *lessen* the pressures and allow an atmosphere to arise in which the paranoia can give way to some type of normalcy? As long as the Soviet Union feels itself besieged by hostile powers with not only nuclear and conventional superiority but a declared willingness to push the button first, it will continue to live under a 'war communism' in which freedom is unlikely ever to exist.

If those in the West criticising the Soviet Union for human rights violations are truly sincere in their belief that human rights—as they define them—should be given to all peoples, then they should be willing to create the atmosphere of tolerance in which human rights can develop. The flower of freedom can only flourish in a climate of peace.

One would think that this truth would be self evident. However, this is not the case. Even as people in their 'right mind' in the USSR acquiesce and allow the Communist Party to maintain near absolute control, so people in their 'right mind' in the West argue that the only way to keep the Soviet system from encroaching upon us is to threaten it with so much destruction that civilisation itself is held hostage against it. The only way to do so is by increasing our nuclear kill capacity. But either acquiescing to dictatorship or threatening to destroy all planetary life if that dictatorship attacks are ultimately acts of cowardice. 'Better dead than red' is simply not good enough. Neither is 'better red than dead'. What we must do is to come to terms with (1) the pervasiveness of human depravity, whether manifest in the socialist camp or a capitalist multi-national; (2) that nuclear weapons merely out-terrorise the existing terrors thereby perpetuating rather than eradicating violations of human rights; and (3) the truth that it is the strength of people, not the power of bombs, that gives a nation its best defence against tyranny.

The first point is in many ways the hardest to admit. Human rights violations in the West are so much more easily explained away than they are in the Soviet Union. After all, we are the children of the Enlightenment, the defenders of the truth that all people are created equal; that all people are entitled to the pursuit of health, wealth and happiness; and that all people must be assured the basic freedoms of speech, religion, assembly and travel if their happiness is to be fulfilled. We pride ourselves for our democratic institutions and openness to differing points of view, vowing yet again that 'I may disagree with what you say but I will die defending your right to say it'.

What we often forget is that our democratic notions, while grandiose in the *abstract*, have been very carefully and narrowly applied in *real life*. The Americans, for instance, while adopting a Constitution guaranteeing a Bill of Rights to all in 1789, *in fact* gave the vote only to males above the age of 25 who owned property. Women and slaves were excluded. Blacks did not begin to get the vote till the late 1860s and women did not win the right to vote until the 1920s. Women in the US, as elsewhere, do not yet have equal protection even under the law, even though equality before the law forms the basis of the whole legal system.

Moreover, the rights won in the West have not been 'given' by the government. They have been demanded and then fought for by the people themselves, often at great cost. The Enlightenment credo 'Liberty, Fraternity, Equality' was emblazoned on the European mind by the fires of the French Revolution. Countless uprisings since then have been necessary to ensure that the flame of freedom does not go out. Governments invariably seek to control; the people seek to create and live out their individual lives. Social reality is lived out somewhere on the continuum between national security on the one hand and individual freedom on the other; between centralised control and anarchy; between subservience and insurrection. The history of the world has been the tale of human beings seeking to work out a proper balance between the individual and the collective. Out of this history, democracy has only recently been born. It is still unaccepted by most; and only tolerated within certain carefully designed structures by those who do.

Human rights violations, not human decency and freedom, are still the norm. From 1976 to 1981, Amnesty International collected documented evidence of torture in sixty different nations, including the United States and nations in the NATO alliance. In more than 50 countries in the world today citizens can be held without charge or trial, and in 134 countries the death penalty is still in force. We are a species only now emerging from an atavistic past. We are territorial, aggressive, relentlessly cruel, and frightened. How else can one explain the following testimony of a young woman arrested for political charges in Turkey.

I was attacked by several people in the street. My eyes were covered by a special black band and I was forced into a minibus. The vehicle did not move for a few minutes. During this time I noticed that the people around me were addressing each other with expressions like 'my colonel', 'my major'. They started asking me questions from the first moment they put me into the minibus. When I did not answer, they started threatening me in the following manner. 'You don't talk now,' they would say; 'in a few minutes, when our hands will start roaming in between your legs, you will be singing like a nightingale.' The vehicle travelled for quite a long time before it stopped before a building I could not recognise. When I got off the minibus, I realised that I was in a relatively high open space. I was then taken into the basement of the building before which we had stopped, and then into a rather spacious room. I was surrounded by people whom I guessed to be military officers from the ways they addressed each other. They asked me questions and kept saying that unless I spoke it would be quite bad for me and that we would have to do 'collective training' together. After a short while they forced me to take off my skirt and stockings and laid me down on the ground and tied my hands and feet to pegs. A person by the name of Umit Erdal beat the soles of my feet for about half an hour. As he beat my soles he kept on saying, 'We make everybody talk here, you think we shall not succeed with you?' and insulting me. Later, they attached wires to my fingers and toes and passed electric currents through my body. At the same time they kept beating my naked thighs with truncheons. Many people were assisting Umit Erdal in this. One was a rather large man, tall, with curly hair and a relatively dark skin. A second was a small man with a relatively dark skin, black hair and a moustache. The third was a young man with a fair skin, dark hair and a moustache. The fourth was rather elderly, of middle stature, and of a dark complexion. He constantly wore dark glasses. The fifth was rather old, fat, of middle stature and with blue eyes and grey hair. At the same time, during the tortures, a grey-haired, stout and elderly colonel, and a grey-haired, blue-eyed, tall and well-built officer would frequently come in and give directions. After a while, they disconnected the wire from my finger and connected it to my ear. They immediately gave a high dose of electricity. My whole body and head shook in a terrible way. My front teeth started breaking. At the same time my torturers would hold a mirror to my face and say: 'Look what is happening to your lovely green eyes. Soon you will not be able to see at all. You will lose your mind. You see, you have already started bleeding in your mouth.' When they finished with electric shocks, they lifted me up to my feet and several of those I mentioned above started beating me with truncheons. After a while I felt dizzy and could not see very well. Then I fainted. When I came to myself, I found out I was lying half-naked in a pool of dirty water. They tried to force me to stand up and run. At the same time they kept beating me with truncheons, kicking me and pushing me against the walls. They then held my hand and hit me with truncheons in my palms and on my hands, each one taking turns. After all this my whole body was swollen and red, and I could not stand on my feet. As if this was not enough, Umit Erdal attacked me and forced me to the ground. I fell on my face. He stood on my back and with the assistance of somebody else forced a truncheon into my anus. As I struggled to stand he kept on saying 'You whore! See what else we will do to you. First tell us how many people did you go to bed with? You won't be able to do it any more. We shall next destroy your womanhood.' They next made me lie on my back and tied my arms and legs to pegs. They attached an electric wire to the small toe of my right foot and another to the end of a truncheon. They tried to penetrate my feminine organ with the end of a truncheon. As I resisted they hit my body and legs with a large axe handle. They soon succeeded in penetrating my sexual organ with the truncheon with the electric wire on, and passed current. I fainted. A little later, the soldiers outside brought in a machine used for pumping air into people and said they would kill me. Then they untied me, brought me to my feet and took me out of the room. With a leather strap, they hanged me from my wrists on to a pipe in the corridor. As I hung half-naked, several people beat me with truncheons. I fainted again. When I woke, I found myself in the same room on a bed. They brought in a doctor to examine me. They tried to force me to take medicines and eat. I was bleeding a dark, thick blood. Some time later they brought in Nuri Colakoglu, who was in the same building as myself, to put more pressure on me. They wanted to show me into what state they had put him. I saw that the nails of his right hand were covered with pus. I realised that they had burnt him with cigarette butts. They themselves later confirmed this. The sole of one of his feet was completely black and badly broken. The same night we were transferred to Istanbul together with Nuri Colakoglu. The next morning, the colonel I have already described came into my cell (I do not know where the cell was). He beat me and threatened me. 'Tonight I shall take you where your dead are. I shall have the corpses of all of you burnt. I will have you hanging from the ceiling and apply salt to your cut soles.' When he did not like the answers I gave him, he beat me again; then he had my eyes tied and sent me to another building. I was brought into a small room with my eyes tied. I was tied on the ground to pegs from my arms and ankles and electricity was passed through my right hand and foot. Then thay administered falanga. During the whole time I was in Istanbul, my hands were tied to chains. Because of this and because my tongue was split, I could not eat. A doctor would occasionally come to look at me and suggest first aid. One night I heard the sound of a gun and the sound of a man fall and die on the ground very close to me. I cried out, 'Whom have you killed?' They answered: 'It is none of your business. We kill whomever we want and bury him into a hole in the ground. Who would know if we did the same to you?' As I knew already, there was no security for my life.

During the ten days I stayed at MIT (the Turkish Secret Service) the same torture, insults, threats and pressure continued. On 28 April I was sent to the house of detention. Despite the fact that I went to the doctor at the house of detention and explained that I was badly tortured, that my right hand did not hold and that I had other physical complaints including the fact that I had no menstruation for four months in the following period, I was given no treatment. Some of my physical complaints still continue.[1]

(signed here and at every page)
Semra

We should pause at this account, for the Turkish government is supposed to be on 'our' side. It is a member of NATO; it trades with the US and the EEC; and it seeks, with us, to protect itself from the 'Russian threat'. Yet it is guilty of violations of human rights that, as just recounted, almost defy belief.

Britain's treatment of prisoners in Northern Ireland is another example, not only of inhumane treatment but of how governments can turn a blind eye to their own cruelty while criticising others. Internment without trial was introduced in Northern Ireland on 9 August 1971. On that day, 342 arrests were made, and large numbers of arrests continued for several days. By the end of the week, the first reports of brutality on the part of the British Army started to find their way into the media.

On 31 August 1971, the British Home Secretary appointed a three person committee, chaired by Sir Edward Compton, to investigate. The committee did conclude that loud noise, sleep deprivation and hooding had been employed by British security forces to 'aid' in the extraction of information from the prisoners but it asserted this behaviour only constituted 'physical ill-treatment'. It was not 'brutality', said the committee, because 'we consider that brutality is an inhuman or savage form of cruelty, and that cruelty implies a disposition to inflict suffering, coupled with indifference to, or pleasure in, the victim's pain'.[2] According to this definition, the regretted use of electric shocks to extract information would be neither brutal nor cruel and would be called necessary under the circumstances.

Amnesty International also conducted an investigation. Its conclusions presented medical and psychiatric evidence of long-term damage due to the 'physical ill-treatment' of the Irish prisoners. "It is a form of torture," the report said, "to force a man to stand at the wall in the posture described for many hours in succession, in some cases for days on end, progressively exhausted and driven literally out of his mind by being subjected to continuing noise, and being deprived of food, sleep and even of light."[3] In 1976, the European Commission on Human Rights also found the British distinction between 'physical ill-treatment' and cruelty a little esoteric. Its verdict on British behaviour: guilty of "torture, inhuman and degrading treatment". Moreover, the Commission found that the use of torture was an administrative practice, with a history of condonement by the British authorities.

British use of torture continues in Northern Ireland. There are continued reports of Irish prisoners being subjected to extreme brutality in the effort to extract information from them; extended periods of solitary confinement, forced sleeplessness, sensory deprivation, long exposure to the cold, frequent beatings, the use of electric shocks, and threats to the families of the prisoners.

Similar examples and trends can be found in virtually every other West European country, particularly West Germany. It is also true in the United States, particularly against the American Indians, who over the last several centuries have been subjected to what can only be described as attempted genocide.

Besides having one of the worst records of brutality and violations of human rights based on racial prejudice, the United States has perhaps the worst record in terms of keeping computer data on its citizens and conducting electronic surveillance against them. The Georgia Power Company, for instance, began keeping files on 'subversives' and 'sexual deviates, sickos and pinkos' in 1973. It operates an undercover intelligence unit with an annual budget of $750,000. Staffing the unit are former agents of the Federal Bureau of Investigation (FBI), the Central Intelligence Agency (CIA), Army Intelligence, the Federal Bureau of Alcohol, Tobacco and Firearms, and the Georgia Bureau of Investigation. Each Georgia Power surveillance car is equipped with a pistol, shotgun, two way radio, camera for infra-red photography in darkness, and a special device that can change the configuration of the headlights to confuse the driver of the car being followed.

The Georgia Power Company is not alone. It is plugged into a national network that circulates information on so-called dissidents. One link in this network is a thirty-page bi-weekly newsletter called 'Information Digest'. This newsletter develops dossiers on literally thousands of Americans who have neither committed a crime nor are suspects. It acts as the processing centre for a network of hidden informants whose information is recorded by police departments throughout the nation without the individual knowing that he or she is being watched. There is also no independent checking by police as to the validity and source of the information obtained.

The CIA, FBI, Internal Revenue Service (IRS), the National Security Agency, the Drug Enforcement Agency, and the US Customs all use 'Information Digest'.

There is also what is called the Law Enforcement Intelligence Unit (LEIU), a private intelligence system that collects information on known criminals and 'terrorist suspects'. It links the intelligence units of most of the police forces in the US and Canada. It has contacts with the US Department of Labor and Air Force and Coast Guard Intelligence. As a private club, however, the LEIU is not subject to federal, state, or citizen control. Therefore, it can be essentially a law unto itself, capable of actually doing the 'dirty tricks' that the official agencies like the FBI and CIA are legally precluded from doing. It is also linked with the security forces of the major corporations, particularly those working for the Pentagon and especially in the nuclear industry—like Lockheed and Kerr-McGee.

The LEIU was founded in 1956 by policemen as a way to break the FBI's monopoly on the files of criminals and suspects. By 1975, the LEIU had almost become a mini-FBI, with some 225 law enforcement agency members. New applicants must be sponsored by one LEIU member and endorsed by at least three more. Before admittance, the applicants are extensively vetted to see if they are trustworthy and leakproof. Once accepted, only one person in the unit receives LEIU secret suspect files. These are 5-by-8 inch index cards with background information on the suspect and a source to contact for more information.

When the LEIU representative in a particular police unit leaves, membership is suspended until another trustworthy representative can be appointed and approved. If any LEIU member organisation either breaks security or gives files to non-LEIU members, it can be suspended. Several LEIU members have been charged with illegal wiretapping and surveillance. This includes city police departments in Chicago, Baltimore, Houston and Fairfax, Virginia and the state police in Michigan.

Despite its non-governmental status, record of illegality and secrecy, the LEIU has been the recipient of government funds. The Law Enforcement Assistance Administration, a Justice Department programme, has been allocating tax payers' money into the LEIU for over a decade. One allocation was a $1.7 million grant to the Californian Department of Justice to put LEIU files on a central computer at the Michigan State Police headquarters in East Lansing. Altogether, a national network with thirty known on-line computer terminals in various parts of the United States has been set up under the codename 'Project Search'.

A similar situation is emerging in Western Europe. Beginning in 1975, the nine nations of the European Economic Community (EEC) have been developing increasingly close co-operation between their police forces. In 1977, the European Convention on the Suppression of Terrorism was signed. It aimed at making extradition automatic for an extensive number of offences by stating that a variety of acts could be considered 'political' no matter who committed them or why. In effect, political asylum between signatory countries was seriously curtailed.

In 1979, the Dublin Convention was secretly signed during a European Council meeting in Dublin, Ireland. The text of this agreement introduced automatic extradition for *all* crimes for which the maximum penalty is imprisonment of a year or more. French President Giscard D'Estaing hailed the agreement as the first stage towards a European 'judicial area'. The European Convention on the Suppression of Terrorism and the Dublin Convention seek to establish a police enforcement link between the nine countries of the EEC not subject to either parliamentary or judicial control at either the national or the community level.

Like the US, Western European governments purport to share a commitment to democratic principles. Like the US, Western European governments are concerned with the threat of the 'terrorists' who are not so much against a particular national regime, as against the very political and economic system common to Western Europe and the United States. The terrorists violently threaten the democratic and capitalist institutions upon which the society of the West relies. Ironically, in the battle against 'terrorism', western governments are destroying the very liberties they claim to protect against terrorism. What is more, they are not inhibiting terrorism; they are curtailing the rights of citizens.

The governments pushing hardest for the creation of a European 'judicial area'—Britain, France and West Germany—are setting in motion a series of inter-related attacks on civil liberties. One is a steady expansion of the notion of who is 'suspect'. Another is the growing erosion of privacy through widespread use of surveillance techniques, including phone tapping, and growing use of computers and data-banks. Thirdly, there is a sustained erosion of the rights and guarantees of those who have been found to be 'suspect' and those who have been accused or sentenced. Rights of defence lawyers are being curtailed and inhuman and degrading treatment of prisoners is increasing, particularly in the area of isolation techniques. Bobby Sands, imprisoned by the British authorities for 'subversive' activities in Northern Ireland, was kept in solitary confinement for nearly two years.

Of all Western European countries it is West Germany which has led the way in creating the essential components of a police state. The German *Berufsverbot* is a case in point. It was made law in 1972 in order to exclude 'communists' from public service jobs. Since then, literally millions of people have been investigated. Tens of thousands have been either refused employment or sacked from their jobs on the basis of the investigations made.

Victims of this law have not been communists so much as militant unionists, progressives within the different political parties, campaigners for ecological protection, the gypsies, people in the anti-nuclear movement, and advocates of non-violence—all those who are potential dissidents and centres of various streams of dissatisfaction within the system.

What this has meant has been the creation of a vast apparatus by which applicants to all government jobs and most industry posts can be given careful ideological screening. The dossiers which have been accumulated record a wealth of private information, not only about the person's political activities and opinions, but about his or her personal relationships, finances, background and character traits. An investigation done by a business consultant for the German business weekly, *Wirtschaftswoche* showed the ways that applicants are selected or rejected on the basis of opinions and prejudices. Stricter criteria are applied when recruiting for any section of industry connected with the nuclear weapons-nuclear energy complex.

The body that is central to the West German apparatus of political surveillance is called the *Verfassungsschutz*—the 'defenders of the Constitution'. Legalised in 1950, it is separate from the various German police agencies and from the Federal Secret Service. The Ministry of Interior describes it as a 'secret intelligence agency'. Its existence reflects the German government's concept of democracy and how that is to be defended.

The Federal Constitutional Court has said in a ruling: ' . . . Germany is a democracy which will not accept abuse of basic rights to fight against the free principles of the Constitution, which also expects its citizens to defend these principles, and will not tolerate opponents of these principles *even if they remain within legal boundaries'*.[4] Federal German courts have ruled that persons who use violence are 'enemies of the state'. Few would quarrel with that. But the courts have also defined what violence is. They ruled in 1972 that 'the use of violence is considered illegal *even if it is in the form of passive resistance (sit-in strikes)'*.[5]

It is against this background that the *Verfassungsshutz* works. Its

Groups	Criteria	Steps to be taken
Smokers	Greater liability to illness Greater nervousness	Observations at interview
Homosexuals	Unsympathetic, unsuitable for certain positions, e.g. instructor, personnel manager	Psychological tests, employ detective, reference
Severely disabled	Difficulties in event of dismissal, general prejudice against disabled	General observations at interview, tax card
Wrong or no religious denomination stated	Dislike of certain denominations, regional and local considerations	Driving licence, interview, psychological tests
Wrong regional origin or dialect	Presumed difficulties of making contact in different environment	Telephone interview interview
Women	Presumed unsuitability for executive positions, possible pregnancies, general prejudice	General observation
Foreigners	Presumed unreliability, customer prejudices	Curriculum vitae, interview
Members of left-wing organizations	Presumed causers of unrest, agitators	Psychological test, employment of detective
Graduates of certain faculties of the Free University of Berlin or of Bremen University	Products of presumed hotbeds of Marxism	Degree, curriculum vitae
Graduates of international business schools	Presumably too ambitious for small firms	Degree, analysis of curriculum vitae
Bachelors	Presumption of irregular life	Analysis of curriculum vitae, interview
Divorced	Presumption of unreliability	Analysis of curriculum vitae

(From: *The Nuclear State* by Robert Jungk)

activities are officially limited to the gathering of information without any executive powers—arrest, interrogation, search, etc. But its links are so close with the people who do have executive power—the police and the courts—that *Verfassungsshutz* acquires the mantle of secret police. It has three main targets: all those criticising or working against the democratic system as defined by the Federal government; all foreigners belonging to extremist groups; and those suspected of being agents of foreign powers.

West Germany has gone further in the use of computers by the police than any country except the United States. Police began installing them in 1968. Computers totally change two key factors in police work: the amount of information that can be stored and the time required for retrieval of that information. Information on 8–9 million people is already stored in secret computer banks and legislation under debate would have *every* citizen write out a 200 item registration form for police use. The potential of the computer is revealed by Horst Hevold, president of the German Federal Criminal Investigation Department:

> ... the police possess the privilege of having access to knowledge superior to all other organs of the state, making it possible to gain insight into abnormal forms of behaviour and defect structures in society. Their ability to diagnose important aspects of social developments frees them from the executor role which they were forced to carry out and obey till now. Society's increasing knowledge is also being put to use by the police—*to the advantage of all*: the police force of the future will be a different one, of a higher level, one *with a function caring for the health of society.*[5]

There are no less than four major computers keeping track of people in West Germany. NADIS, the *Verfassungsschutz* computer, was known in 1979 to have 2.5 million people on file, mostly applicants for civil service jobs. The NADIS computer keeps records of all who are considered a security risk. This includes anyone who has ever travelled to a socialist country or who has relatives who have. NADIS also collects information on people with characteristics considered questionable by *Verfassungs-schutz*—mental disturbances, criminality, drunkenness, drug use, gambling debts, talkativeness, sexual abnormality.

INPOL, the computer for the Federal Criminal Investigation department, was installed in 1972. INPOL has 1,527 terminals in various police stations, border controls and airports. Mobile terminals are being installed in every police car at a cost of DM 30,000 each. INPOL information includes a Central Person Index; a Person Identification Centre for Terrorist Violence (known to number 3,600 in 1979); a Wanted Persons Register, which includes the category of 'demonstrators'; Objects Register, which covers all lost or stolen goods; and a Register of Arrests, covering all those in prison and all those admitted for psychiatric treatment.

PIOS (Persons, Institutions, Objects, Things) is a section of the INPOL computer recording data about anyone or anything involved in any way with 'terrorism'. This includes members of support committees for political prisoners, firms that 'terrorists' once worked for, and an index to 12 million pages of court files. PIOS also registers all who carry out 'violent demonstrations', which includes any anti-nuclear demonstrators. PIOS is also known to have registered 1,000 communes and the people living in them.

INPOL has been spreading across Europe. It now has terminals in Paris, Rome and Rotterdam. All stolen vehicles and lost passports in all Western European countries go on the INPOL computer. There is growing evidence that INPOL is destined to act as a central information depot for Western Europe.

The INPOL computer is so voracious that one member of the police computer staff is quoted as saying that in the early days there was an office party for every further 100,000 entries. By 1976 there were 3.2 million people on file, plus fingerprints and photographs. That's one party every six weeks.

The other two computers in use by *Verfassungsschutz* and the West German authorities are the computers of the Federal Secret Service Agency which concerns itself with foreign espionage; and the computer of the Military Intelligence service, known as MAD, which has data on more than 3 million Germans who have done military service.

The *Verfassungsschutz* goes to great lengths to collect information. Since 1978, mass controls at road blocks have been legalised; all who rent cars have been subjected to security checks; and all hotel guests have had to fill out their registration forms in handwriting so as to allow for police handwriting checks. Recently, the notion of the 'friendly local cop' has been introduced. Policemen are given small areas to patrol and are directed to be 'helpful' and gather as much information as possible.

The other European country heavily involved in the computer and electronic surveillance of its citizens is Britain. A branch of British Security Service, the MI5, has the largest government databank in Britain. Their computer—a 'dual' ICL 2980—has a computer memory, which even by the standards of an industry accustomed to superlatives, can only be described as gigantic. Its 'discs' can store 20,000 million characters, or 20 'gigabytes' of information. This is the equivalent of the information contained in about 50,000 paperback books. Or, it could store personal dossiers on more than 20 million people, if the dossiers consisted of identifying particulars and about 150 descriptive words.

This MI5 computer is two and half times as big as the Police National Computer (PNC). The PNC itself has some 40 million personal records and is checked tens of thousands of times daily by police and government officials. MI5 files are also in addition to the 1.3 million Special Branch files already on computer at the New Scotland Yard. MI5 have authorisation from the Prime Minister for access to these other government databanks.

In 1980, it was estimated that there were over 200 separate government computers in use for 'general and administrative' purposes. A 1975 White Paper listed 220 databanks with information about people outside government employment. The MI5 charter, issued by the Ministry of Defence and made public in Australia but not in Britain, gives the Director-General specific access to all these other government files:

> You will arrange to have such access to the records of Government Departments and agencies as you may deem necessary for the purposes of your work ... You will establish a comprehensive set of security records. In order to do this you will arrange that all Government Departments and agencies submit to you for inclusion in your records all information bearing on security which may be, or come into their possession.[6]

A major part of the MI5 computer's retrieval system is by a technique called Free Text Retrieval (FTR), which enables the user to gather information on any subject or combination of subjects almost instantaneously. A 1978 Government report stated that the FTR systems "provide an easy method of browsing through collections of information (and) are well suited to surveillance requirements such as criminal intelligence or the preservation of national security .... They are ideally suited to the retrieval of every occurrence of particular items of information from a large mass, and for discovering the relationship of one piece of information with another".[7]

The key to the linkage of personal files on the hundreds of computers the MI5 computer has access to is a person's National Insurance number. Because each person must have one to be gainfully employed, the MI5 has access to most of the adult population of Britain. This was clearly shown in 1980 when a London magazine was inadvertently sent a copy of a letter from Special Branch detectives in Dumfries to Box 500 in London—the codename for MI5. MI5 had sought information about a young left wing shop steward in the Dumfries area, James Hogg. To each reference to his name was appended his National Insurance number.

The cost of building the MI5 computer is estimated at between £15 and £20 million. This money is carefully laundered through 'miscellaneous' programmes in the Ministry of Defence budget. When questioned about using funds not open to public scrutiny but used to scrutinise the public, MoD Permanent Secretary Sir Frank Cooper claimed that such an arrangement was legitimate. Covert use of MoD funds for the MI5 were 'fully accountable in every sense of the word'.[8]

This claim is strange one, since no questions about MI5 are ever even *allowed* in Parliament.

Connected with computers is the use of electronic surveillance devices to monitor people's activities and conversations. Phone tapping was made legal in West Germany in 1968, subject of course to 'ministerial control'. It has been Britain, however, that has been the most flagrant violator in this area of electronic surveillance. In 1979, the weekly *New Statesman* revealed the existence in London of a special building with the equipment necessary to tap up to 1,000 phone lines, to apply voice-recognition techniques, and to automatically type out suspect conversations. In July 1980 the British Postal and Telecommunications Workers Union warned that phone tapping was getting out of hand. It drew attention to the fact that the US National Security Agency was operating inside Britain, monitoring *every* call made from Britain to another country as well as tapping into the Western European communications network on a massive scale.

Once a person becomes suspect, his or her right to defence begins to be increasingly curtailed. While in France and Britain the lawyer is identified with his or her client, in West Germany the legal tradition has implicitly expected the lawyer to be on the side of the established system. Because of this, West Germany has gone the furthest in eroding the rights of the accused persons. Lawyers are hindered from defending those accused of 'terrorism'. Lawyers are forbidden to defend more than one client simultaneously. Lawyers are often refused access to the accused and are frequently themselves charged with being 'accomplices'. Before seeing their clients in prison, they are frequently subjected to body searches.

The German model is being followed in other countries. In Italy, pressure and attacks against lawyers defending persons accused of terrorism became so great that in April 1980, one lawyer, Apazzali, was arrested and one, Arnaldi, committed suicide. In Belgium, Michel Grainderge, a lawyer with 'left wing sympathies' was arrested. Even in the Netherlands, lawyers came under fire for being 'accomplices' when they protested against illegal interrogations by German police of suspected 'terrorists' arrested in Holland.

The accused themselves are being subjected to increasingly harsh treatment. British and Turkish torture methods have already been detailed. In West Germany scores of people suspected of being 'terrorists' have been subjected not just to solitary confinement but to various techniques of sensory deprivation which can lead to physical illness and ultimately to insanity. In France, five women were arrested in Paris as 'suspected terrorists' in June 1981, at the request of the West German police. They were held in solitary confinement for 23 hours each day for the several weeks it took to conduct the extradition hearings. Moves by French lawyers to have the women treated normally and to find out who had ordered this special confinement yielded no results.

The growing erosion of civil liberties in Western Europe and the United States is closely linked with the nuclear energy-nuclear weapons complex, which mandates a psyche all its own. This complex creates the necessity for secrecy on the one hand and greater protection of investment on the other. Not only are there high financial and environmental risks but also potential ramifications beyond national boundaries. Because of the 'plutonium culture' generated by the nuclear complex , the age old dilemma of striking a balance betwen state authority and the rights of the individual is being forced to opt for increasing state control, and diminishing individual freedom. The plutonium culture allows for no other choice.

Each operating nuclear reactor produces between 400 to 600 pounds of plutonium waste each year. Less than one millionth of a gram, if ingested, can cause cancer and/or genetic mutation. Twenty pounds, if properly fashioned, can be made into a nuclear bomb. Because of this, *the different aspects of the plutonium economy must be as tightly guarded as nuclear weapons themselves*. Nuclear weapons are kept at military facilities generally away from population centres and specifically under guard in a military system predicated upon discipline, hierarchy and authoritarian leadership. Similar protection for the 'atoms for peace' programme will have a devastating impact upon the democratic freedoms and civil liberties of the citizens.

The potential problem with the plutonium economy and its relation to human freedom has been succinctly expressed by a statement made by Dr. Bernard Feld, Chairperson of the Atomic and High Energy Physics Department of the Massachusetts Institute of Technology:

> Let me tell you about a nightmare I have. The Mayor of Boston sends for me for an urgent consultation. He has received a note from a terrorist group telling him that they have planted a nuclear bomb somewhere in central Boston. The Mayor has

confirmed that 20 pounds of plutonium is missing from Government stocks. He shows me the crude diagram and a set of the terrorists outrageous demands. I know—as one of those who participated in the assembly of the first atomic bomb—that the device would work. Not efficiently, but nevertheless with devastating effect. What should I do? Surrender to blackmail or risk destroying my home town?[9]

The dangers are real, so real that government planners in every country with nuclear programmes have undertaken steps to be prepared for Dr. Feld's scenario. In 1975, the Nuclear Regulatory Commission (NRC) commissioned a specific study of the problem. One of the participants, Professor John Barton, Professor of Jurisprudence at Stanford University Law School, prepared a paper entitled 'Intensified Nuclear Safeguards and Civil Liberties'. The document began by stating that:

Increased public concern with nuclear terrorism, coupled with the possibility of greatly increased use of plutonium in civilian power reactors, are leading the US Nuclear Regulatory Commission (NRC) to consider various forms of intensified safeguards against theft or loss of nuclear materials and against *sabotage*. The intensified safeguards could include expansion of personnel clearance programs, a nationwide guard force, *greater surveillance of dissenting political groups*, area searches in the event of a loss of materials, and creation of *new barriers of secrecy* around parts of the nuclear program.[10]

It is important to be clear what the above statement implies. The governments supporting nuclear power are attempting to protect the plutonium economy from two perceived enemies: first, those who would use the nuclear materials to terrorise the country through some type of nuclear sabotage; and second, those who seek to stop nuclear power, meaning anti-nuclear 'dissenting political groups'. This requires a nationwide guard force to be created specifically to deal with any terrorism and the erection of new barriers of secrecy around the nuclear programmes to keep public knowledge and participation at a minimum. Both sets of enemies would be subject to greater surveillance through electronic listening devices such as phone taps.

In Britain, for instance, it is accepted as a matter of course that anyone working for the Atomic Energy Authority be 'positively vetted' before being appointed. The Official Secrets Act, moreover, allows the government and the atomic industry to keep the nuclear installations cloaked in secrecy and the employees forbidden to communicate anything about their work. In 1976, Britain also became the first country to establish by law a nationwide guard force of constables under the direct control of the atomic authorities in order to guard nuclear facilities and specifically the plutonium stores. This guard force has privileges in relation to carrying weapons not granted to any other British police unit. Indeed, so sensitive are these privileges that under the Official Secrets Act, information about them has not been made available to the public. This force is mandated not only to guard against possible terrorism but to keep tabs on 'dissenting political groups'.

Jonathan Rosenhead, of the London School of Economics, points out that this type of political control is very easily overlooked by the general populace because it is specifically designed and intended to be used as inconspicuously as possible. In America, political scientists refer to this technique as the "politics of the iron fist in the velvet glove". "What the ruling groups prefer", he says,

is to produce a situation in which no one dares oppose their plans. Their favourite methods are therefore to exploit people's dependence on consumer goods and on their jobs and exercising prevention controls by means of intensive surveillance. In the event of open conflict breaking out in spite of that, they would hope at least to contain it by 'limited operations'.[11]

What needs to be remembered in assessing this state of affairs is that plutonium, if it is to be used, must be protected by police state methods. We just cannot have something that can be used for nuclear bombs and can damage and mutate human life with the lethalness of millions of cancer doses per pound floating about in a free society. *A plutonium economy and a free democracy are a contradiction in terms.* This is a fact that has been recognised by leading legal experts and politicians alike. Writing in the *Harvard Law Review*, Russell Ayres states flatly that 'plutonium provides the first rational justification for widespread intelligence gathering against the civilian population'.[12] The reason for this is that the threat of nuclear terrorism justifies such encroachments on civil liberties for 'national security' reasons. It is inevitable, therefore, says Ayres, that "plutonium use would create pressures for infiltration into civic, political, environmental and professional groups to a far greater extent than previously encountered and with a greater impact on speech and associated rights". Sir Brian Flowers, in Britain, has come to similar conclusions. At the end of his environmental impact statement for the plutonium economy in the United Kingdom, known as the Flowers Report, he made it quite clear that Britain could not have both plutonium and civil liberties. Rather, he said, to adopt the plutonium economy would make 'inevitable' the erosion of the freedoms that British people had fought for over the centuries and have come to assume and accept as inalienable rights.

What is happening to Western Europe and the US should not be seen as an abnormal occurrence; rather, it should be viewed as the *logical progression* of what the adoption of the plutonium economy in any country implies. There are certain psychological implications inherent in the use and development of nuclear weapons. There are direct physical results on both workers and public alike from the nuclear fuel cycle. So, too, the plutonium economy makes inevitable the erosion of human rights.

Observers in the Netherlands and West Germany refer to the decline of the *Rechtsstadt* (meaning a state guided by laws which are both just and accepted) and the rise of the *Machtstadt*, where state authority is based on power equations. In the US, it is sometimes referred to as a 'national security state'. We prefer the term *totalitarian democracy* to characterise the governments of the US and Western Europe. It denotes a governmental system of parliamentary democracy within which the official bureaucracy, the police, and the legal authorities are vested with almost total power over the individual.

It has been apparent for some time that the drive in the West for all-out growth, dictated by the need for capital accumulation and profits, has been creating problems that existing institutions, be they national or international, are simply not equipped to handle. These include:

— the alienation through and ruthlessness of the multinational corporations;
— the frustrations of an economy where automation and machinery are replacing human skills and ingenuity;
— the gnawing fears and anxieties aroused by the 'diseases of affluence', notably cancer, heart disease and stress;
— and the looming threat of environmental destruction, be it at the local or planetary level, from chemical pollution, or the plutonium economy.

As long as the boom lasted, and Western affluence was sustained these pressures could be ignored. But that 'boom-balloon' has burst. The energy crisis is deepening. The economic reality of increased unemployment and inflation is becoming more and more depressing. The pressures of burgeoning populations, as also the youth demanding employment and a piece of the good life, are becoming unbearable.

In order to survive this 'crisis of capitalism', the dominant forces in industry and government are forcing through a ruthless restructuring and re-grouping of the economic system. In Western Europe this is reflected in the wholesale writing-off of vast sectors of traditional industry such as steel and textiles and the resultant social decline of whole areas. The trend is to form blocs such as the EEC but this in turn places increased strain on the member states and does little more than paper over the fundamental problems with another layer of bureaucracy. Under this weight, the welfare state that grew up in the decades after World War II is being dismantled, to squeeze just a bit more money to spend, as often as not, on more weapon systems. In the process, yet another safety net is removed for the individual who is the victim of the capitalist system. If it is any consolation, Marxism hasn't come up with any answers either.

Those in power know they have no way to solve the problems or meet the demands of their youth, of the millions of unemployed, of the anti-nuclear movement, of the populations in economically depressed areas, of the victims of industrial disasters, or of any other discontented groups. The only valid answers are ones which involve fundamental changes in our thinking and in our system itself, and these are ones which those in power are not in a position to offer. So they placate their constituencies with promises which they know they cannot fulfil.

This only adds to the frustration of those who can no longer wait. The next stage after fruitless protest cannot fail to be a challenge to that part of the system of which the individual has become the victim. If this challenge is met with either refusal or with repression, the frustration of those in protest can lead to violent action. Protest by violence against the system which cannot meet their demands when peacefully presented is labelled by those in power as 'terrorism'.

Foreseeing this scenario, the reaction of the dominant groups is to proclaim the necessity to prepare in time to deal effectively with those who are discontented. When there are violations that cannot be put right, then freedom to criticise and, in the end, democracy itself become hostage to 'effective governance'. It is an axiom of history that when the people begin to question the right of their leaders to govern, the leaders question the right of the people to question.

The irony of this situation within the conflict of East-West relations is that although the starting point of their analyses are different, the conclusions drawn by the Soviet leaders and the governing groups in the West are the same: both regard effective governance as being hindered by a genuine democratic government. The result in the East has been the 'dictatorship of the proletariat'; in the West, 'totalitarian democracy'.

While it is true that the system of repression in the West is not as extensive or as brutal as in the East, except in isolated cases, what is necessary to remember is that the *mentality* of the oppressor, whether in the Kremlin or in 10 Downing Street or in the White House, is the same. What is different are the *mechanisms* which oppress the people below. In both cases what is achieved is the setting up of a *standard of behaviour* which, because there are no alternatives allowed, becomes the *pattern of behaviour*. This creates a dangerous person-into-machine social norm. In the Soviet Union this has been done with a ruthlessness that needed only the unity and discipline of the Party; in the West mass control has been achieved by subtle manipulation that needs either public ignorance or public apathy to be effective. Social control is justified, particularly as far as the plutonium economy is concerned, by the over-riding necessity to avoid the catastrophe which might occur either through carelessness, disobedience, or 'terrorism'. This cultivated attitude enables the Western technocrats to represent themselves to the public as the guardians of the society in the emergency situation they themselves inspired and engineered.

The tragedy of the Russian people is the suffering of individuals endowed with a passion for personal freedom so profound as to verge on the anarchic, and yet who have been forced to live under a despotism resolutely intent upon the suppression of that freedom.

The tragedy unfolding in the West is of a people who achieved liberty at great cost, but who now, faced with the despotism inherent in the plutonium economy, are abnegating it. They are rendering themselves subservient to those few who wish to build a national security state supplied with nuclear energy and armed with nuclear weapons. Our leaders are depriving us of the very liberties they have been entrusted to defend. Moreover, they are manipulating the 'Russian threat' to justify such actions, all the while claiming that they are protecting democracy. Never before have so few asked so many for so much for the sake of so little.

7 The Rise and Fall of the 'Soviet Threat'

Daniel Yergin, in his study of the cold war, *Shattered Peace*, coined two terms—'Riga axiom' and 'Yalta axiom'—with which to distinguish different western perceptions of Soviet behaviour. 'Riga' is the capital of Latvia and the term 'Riga axiom' signifies the perception of the Soviets as aggressively hostile and expansionist.

The 'Yalta axiom' signifies another perception. Named after Yalta, the city at which Roosevelt, Churchill and Stalin settled the nature of the post-war world, this axiom sees the Soviet Union as a rival but one which can be addressed as much through mutual accommodation of interests as by military strength. It was in the spirit of the 'Yalta axiom' that the SALT I and II agreements were negotiated; that Nixon and Brezhnev worked out the agreements that constituted the era of detente; and which allow normal embassy and diplomatic exchanges to take place. The difference between the Riga and Yalta perceptions is not in the degree of hostility, but in terms of the *appropriate response* to the other superpower. The Riga axiom implies military confrontation. The Yalta axiom leads to diplomatic dialogue. Perceptions of the Soviet threat in the West have tended to fluctuate between both these extremes.

A rise in the Riga axiom generally begins when (a) some important group of policymakers, either officially or unofficially, makes a report claiming that the Soviets are getting stronger and the NATO alliance and/or the US are getting weaker; and (b) something is actually done to demonstrate US and NATO resolve in the face of the threat the report describes. In 1945, for instance, the famous 'long-telegram' written by George Kennan from Moscow reminded the US State Department about the "inherent tendency" of the Soviet Union to expand. In 1950, the National Security Council document NSC–68, a top secret report on Soviet intentions, warned that

> The Kremlin's policy towards areas not under its control is the elimination of resistance to its will and the extension of its influence and control. It is driven to follow this policy because it cannot ... tolerate the existence of free societies; to the

Kremlin the most mild and inoffensive free society is an affront,
a challenge and a subversive influence. Given the nature of the
Kremlin, and the evidence at hand, it seems clear that the ends
towards which this policy is directed are the same as those
where its control is already established.[1]

NSC–68 denied that the USSR could ever act like Britain, France,
Germany or the US who by choice would maximise their influence
in certain places and allow others to do the same elsewhere.
NSC–68 asserted it was in the very core of Soviet character to
expand *everywhere*. The model of totalitarianism used by NSC–68
to analyse Soviet intentions was that of Nazi Germany. That the
Soviet Union was a completely different social structure in a
different historical context was ignored.

Although NSC–68 was never officially adopted by the Truman
administration, it is generally viewed as a turning point in US and
Western European assessment of Soviet intentions and behaviour.
Its effect was to cause two transformations of perception. First, it
called for major increases in defence spending to counter the
Soviet threat; and second, to quote former Secretary of State Dean
Acheson, it was used "to bludgeon the mass mind of 'top
government' so that not only could the President make a decision
but the decision could be carried out".[2] After NSC–68, dissenters
from the Riga axiom had a very difficult time getting a hearing.
Now more united, and having an authoritative document to use
for bludgeoning, the governing elite could convey the impression
of the Soviet threat with greater clarity to the public of America and
Western Europe. Thus they could obtain support for the particular
foreign policy programmes they wanted.

Subsequent to NSC–68 other documents have appeared. They
have reiterated the same basic themes during times when the
government elites of either the US or NATO countries needed to
remind their people just how bad the Russians really are. The best-
selling books of Henry Kissinger and General Maxwell Taylor
during the 1950s prophesied US and NATO weakness in the face
of the Soviet threat. In 1957, the Gaither Report warned that the
US and NATO were actually falling behind the Soviets and the
WTO. Re-affirming the NSC–68 consensus, the Gaither Report
made one point in particular which has haunted US and NATO
policymakers ever since: that the Soviets soon would have enough
ICBMs to overwhelm NATO and American defences. In the
strongest possible terms, the Gaither Report urged higher defence
budgets and the immediate indoctrination of the public to the
dangers at hand.

Since then other reports have come out. In 1976, a group calling
itself the Committee on the Present Danger was founded in the

US. It was composed of high ranking conservative political and military specialists, military planners and foreign policy experts. Warning that a new wave of Soviet expansionism was beginning, its report stated: "The principal threat to our nation, to world peace, and to the cause of human freedom is the Soviet drive for dominance ... The Soviet Union has not altered its long-held goal of a world dominated by a single centre—Moscow".[3]

After a document such as NSC–68 or the Gaither Report is read and debated, a new consensus forms about the Soviet threat. As a result, the second component of the cluster of events takes place which makes the Riga axiom a reality—this involves the concrete steps the US and/or NATO take to express concern. This generally occurs in two ways: first, a rise in defence spending takes place; and, secondly, a decision is taken to demonstrate US and NATO 'resolve' in some specific way.

In the wake of the Gaither Report, for instance, President Kennedy was elected. During his first year in office, he increased the defence budget by 15%; he tripled draft calls; he asked for the power to call up reserves; and he supported a civil defence programme. Various authors of both NSC–68 and the Gaither Report were given high ranking posts in the State and Defense Departments as well as the NATO command structure. Kennedy also gave his Secretary of Defense MacNamara virtual free reign in making US military power more 'useable' in controlling world events. In particular, he supported the sending of 'Special Forces' to engage in counter-insurgency warfare whenever US interests were threatened. In early 1963, Kennedy sent a 1200-strong 'Special Force' to Vietnam.

Alan Wolfe, a military analyst, has noted two peaks, two valleys and a present peak in the Western perception of the Russian threat.[4] He identifies the peaks and valleys of the Soviet threat as follows:

1) The first peak followed the end of World War II. It involved the 'long-telegram' of George Kennan and NSC–68, which reminded the West that the Soviet Union was inherently expansionist. To counter this expansionism, Truman enunciated his 'Truman Doctrine' which called upon Western Europe and the US to unite against the Soviets in Korea and China and over such matters as Trieste, Iran and reparations. NATO was formed and the decision to construct the hydrogen bomb was taken. This first peak of anti--Soviet sentiment created certain negative elements which have remained embedded in the US and Western European perceptions of the Soviet Union ever since. This peak inaugurated the Cold War.

2) The first valley involved the retrenchment under Eisenhower

from 1952–1957. This might seem strange, given the fact that Secretary of State, John Foster Dulles, was so vehemently anti-Communist. Yet Nikita Khrushchev in his *Memoirs* records the following observation about Dulles:

> Dulles often said that the goal of the United States was to push Socialism in Europe back to the borders of the Soviet Union, and he seemed obsessed with the idea of encirclement .... However, I'll say this for him: Dulles knew how far he could push us, and he never pushed us too far. For instance, when the forces of our two countries confronted each other in the Near East during the events in Syria and Lebanon in 1958, Dulles stepped back from the brink of war, the reactionary forces of the United States and England pulled back their troops, partly as a result of Dulles' prudence.[5]

In defence policy, the US repudiated the doctrines of NSC–68 in favour of what Eisenhower termed the 'new look' in military strategy which meant 'stability of expenditures' and 'maximum protection at bearable costs'. Overall, this period of retrenchment saw a greater number of foreign policy adventures than during Truman's administration, 57 in eight years as opposed to 35 in six. However, a majority of US interventions were to save the world for US economic interests rather than from Soviet political influence. Guatemala 1954 is a case in point. The Suez Canal Fiasco also occurred during this period. Britain intervened not to stem the tide of Soviet aggression but to protect British interests.

3) The second peak in anti-Soviet sentiment occurred between 1957–1963. The authors of NSC–68, extremely disenchanted with Eisenhower's retrenchment, regrouped and conducted another top-secret review of Soviet capabilities. This was the Gaither Report, already discussed, which projected that the Soviet Union would soon 'surpass' the US military capabilities.

President Kennedy's militarism in the wake of the Gaither Report and the books by Henry Kissinger, Maxwell Taylor et al, would not have been possible without this rekindling of the image of the Soviet Union as a threat. US Secretary of State Dean Rusk enunciated the domino theory and made it a pillar of US foreign policy. He believed that if one country 'falls' to the Communists, others will necessarily follow. All conflicts were seen as tests of US resolve in the face of communist 'aggression'. In a period of just two years, Kennedy faced more foreign policy crises than Eisenhower had in his whole eight years in office. What is interesting to note is that the Soviets did not seem any more 'aggressive' than before. Despite his boasting, Khrushchev in fact downplayed military spending in favour of expansion of consumer goods. In 1956, he repudiated Stalinism and relaxed the Soviet hold over Eastern Europe, although after a time he sought to regain control. He enunciated a policy of 'peaceful coexistence'. It was characterised by attempts to win the favour of the newly independent Third World countries in the face of stiff competition from the erstwhile colonial powers, while trying to find some sort of compromise between cooperation with and challenge to the US. The policy of peaceful coexistence was the precursor to the Helsinki Agreement and 'detente'.

But Kennedy and his advisors chose to ignore the double aspect of Soviet policy in favour of the negative view set forth in the Gaither Report. It had warned of a Soviet superiority in intercontinental ballistic missiles (ICBMs) . Kennedy actually participated in mass scale propagation of this information, known at the time to be false, by capitalising on the so-called 'missile gap' in his campaign against Richard Nixon in 1960.

4) The second valley in the Soviet threat occurs during the years of detente, 1963–64, 1968–78. There is reason to believe that Kennedy had begun to revise his hard line anti-Soviet views. In a famous speech given on 10 June 1963, he stressed the importance of searching for areas of cooperation with the USSR. He then signed the Nuclear Test-ban Treaty with the Soviet Union and Britain. He also gave secret executive order, reported to be his last one, to withdraw the 'Special Force' he had sent to Vietnam. Before that could be implemented, Kennedy was assassinated in Dallas, Texas. With his death this order became null and void. At that point Lyndon Johnson took over the administration and within four years there were 500,000 US troops in Vietnam.

The escalation of hostilities in Vietnam postponed serious detente during the Johnson administration. However, when Nixon was elected detente began in earnest. Nixon's 1972 trip to China, for instance, marked a watershed in US foreign policy, for it brought to an end America's 20 year attempt to act as if the world's most populous country did not exist. Moreover, Nixon and Kissinger moved with determination to negotiate the SALT II Treaty, after obtaining ratification of SALT I. Indeed, more than any President before him, Nixon embraced the Yalta axiom in his perceptions of the Soviet Union.

This approach was due largely to the influence of Kissinger who, schooled in the Germanic tradition of political theory, believed power to be inherently conservative. Kissinger argued that leaders of countries attempt to protect their positions and are inherently suspicious of any challenges to their authority. This being the case, he recognised that both the US and USSR, despite differences in ideology, are basically two imperial powers who would act as conservative, not revolutionary forces. Kissinger argued that while there were many lesser powers throughout the world, the US and USSR were so overwhelmingly superior that they could ensure 'stability'. Rather than worrying about Soviet intentions, therefore, or seeing every local conflict as a test of US will against world communism—which Kissinger said merely 'confuses the debate'— the US should 'discipline power so that it bears a rational relationship to the objectives likely to be in dispute'.[6]

Kissinger's *realpolitik* ended the ideological excesses of the Kennedy-Johnson era and began the rhetoric of detente. While the eight years of Kennedy and Johnson administrations saw 88 foreign policy adventures, the Nixon and Ford administrations were involved only in 33. Expenditures on national defence as a percentage of Gross National Product fell from a high in Johnson's last year of 8.89% to 5.09% in 1976, when Ford left office.

To a large degree the reluctance of Nixon and Ford to use military force as an instrument of foreign policy was due to the public's reaction against Vietnam. But it also followed from the relaxation of tensions the era of detente implied. Without a hysterically negative view of the Soviet Union, it was difficult to justify an activist foreign policy.

The document that symbolised the spirit of detente more explicitly than perhaps any other was signed by Nixon and Brezhnev at the Soviet-US summit conference in May, 1972, when Nixon visited Moscow. Called the Basic Principles of Mutual Relations between the USSR and the USA, it formalised two fundamental principles between the two superpowers: the principle of peaceful coexistence and the principle of equality. The document stated that both countries

> will proceed from the common determination that in the nuclear age there is no alternative to conducting their mutual relations on the basis of peaceful coexistence. Differences in ideology and in the social systems of the USSR and the USA are not obstacles to the bilateral development of normal relations based on the principles of sovereignty, equality, non-interference in internal affairs and mutual advantage.[7]

Both sides pledged to continue efforts to limit armaments, noting that both regard as the ultimate goal of their efforts, the achievement of general and complete disarmament and the establishment of an effective system of international verification in accordance with the purposes and principles of the United Nations.

Both the USSR and US agreed to actively promote commercial and economic ties, contribute to the improvement of sea and air communications, develop cooperation in the fields of science and technology, expand cultural relations, and improve conditions for tourism. In all, the US signed nearly 70 agreements with the Soviet Union during the era of detente.

This spirit reverberated throughout Europe. In West Germany, a whole new era was ushered in with the USSR-FRG treaty of 12 August 1970, signed in Moscow by Chancellor Willy Brandt and President Brezhnev. After twenty-five years of uncertainty and friction over the status of the two Germanys and the border between East Germany, and Poland, the treaty stated that the Oder-Neisse line between Poland and East Germany, and the frontier between East Germany and West Germany would be "inviolable" and that "peace in Europe can be maintained only if no one encroaches on the present frontiers". At long last there was official recognition on both sides that the present borders of European countries should remain as they are.

The improvement of the general international situation made it possible to settle the specific question of West Berlin. Beginning with the crisis of 1948 when an attempt by Stalin to cut it off from the West was met with a US air lift, Berlin had been a constant source of friction. On 3 September 1971, after almost 17 months of difficult negotiations, the USSR, US, France and Britain signed a quadripartite agreement on West Berlin. The central element of agreement was the recognition that West Berlin does not belong to the Federal Republic of Germany. It also stipulated that all four powers would refrain from using force in solving future disputes over the city. The Soviets and East Germans also agreed to widen communication and transit links between Berlin and the West as well as to liberalise restrictions on travel and people-to-people contacts.

In Britain, too, there was a spirit of detente. During his period in office Harold Wilson visited the Soviet Union thrice, and the British Foreign Secretary went to Moscow four times. Soviet Foreign Minister Gromyko came to Britain in March 1965, and Premier Kosygin in February 1967. By 1965, Soviet-British trade grew to three times its 1958 level, and for a time Britain moved up to the first place in the USSR's trade with developed capitalist countries. In 1965–1969, both countries signed a Consular Convention, agreeing to exchanges in the fields of science, education and culture; signing a treaty on commercial shipping; agreeing to establish a direct teleprinter link-up between the Kremlin and 10 Downing Street; and increasing exchanges at departmental and ministerial levels.

Similar patterns can be traced in the Soviet relations with the rest of the NATO countries, with France, and with Japan. Indeed, so pervasive was the spirit of detente that at a meeting in Budapest on 17 March 1969, the Warsaw Treaty member states adopted a statement in which they called upon all European nations to begin the practical preparations for a Europe-wide conference. On 9 May 1969, the government of Finland sent a memorandum to all European countries and the USA and Canada, declaring that it was prepared to play host to such a European conference in Helsinki.

This initiative resulted in the European Conference on Security and Cooperation, attended by 33 European states (Albania was the only country to refuse to participate), the US and Canada. Final deliberations ended on 21 July 1975. Altogether, ten principles were established which were to govern the future of Europe: 1) the sovereign equality of all the 33 signatories and respect for the rights inherent in that sovereignty; 2) refraining from the threat or use of force; 3) the inviolability of frontiers; 4) the territorial integrity of states; 5) the peaceful settlement of all disputes between nations; 6) non-interference in the internal affairs of other nations; 7) respect for human rights and fundamental freedoms, including the freedom of thought, conscience, religion and belief; 8) equal rights and the self determination of peoples in accordance with the purposes and principles of the United Nations Charter; 9) cooperation between states at different cultural, economic and political levels; and 10) fulfilment in good faith of obligations under international law.

The Helsinki agreement accorded recognition to the situation as it had existed since the end of the Second World War. At Soviet insistence, existing boundaries were recognised and the principle of non-interference in the internal affairs of other states was accepted. At the same time, the demand by the US, Canada and the West European countries was met ensuring recognition of the basic freedom of thought, conscience and religion. Sovereign rights blended with human rights to make Europe a champion of both peace and freedom.

Yet within a few short years from Helsinki, even the term 'detente' had been banished from the US diplomatic lexicon. Why, after all it had achieved, did 'detente' become a dirty word?

On 8 June 1976, Leonid Brezhnev attempted an explanation: Detente has now become a visible reality. It has undoubtedly sunk deep roots. The prerequisites exist for making detente really irreversible. But one must see something else, namely, that the adversaries of detente have lately grown much more active. It was as though they had suddenly woken up to the realisation that their card has been trumped. In order to wreck detente they are going to all lengths to slander the policy pursued by the Soviet Union and the other socialist countries. They are having recourse to the battered cold war accusations of 'aggressive designs', of 'hegemonistic' ambitions, and the like.[8]

Detente could not last. There were forces building up in the

United States in particular which believed detente to be 'appease-ment' in face of Communism. They argued that the SALT II proposal being worked out between the superpowers would 'lock in place the Soviet superiority in the arms race'. After the heights in the Yalta doctrine the historical pendulum began to swing inex-orably back to embrace the Riga axiom. It is this momentum that embraces all of us today.

5) The breakdown in detente and the build-up of the current peak in anti-Soviet attitudes and behaviour began to take shape, coinci-dentally enough, around the time of Brezhnev's speech of 8 June 1976. It was crystallised in a report known as the 'Team B Report', commissioned by President Ford. Like NSC–68 and the Gaither Report before it, the Team B Report signalled a new era of anti-Sovietism. Its composition and context are interesting, and give an insight into the present crisis.

We have mentioned before the CIA estimates concerning Soviet strength. Called National Intellegence Estimates (NIEs), these reports generally become the official basis for Pentagon strategic planning. Towards the end of President Ford's tenure in office, one particular NIE came under scathing criticism by Soviet policy makers who were even more conservative than the CIA analysts.

In response, President Ford appointed another group, known as Team B, to analyse the same data. Several members of Team B had been involved in both the NSC–68 endeavour and the Gaither Report, Paul Nitze, for instance. Besides Nitze, several others such as Harvard Professor Richard Pipes and General Daniel Graham, were to later form the core of the Committee on the Present Danger, and go on to become the closest advisers to President Reagan. President Ford's directive to them was to see if a more conservative interpretation of the data was possible than that which the CIA had concluded. Not surprisingly, it was; and a new consensus began to consolidate concerning America's and NATO's 'weakness' in response to an ever growing Soviet and Warsaw Pact threat, both conventional and nuclear.

On the basis of information gathered from coordinating Soviet missile telemetry intercepts with radar monitoring of the trajectories of Soviet missile tests, the CIA NIE was revised to show a substantial improvement by 1982 in the Soviet 'hard-target kill capability', meaning the accuracy yield combination of Soviet warheads. Over the years 1978–1985 terrifying improvements were projected for Soviet missile accuracy, from 1,500 feet to 600 feet. Beginning in 1980, Team B projected a dramatic shift in the strategic balance between the US and USSR in favour of the Soviets.

Because the Team B report was corroborated by the Strategic Air Command, the Committee on the Present Danger and several outspoken Congressional hawks, their assertions concerning the 'Soviet threat' were believed, proving that a lie repeated often enough becomes the accepted truth. Forgotten was the fact that President Ford's directive to them was to examine the possibilities of a more conservative interpretation of the data than that of the CIA.

In reality the Soviet actions did not present a clear cut menace. The Soviets had been increasing their defence spending, but most of the allocations were going into defending the Chinese border. Economically, they were facing a crisis. The Soviet agricultural system was so dilapidated that it was having to import massive amounts of food. It was in debt to the West and was failing in its attempt to trade competitively. In fact, its overriding political goal in its relation with the US seemed to be detente and the signing of SALT II. If one looks at the situation geo-strategically, the US rapprochement with China had put the Soviet Union in a besieged position. Indeed, some conservatives argued that it was precisely because the Soviets were *weaker* that they were becoming *more hostile*.

Initially, newly elected President Carter downplayed the Soviet threat. He avoided the committee on the Present Danger in naming his foreign policy advisors. Then, when the right wing gathered strength, he attempted to balance both sides with the position that the US and NATO should seek to both cooperate and compete with the USSR.

His confusion was expressed in his Presidential Review Memorandum (PRM) 10, a document intended to rival NSC–68 and the Gaither Report but which achieved little beyond heightening the contradictions within Carter's administration. On the one hand, PRM–10 argued that there was "essential equivalence" in nuclear weapons and that the SALT II treaty should be signed. On the other hand, PRM–10 argued that the US should continue to gain geostrategic and commercial superiority over the USSR in places like Europe and the Middle East.

Meanwhile, the Team B Report continued to gain increasing credibility. What had begun as a speculative revision of a CIA National Intelligence Estimate has become an enormous albatross around Carter's attempt to gain Senate ratification of SALT II. Unable to gain the offensive, the Carter Administration defeated itself. For the duration of the treaty period and beyond, Department of Defense charts showed a substantial Soviet superiority in 'pre-attack' forces, in forces remaining after a Soviet counterforce first strike, and in forces remaining after US counterforce retaliation. Why then, argued the hawks—with Ronald Reagan among them—should the Senate ratify a treaty codifying this emerging condition of US 'inferiority'? The Carter people responded that there was nothing in the treaty which would prevent the United States from taking steps to haul itself out of the strategic bathtub. To this end they borrowed an idea from Paul Nitze's book and offered the MX-missile system as the appropriate panacea.

There were other complications. The Soviets reacted to Carter's pronouncements on human rights, his attempts to further arm NATO, and his recognition of China in January 1979. There were also heightened American concerns about Soviet 'adventurism' in the Third World, particularly when Soviet advisors and Cuban troops intervened in Angola and the Horn of Africa. Nevertheless, Carter and Brezhnev signed SALT II in Vienna on 18 June 1979. This complicated treaty limited each side to 2,250 strategic missiles and 1,320 missiles with multiple warheads.

Mutual hostility and suspicion was so high, however, that the very next month Carter announced he was going to set up a 110,000 strong Rapid Deployment Force in the Indian Ocean area. He also threatened to use tactical nuclear weapons in the area if US 'vital interests' were threatened. Then in early December the Committee on the Present Danger drummed up what became known as the 'Combat Brigade in Cuba Affair'. They accused Russia of stationing in Cuba a 'combat brigade' of 3,000 soldiers besides the 6,000 Soviet troops already there as trainers and instructors.

While there was little prospect that the Soviet could do anything more with their 'combat brigade' than training, a great furore ensued. Carter demanded their withdrawal. Brezhnev refused, pointing out they had been there since 1964 with US knowledge. Soviet suspicions that this affair was a part of some internal US wrangle between Carter and the Team B players were heightened when the issue was abruptly dropped at the end of October, even though the 'brigade' remained in Cuba. As was characteristic for Carter generally, indecisiveness reigned.

By then Brezhnev was trying to persuade the West Europeans into encouraging Washington to ratify the treaty. At the same time, Brezhnev attempted to pressurise them to resist the American plan to deploy Cruise and Pershing II missiles in Europe. To demonstrate good faith, Brezhnev withdrew 20,000 Soviet troops and 1,000 tanks from East Germany. Carter, now overwhelmed by the hawks, was forced to call Brezhnev's move a "fraud". On 12 December 1979, NATO agreed to deploy 464 Cruise missiles and 108 Pershing II's. On 24 December 1979, the Soviet soldiers marched into Afghanistan.

> SALT II was dead.
> Detente was over.
> A 'new' cold war had begun.

8 Domestic Reasons for the 'Soviet Threat'

Opposition to communism is a basic tenet of a capitalist system. The American and NATO societies derive from and thrive on this system, taking on intellectual, social, cultural and psychological colouring from the capitalist economy. Hence an anti-Soviet stance in the US and NATO countries is understandable. The fact that the Soviet system opposes the US and NATO system is only axiomatic. Therefore, one ought not to be surprised to find that anti-communism is a permanent fixture within the American and NATO foreign policy. This anti-communist/anti-Soviet perception fluctuates between the Yalta axiom, which seeks to relate to the Soviet Union through negotiation, and the Riga axiom, which demands development and expansion of military conflict. The latest rise of the Riga axiom has been used to deploy Cruise and Pershing II missiles in Europe. It is important to note that those arguing for the Riga axiom never change their views. What changes is the degree to which the public and the political leaders believe these views.

Anti-Soviet perceptions do not seem related to fluctuations in Soviet aggressiveness. Evidence of such aggressiveness is put forward, of course, such as the Soviet deployment of the SS–20s to justify the NATO deployment of the Cruise and Pershing II missiles, but close examination of the facts either refutes such justifications or indicates that the situation is at best ambiguous, allowing for either a Yalta or Riga perception, depending on the internal political realities of Washington, London, Bonn or Paris. What matters is not so much Soviet behaviour but the way in which the Western leadership decides to interpret it. At each rise in the Riga axiom, evidence existed to support the Yalta axiom. In the late 1940s, when NSC–68 was written, Stalin was indicating his intention to cooperate and negotiate. At the time of the Gaither Report in the late 1950s, Khrushchev had been downplaying military spending in favour of consumer goods and was indicating willingness to negotiate a test ban treaty. During the latest rise in anti-Soviet perception, the Soviets have indicated an overwhelming desire to maintain detente. At the 25th Party Congress in 1981,

Brezhnev called for a meeting with Reagan on armament limitations, only to be snubbed by the newly elected US President and
his Secretary of State. Rather than pursuing the peaceful options,
Reagan argued for acceptance of a renewed Soviet threat, pointing
to the invasion of Afghanistan and Soviet conduct concerning
Poland. He also made it quite clear that the civil war in El Salvador
and the 'communist conspiracy' in Central America directly
threatened US security and that both are inspired by the Soviet
Union. One wonders why the Reagan administration chose the
path of confrontation.

Anti-Soviet perceptions do not reach a peak only because
policymakers intentionally engage in a campaign to paint the
Soviets black. Various 'constellations of forces' also come together
to give greater credence to a more negative analysis of the Soviet
behaviour. Political convenience rather than a right wing
conspiracy produces and promotes the Soviet threat.

In face of evidence that Soviet hostility, at best, is ambiguous and
that the US strength remains overwhelming, it needs to be
understood why the more negative perceptions develop and
predominate in the Western corridors of power. This can be gained
by examining the different groups in the West that benefit from the
'Soviet threat': the scientists; the corporations; the military; the
politicians; and the strategists.

THE SCIENTISTS

When World War II ended, the political leaders who had
appreciated the work of scientists during the war wished to involve
them in the post-war reconstruction. Major advances had been
made in war technology by scientific help. This help could now be
directed to post-war 'security', particularly since military technology, like most other things, had entered the nuclear, micro--
electronic and computer age. With more and more scientific
knowledge being applied, military equipment had become even
more complicated. Scientists were now indispensable in maintaining current systems; developing better and new ones; and explaining them to the politicians who felt that the more they had the
stronger they were but who really did not understand the complex-
ities involved. An overwhelming number of scientists did not
return to their university laboratories after the war; they continued
working in defence research establishments. Many of those who
did return, worked on defence-related projects.

This created a whole new phenomenon within the scientific
establishment: a large body of technicians, engineers and research-

ers wholly dependent on military funds for their livelihood, professional status and *raison d'être*. At first working for the military—as the scientists did during the Manhattan Project which created the atom bomb—these scientists soon became the ones who initiated new developments, unsolicited by the military in many cases, and who created new military technology for which the Generals later offered a strategic rationale. The scientists became the begetters of a new world order. By their ability to produce new technological advances, they became the propagators of military realities to which the soldier had to adapt and to which the politicians had to relate the new economic and political order.

One of Einstein's great regrets was that he had made the atomic bomb a scientific possibility. He said that had he known what his equations would produce he would have remained a watchmaker. There is an old saying that the road to hell is paved with deep regrets and noble intentions. Lord Zuckerman, who as Chief Scientist to the British Government was integral to post-war military developments, states categorically that "The nuclear world with all its hazards is the scientists' creation; it is certainly not a world that came about because of any external demand".[1]

Herein lies the problem, says Zuckerman. Means have become ends, and scientists and technologists have not only been *expanding* human knowledge indiscriminately, they have also been *applying* this knowledge indiscriminately. Consequently, the major issues confronting the world today are largely the result of unplanned and unrestrained technological exploitation of scientific knowledge, whether they be in the field of gene splicing and recombinant DNA or the nuclear arms race.

Zuckerman goes even further when it comes to the nuclear arms race in particular. In this area, he says, the military chiefs are merely the channels through which the scientists transmit their views. It is the researchers in the laboratories—not the generals or the politicians—who initially propose improvement on an old warhead or the design of a whole new one; and if a new warhead, then a new missile, then a new system within which it fits. "It is he, the technician, not the commander in the field, who starts the process of formulating the so-called military need. It is he who has succeeded over the years in equating, and so confusing, nuclear destructive power with military strength . . . ."[2] The result is that "the men in the nuclear weapons laboratories of both sides have succeeded in creating a world with an irrational foundation, on which a new set of political realities has in turn to be built".

What is more, scientists at the highest levels have been involved with the political manipulation of the 'Russian threat' in order to keep the defence contracts coming to the laboratories which pay their high salaries—and to justify their new designs and improvements. George Kistiakowsky, chief scientific advisor to President Eisenhower, recalls that Eisenhower's policies of rapprochement in Europe were being frustrated continually by people who exaggerated the Soviet military threat.[3] Harold York, the first Director of Defense Research and Engineering at the Pentagon, tells of witnessing a steady flow of phony intelligences coming from a variety of sources to justify political agendas and new weapons systems. Ironically, says York, "those who had all the facts of the matter and knew there was no real basis for any of these claims were hamstrung in any attempts being made to deal with them by the secrecy which always surrounds real intelligence information".[4] Herbert Scoville, who was in charge of scientific intelligence for the CIA during the 1960s, confirms York's claims.[5]

The interconnection between scientific research and the Pentagon's manipulation of the 'Soviet threat' has been brought out by Robert Aldridge in his recently revised book, *The Counterforce Syndrome*.[6] He gives the example of missile improvements to demonstrate this interconnection.

Scientifically considered, he says, the trajectory of an intercontinental ballistic missile is made up of three parts: powered flight, coasting through space, and re-entry into the earth's atmosphere. Early missiles flew a preprogrammed trajectory from a given launch point to a given target. After the initial blast-off, the missile would shoot towards its target like a bullet; hence the term 'ballistic'.

A major scientific breakthrough occurred when US scientists developed multiple individually-targeted re-entry vehicles (MIRV's). This involved putting several different nuclear warheads on the front of a single booster rocket, called a 'bus'. After the last booster motor burns out and separates, the nose cone covering the warheads is also ejected. The bus continues through the coast phase and at periodic intervals different warheads are shot off at different targets.

When the military first heard about this scientific advance, they were not sure what to do with it. They were enticed by the idea that a MIRV system would be a step forward in the Pentagon's ultimate aim of developing a first-strike capability against the USSR. But the public was being told officially that the US policy was that of deterrence—being able to hit the Soviets back after a Soviet attack, not a policy of the US being able to attack the USSR first—so the generals were at first unable to think of a tactical reason acceptable to both the public and the Congress that would lend legitimacy to a programme to put multiple warheads on the US ICBM system. Finally, they argued in Congress that MIRVs

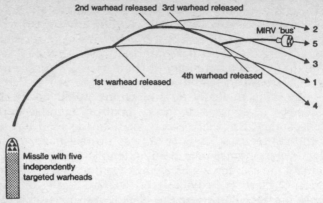

Missile with Five Warheads.

were 'urgently needed' to penetrate Soviet interceptor missiles such as those being stationed around Moscow. Congress and the public bought this reason and the MIRV system was adopted. No one bothered to ask what the connection was between US MIRVs and the Soviet anti-ballistic missile system. It was enough to raise the 'Russian threat' in any area to get approval of virtually any new system. To refuse to do so, would be to risk 'vulnerability to Soviet attack', to say nothing about being unpatriotic.

One particular aspect of missile technology that challenged scientists was precision. Accuracy is of secondary importance if one is interested in a deterrence strategy, for the destruction of urban industrial centres can be easily achieved even with rather large margins of error. However, if the strategy is that of attacking *first* and attacking specific military *targets*, then accuracy is imperative.

No matter how accurately the missile and the warheads it carried were targeted, the re-entry stage into the earth's atmosphere was generally turbulent enough to cause the warhead to miss its target, even if by only a little. Uneven erosion or ablation (the melting away of the warheads' surface by air friction) or wind patterns, air turbulence, rain or sleet, all affected accuracy. The scientific problem, therefore, was to find a way to enable a warhead to *manoeuvre* during the final re-entry phase.

The scientists at the Lockheed Missiles and Space Company, a major defence contractor, began to investigate this problem in 1968. The challenge was to design a manoeuvring re-entry vehicle (MARV). They came up with a Special Re-entry Body (SRB) which had a bent nose so that the warhead would fly at a slight angle during re-entry. This angle provided an aerodynamic lift similar to that of wings on an airplane, although because of its high speed, the SRB did not need wings. Inside the body of the SRB was a counterweight. If it was kept in the middle the warhead would fly straight, if it moved to one side the combination of gravity and air pressure caused the warhead to roll accordingly. By careful programming, scientists could use the counterweight to cause various manoeuvres.

Like MIRVs, MARVs were not solicited by the military. Scientists first developed it and then the Lockheed Corporation sold the idea to the Pentagon for profit. Once convinced, the generals, in turn, went to Congress, arguing that MARVs were necessary to avoid the anti-ballistic missiles of the Soviet Union. As with the MIRVs, the real reason was to increase accuracy to the point of developing a first strike capacity against the Soviet Union.

In 1970, Lockheed scientists began 'concept studies' for the MARV to be used on the Trident submarines. Known as the Mark–500, the missile used the same bent nose and shifting weight as the SRB but in a much more sophisticated fashion. The people of the United States were told that these 'concept studies' were essential for evasion of Soviet interceptor missiles. The real reason again was to improve missile accuracy to be able to launch a first strike against the Soviet Union.

Lockheed Corporation and the Pentagon got caught in their own rhetoric. The anti-ballistic missile (ABM) treaty was signed between the US and USSR in 1972, limiting each country to 200 interceptor missiles. Lacking obvious justification, the Mark–500 had to be temporarily shelved.

1972 was also the year that the Defense Department awarded Lockheed the prime contract to build the first generation of Trident missiles. Because of Lockheed's cosy relationship with Congress, the Pentagon did not even ask for competitive bidding, the usual practice. To pacify any concern about this in Congress, the Trident contract stipulated that Lockheed share some of the work with other corporations. Under this proviso the Mark–500 programme was quietly shifted to General Electric (GE). GE scientists had been engaged in their own MARV research, financed by the Advanced Ballistic Re-entry Systems programme of the US Air Force. Rather than using counterweights, they had developed a MARV that used twin flaps on the bottom side of the warhead. Moving both flaps in the same direction caused the vehicle to pitch up or down; when they worked scissor-fashion, the warhead would turn sideways. Combining these two movements allowed for precise man-oeuvering.

A Congressional critic, Les Aspin, publicly challenged the GE development of the Mark–500 programme in January, 1974. He announced that the Navy was secretly planning to use a MARV on the Trident missile, which suggested to Aspin that the Navy was tacitly intending a first strike capability for its Trident programme. With the ABM treaty, there was no other explanation. The Defense Department replied that "there is no plan to deploy a MARV on-target at this time ...".[7] They then claimed that while a first strike capability was not in accordance with official US policy, the purpose of the Mark–500 programme was to develop the basic technology just in case the ABM treaty was ever cancelled and the US would need to defend its missiles against Soviet interceptors. In view of the fact that the ABM Treaty was modified in 1974 to allow for only 100 ABMs per side (the Soviets having built only 64) this argument was spurious. Nevertheless, Vice Admiral R.Y. Kaufman announced that the Mark–500 had been renamed 'Evader' in order to clarify its real purpose—the evasion of Soviet interceptors. Under the new name testing and design improvements continued.

In February 1976, the Pentagon was claiming that the Mark–500–Evader was an evasive system—not one designed for accuracy and first strike. Dr. Malcolm Currie, Director of Defense Research and Engineering at the Pentagon, told the House Armed Services Committee: "We have our Mark–500 ... we hope it will discourage the Soviets from deploying their ABM developments."[8] In March, however, the rationale for the programme changed. The Navy told the Senate that Mark–500 was a rudimentary MARV intended to out-manoeuvre *anti-aircraft* missiles, which it claimed the USSR was upgrading to use against US missiles. To expect a surface-to-air missile designed for use against airplanes travelling at mach–2 to be able to be 'upgraded' for use against missiles travelling at mach–20 strained the credulity of even those who *believed* in the reality of the Soviet threat. Finally, the Chairman of the Joint Chiefs of Staff, General George S. Brown, revealed the Navy fabrications for what they were. In his military posture statement for 1978 he stated: "There is no present indication that the USSR has adapted its extensive surface-to-air (SAM) network to ABM defense, nor that it is currently suitable for that role."[9]

Despite the zigzags in official policy, scientific research and development continue for both MIRVs and MARVs. There is now the Advanced Manoeuvring Re-entry Vehicle (AMARV) which has radar-based sensors installed in the warhead so that its trajectory can be corrected for a no-miss strike. Scientists consider a no-miss strike one that gets the warhead to within 30 metres of its target. Considering that most warheads carry between 10 and 20 times the explosive power of the Hiroshima bomb, this degree of accuracy ensures a US capacity to obliterate any target of its choosing.

The thrust of US military doctrine and scientific research has not been that of building a credible deterrent against the 'Soviet threat'. Rather, while justifying various systems with the 'Soviet threat', the US has been quietly applying its scientific and technical knowhow and its superior economic resources to developing the capacity to mount a devastating nuclear first strike against the Soviet Union.

THE CORPORATIONS

The scientists are responsible for designing the new weapons systems. The corporations profit from their production. The scientists are often working for either the corporations doing business with the military or are in the military itself; and the directors of the corporations are often former military people and vice versa. Together they form a very powerful elite which is perhaps the single greatest impetus in the arms race, both nuclear and conventional.

In fiscal year 1980, the Pentagon placed contracts with various branches of the US business community for over $83 billion. Nearly half of this sum went to the 25 largest arms manufacturers, including McDonnell-Douglas, United Technologies, General Dynamics, Boeing, General Electric, Ford Motor Company, General Motors and Rockwell International. But this is only the tip of the iceberg. 25,000 contractors and more than 50,000 subcontractors are engaged in fulfilling Pentagon orders for arms, equipment and supplies. In 1981, Pentagon payments for military-related contracts amounted to over 30 per cent of the entire general engineering output in the US. 75 per cent of what the federal government buys is purchased by the Pentagon.

Each of the main defence contractors specialises in certain types of weapons systems. Boeing Aerospace, General Dynamics and Rockwell International specialise in missiles and bombers. Grumman and Vought specialise in fighters for the Navy. McDonnell-Douglas and General Dynamics specialise in fighter jets for the Air Force. Lockheed specialises in heavy air transports and submarine-based missiles. Chrysler and General Motors build battle tanks. Dassault in France, British Aerospace and MBB in Germany specialise in combat aircraft. Fokker of Holland builds transport aircraft. Westland of Britain, Aerospatiale of France, and United Technologies, Bell, Boeing Vertol in the US make helicopters. Electric Boat, a divison of General Dynamics, specialises in submarines (it is currently building the Trident) and Newport News makes aircraft carriers. Etcetera, etcetera.

The 20 leading industries in the US defence business

Industry	Defence business (Billions of 1980 dollars)		Estimated average annual growth (per cent)1981-87	
	1981	1987	Defence business	Non-defence business
Radio, TV equipment	$12.1	$25.2	13.0	4.1
Petroleum products	7.8	12.3	8.0	0.9
Aircraft	7.8	16.4	13.2	5.0
Aircraft parts, equipment	6.8	13.5	12.0	3.9
Aircraft engines, parts	6.4	13.2	12.7	4.1
Guided missiles	6.2	12.8	12.9	0.4
Shipbuilding, repairs	4.9	7.6	7.5	3.8
Misc. business sevices	4.8	9.1	11.3	4.8
Crude oil, natural gas	3.2	5.1	7.7	0.7
Steel	2.9	5.3	10.4	3.6
Truck transport	2.9	4.6	8.3	4.5
Electric power	2.8	5.0	10.1	2.7
Electronic components	2.6	6.0	14.9	8.2
Ammunition (excluding small arms)	2.3	5.3	15.0	6.7
Maintenance, repair	2.3	4.0	9.6	2.6
Professional services	2.3	4.7	12.2	4.3
Chemicals	2.1	4.0	11.3	4.4
Ordnance, accessories	1.8	3.7	12.6	6.7
Communications (excluding radio and TV)	1.7	3.3	11.6	5.3
Tanks, components	1.5	3.7	12.6	4.5

Source: US Defense Department.

Typical of these companies who are dependent upon military contracts for livelihood is the Newport News Corporation—an unlikely name for a Corporation engaged in nuclear weapons production. In congressional testimony, the president of the corporation proudly testified:

> What we have built at Newport News is a unique ship-manufacturing complex—the only one in the United States that has the facilities, equipment and human resources to build, repair, overhaul and refuel the full range of Navy vessels and the only one now building nuclear-powered surface ships. Newport News is truly a national asset.[1]

Very often prime contractors and their subsidiaries dominate a region, so that the impact of their weapons production upon the economy is both immediate and substantial. Boeing Aerospace, for instance, is the largest company in the State of Washington. Its production of the Cruise missile is keeping the economy of the area out of a recession. If Boeing closes, Seattle dies, and Vancouver mourns. Lockheed, Rockwell and Douglas dominate the economy of Southern California. Indeed, so great is the presence of the military–industrial complex in California that it is estimated that 40% of the work force works either directly or indirectly for defence contractors. McDonnell dominates manufacturing in St. Louis, Missouri. Bath Ironworks is the largest employer in the state of Maine. Rockwell International employs 13,000 directly nationwide and 40,000 through subcontractors. There is not a single US congressional constituency that is not tied to some locally based defence-related industry.

What is unique about this armaments industry is that while its business is weapons systems, most of the weapons it produces are never used in the crucible of war. The consequence is that the complex is almost completely self-contained and introverted. Its momentum is not towards the defeat of the enemy but the perpetual perfection of itself. Submarines are made larger, faster, quieter; aircraft are made more complex, versatile, long-range; and missiles are made more accurate, sophisticated and deadly. But there is little or no strategic value in any of the improvements made. Rather, any improvements must be seen as the result of corporate and scientific competition within the armaments industry itself.

What has been created by the armaments industry has been what

British Aerospace and the electronics companies' main arms projects

Project	Cost (approximate)	Company
Tornado GR1 & F2 plane	£9,500m	BAe/GEC Marconi
AV8B plane[1]	£1,000m	BAe
Sting Ray torpedo	£ 920m	GEC Marconi
Type 42 Destroyer equipment	£ 680m	Ferranti/GEC Marconi
Heavyweight torpedo[2]	£ 500m	GEC Marconi
Nimrod planes	£ 360m	GEC Marconi
Sea Eagle missile	£ 350m	BAe/GEC Marconi
Rapier missile update	£ 320m	GEC Marconi
New sonar systems	£ 240m	Plessey
Sea Skua missile[2]	£ 200m	BAe
Blow Pipe missile	£ 200m	Shorts
Ptarmigan communications[3]	£ 150m	Plessey

Notes
1 Estimated value of work going to UK.
2 Total development and initial production costs.
3 First phase only.

Mary Kaldor calls a "baroque arsenal"—weapons systems so complex and expensive that they have become untenable.[2]

The F–4, F–14 and F–15 are very expensive and complex flying machines requiring some 70,000 spare parts. A recent Pentagon exercise, known as Air Missile Intercept Evaluation, demonstrated that despite the versatility and sophistication of these fighter aircraft what mattered was manoeuverability, not complexity. In close engagements, the planes consistently destroyed one another. "It doesn't make much difference how fast your airplane is or how high it will fly", explained a Major General Frederick C. Blesse, who observed the exercise. "Once you get inside your enemy's missile envelope, you're not likely to escape."[3] Pilots were simply unable to use the many theoretical capabilities of the planes when it came down to actual combat.

Baroque weapons systems abound. The F–111, which was to have been the main combat aircraft of the US Air Force and Navy during the 1970s was expected by the Tactical Air Command to be capable of:

—taking off from short rough landing strips;
—flying the Atlantic non-stop;
—flying at tree top level;
—engaging in aerial combat at high altitudes and at speeds in excess of 1,700 miles per hour;
—having a large carrying capacity;
—*and* carrying a load of nuclear weapons.

The B–1 bomber is another weapon in the baroque style. It has been justified because it is supposed to be able to penetrate Soviet air defences. But by the time it becomes operational, the B–1 will only be able to penetrate Soviet defences for at most a year, since the Soviets, also caught in this baroque spiral, are in the process of strengthening their air defences. $30-50 billion for a viability of 365 days?

The US Army plans to buy 7,058 M–1 tanks at an estimated $19 billion. Yet the tank's transmission system is so delicate that the vehicle cannot dig itself into a 'hull-down' position necessary for combat. This 'drawback' has forced the Army to buy high speed bulldozers—called 'armoured combat earthmovers'—to help the tanks dig-in. Price tag: $1 million apiece. Moverover, because the M–1 tank consumes 3.86 gallons of fuel *per mile*, the Army has been forced to begin acquiring a new fleet of tankers to keep its armoured divisions operational in the field. As if this were not enough, the Government Accounting Office has revealed that the the M–1 requires "costly maintenance and frequent replacement". It has to stop for repairs every 43 miles and its track life is only 1,400 miles.

The British cruiser *Invincible* and its sister ships *Indefatigable* and *Ark Royal* are expected to combine the roles of command, control and coordination of both the British and NATO maritime forces; the deployment of anti-submarine warfare aircraft; and the capacity to carry 1,000 commando troops.

The European Multi-Role Combat Aircraft, jointly built by Britain, Germany and Italy had to fulfil the following expectations:

—Britain wanted it for long-range strike and strategic air defence against bombers;

—West Germany wanted it for close air support;

—and Italy wanted it for air superiority against other fighters.

By the time it was built it could barely fly. It has been described as an "egg-laying, wool-producing, milk-giving sow".

As soon as work is completed on one weapons system, work begins on its successor. Boeing produced the B–47, followed by the B–52, followed by the Intercontinental Ballistic Missile. Lockheed produced the F–80, followed by the F–104 fighters and a whole series of heavy transports. North American produced the P–51 Mustang, followed by the F–86, followed by the F–100. As one Air Force colonel has said, "there is always someone working on the follow-on at the Pentagon, it's an article of faith".[4]

For corporations which are 'defence-dependent', the drive for new contracts becomes compelling. By the time a firm has developed the personnel, complex equipment and expensive facilities to handle programmes budgeted for hundreds of millions or billions of dollars, the management must keep the firm operating at or near full capacity or risk serious losses. Because many firms have not developed products able to compete in the civilian sector of the economy, they have no other choice.

To ensure continuous work, all defence-dependent companies have planning groups, whose sole function it is to choose appropriate successors for the weapons that are currently being produced. They work with similar groups in the particular branch of the military they are involved with. The planning group is supposed to predict what a particular service branch might require when the current contract is fulfilled, and the ways that the corporation might fulfil that requirement. These predictions generally become self-fulfilling prophecies.

In fact, corporate planning groups often assist government staffs in writing the Requests for Proposals which are eventually issued to potential contractors. Industry officials research areas to which their particular company's skills might be applied and then identify the key government offices which would welcome their proposals. They also attempt to discover what funds are actually or potentially available for particular programmes and tailor their proposals accordingly. Intelligence information concerning defence funding is a highly valuable factor in the preparation of cost estimates submitted by industry to the Defense Department. One corporate vice-president said the government "depends on companies like ours to tell them what they need".[5]

What complicates, and sometimes corrupts the competition between the corporations is the fact that it is no longer possible to discern where the 'military' ends and the 'industrial' begins. Between 1970 and 1979, 1,942 people moved back and forth between the US military and those corporations which have become 'defence dependent': Boeing, General Dynamics, Grumman, Lockheed, McDonnell-Douglas, Northrop, Rockwell International, and United Technologies. This is not surprising says former Admiral Rickover: "the great difficulty in conducting defense business is that the top (Pentagon) officials come from industry and have an industry standpoint".[6]

A handbook on defence/space research compiled by a group of defence-industry executives states:

> Strong competition in the defense/space market necessitates close working relationships with the customer. It means not only frequent contacts but considerable participation with the customer in development of his performance and product requirements. It is necessary to attempt to work with the customer on study contracts and feasibility studies in order to help analyse the required characteristics of products and performance for which the customer issues requests for proposals. Market research activity must provide sufficient lead time to guide research and development efforts in the directions in which requests for proposals are likely to be forthcoming. Hence, considerable contact with the customer during the formulation of product requirements is an extremely important function of market research activity in the defense field.[7]

The "customer" in this case is the Pentagon.

THE MILITARY

Further insight into the armaments industry can be gained by examining the relationship between the different corporations and the various branches of the military. It was President Eisenhower who first drew attention to this complex relationship. In his last speech as President he said:

> we have been compelled to create a permanent armaments industry of vast proportions .... We must not fail to comprehend its grave implications .... In councils of govern-

ments we must guard against the acquisition of unwarranted influence, whether sought or unsought, by the military-industrial complex.

Eisenhower warned the American people that this complex would seriously undermine their way of life, if not kept in check.

It has not been kept in check.

As a result the military-industrial complex has transformed strategic thinking, war planning, weapons production, combat operations, and the very structure and direction of the economy.

Each of the corporations involved in this complex represents a certain type of manufacturing experience, a particular combination of plant, equipment and staff, specific management structure, and *a particular relationship with the military branch it serves* and the politicians with whom it has to deal.

This is important to stress because the military branches themselves have their respective emphases. The Army demands troop movement carriers, amphibious assault carriers and airborne missions. The Navy calls for ships and submarines, although it specialises in the ability to fly aircraft and land marines. The Air Force wants all manner of bombers, missiles and aircraft able to make deep penetration raids. It is essential to know that both the Navy and Army insist on being able to conduct airborne operations; the Navy clings to the right to land marines; and all branches are in the missile business. The Cruise missile, for instance, is being especially adapted for firing from airplanes for the Air Force, from ships and submarines for the Navy, and with chemical warheads for the Army.

Competition between corporations has led to departmental/ operational rivalry between these different military establishments and vice versa. It has also led to institutional expansion of both the military branches within the Pentagon and the corporations they are interlocked with, often resulting in considerable overlapping. Lockheed, Litton, and General Dynamics, for instance, although chiefly aerospace companies, have acquired shipyards. North American Aviation merged with Rockwell International, which makes axles for army trucks. Ford Motor Company has acquired an aerospace subsidiary.

The result of this is that although fighting a modern war requires military operations which can *coordinate* land, air and sea actions, the particular services involved are in fact *competing* bureaucratic empires with their own popular constituencies, contractors, supportive interest groups, legislators, and ideologues, which can be mobilised to make sure the particular service in question gets its 'fair share' of the defence budget. Sometimes conflicts within the five walls of the Pentagon rival real wars in their ferocity. These conflicts have political impact. They mould economic reality. And the 'Russian threat' is used to justify their discordant influences.

Since World War II in particular, there have been repeated attempts to establish and dis-establish the inter-service equilibrium in the US. Sometimes one branch will sponsor a 'reorganisation' plan which is designed to solidify its powers over the other branches. Alternatively, another branch, feeling it is lagging behind, will scheme to gain additional ground. In either event, it will be in the interest of somebody to exaggerate negative perceptions of the Soviets, either to hold on to what they have or to gain what they want. The external 'Soviet threat' has risen whenever the internal equilibrium among the military branches has been shaken.

The inter-service wrangling is exacerbated because each has traditional links with different political parties. The US Army, for example, is traditionally rooted in the South and is therefore generally Democrat in political orientation. Furthermore, because the Army is so labour intensive, drawing large numbers from working class and poor backgrounds, it has generally been politically the most moderate. Army leaders often have supported the welfare state and believed in active presidential power. The power of the US Air Force, in contrast, lies in the West, where both right-wing conservatism and isolationism are traditionally strong. Most Air Force leaders have been Republicans and inter-linked with defence contractors who wished to arm the US in a kind of 'Fortress America' style. The Navy, on the other hand, has tended to find support among the patrician families of both parties along the East Coast.

The relationship between inter-service wrangling and the corporations interlocked with the military was given classic expression in the rise of the Air Force in the years immediately after World War II.

At the end of World War II, the US military budget was drastically reduced. Thousands of workers throughout the armaments industry were laid off. Many corporations were able to adapt to a civilian economy, particularly the automobile manufacturers and companies making domestic appliances, electrical equipment and chemicals. However, adjustment proved very difficult for the aircraft companies, the naval shipyards and certain specialised companies like Raytheon, which made radar.

Many aircraft companies tried to develop civilian transports but the market was glutted with planes left over from the war. During 1945, employment at Republic Aviation, which had built P–47 fighters by the thousands, plummeted from 10,000 to 3,700. Employment at North American Rockwell, also involved in war-time production of fighter aircraft, fell from 102,000 to 9,000.

For a brief period, these companies were able to keep solvent with accumulated wartime profits. But the technical core that remained, composed of scientists at specialised facilities, could only be kept going if there were more contracts. For the corporations, development work had always been considered a form of investment. It was production that brought profits. However, for the government it was difficult to justify development contracts with aerospace firms without a military reason for procurement of their products.

Despite the absence of a strategic reason for a new programme of military aircraft production, pressures began to build-up for procurement. The National Planning Association reported in 1946 that "unless a substantial volume of military production is maintained at this time, this country runs the risk of doing irreparable damage to its aircraft manufacturing industry".[1] The Aircraft Industries Association, the President's Air Policy Commission (Finletter Commission) and the Joint Congressional Air Policy Board all made similar statements.

William M. Allen, President of Boeing Corporation, went on to argue in a letter to Boeing stockholders that

there is a growing realization on the part of the American public and government leaders that from the standpoint of national defense alone it is essential that this country have an industry capable of producing military requirements. There must be not merely an industrial mobilization plan to be put into effect on some future signal but a continuing program of development, perfection and proving of new experimental models, and continuing production of the required quantity of the latest accepted and operating types of aircraft.[2]

The Finletter Commission agreed with Boeing. It conceded that war was unlikely.

However, we cannot be sure. The world situation is dangerous. A nation in the position in which United States finds itself to day has no choice but to follow policies which may lead to friction with other nations. There is, moreover, such a thing as blundering into a war. ... Sometimes, events get out of hand and war happens when neither side wants it.[3]

Stating that "a strong aircraft industry is an essential element in the Nation's airpower", the commission argued against a reduction in the number of aircraft companies. However, because all these companies were dependent on the government, the government, through "proper planning, adequate volume and abandonment of uneconomic procurement practices", could "create an atmosphere as conducive as possible to profitable operations in the aircraft manufacturing business". What made government approval for the Finletter Commission recommendation a certainty was the growing power of the US Air Force.

The Air Force was convinced that it was the vanguard of the future after World War II. Nuclear weapons were the ultimate in military power, and immediately after the war the logical way to deliver them was by airplane. Although the Air Force was only created as a separate branch at the end of the war (formerly it was part of the Army) it quickly sought a dominant position. Prominent Air Force officials began distorting the Soviet threat, for they needed a credible external enemy to rationalise their national campaign. General Carl Spaatz, who led the fight for the new service, stated the case as follows:

> The low grade terror of Russia which paralyzes Italy, France, England and Scandinavia can be kept from our own country by an ability on our part to deliver atomic destruction by air. If Russia does strike the US, as she will if her present frame of mind continues, only a powerful US air force in being can strike back fast enough, and hard enough to prevent the utter destruction of our nation.[4]

The war scare which broke out over Czechoslovakia in 1948 gave the Air Force its *raison d'être*. Air Force Secretary Stuart Symington created the 70–Group to lobby for greater funds from the Congress. In 1949, the share of the defence budget going to the Air Force was doubled.

Many of the important contracts for aircraft were signed during 1948 and 1949. Boeing received orders for the B–50 Superfortress, the new B–47 bomber and the C–97 stratocruiser transport plane. North American was contracted to develop and produce the F–186 fighter. And McDonnell Douglas, Grumman and Vought received contracts for a series of carrier based aircraft.

The Navy also profited from this peak of anti-Soviet campaigning. The maritime industry was in almost as bad a shape as the aircraft firms. Immediately after the war there were few orders for merchant ships because the US Merchant Marine was glutted with wartime Liberty and Victory vessels. Similar arguments were expressed on behalf of the shipyards, although somewhat less vociferously. Nevertheless, in 1948–49, the Navy ordered two new anti-submarine-warfare cruisers; four new destroyers from Bethlehem Co. and Bath Iron Works; and nine new submarines from Electric Boat New York Shipbuilding Co., and Portsmouth and Mare Island Naval Yards.

All of these Navy and Air Force contracts were signed *before* the formation of NATO and *before* the outbreak of the Korean War. However, they were not merely a response to the problems of the arms industry. They were also a part of a wider US geo-strategic policy, heralded by the Truman Doctrine of 1947, in which US world leadership, combined with a vigorous economy and military production at home, was seen as the winning political coalition. Gone forever was the non-interventionist, isolationist conceptions of Roosevelt's New Deal era. These contracts signalled the creation of the military-industrial complex of which President Eisenhower was eventually to warn. It may well be that both NATO and the Korean War were an effect of the emergence of this military-industrial complex rather than its cause.

The Air Force went on to exploit the famous 'bomber gap' of the mid-1950's. There are two theories as to how the gap came to be. One is that the Soviet Union repeatedly flew the same bombers towards American defensive radars, round in a circle and in again, thus causing the US to have an exaggerated impression of Soviet air power. Another story is that Soviet bombers were repeatedly flown over Moscow in a May Day Parade, giving rise to exaggerated CIA estimates. When the US Air Force finally closed the 'gap', it had 1,800 B–47 and 850 B–52 long-range bombers. As it turned out, the Soviet Union only had 120 Bison jet heavy bombers and 70 Bear turbo-prop bombers.

Needless to say, the CIA's Board of National Estimates (BNE) was badly buffeted by all the conflicting claims and the fact that the *reality* showed a US superiority, *not* a Soviet one. When challenged on this one BNE official stated that "our answer is to say nothing is going to happen in the forseeable future, and say it in the most alarming way possible".[5] The result of this approach was one National Intelligence Estimate (NIE) after another predicting a huge Russian bomber fleet down the road.

In 1955, the US Strategic Air Command (SAC) discussed a plan to launch a first strike nuclear attack on the Soviet Union with all its new bombers. According to Navy and Air Force documents only declassified in 1982, the exact battle plan of the SAC's 'bomb-as-you-go' strategy was known only to General Curtis Lemay, who had sole authority to conduct such a mission.

The SAC plan called for an all-out coordinated attack by 735 bombers that would overwhelm Soviet defences. The aircraft would drop 600 to 750 nuclear bombs. Chief targets would be Soviet airfields and atomic installations, but an estimated 118 big cities were also to be destroyed and 60 million people killed.

A Navy Memorandum, written by Capt. William Moore, on a US Air Force briefing held on 15 March 1954, stated: "Many heavy lines, one representing each (bomber) wing, were shown progressively converging on the heart of Russia with pretty stars to indicate the many bombs dropped. . . . The final impression was that virtually all of Russia would be nothing but a smoking, radiating ruin at the end of two hours."[6]

The Soviets never produced long-range bombers; they emphasised missiles instead. The BNE was slow to catch on, partly because the Air Force was not interested in missiles. It was dominated by World War II bomber generals who liked to fly. They grudgingly funded a low-level missile-research programme, largely to make sure that the Navy did not get into the field and encroach on the Air Force's strategic bombardment mission.

Deep down inside the Air Force, however, there were a few colonels who were convinced that missiles were both cheaper and more effective than bombers. In love with missiles, they concluded that their Soviet counterparts were too. In the intelligence business this is known as 'mirror-imaging'.

Writing in the April 1982 edition of *The Atlantic*, Thomas Powers reports that during the Korean War, when funds for missile research had slowed to a trickle, one particular colonel concluded that nothing would budge his Air Force superiors but a fear of a Russian missile. He routinely asked the Air Technical Intelligence, at Wright-Patterson Air Force base, for more information about Soviet missile research, but nothing came back. So the colonel *invented* a Russian missile, fuelled by oxygen and hydrocarbons and producing 100 tons of thrust. He then gave these designs to a buddy in intelligence, asking him to include the hundred-ton rocket in his next briefing. He did so, solemnly telling a group of Air Force generals at Wright Field about this latest alarming development in Russian weaponry. Funds began to flow in the colonel's direction. It may well turn out that the first Soviet missile was designed in the United States.

By the late 1950s, as the second peak in anti-Soviet hostility was building up, the Army demonstrated how a branch losing ground could recoup it by using the Soviet threat. Army Chief of Staff Maxwell Taylor launched a campaign to reassert Army prestige. He argued that while the Air Force was right in claiming the supremacy in delivering nuclear weapons, they were unlikely ever to be used. Relying on them was making the US weaker, not stronger, for it was putting too many eggs in one single fragile basket. The answer lay in building up the US conventional forces. Moreover, since Europe was more or less secure from nuclear conflict, it was argued that the US should direct its attention to the countries of the Third World.

The only flaw in the Army's analysis was that it was unclear how US interests were connected with the peripheral countries of the Third World, other than the obvious interest the US multinationals had in markets. Eisenhower and the Joint Chiefs had specifically rejected any intervention in Vietnam in 1954, asserting it would not be worth the cost. In order to give these countries an appearance of vital US interest, Taylor claimed that the real enemy was the

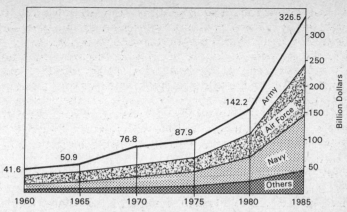

U.S. Defense Department Allocations (*Source:* Whence the Threat to Peace)

USSR. Any revolution in the Third World was perceived as a victory for the Soviets, since it curtailed the US power base and threatened its commerce.

In fact, the USSR was as concerned with the instability of the Third World as the US and was not sure what to make of the nationalistic rebellions sweeping through former colonies. But Taylor and other cold war hawks such as Walt Rostow insisted on seeing Russians behind every revolution and palace coup. In so doing, they created a self-fulfilling prophecy: since Russians had to be shown to be involved, the US acted as if they were, whether they were or not. In other words, US propaganda moulded US policy. Facts, if not created, were interpreted to justify a policy. The Army, the most appropriate service for "counter-insurgency warfare" argued Taylor, would have to expand to give the US greater direct intervention capability in the Third World. As a Democrat, President Kennedy leaned towards the army view of things and appointed Maxwell Taylor to be a major figure in his administration. The Army budget dramatically increased, and the "counter-insurgency warfare" in Vietnam began.

After initially trying to bomb the North Vietnamese into submission, President Nixon began the painful process of disengaging US forces from Indo-China. He downplayed Taylor's emphasis on guerilla wars and increased the importance of the Air Force within the context of a renewed interest in strategic parity with the Soviet Union. President Carter tended to favour the Army. He cancelled the B–1 bomber project and gave a more prominent role to the build-up of conventional arms. The Army made much more of the Soviet invasion of Afghanistan than did the Air Force. The Navy was also quick to emphasise the Soviet threat to US security in the Indian Ocean. Carter's scheme for a Rapid Deployment Force

(RDF) in the Middle East favoured both these services. And what Carter started with reluctance, Reagan has escalated with a flourish.

THE POLITICIANS

The politicians consider it to be their duty to sanction the expenditures of money needed by the constantly expanding military-industrial complex. It is up to them to assuage public concern and to justify to the public the use of the taxpayer's money for a baroque arsenal too complex to operate effectively and too lethal to use without endangering all planetary life.

Politicians rise to this challenge because in many cases they are themselves part of the problem; in some cases they are the problem. They use the 'Soviet threat' to justify political agendas. This can be seen in three ways: first, in the pattern of party politics; second, in the cycles of presidential strengths and weaknesses; and third, in the formation of foreign policy coalitions.

The Pattern of Party Politics

It is a striking feature of the three peaks of anti-Soviet hostility between 1945 and 1979 that Democrats rather than Republicans held the US presidency at the relevant time. The dynamic is fairly straightforward. After a Democrat assumes office, the right wing organises itself around the notion of the 'Soviet threat', a politically safe issue for them because they are out of power and need not deal with the difficulties of putting policies into effect. This pressure from the right makes the newly elected president vulnerable, particularly if there is not an equally strong left wing putting pressure for smaller defence budgets and increased spending in the domestic sector. Unfortunately, the left wing in the US has always been weak, forcing even liberal Democrats to adopt an aggressive foreign policy as a way of protecting their political base. Such a stance cuts down the need to adopt innovative domestic programmes which would antagonise conservative interest groups and the corporations. The structure of the political alignments before and after elections contribute as much to the increase in the 'Soviet threat' as any actions taken by the USSR itself.

In many ways, President Truman, a Democrat, set the tone for the pattern which has developed since. He became president with the death of Franklin Roosevelt, and was quickly aware that there was a resurgence of conservative sentiment sweeping the land as the Second World War drew to a close. This conservative sentiment crystallised, at least in foreign policy terms, with NSC–68.

Without Roosevelt's personal magnetism, Truman realised he could counter the right-wing offensive only by attempting to unify the New Deal Coalition Roosevelt had put together and face the right wing head on or by moving to the right and co-opting it. Either option entailed difficulties and risks, and Truman searched desperately for middle ground, one that would forestall both extremes and allow him to build a new political coalition. Truman succeeded in his endeavour and a new centrist coalition did come to power. Called 'Cold War Liberalism', this coalition has dominated the Democratic Party and to a larger extent US politics ever since. Its main features entail a moderate support for the welfare system and a strong support for a cold war foreign policy. The coalition comprises business, labour, intellectuals and the military and has kept together because of one basic denominator: the 'Soviet threat'.

That anti-communism and the spectre of the Soviet threat could unite heretofore disparate groups can be seen in the inclusion of US business interests in the coalition. American business rejected Keynesian economics as subversive. It argued that using government to stimulate the economy would undermine free enterprise and mean higher taxes. The dilemma Truman faced was that of involving the state in macroeconomic management—something that the left wing of the US political spectrum demanded—without unduly antagonising the conservative business sentiment of the country. High defence budgets came to the rescue, for they could be used to stimulate the economy without invoking opposition. While Truman remained unconvinced personally, the political logic was compelling. During his presidency, defence spending ceased to be primarily for the defence of the realm; rather, it became an acceptable economic stimulant. Spending this money in the South and West brought both Southern Conservatives and former isolationists into the coalition, thus keeping the extreme right wing from seriously challenging the new centrist consensus.

Cold War liberalism was deeply engrained in the American political tradition by the time of Kennedy's election in 1960. Like Truman, Kennedy was elected in the aftermath of a right wing resurgence, characterised by the Gaither Report. With the conservative bloc strong, and with little room for manoeuvre, Kennedy took the course of waging full scale battles against the one universally recognised enemy: the Communist Menace. He capitalised on the famous 'missile gap' during his 1960 Presidential campaign, fiercely attacking the Eisenhower administration (of which Richard Nixon was Vice-President) for 'neglecting' the nation's defences.

Kennedy had not created the 'missile gap' of course. It had arisen in 1957 after the Soviet Union had launched Sputnik, the first human-made device to be put in orbit around the earth. This caused an hysteria bordering on panic in the US. The launching of Sputnik marked the first time the USSR had established a 'first' in the technological competition. What followed were enormous estimates of the future number of Soviet missiles.

The extent of exaggeration about the number of Soviet missiles was staggering. The following table gives the variance between the estimates—offered by the Gaither Report, the Air Force and newspaper columnists such as Joseph Alsop—and the reality:

	United States	Soviet Union	Balance (+ = United States superiority − = Soviet superiority)
		A. Missile Gap Projection	
1960	30	100	− 70
1961	70	500	− 430
1962	130	1000	− 870
1963	130	1500	−1370
1964	130	2000	−1870
		B 'Actual' Figures	
1960	18	4	+ 14
1961	63	20	+ 43
1962	294	75	+ 219
1963	424	100	+ 324
1964	834	200	+ 634

Sources: Missile gap projection of J. Alsop from Ralph E. Lapp, *The Weapons Culture*, p. 32; 'actual' figures: 1960 and 1961 from Lawrence Freedman, *U.S. Intelligence and the Soviet Strategic Threat, pp. 73 & 100*, and Lt. Gen. Daniel O. Graham, *Former Director, United States Defence Intelligence Agency, Air Force*, May, 1976, p. 35; later years from IISS *Military Balance 1969/70*.

John Kennedy not only exploited the 'missile gap', he also lied about it after he assumed office and the 'gap' had disappeared. Shortly after his inauguration, his Secretary of Defense McNamara caused a stir by stating that there was no missile gap. The next day, Kennedy contradicted McNamara's claim, stating that no study of the subject had been concluded. When asked what he thought about press briefings of the kind at which Mr. McNamara had made his statement, Kennedy replied, "Well, they are hazardous in many cases—(laughter)—and I think our Mr. McNamara might agree with that now".[1] He then promised that a "new" appraisal would be given when the review of the defence budget inherited from the outgoing administration had been completed. When that review was completed, it contained no new appraisal of the missile gap. All that was said was that "It would not be appropriate at this time or in this message either to boast of our strength or dwell upon our needs and dangers".[2] However, it was in this same message to Congress that Kennedy announced accelerated programmes for Minuteman intercontinental ballistic missiles, Polaris nuclear submarines and an increase in the alert bomber force. These were the first in a series of decisions which led to the ordering of 1,000 Minuteman missiles and 41 Polaris submarines. Kennedy also increased the number of 'tactical' nuclear weapons in Europe from 2,500 to 7,000.

When McNamara left the job of Secretary of Defense, he argued that it was "lack of accurate information" about the Soviet Union's future nuclear plans, combined with necessary "conservatism" which caused the US to build a larger nuclear arsenal than it needed.[3] He also revealed that the US Air Force used the spectre of "Soviet Threat" to first argue for and later actually develop a first strike capability.[4]

Lyndon Johnson inherited Kennedy's cold war liberalism and took it to its extreme. On the one hand, his Great Society programmes brought about a fundamental liberalisation in the domestic sector, providing federal money for welfare, medical, educational and housing needs for millions of people. On the other hand, Johnson did all he could to prove how aggressive he could be overseas, sending US marines into the Dominican Republic in 1965 and then turning Vietnam into an all out war.

According to a former CIA officer, President Johnson and the CIA deliberately fabricated evidence in 1965 to 'prove' that the war in Vietnam was being fuelled by outside arms. The officer, Philip Liechty, came across CIA documents early in his 15 year career with the CIA that dealt specifically with how such fabricated evidence could be used to set the stage.[5]

Liechty joined the CIA in the summer of 1963. His first two years there were spent searching CIA "personality files" looking for what he calls "derogatory or inflammatory information on individuals that other branches of government are seeking information about". One day Liechty said he pulled a misplaced file, and there was a quarter-inch of documents inside relating to Vietnam operations. The top three or four pages were an operating plan of a new agency proposal to fabricate evidence of outside support of the Viet Cong effort in South Vietnam. This was no rough draft. It was a carbon copy of a final proposal and his recollection is that it was written in response to directions from the White House and could not have happened without Johnson's approval.

When he first saw the documents, he said, he had "no idea where these guys were going". But later, he said, it became "clear what they were doing. This was intended to con the Congress and the American people". It was supposed "to support the view that what was going on was all instigated, supported and controlled from the outside".

Liechty did not release this information until March 1982. He finally decided to break silence, he said, because "the point is that what is happening now in El Salvador looks so similar to what I saw of the agency role in preparing the groundwork for a big US involvement" in Vietman.

One set of documents Liechty saw involved a plan to take large stocks of communist-bloc arms the CIA had collected, load them into a Vietnamese boat, fake a fire fight in which the boat would be sunk in shallow water, and then call in Western reporters to see the captured weapons as 'proof' of outside aid to the Viet Cong. Another plan involved the printing of a large number of North Vietnamese postage stamps showing Vietnamese soldiers shooting down a US Army helicopter. Letters written in Vietnamese and bearing these stamps were then mailed all over the world. The CIA was to make sure journalists saw them.

On 28 February 1965, a US Government White Paper, entitled 'Aggression from the North', was released. It contained an account of a "suspicious vessel . . . carefully camouflaged and moored just offshore along the coast of Phu Yen province" in South Vietnam. The cargo vessel was "sunk in shallow water" after an attack by South Vietnamese forces. Investigation revealed over 100 tons of military supplies, "almost all of Communist origin, largely from Communist China and Czechoslovakia as well as North Vietnam". The white paper noted that newspeople visited the site and saw the armaments.

Publication of the White Paper turned out to be the key component in CIA and Johnson Administration efforts to 'document' charges that the civil war in South Vietnam was being instigated, controlled and armed by North Vietnam in consort with 'world communism'. The document, as well as the postage stamp caper—the North Vietnamese stamp emblazoned the cover of *Look* magazine on 26 February 1965—were designed to prepare US public opinion for what was to follow: the commitment of US combat forces in Indo-China.

Had Johnson carried over into foreign policy the lessons of the Great Society—that America is not so conservative that the people will not support changes in political practice—he could have broken the cold war liberal consensus and its need to exaggerate the Soviet threat. Instead he was forced to retire in disgrace, his Great Society in shambles and the Vietnam war out of control.

In contrast to these peaks in anti-Soviet perceptions as a result of cold war liberalism, the valleys are also interesting. The valleys have been dominated by Republicans with their own political programmes. Because Republicans are generally from the conservative bloc, Presidents Eisenhower and Nixon did not have to worry about their right flanks as did the Democrats. To call someone like Nixon 'soft' on communism would be so ludicrous as to have no effect. Because of this, neither Eisenhower nor Nixon had any particular interest in further fanning the flames of the Soviet threat. The result was far fewer foreign adventures and the resurgence of the Yalta axiom.

Jimmy Carter took office after eight years of detente with the USSR and the opening of a realistic China policy. By relaxing tensions around the world, Nixon did what no Democratic liberal had ever done, namely, prepare the ground work for some reasonable world order and a new domestic consensus on the Soviet threat. Indeed, because of Nixon and Kissinger's policies of detente and their negotiations of SALT I and II, Nixon placed Carter in the position of being the first President who did not need the cold war.

Carter's inability to carry on where Nixon and Kissinger left off may well turn out to be one of the biggest political tragedies of modern times. It is of course fair to point out that by Carter's time, the cold war consensus had transformed American life. The Soviet threat had become an indispensable part of both left and right wings. Defence plants and the hundreds of corporations that lived off ever-increasing defence budgets and contracts for new weapons systems had turned the military-industrial complex into the cornerstone of American economic and political life. This, combined with hawkish labour unions, macroeconomic management of the economy by the federal government, and the spreading influence of the Pentagon, which by the late 1970s had two full time lobbyists for each member of Congress, produced an ever expanding consensus about the Soviet threat and the need for bigger defence budgets. Carter's influence was peanuts compared to the momentum generated by the military-industrial complex.

What is unique about the present situation is that Ronald Reagan was elected to the White House at the peak of the latest anti-Soviet wave. Unlike the Democrats before him, who were motivated more by political expediency, Reagan seems actually to believe his anti-Soviet rhetoric. His administration moved quickly to capitalise on the Soviet threat. On April 20, 1981, his Secretary of Defense, Casper Weinberger, even announced contingency plans to fight a protracted conventional and nuclear war with the Soviet Union. This was after announcing SALT II to be dead and that the US was committed to achieving nuclear superiority over the USSR.

Foreign Policy Coalitions

There has always been a debate in the US about the most important focus of foreign policy. One of the major disagreements
during the 1940s was between those giving priority to Asia and
those giving priority to Europe.

Asia-firsters tended to be businesspeople interested in expanding into new territories and creating new markets. They were
generally from the new and more competitive industries located in
the American West, were conservative politically and suspicious of
any big government other than one which would protect their
business interests. Since European markets had been tied up for
centuries, these people viewed the Third World as a vast potential
market for US goods and technology.

European-oriented policymakers, on the other hand, were
concerned much more with geo-political stability than new
markets and high profits. They had ties with both the financial
world and the monopoly sector and were thus far more inclined to
believe in a powerful central government which would organise
the world in order to preserve the existing system. They viewed
the world in terms of nation states and spheres of influence, not
specific corporations. They believed America should be the world's
only superpower.

An important dimension of the debate between the Europhiles
and the Asiaphiles were fundamental differences in economics.
The Europhiles tended to be free traders, i.e. they believed capital
should be free to move, regardless of national boundaries. But they
were also aware that no system of free trade could work unless the
US was powerful enough to enforce it, as Britain did in the nineteenth century. This position was opposed vigorously by the Asia-
oriented business people who needed tariff protection in order to
compete on the world market. Opposition also came from labour
unions who wanted US jobs protected, and also from those isolationists who did not want their tax dollars propping up other
governments around the world. This economic nationalism had
great popular appeal because it put America first.

The first test of the comparative strengths of these two positions
after the war came in 1946 when the US Congress was asked by
Truman to support a massive loan for Britain. Conservative
opposition, led by Ohio Senator Robert Taft, was strident and
strong. Truman's advisors told him that the only way to get the bill
passed was to make a strongly anti-Soviet speech claiming that
without aid, Britain's future was in danger from Soviet subversion.
Still inexperienced at using the 'Soviet threat', Truman refused,
although approval was given for Congressional leaders to make

the claim. They did and the loan was approved. Britain was saved from the Soviet menace.

The Conservatives worried that the British loan was merely the first in a massive economic aid programme to Europe. They were right. Shortly thereafter, Secretary of State George Marshall announced his plan under which the entire West European economy was to be reconstructed with massive helpings of US dollars.

Knowing the Marshall Plan would give pre-eminence to Europe, the Asia-oriented policy makers and fiscal conservatives, labour unions, and isolationists mobilised enormous opposition. It was clear that the Marshall Plan could not be passed without the aid of the 'Soviet threat'. Even Truman could not refuse to use it. Like the Air Force, he opted to manipulate the crisis in Czechoslovakia in February, 1948, in order to gain support. Top secret studies done by the National Security Council indicated that the Soviets were expected to control Czechoslovakia and that no change in the balance of power would occur. In fact, US officials had concluded that Czechoslovakia had been Communist before February, 1948, and had refused to give it foreign aid on those grounds. Nevertheless, Truman delivered a stridently anti-Soviet speech in March, 1948, claiming that a freedom loving country had been invaded by a totalitarian dictatorship. Without the Marshall Plan, he warned, the USSR might take over other countries as well. In the end the Plan passed but the Conservatives got their pound of flesh by the inclusion of Japan.

The Marshall Plan was one that required massive amounts of money, some $26 billion spread over several years. Congressional authorisation was necessary for each new expenditure. Because of this, the Marshall Plan did not need the 'Soviet threat' only once; rather it institutionalised it, and 'proof' of the Kremlin's evil designs were furnished each time Congress was asked for more money. These events surrounding the Marshall Plan and the development of a free trade economy in Western Europe offer a clear example of how anti-Soviet perceptions in attaining foreign policy objectives were in fact peripheral to a direct concern with Soviet behaviour.

The second peak of anti-Soviet hostility, under Kennedy and Johnson, had a foreign policy dimension as well. Only in this case, attention was directed to Asia and the unrest sweeping the Third World. The 'Soviet threat' was exaggerated to gain support for a foreign policy with an Asia-orientation just as it had been to win support for the Marshall Plan and a European orientation.

After Vietnam, a major debate in policymaking circles occurred concerning the future locus of US foreign policy. Some argued, such as Carter's Secretary of State Cyrus Vance, that the US had over extended itself in Vietnam and should concern itself with 'core areas' such as NATO and the Middle East, relying on non-interventionary solutions in other parts of the world, particularly Africa. Others argued that what occurred in Vietnam was a failure of will, and that the US must renew its commitment to the principles of the cold war.

Carter seemed to side with the position emphasising core areas and came to office with two apparent objectives. First, to restore Europe to a place of prominence after the years of US fixation with South East Asia and counter-insurgency warfare; and second, to develop a new foreign policy stance vis-a-vis the Third World. The first objective was urged most strongly by the Trilateral Commission, to which Carter, Vice-President Walter Mondale, National Security advisor Zbigniew Brzezinski and Secretary of State Cyrus Vance belonged. The programme of the Trilateralists represents a return to the free trade principles of the Marshall Plan; a solidification of the alliance between North America, Western Europe and Japan, the so-called 'industrial democracies'; and the setting up of 'client states' in the Third World which will integrate themselves both politically and economically into the US–NATO–Japan dominated political and economic bloc.

The post war history of the US has demonstrated that it is impossible to have a free trade programme without the cultivation of the Soviet threat. Such a programme undermines the security of American jobs and income overseas, and it runs counter to the strong feelings of nationalism. Only if people are convinced that an overwhelming danger exists can their support be gained for a programme which undermines their economic security. Realising this, the Trilateral Commission has used the 1940s language about Soviet aggression. This has been done particularly by Brzezinski, an original architect of the Trilateral Commission.

Reagan's foreign policy is clearly of the school that America lost in Vietnam, not because of over extension but because of 'failure of will'. He has invoked the image of Soviet subterfuge behind any unrest, whether the civil war in El Salvador, the uncertainties in the Persian Gulf, or the current debate over the Cruise missiles in NATO. He is determined to make America 'Number One' again and to develop a 'global strategy' rather than one that fluctuates between Europe and Asia.

It is sometimes difficult to believe that the people who become responsible for political leadership in democratic societies would be so susceptible to the pressures of the military and economic interests. But such is the case. Legislators on key government committees manoeuvre ingeniously to protect the vested interests of their constituencies.

The chief asset of Vint Hill Farms, a small intelligence station in Virginia's Shenandoah Valley, for instance, is its top-flight commissary. When the Pentagon decided to close the station and move the staff to Fort Meade, Maryland, for a saving of several million dollars, the district's Republican Representative, Kenneth Robinson, blocked the move. He used his position on the House Defense Appropriations subcommittee to stop funds for building a new commissary at Fort Meade. If the Vint Hill commissary closed, said Robinson, "all the people who do business there would be on their congressman by the thousands".[6]

Once the Pentagon has pushed a new weapon on Congress, it is often stuck with it. The Navy sought to replace the A–7 bomber with a new F–18 bomber. However, when the costs of the F–18 skyrocketed to $32 million per plane, the Navy considered abandoning the programme. The politicians blocked the move. F–18 engines are built in Lynn, Massachusetts, next to the district of House Speaker Thomas P. O'Neill. As for the A–7, it is also still in production. The LTV Corporation, which builds the plane, is in the district of House Majority Leader James Wright.

To help win approval of its Trident nuclear submarine programme, the Pentagon selected Kings Bay, Georgia, for the Trident's East Coast support station. Kings Bay is the home of House Military Construction Appropriation Subcommittee Chairman Bo Ginn. While the Trident programme has been delayed by more than three years, Ginn's subcommittee has rebuffed all Pentagon efforts to stretch out construction of the $156 million base.

The corruption of politicians interlocked with the military-industrial complex is exceeded perhaps only by their ignorance of what would occur if the weapons systems they so glibly build were ever used. Many lack rudimentary knowledge even of the political forces at work that could result in a nuclear war. Because of this, any nuclear exchange will probably not be initiated by a well organised meticulously prepared 'bolt out of the blue'; it will probably be the result of political negligence, strategic inefficiency and gross ignorance about the real effects of nuclear weapons. This is the fear of William Hyland, a longtime strategic specialist for the Nixon, Ford and Carter administrations and now a senior associate at the Carnegie Endowment for International Peace. He fears that World War III might begin not as World War II did, with a Nazi blitzkrieg in the West and a Japanese sneak attack in the East, but as World War I did, with a combination of bumbling, inadvertence, events getting out of control and just plain bad luck. "If there is ever a nuclear war," he says, "it will be like August 1914—a gradual losing of control. There would be rival alerts, no one backing down, no one wanting to fight, but a mounting confrontation that could lead to fighting."[7]

Such a scenario becomes plausible when one considers politicians in high places such as William Clark. Shortly after he took office, President Reagan nominated Clark to be Deputy Secretary of State. The only problem was that Clark knew even less than the average American about foreign affairs. During his nomination hearings before the Senate Foreign Relations Committee he could not name the prime ministers of South Africa or Zimbabwe, knew little about the nuclear non-proliferation policy of Congress, and seemed at a total loss to explain the US relationship with its NATO allies. His ignorance was so embarrassing that only Republican party discipline voted him in. The Republican committee chairman, Charles Percy, stated, however, that "never again can we accept a candidate who professes ignorance in any area where he is to be given responsibility".[8]

After this humiliating debut, Clark took care to avoid any further public scrutiny. He gave no open press conferences and refused to testify in Congress again. Such action by a Deputy Secretary of State was without precedent. Warren Christopher, who had the job before him, testified four times during his first year and 44 times thereafter.

Clark did prove himself to be a good 'team player' in the Reagan administration, acting as a bridge between the Secretary of State Haig and the White House staff. When National Security Advisor Richard Allen resigned under pressure in January 1982, Clark was quickly appointed to take his place. A man, who a year before had displayed gross ignorance, was named by Reagan to the most sensitive foreign policy post in the land. As National Security Advisor, it is Clark's role to brief the President every morning about what is happening around the world.

Within days of his appointment, Clark imposed the tightest restrictions ever attempted in peace time on reporters' access to foreign policy documents. Clark also added two more military men to the National Security Council, Marine Colonels Robert McFarlane and Jeremiah O'Leary, who were to act as his personal assistants. William Buckley and Thomas Reed were hired as his consultants. Buckley had just been successfully litigated against for fraud and stock manipulation, and Reed had spent 1981 under government investigation for illegal stock market dealings.

Clark also brought William Casey into the White House foreign policy process. Casey is a former representative of Indonesian interests in the US and the former CIA director still under government investigation for stock manipulation and fraud. Michael Deaver, the Deputy Chief of the White House staff, also sits at Clark's table. Deaver used to be a paid agent of Amigos del Pais, an organisation of Guatemalan plantation owners and junta officers.

As his advisor on Morocco, Guatemala and Brazil, Clark has General Vernon Walters, former Deputy Director of the CIA. Walters collected commissions for US arms delivered to Morocco; and he received fees from International Basic Resources, an oil company, for seeking increased oil production quotas in Guatemala. Walters also boasts of having engineered the 1964 coup that overthrew a democratically elected government in Brazil and established a military junta.

Advising Clark on Latin American affairs is Lieutenant General Gordon Sumner, who resigned from the Inter-American Defense Staff in protest against the Carter administration's 'softness' in the Western Hemisphere. Gordon makes his living by dividing his time between Clark and working for a New Mexico consulting firm called La Mancha, which sells advice on Washington policy to Latin American governments.

It is rare, even by White House standards, to find a team of such disreputable people in such reputable positions. The scene in Clark's National Security Council could almost be a re-enactment of the palace of a banana republic, where wealth is the prerogative of the local plantation owners, and injustice is delivered out of the barrel of a gun. All these men have been assembled to 'advise' the man who 'guides' the President. They are also there to assist the man who described his political philosophy to the *New York Times* as "remembering how government decisions affect the little guy".

THE STRATEGISTS

If American nuclear power is to support US foreign policy objectives, the United States must possess the ability to wage nuclear war rationally . . .

US strategic targeting doctrine must have a unity of political purpose from the first to the last strikes. Strategic flexibility, unless wedded to a plausible theory of how to win a war or at least ensure an acceptable end to a war, does not offer the United States an adequate bargaining position before or during a conflict and is an invitation to defeat. Small, preplanned strikes can only be of use if the United States enjoys strategic superiority—the ability to wage a nuclear war at any level of violence with a reasonable prospect of defeating the Soviet Union and of recovering sufficiently to insure a satisfactory postwar world order.

This statement by two military strategists, Colin Gray and Keith Payne of the Hudson Institute, summarises the rationale behind the production and maintenance of the constantly increasing baroque arsenals.[1] The designs of the scientists, the machinations of the generals and the politicians, and the greed of the corporations are all given a purpose by the strategists. And the purpose is to provide for the 'defence of the free world' against the 'Russian threat'.

Weapons systems need a reason. Absolute weapons need an absolute enemy. However unusable, they must serve a purpose in strategic planning. The paradox of nuclear weapons is that while they were first developed by strategic design, once their destructive capacity became evident they began to dictate a strategic rationale. The strategic purpose of developing the atomic bomb was to defeat the Axis powers in World War II. When the bombs produced wiped out Hiroshima and Nagasaki in single blasts, everyone was stunned, including the scientists. "Physicists have now known sin" was Robert Oppenheimer's reaction, who had headed the Manhattan Project which produced them. Nevertheless, the atomic bomb gave the Americans supreme power for a few years, and with it the strange sense of security that came from knowing they were the sole possessors of a weapon that could destroy the world. During the 1940s and the 1950s, the strategic reason advanced for keeping this weapon was that the US could then have the power of 'massive retaliation'. Only through this, it was argued, could the US and NATO have an effective 'deterrent' against possible Soviet attack.

This strategic rationale for nuclear weapons has remained engraved in the public mind almost as deeply as the stark images of Hiroshima and Nagasaki. Indeed, some forty years later most people still think that the strategic policy by which the American and NATO nuclear arsenals are governed is that of deterrence. We are told that the Russians will attack at the first sign of weakness. NATO and US defence is based on the ability to strike back so hard and fast that the Soviets will be deterred from ever attacking in the first place. Deterrence is consequently a defensive measure, and the public is talked into supporting the respective arsenals of nuclear weapons on this basis—the ability to inflict unacceptable damage on any attacker. Only behind this 'nuclear shield', we are told, can the West preserve its democracy.

What would the Soviets consider unacceptable damage, such that they would be deterred from ever attacking first?

This question was put to US Secretary of Defense Robert McNamara in 1967. In Congressional testimony, he replied: "It seems reasonable to assume that in the case of the Soviet Union, the destruction of say, one-fifth to one-fourth of its population and one-half to two-thirds of its industrial capacity would mean its elimination as a major power for many years."[2] This would amount to several times the damage the Soviets experienced in World War II.

Nearly one-fourth of the Soviet population and one-half of its industrial capacity are concentrated in and around its 100 largest cities. One 50-kiloton bomb, dropped within half a mile of the centre of any of these cities would incinerate far more than 25% of its population and would devastate more than 50% of its industry. Clearly, all that the US and/or NATO need to constitute an effective deterrent is a stock of just 100 fifty-kiloton bombs.

The demographic fact is that going beyond the destruction of the largest 100 cities would not add to the unacceptable damage. The remaining cities are much smaller, the economic sites widely dispersed. To kill another 25% of the Soviet population and more industry would require ten times the effort without yielding corresponding results.

McNamara's advisors further calculated that 400 'equivalent megatons' of nuclear power were necessary to do the job. They reasoned that the US could feel 'secure' if it possessed this 'damage potential' three times over—once for each 'leg' of its 'Strategic Triad'. This Triad consisted of B–52 *bombers*, which carry nuclear weapons and can fly over Soviet territory; *land-based missiles*, deployed in the Midwest and aimed at the USSR over the North Pole; and Polaris and Poseidon *submarines*, each equipped with sixteen nuclear missiles.

McNamara and Kennedy implemented this strategy by building a force of 300 bombers, 41 submarines, and 1,000 Minuteman missiles. This was enough, they felt. "Once we are sure that, in retaliation, we can destroy the Soviet Union and other potential attackers, as modern societies, we cannot increase our security or power against them by threatening to destroy more", explained two of McNamara's strategists, Alain Enthoven and K. Wayne Smith.[3]

Thus far strategy seemed to control technology. This was to be short-lived, however. In the mid–1960s, scientists perfected the MIRV technology, and since then improving nuclear technology has been leading strategy by the nose. McNamara's Strategic Triad allowed for the 41 nuclear submarines to carry 16 missiles apiece. This gave them 656 missiles. After the MIRV breakthrough, the 656 missiles carried 5,300 warheads. The 1000 Minuteman missiles now carry more than 2,000 warheads. Within only a few years, the US had acquired nearly 10,000 warheads in its strategic and nearly 20,000 warheads in its tactical arsenal. This represents vastly more 'equivalent megatonnage' than thought necessary in the early 1960s.

Other technological breakthroughs allowed for greater precision, accuracy and reliability. This allowed strategists to begin articulating a doctrine of hitting specific targets, such as missile silos, military bases, industrial complexes, submarine ports, government centres, and communications networks. US strategic doctrine began to mix a 'counter value' strategy—hitting cities— with a 'counter force' strategy—hitting specific sites. These two strategies are integrated into the Single Integrated Operation Plan (SIOP), known only to the US Joint Chiefs of Staff. It contains a complete list of targets the American warheads are programmed to hit in various nuclear exchanges. Several of the SIOP options are scenarios which were not considered realistic before the scientific breakthroughs of MIRV, MARV and improvement in accuracy. These are the options of 'first strike' and 'limited' nuclear war.

What must be borne in mind about American nuclear strategy is that it is part of a global design. After the Second World War, the US quite literally controlled the oceans of the world and was the single greatest power on earth. The only area beyond the US influence was the land controlled by the USSR. Since then, the US has employed what the Pentagon calls the 'Global Options Strategy' to maintain US supremacy abroad.

In a statement entitled 'Perspectives on Security and Strategy in the 1980s', given before Congress on 6 February 1981, General David Jones, Chairman of the Joint Chiefs of Staff at the time, clarified what this Global Options Strategy implies.[4] "In the early years of our country's development," he said, "the oceans off our shores were both a bridge linking us with trading partners abroad and a barrier shielding us from the conflicts that ravaged much of the rest of the world. In a modern age of supersonic transoceanic travel it is often overlooked that the US is still fundamentally a maritime power." As "a superpower with worldwide interests and global commitments, the US needs unimpeded access across and over the seas to protect whatever military power may be needed to protect" its vital interests. The major problem, Jones said, is that

> our former protective barrier no longer exists; although we cannot be conquered by invasion, the technology of strategic weapons has made us (and all nations) subject to devastating attack from intercontinental distances. The expanse of the ocean has, in many respects, become a US liability in our changed world. Western Europe, the largest industrial concentration in the world—and East Asia, the most populous, are closer to the USSR than to the US. So is Southwest Asia on which the other two depend for the majority of their energy needs.

Complicating the problem is the fact that the US is heavily dependent on these far-away places for the resources it needs for its economy. The nation's reliance on imports of minerals and metals (apart from oil) has risen sharply since the 1960s. Of the top 25 such imported commodities, US dependence now averages 70%, up from 54% in 1960. The US depends on foreign sources for 20 of the 36 minerals it regards as strategic. The US imports 98% of its columbium and tantalum, 97% of its manganese ore, 95% of its cobalt, 93% of its bauxite, and 91% of its chromite. These are essential to the production of specialty steels, jet engines, missiles, turbines, gun barrels, armour plate, and aircraft fuselage.

The US is not an exception. Most of the NATO countries also are dependent to a varying, but vital degree upon resources produced and shipped from far-away shores. Moreover, the increasing sophistication of Western technology has made economies more dependent on these essential imports, thus making defence programmes more vulnerable to disruption.

Geography confers a different set of strategic advantages and liabilities on the Soviet Union. It is much closer than the Western nations to being economically self-sufficient with the notable exception of its agriculture. Moreover, it enjoys greater relative proximity to countries upon which the US and NATO depend for their key resources.

As Soviet power "continues to widen to more distant parts of the world," Jones warned, "supported by an increasingly more sophisticated Soviet force projection capability, the danger of attempted infringement on the most vital interests of the US and its allies increases proportionately".

This leaves the US and NATO with two choices: "either taking cooperative security action to offset this asymmetry (and permit market forces to determine access) or living in perpetual risk of seeing an unfriendly hand grip their economic lifeline." General Jones counselled for the first option. "During the past year," he said,

> much of the world has rediscovered a principle that some had mistakenly thought obsolete in the 60s and 70s: *military strength counts*. We still live in a world in which the use and potential use of decisive military power can influence policies, alignments, and actions. What has sometimes been overlooked is that such influence can be either constructive or disruptive for our security interests, depending on who is wielding it and towards what end.

When it comes to military strength,

> the United States has formidable and highly professional military capability. However, we are not well configured for

certain kinds of combat in certain areas of the world, particularly
if we must project and sustain forces close to the Soviet
periphery. There are a number of shortfalls across the board and
major improvement programs that we must initiate or accelerate
in our strategic, theater, and conventional forces.

The US, Jones argued, must modernise its strategic nuclear
forces; better prepare itself to fight "limited" nuclear wars in
particular "theatres" of combat; deploy chemical warfare weapons
both defensively and offensively; and improve its conventional
capabilities.

In the event of conflict, our strategy should be to apply our
strengths against the weaknesses of the adversary, not just
necessarily at the point of attack (which may be the enemy's
strength) but across a wide array of painful vulnerabilities. The
Soviets must be continually faced with the certain prospect that
a military move against US or allied interest risks a conflict that
could be wider in geography, scope, or violence than they are
prepared to deal with. In particular, they must be convinced
that an infringement on our vital interests in Southwest Asia
would trigger a confrontation with the United States that would
not be confined to that region.

The strategy put forth by General Jones as the keynote of
President Reagan's foreign policy is a strategy that calls for a
dramatic escalation in the arms race. It emphasises conflict in
'limited' nuclear exchanges. It also plans for the deployment of
both offensive and defensive chemical weapons.

It is clear from Jones' testimony and the plan of President Reagan
to spend $1.6 *trillion* (not counting the $750 billion projected over-
run) between 1981 and 1986 on defence that American strategists
have something big in mind. On 13 August 1981, the *New York
Times* revealed that Defense Secretary Weinberger was preparing
"a secret plan for a ten year strategic build-up that would enable
the United States to regain nuclear superiority over the Soviet
Union within this decade ... to build a capacity to fight nuclear
wars that range from a limited strike through a protracted conflict
to an all out exchange". What this means for the US taxpayer is
$20,000 per household over the next five years.

It is this strategy that motivated President Reagan, in accord with
the US National Security Council, to decide on 19 July 1982 not to
continue negotiations with Britain and the Soviet Union on a
comprehensive ban on nuclear weapons testing. In 1963, nuclear
tests were banned above ground, under water and in outer space
by a treaty signed by 120 nations. In 1974, the US and USSR agreed
to prohibit testing of any bombs bigger than 150 kilotons (the

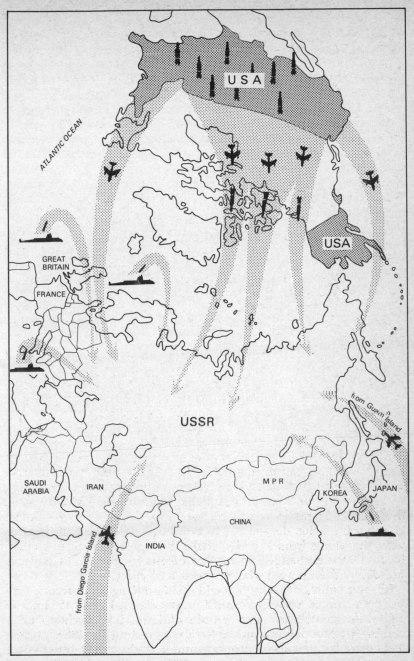

Reason for Soviet Fears: based on Soviet interpretation of major military exercises held during 1970 – 1980. (*Source:* Whence the Threat to Peace)

Hiroshima bomb was 12 kilotons), although the US Senate did not ratify the Treaty. In 1976, the Peaceful Nuclear Explosion Treaty was signed (although again not ratified by the Senate) banning nuclear explosions greater then 150 kilotons for 'peaceful purposes'. Negotiations for a complete ban on *all* nuclear weapons testing *anywhere* have been underway since 1977. President Reagan is the first President since President Kennedy to refuse to voice a commitment to negotiate a comprehensive test ban to prevent the further proliferation of nuclear weapons. Although publicly he said his reason was that he wanted to strengthen 'verification measures' of the two previous treaties, the *real* reason, according to officials, was his refusal to accept a treaty that would prohibit further nuclear weapons research and production. Both the Soviet Union and Britain are prepared to negotiate such a treaty. President Reagan has instead ordered the production of 17,000 new nuclear weapons, taking total numbers to over 50,000. The megatonnage of this arsenal will equal *one million* Hiroshimas.

Preparing for a nuclear war generally and a pre-emptive nuclear first strike against the Soviet Union in particular is an integral part of US strategic doctrine. Consider, for instance, the strategic ruminations of William L. Dickinson, the ranking minority member of the House Armed Services Committee:

> I think it is ludicrous for us to tell the world that we will not make a first strike .... I think that whether we are going to fire, respond under warning or under attack, or even have a pre-emptive capability, is our prerogative, and we don't have to signal our intent to anyone.
>
> Can we fire on warning and perhaps put a missile in orbit that can be recalled? I think this is a very interesting concept, and in talking to the technical community I am told that this is possible. This is technically feasible.[5]

Colin Gray and Keith Payne of the Hudson Institute not only state that "nuclear war is possible" but go on to assert that the "recognition that war at any level can be won or lost, and that the distinction between winning and losing would not be trivial, is essential for intelligent defense planning".[6]

"Nuclear war is unlikely to be an essentially terminal event," Gray and Payne state.

> Instead it is likely to be waged to coerce the Soviet Union to give up some recent gain. Thus, a president must have the ability not merely to end a war, but to end it favorably. The United States would need to be able to persuade desperate and determined Soviet leaders that it has the capability, and the determination, to wage nuclear war at even higher levels of violence until an

acceptable outcome is achieved. For deterrence to function during a war each side would have to calculate whether an improved outcome is possible through further escalation.

Believing that 'victory is possible' these strategists urge that the

United States should plan to defeat the Soviet Union and to do so at a cost that would not prohibit US recovery.Washington should identify war aims that in the last resort would contemplate the destruction of Soviet political authority and the emergence of a postwar world order compatible with Western values.

The most frightening threat to the Soviet Union would be the destruction or serious impairment of its political systems. Thus, the United States should be able to destroy key leadership cadres, their means of communication and some of the instruments of domestic control. The USSR, with its gross overcentralization of authority, epitomized by its vast bureaucracy in Moscow, should be highly vulnerable to such an attack. The Soviet Union might cease to function if its security agency, the KGB, were severely crippled. If the Moscow bureaucracy could be eliminated, damaged, or isolated, the USSR might disintegrate into anarchy, hence the extensive civil defense preparations intended to insure the survival of the Soviet leadership.*Judicious US targeting and weapon procurement policies might be able to deny the USSR the assurance of political survival.*

Once the defeat of the Soviet state is established as a war aim, defense professionals should attempt to identify an optimum targeting plan for the accomplishment of that goal. For example, Soviet political control of its territory in Central Asia and in the Far East could be weakened by discriminate nuclear targeting. The same applies to Transcaucasia and Eastern Europe.

Gray and Payne do not believe that the US should attack the USSR at any cost. They state clearly that "a US President cannot credibly threaten and should not launch a strategic nuclear strike if expected US casualities are likely to involve 100 million or more American citizens". What Gray and Payne make painfully clear is that up to a hundred million US citizens would be an acceptable price to pay for destroying the Soviet Union.

In 1981, Mr. Gray was appointed by President Reagan to the advisory board of the Arms Control and Disarmament Agency and as an adviser to the State Department.

The second aspect of America's global options strategy for the 1980s is the development of the capability to fight 'limited' nuclear wars in particular 'theatres' of conflict. Both the Cruise and Pershing II missiles are considered by the American strategists to be a part of what General Jones calls a "Long-Range Theatre Nuclear Force" (LRTNF). For the Americans, public opposition in Europe against these missiles is merely an inconvenience; and the arms control discussions with the Soviets in Geneva merely a ploy, so that when the talks fail, the Russians can be blamed for 'bad faith'. General Jones has stated categorically that the "464 Ground-Launched Cruise Missiles and 108 Pershing II Launchers *will eventually be deployed* to several European nations".[7]

Many NATO nations are naively under the misapprehension that they are 'full partners' with the US in an 'alliance of equals'. For the Americans, Western Europe is one of many 'theatres' the US has in its encirclement policy against the Soviet Union.

The newest 'theatre' to be developed has been that of the Indian Ocean and Persian Gulf area. During the 1970s, the US presence in the Persian Gulf area was composed of only three destroyers. The US now has two aircraft carrier groups permanently in the area, even though the USSR has been reducing its presence in the Indian Ocean. In 1981 the Soviets had only 21 ships there, most of which were noncombatant. In Singapore, Sri Lanka, Mauritius and Kenya, thousands of US sailors, soldiers and marines swarm ashore on 'visits' every month. On Diego Garcia, the coral island in the Indian Ocean which serves as the coordinating centre of the US presence in the Indian Ocean, construction is under way for runways for B–52 bombers and port installations for ships carrying up to 12,000 sailors at a time. US Marines have taken part in military exercises in north-eastern Kenya and the US has signed agreements with Australia, Kenya, Somalia and Oman to use their bases in exchange for 'assistance and cooperation'. US B–52s have begun regular flights over the Indian Ocean from bases in Guam and Australia and a new surveillance satellite monitoring the ocean was launched in March 1981. A new military assistance package for Pakistan has been negotiated, and for the first time ever, military discussions are being held with South Africa, which commands the south-western approach to the Indian Ocean. Even Sudan and Israel, which control the access to the Red Sea, have declared their readiness to let US forces use bases 'under certain circumstances'.

All told, the US has over 60,000 troops in the Indian Ocean region, and the build-up is continuing. Pleas to demilitarise the region are being ignored. A 45 member United Nations committee on the Indian Ocean was to have held a conference in the summer of 1981, in Colombo, Sri Lanka, in order to discuss the creation of a 'zone of peace' in that area. However, at a committe meeting in New York in March 1981, the Western members, represented by Australia, made it clear that the existing atmosphere was 'not conducive' to convening such a conference. The US also ignored

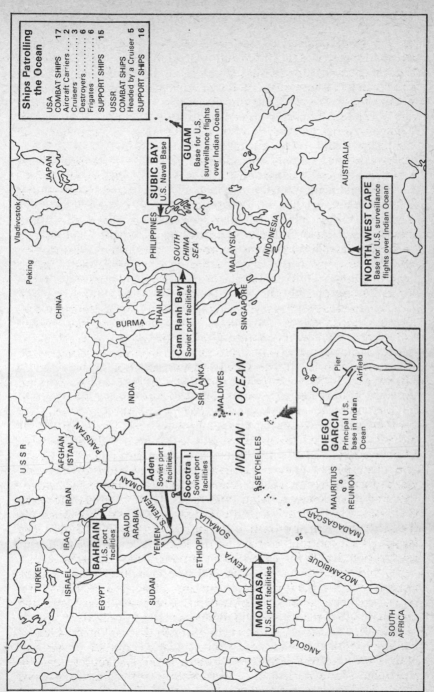

The Strategic Importance of the Indian Ocean.

Ships Patrolling the Ocean

USA
COMBAT SHIPS 17
    Aircraft Carriers 2
    Cruisers 3
    Destroyers 6
    Frigates 6
SUPPORT SHIPS 15

USSR
COMBAT SHIPS
    Headed by a Cruiser 5
SUPPORT SHIPS 16

SUBIC BAY
U.S. Naval Base

GUAM
Base for U.S.
surveillance flights
over Indian Ocean

NORTH WEST CAPE
Base for U.S. surveillance
flights over Indian Ocean

Cam Ranh Bay
Soviet port facilities

DIEGO GARCIA
Principal U.S.
base in Indian
Ocean

Pier

Airfield

Aden
Soviet port
facilities

Socotra I.
Soviet port
facilities

BAHRAIN
U.S. port
facilities

MOMBASA
U.S. port facilities

JAPAN
Vladivostok
Peking
CHINA
USSR
AFGHAN ISTAN
PAKISTAN
IRAN
IRAQ
TURKEY
ISRAEL
EGYPT
SUDAN
SAUDI ARABIA
OMAN
YEMEN
S. YEMEN
ETHIOPIA
SOMALIA
KENYA
MOZAMBIQUE
ANGOLA
SOUTH AFRICA
MADAGASCAR
MAURITIUS
REUNION
SEYCHELLES
MALDIVES
SRI LANKA
INDIA
BURMA
THAILAND
BURMA
PHILIPPINES
SOUTH CHINA SEA
MALAYSIA
SINGAPORE
INDONESIA
AUSTRALIA
INDIAN OCEAN

an appeal by Madagascar for a meeting of world leaders about the Indian Ocean. The USSR endorsed both the UN conference and the Madagascar appeal, although it showed no sign of withdrawing troops from Afghanistan, which the US is using as the reason for its build-up in the Persian Gulf.

The Pentagon has used the Russian presence in Afghanistan so effectively that it has succeeded in setting up a whole new command structure in the Persian Gulf region. The purpose of this new command, argued Secretary of Defense Weinberger is "to send a signal of determination to the Soviet Union".[8]

The Rapid Deployment Force based in the Indian Ocean, makes it clear that the US is in the area to stay. It has added another 'theatre' to its 'global options strategy'. Similarities with its Western European 'theatre' are striking. It is held together by a massive US military presence which is said to be in the region to counter a 'Soviet threat'. The Carter Doctrine of 1980 enunciates for the Persian Gulf what the US Doctrine has long enunciated for Western Europe: that the US is prepared to use nuclear weapons first in the region to protect US 'national interests'. This military presence and policy of nuclear first strike is given official sanction by a host of bilateral and multilateral treaties the US has signed with individual nations in the region.

Besides the all-out drive to attain nuclear superiority and the means to fight 'limited' nuclear wars, US strategy for the 1980s also calls for a dramatic increase in chemical warfare capabilities, both for defensive and offensive use.

Chemical warfare may well equal nuclear warfare in its hideous consequences. After only a brief exposure to nerve gas, for instance, victims bleed profusely from the mouth and nose and go into severe convulsions. They die mercifully within minutes, or after days of agony. Even the most primitive chemical weapons used during World War I proved so brutal that every major nation—including the US and the USSR—ratified a 1925 Geneva protocol banning their use. Officially, they have never been used since.

On 25 January 1982, however, an unpublished Air Force history was brought to light which reported that the United States secretly sprayed herbicides on Laos during the Vietnam War and openly sprayed them on South Vietnam.[9] It did so only after debating whether other nations would denounce the move.

The account says that in the early 1960s, thousands of gallons of military defoliants were secretly brought into South Vietnam by the United States in violation of the Geneva protocol of 1925 and the inspection provisions of the Geneva accords of 1954, designed to end hostilities in Indochina.

It was during the height of the Vietnam war in 1969 that President Nixon officially halted all production of chemical weapons. In 1972, the US and the USSR signed a convention against the use of chemical weapons, although both reserved the right to possess them as 'deterrents'. In February 1982, President Reagan formally notified the US Congress and the world that the Pentagon plans to produce a 'new' generation of lethal chemical munitions beginning in 1984. The Pentagon wants over $2 billion in taxpayers' money over the decade of the 1980s to build a store of 'binary' weapons—made of two non-lethal substances activated only when they are brought together. Reagan earmarked a $30 million 'start-up' sum in his 1983 budget request.

International consternation about the Reagan plan erupted when Ms. Anoretta H. Hoeber, Principal Deputy-Assistant Secretary of the US Army, announced the Pentagon was discussing plans to deploy some of the new chemical weapons in Britain, perhaps at the Lakenheath Air Base. The US immediately denied any such plan and publicly contradicated General Jones' testimony to Congress that US chemical weapons would be offensive as well as defensive. To allay public concern, the Pentagon insisted that the US would never be the first to use its chemical weapons.

Discussion of "the use of gas frightens people", one Pentagon official told the *New York Times*, "but it could be considered a cheaper substitute for nuclear warfare that would do far less damage outside the battlefield".[10] Besides, he added, having already decided to produce chemical weapons, the US "can't stop now".

The justification given for this new US strategy is that the Soviet Union has a chemical warfare force of 60,000 troops, and that every Soviet division in Central Europe possesses elaborate anti-gas equipment. US officials charge that the USSR has used chemical mycotoxins—called 'yellow rain'—in Laos, Kampuchea and Afghanistan. By contrast, the 630,000 warheads in the 'ageing' US chemical arsenal are leaky and rapidly becoming 'obsolete'. Most were made for use with a 105 mm howitzer that is being phased out or for use in the M–55 rocket which no longer has a launcher. Pentagon strategists warn that the Soviet's chemical forces give the USSR a 'significant edge' in conventional warfare. They insist that only a matching US capability can deter a Soviet chemical first strike.

When asked to prove Soviet use of chemical warfare techniques, the best the Defence Department could do was produce a few leaves, said to be from Kampuchea, containing a trace of mycotoxin of only 50 parts per million. It is highly likely, however, given US use of herbicides in the area during the 1960s, that the

US has merely uncovered residual remains of some of its own chemical warfare. It is a twist of genius that it is now blaming that on the Russians to justify an increase in its own lethal capacity.

On 17 June 1982, a senior White House adviser, Thomas C. Reed, disclosed that the overall strategic objective of President Reagan's national security policy was to 'prevail' over the Soviet Union.[11] Mr. Reed dismissed the policies of containment and detente, which served as the foundations of earlier security strategies, the first initiated by President Truman, the second by President Nixon.

"Through both of those policies ran the unspoken fear that the Soviet military-industrial locomotive might be unstoppable," he said. "That is no longer our view. 'Prevailing with pride' is the principal new ingredient of American security policy." Following an economic theme, Mr. Reed said:

> There is a crisis in the Soviet Union, where the demands of the economy are colliding with those of the political order. The Soviet Union is an economic basket case, and yet the Soviet leadership continue to pour resources into its military establishment. Despite its immense size, it cannot feed its own people, and it is hard-pressed to finance the import of food and other products necessary to prop up its mismanaged and misdirected economy.

In economic dealings with the Soviet Union, Mr. Reed said "we should not provide the trade and credits necessary to prop up the Soviet economy except in exchange for specific and meaningful Soviet actions that promote stability, peace, and the well-being of everyone, including the citizens of the Soviet Union".

The key word of the revised policy—prevail—also runs through the strategic guidance that Secretary of Defense Caspar W. Weinberger recently approved for the armed forces, where it was applied to the administration's strategy for protracted nuclear war.

Mr. Reed cautioned Soviet leaders that the administration is moving ahead with a communications system that would ensure the ability of the president or his successors to control US military forces even during nuclear attack.

"We have, we exercise, and we are improving a plan for the continuity of government," he said.

> There should be no doubt in the minds of Soviet planners that any attempts to disconnect the national command authorities from control of American weapons in time of crisis will fail. Likewise, the American people should be assured that the presidency, as an institution, can survive.

This is not idle talk.

By the summer of 1982, the Pentagon—on orders from the

President—completed a strategic masterplan to give the United States the capability of 'winning' a 'protracted' nuclear war with the Soviet Union. The new masterplan essentially provided a 'how-to' treatment of the Gray and Payne article. For example, the new plan devotes considerable space to destroying Soviet political and command centres while preserving US centres. The Reagan administration budgeted $18 billion for the purpose of protecting US military command, control and communications facilities, known as C–3 to strategic planners. Only with a secure C–3 complex can the national political and military leaders maintain communication with the troops in physical control of the nuclear arsenal.

The implications of Reagan's shift in strategic thinking about nuclear war were spelled out by Gen. James W. Stansberry, Commander of the Air Force Electronics Systems Division: "In previous years", he said at an Air Force conference, "the concept for C–3 was that it only had to be able to get off a launch of US strategic weapons in response to a first strike before damage was unacceptable. The idea that there was no way to win a nuclear war exchange sort of invalidated the need for anything survivable. There is a shift now in nuclear weapons planning, and a proper element in nuclear deterrence is that we be able to keep on fighting."[12]

The top political and military leaders of the United States appear to believe that a nuclear war might be fought over a period of several months with selective 'surgical' strikes at primary military targets and command centres. In the end, they hope, the United States would emerge victorious, with enough of its resources and population to begin again.

U.S. Base (*Source: Social Alternatives, Queensland*)

9 The Soviets Strike Back

WAR COMMUNISM

Those who fall behind get beaten .... The history of old Russia was the continual beatings she suffered for falling behind. She was beaten by the Turkish beys. She was beaten by the Polish and Lithuanian gentry. She was beaten by the British and French capitalists. She was beaten by the Japanese barons. All beat her—for her backwardness, for industrial backwardness.... Such is the jungle law of capitalism. You are backward, you are weak—therefore you are wrong; hence, you can be beaten and enslaved. You are right; hence, we must be wary of you. That is why we must no longer lag behind.

So said Stalin in 1931.[1] Rapid industrialisation of the Soviet Union under Stalin in the late 1920s and 1930s was aimed at 'catching up' with the capitalist camps. This mentality dominates Soviet armaments policy. Because they have been encircled, besieged and invaded, they have developed a linear view of progress—the notion that there is only one way of achieving political, economic and military strength, and that is by moving down the same road as trodden by the capitalists, only faster and more efficiently. The effect of this mentality has been to endorse both Western military doctrine and the Western concepts of what constitutes military power. Seeing the weapons system culture in the West, the Soviet Union has felt compelled to build one of its own.

The problem is that the Soviets have never caught up. This can be seen from the following chart:

Any Soviet 'firsts' have only been temporary and of little consequence. For instance, the Soviet Union tested its first intercontinental ballistic missile (ICBM) in August 1957, a few months earlier than the US. But the Soviet programme was plagued with technical difficulties, and only four of their first ICBMs were ever deployed. This was the basis of the famous 'missile gap' during the 1960 election. By 1962, the US had deployed 294 ICBMs, compared with 75 for the USSR. By 1964, the US had deployed 834, com-

ACTION ⟶ ⟵ REACTION
in the Nuclear Competition

The dynamics of the nuclear arms race ensure that development of a new weapons system by one power will in a relatively brief period be followed by a comparable achievement by the other. Both powers have had "firsts". Neither has stayed ahead for long. The US generally has a technological lead of several years, but the futility of the race for short-term advantage is demonstrated by a chronology of developments to date.

US 1945   **atomic bomb**   **1949 USSR**

The nuclear age began with the explosion of a US A-bomb of 12.5 kilotons (equivalent to 12,500 tons of TNT) over Hiroshima, Japan. The single bomb, which destroyed the city, introduced to the world a concentrated explosive force of unprecedented power. Within four years, the USSR conducted its first atomic test.

US 1948   **intercontinental bomber**   **1955 USSR**

By 1948, the US had begun to replace the propeller planes of World War II with long-range jets. The first planes developed for strategic (intercontinental) bombing required refueling to reach another continent. In 1955, the US began deployment of the all-jet intercontinental bomber, and USSR soon followed suit.

US 1954   **hydrogen bomb**   **1955 USSR**

The H-Bomb multiplied the explosive force of the A-bomb 1,000 times. The first US thermonuclear bomb had a yield equivalent to 15,000,000 tons of TNT; a year later the USSR tested a bomb in the million-ton range.

USSR 1957   **intercontinental ballistic missile (ICBM)**   **1958 US**

Following intensive development by both nuclear powers, a land-based missile to carry nuclear warheads intercontinental distances was successfully flight-tested by the USSR in 1957, and by the US a year later. By 1962 both nations had ICBM's with a range of 6,000 miles, each missile able to carry a payload equivalent to 5-10,000,000 tons of TNT.

USSR 1957   **man-made satellite in orbit**   **1958 US**

Sputnik I by the USSR initiated a space race which quickly took on military functions; the first US satellite was launched into orbit the following year. Well over half the superpowers' satellites have been military: for surveillance, targeting, communications, etc.

US 1960   **submarine-launched ballistic missile (SLBM)**   **1968 USSR**

A nuclear-powered submarine which could fire long-range missiles from a submerged position was the third means of strategic delivery. The US produced the nuclear-powered Polaris, with missiles with a range of 1,200 nautical miles. Eight years later the USSR had comparable nuclear subs.

US 1966   **multiple warhead (MRV)**   **1968 USSR**

Multiheaded missiles increased the number of targets a missile could hit. US MRV'd missiles carried three warheads, each with sixteen times the explosive force of the Hiroshima bomb. The USSR had them two years later.

USSR 1968   **anti-ballistic missile (ABM)**   **1972 US**

The USSR deployed 64 defensive missiles around Moscow. The US began construction of the Safeguard system in 1969 and had one site completed when a treaty restricting ABM's was signed in 1972. Generally judged militarily ineffective, ABM's were restricted to one site in each country in 1974. Subsequently the US site was closed.

US 1970   **multiple independently-targeted warhead (MIRV)**   **1975 USSR**

Further development of multiple warheads enabled one missile to hit three to ten individually selected targets as far apart as 100 miles. USSR began to flight-test MIRV's three years after US put them in service and in 1975 began deployment.

US 1982   **long-range cruise missile**   **198? USSR**

Adaptable to launching from air, sea, and land, a new generation of missiles with a range up to 1,500 miles is in production. The cruise missile is small, relatively inexpensive, highly accurate, with the unique advantage of very low trajectory. Following the contours of the earth, and flying under radar, it will be able to destroy its target without warning. The US is reportedly 7-8 years in the lead in this technology.

US 1983   **neutron bomb**   **198? USSR**

This nuclear weapon releases its explosive energy more in the form of an invisible, penetrating bombardment of radiation rather than in heat and blast. The decision to produce and stockpile the enhanced radiation warhead in the US was announced in August 1981. The USSR promptly announced that it has the capability but had deferred a production decision.

US 199?   **anti-satellite weapons**   **199? USSR**

Because satellites play vital military roles, they have also inspired a search for weapons to destroy them. The USSR began testing intercepter satellites in 1968. Both superpowers are attempting to perfect lasers to destroy enemy satellites and nuclear missiles in event of war.

(*Source: World Milit. & Soc. Expenditures*)

pared with 190 for the USSR. Moreover, in 1960, the US began to deploy submarine-launched ballistic missiles (SLBMs); the Soviet Union did not begin deployment until 8 years later.

Nearly all commentators agree that the Soviet Union lags behind the US in military technology. This is a fact recognised even by the Pentagon despite its rhetoric about the 'Russian threat'. In 1972, a Pentagon study showed that the USSR had a technological lead over the US in 11 deployed systems; was equal in 4; and lagged behind the US in 17 systems. Another Pentagon study in 1973 examined 334 areas of military knowledge and application. The USSR led the US in 65 areas; was equal in 129 areas; and lagged behind in 140 areas. In 1977, CIA Director Admiral Stansfield Turner stated in Congressional testimony that

the Soviets trail the US by 3 to 14 years in the introduction of certain electronic technologies. (Security deletion). The technology and fabrication techniques of Soviet computers and electronics are no better than those of the US five years ago. (Security deletion). While the Soviets may match the US in military laser design, they may have difficulty in fielding the equipment as widely. (Security deletion). The design and manufacturing technology incorporated in Soviet aircraft and missiles also lags behind that of the US.[2]

According to General Eugene Tighe, Director of the US Defense Intelligence Agency, the Soviet Union's

principal lag ... is in microminiaturization in computers, the ability to package a lot of complex command and control apparatus in their equipment. They use a great deal of their throw-weight capability today in rather, as I would describe it, very rigid 1960s technology.[3]

The US has roughly a 2 to 7 year lead over the USSR in the field of microelectronics, computer software, and jet engines essential to the development of advanced weapon systems. Soviet technology nevertheless has achieved a level of adequacy with respect to its present military requirements, in part by what is called 'reverse engineering'. This involves the Soviet acquisition of US and Western technology, and then simply copying it. The Soviet RYAD series of computers, for instance, are based on second generation IBM computers. IBM is currently working on its fourth generation equipment. They have copied US, British, West German and Japanese microcomputer and microprocessing equipment and different types of integrated circuits, including computer logic and memory chips. This saves the Soviets money, research and development time. Without this 'reverse engineering' it is estimated that the Soviets would trail the West by a 10–12 year gap rather than the present 2–7. This trailing behind the West is not owed to lack of scientific potential but owed to paucity of sufficient funds to carry on their own research and development which might put the Soviet Union parallel with the West.

The Soviet experience during the Wars of Intervention and during World War II demonstrated to them that despite technical inferiority they could nevertheless attain victory by deploying large numbers of troops and equipment into battles. During World War II alone, the Soviet Union fielded some 12 million troops and produced 140,000 aircraft and 70,000 tanks.

This lesson has remained engraved on the Russian military psyche. As the Soviet Deputy Defence Minister and Commander-in-Chief of Land Forces General Pavlovsky puts it:

> Thirty years have elapsed since the final battles of the Second World War, in the course of which the Soviet Land Forces enriched themselves with experience in the theory and practice of battles and operations ... In spite of the qualitative postwar changes in weaponry and in the methods of their use, this rich experience has not lost its significance and is now an important source of knowledge for training and educating the troops. Scientifically generalized, this experience has found its expression in all manuals of the Soviet armed forces.[4]

In many ways, the Soviet notion of deterrence places an even greater burden on the Soviet economy and culture than does the US notion of deterrence on the West. While Western military power rests on *technical* strength, that of the USSR rests on a continual *mobilisation* of its people and economy to be able to wage protracted war. Because of this, the Soviet economy has been characterised as a 'war economy' in the sense that the centralisation of economic management resembles that of a capitalist economy in wartime. Indeed, the priority given to defence in the Soviet Union is what provides the central justification for such a concentration of economic power and political control.

It was 'war communism' that enabled Lenin to consolidate Soviet power, drive out the British, American, French, German and Japanese troops, and go on to win the civil war between 1918 and 1920. It was 'war communism' again which enabled Stalin to rapidly industrialise and defeat the Nazi onslaught during World War II. And it has been 'war communism' yet again which has enabled the Soviet Union to compete with the United States both militarily and politically during the past forty years of the Cold War. War Communism has produced the Soviet superpower.

The Soviet system, which was largely established with Stalin's first Five Year Plan in 1928, was one in which centralised planning replaced a free market economy and the profit motive. To understand the Soviet economy one must imagine an economy two-thirds the size of that of the United States under the control of one Board of Directors—the Politburo in Moscow. This method has proved remarkably efficient for carrying out certain ambitious tasks, such as development of heavy industry or mobilisation for war or constructing the Siberian gas pipeline.

Centralised planning, however, entails enormous long-term social and economic costs. At factory levels, incentive is replaced by direct instruction—production quotas. Both workers and managers fulfilling their quotas receive material, social and political advantages. The problem is that the central planners cannot take into account all the details of local circumstances necessary to make the local quotas relevant to local needs and capabilities. The centre cannot possibly collect enough information to make correct estimates for appropriate output and input. All along the way misinformation is fed in which exaggerates success and downplays failure. Over-estimation results in wastage; under-estimation causes bottlenecks. The economic process is thus plagued by a morass of overinvestment, duplication, redundancy and corruption. Such a system inhibits technological progress because any emphasis on qualitative innovation would disturb the quantitative fulfilment of the existing quotas perhaps set several years prior to the proposed innovations. It would also disrupt established supply lines and create new supply constraints.

The problems of the Soviet economy are further complicated by the fact that economic planning is caught up with the internal political balance of those at the centre. This has the effect of making economic decisions the result, not of market forces as in the West, but of the relative influence of various sectors and groups in the central bureaucracy. This adds further rigidity to the system: by definition anything that is new and innovative is not yet big and powerful. In many cases, it actually threatens to disrupt the existing and established balance.

In the West, the military—industrial complex serves to uphold declining sectors of the economy (aircraft corporations after World War II, e.g.), and to inhibit the emergence of dynamic new ones. In the Soviet Union, the same tendency results from the operation of the planning systems as a whole. It is in the newest industries such as computers that the USSR lags behind the West the most. Moreover, technical progress is slow both in the new industries as well as in the declining ones. Traditional techniques continue to be used long after the introduction of new ones because in the absence of a free market to judge success or failure there is only the discretion of the political and economic planners of the vast but centralised Soviet bureaucracy.

THE METAL EATERS

In his memoirs, Khrushchev complained about the 'metal eaters' of the Soviet Defence Ministry. "I know from experience", he wrote,

that the leaders of the armed forces can be very persistent in claiming their share when it comes to allocate funds. Every commander has all sorts of convincing arguments why he should get more than anyone else. Unfortunately, there's a tendency for people who run the armed forces to be greedy and self-seeking. They're always ready to throw in your face the slogan 'if you try to economize, you'll pay in blood when war breaks out tomorrow'. I'm not denying that these men have a huge responsibility but the fact remains that the living standard of the country suffers when the budget is overloaded with allocations to unproductive branches of consumption. And today as yesterday, the most unproductive expenditures of all are those made by the armed forces. That's why I think military leaders can't be reminded too often that it is the government which must decide how much the armed forces can spend.[1]

In spite of that, the defence sector in the Soviet Union is the most powerful pressure group just as it is in the US and NATO. Military representation in state and Party committees is high. Defence Minister Ustinov and President Brezhnev both gained their formative experiences in the defence-industrial sector. Military spokespeople have always stressed the importance of heavy industry. For the military, heavy industry is the basis of the entire economy and the cornerstone of state power.

The Soviet defence sector exhibits all the conservative inclinations that pervade the rest of the Soviet economy. Therefore, Soviet defence institutions are even more stable than their Western counterparts, although there is no free enterprise system to induce the technological dynamism which motivates the Western military-industrial complex.

This is not to say there is no institutional pressure for technical innovation. There is. Fierce competition between the military services, various design bureaus and manufacturing firms takes place. Successful designs lead to production contracts, follow-on assignments, and the concomitant increase in prestige, state prizes and monetary and material reward. In his memoirs, Yakovlev, the powerful director of the bureau which designed the MiG–15 fighter, recalled how he used his personal influence with Stalin to concentrate research on modernising the MiG–15, rather than designing a new aircraft. "I was very worried about the situation," he wrote. "You see, behind me stood 100 people, who might lose faith in me as the leader of the design collective."[2]

One of the ways in which the defence industries attempt to by-pass the unreliability of the planning process is to keep as much of the manufacturing process as possible within the ministry concerned. This causes its own tensions and competition because it must be decided which manufacturing firms go to which ministries. Most ministries have their own metallurgical and machine-tool manufacturing facilities. The Electronics Ministry produces its own electrovacuum glass, ceramics, organic film for condensers, cast permanent magnets, etc., because it cannot rely on other ministries to meet either quantity or quality requirements. The Ministry of Aviation Industry includes metallurgical plants, stamping and extruding facilities and plants that manufacture rubber and plastic goods. Of the thousands of components needed to build an aircraft, 90–95% are produced in the aviation industry itself.

The consequence is continuity of both prime contractors and subcontractors. The emphasis is on standardisation and adaptability. But here again there is a built-in inhibition against innovation because any practice other than the norm might involve a change of suppliers which could mean an interminable process of going outside the ministry to obtain new materials and components.

Besides these horizontal relationships *within* the ministries, there are vertical relationships *between* ministries. The activities of research and development establishments are planned and directed by the ministries, who in turn are directed by the Military Industrial Commission. On the military side, the technical administrations work closely with counterparts in the particular military branch they serve. These activities are in turn co-ordinated and directed by the General Staff. Final decisions are taken by the Defence Council, which is subordinate to the Presidium of the Supreme Soviet. The Soviet Politbureau is the ultimate referrent for decisions and policy.

This hierarchical ordering of the Soviet military-industrial complex means that the cooperation between suppliers and customer is organised on the basis of decisions taken at the top which are then transmitted down through the various party, military and industrial channels.

While this tends to induce even more conservatism in the Soviet system it does have the one advantage of being able to shift emphasis when and where needed. This has been necessary to keep up with the different breakthroughs in US military technology. When the US exploded its atomic bomb in 1945, for instance, Stalin re-directed much of Soviet research and development towards obtaining a Soviet atom bomb which was

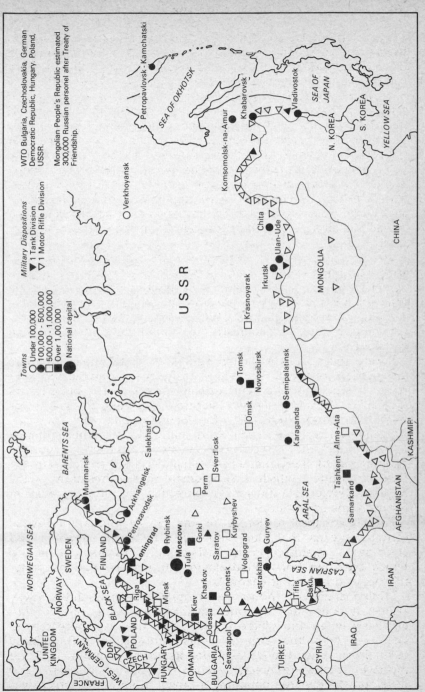

Soviet Military Strength (*Source: The Soviet Superpower, Heinemann Educ.*)

achieved in 1949. Ever since then, as US breakthroughs occurred, the Soviet leadership has re-directed the Soviet military-industrial complex accordingly. The famous Soviet designer of transport aircraft, Antonov once commented, "Have you not noticed that the Party has several times rolled up its sleeves, gone after one industry or another, and, dragging it out of the morass of gradualism, given it a powerful push in the direction the country required?"[3]

Another important result of the hierarchical nature of Soviet power is that the leadership can integrate the military and civilian sectors as the situation demands.

Almost all defence enterprises are simultaneously responsible for substantial civilian production as a matter of policy. Brezhnev, in an oft-quoted statement, has estimated that 42% of defence plants' output is intended for civilian use. On the other hand, it is also estimated that nearly 60% of civilian enterprises are producing for defence needs.

Cooperation between the military and civilian industries began during the 1930s, when Stalin ensured that defence obtained a major share of the budgetary allocations for industry. The defence sector accounted for about 20% of machine tools and steel output and 10% of all chemical industry equipment. The defence sector exerted a decisive influence upon the development of quality iron and steel products as well as upon non-ferrous metals, alloys, fuels, rubber and chemicals. Many civilian enterprises were constructed with the specific objective of convertibility for war effort. Tractor factories were designed to re-tool quickly for tank production. Clock and watch factories were also designed to manufacture fuses. Nearly all civilian enterprises had special units which were responsible for preparing production processes to be adopted in the event of war. These units were authorised to disrupt normal work and reorganise equipment and personnel.

This convertibility requirement led to inefficiency in the organisation of factories. For instance, two of the world's largest tractor plants were built in Stalingrad and Chelyabinsk. While they could both be re-tooled for tank production at virtually a moment's notice, they could never operate at optimum production levels. Moreover, massive absorption of resources by and for the defence sector diverted badly needed resources from civilian use. Nevertheless, this period of the 1930s and 1940s was perhaps the most dynamic time in Soviet economic development. It established the industrial structure which, because of its rigidity, centralisation and conservatism, still shapes the Soviet economy and social system of the 1980s. The military sector remains deeply embedded in the Soviet industrial structure.

Given the age-old Russian experience and fear of invasion, coupled with their need to be able to mobilise quickly, the Soviets do not make hard and fast distinctions between 'military' on the one hand and 'civilian' on the other. To them, all sectors must contribute, or be prepared to contribute, to the national 'defence'.

This ability to mobilise the entire national productive capacity is what motivates the Soviet Union to articulate the notion of deterrence-through-denial, discussed in Chapter 1. While they hope to avoid a general war and have pledged never to strike first, their deterrence has not failed if their armed forces are able to recover from an enemy attack and go on to win the victory.

10 Can There Be Peace?

We have made the Cold War an addiction. The scientists design the weapons for it; the corporations produce and profit from it; the military promotes and grows from it; the politicians rationalise it; the strategists plan for it. The military-industrial complex that has arisen *because* of the Cold War now *generates* the Cold War. It does not serve the interests of the people; people now serve it. And yet it is all of our own making.

Harold York, first director of Defense Research and Engineering at the Pentagon, argues that "the guilty men and organisations are to be found at all levels of government and in all segments of society; presidents, presidential candidates; governors and mayors, members of Congress, civilian officials and military officers; business executives and teachers, famous scientists and run-of-the-mill engineers; writers and editorialists; and just plain folks".[1] He speaks from experience.

York himself at one time was involved deeply in the scientific promotion of the arms race. He speaks from personal experience. The motivation to participate and promote the arms race and to manipulate the 'Soviet threat' to justify it varies from person to person, he says. However, what can be said is that

> nearly all such individuals have had a deep long-term involvement in the arms race. They derive either their incomes, their profits, or their consultant fees from it. But much more important than money as a motivating force are the individuals own psychic and spiritual needs; the majority of the key individual promoters of the arms race derive a very large part of their self-esteem from their participation in what they believe to be an essential—even a holy—cause.... They are inspired by ingenious and clever ideas, challenged by bold statements of real and imaginary military requirements, stimulated to match or exceed technological progress by the other side or even by a rival military service here at home, and victimised by rumours and phoney intelligence. Some have been lured by the siren call of rapid advancement, personal recognition, and unlimited opportunity, and some have been bought by promises of capital

gains. Some have sought out and even made up problems to fit the solution they have spent much of their lives discovering and developing. A few have used the arms race to achieve other, often hidden, objectives.[2]

What emerges is a complex interrelationship between scientists and those they serve; between corporate profits and military need; between personal motives and political agendas; and between objective facts and subjective prejudices. No one is totally to blame but we are all equally responsible.

The US and the USSR are the main protagonists in this war. There are military–industrial complexes on both sides which are not so much similar as inter-locked. They interact with one another, creating a self-reproducing *momentum* that quite literally sucks their respective allies and the Third World into it. The newly fashioned baroque systems on each side summon forth an appropriate response on the other side, which in turn compels a riposte. The hawks of the US feed the hawks of the USSR which feed the hawks of the US . . . . Dr. Henry Kissinger has summed up this reciprocity of fear and response very succinctly. He said,

> The Superpowers often behave like two heavily-armed blind men feeling their way around a room, each believing himself in mortal peril from the other whom he assumes to have perfect vision . . . . Each tends to ascribe to the other side a consistency, foresight and coherence that its own experience belies. Of course, over time even two blind men can do enormous damage to each other, not to speak of the room.[3]

The historian Max Lerner lists ten premises and principles of classical world politics, to reveal that inherent in the *structural* way in which the world has ordered itself in recent centuries, is a *psychological* need for a war mentality.[4]

1. We are within a system that is based on *power* and the uses of power—for supremacy of one nation over the other, for war and the maintenance of peace, for equilibrium within nations and for the changes of rulership both in and between nations. Power is the prime mover and it is also the goal toward which everything in the system gravitates.

2. Since the ruling passion is for power, the underlying assumption is that of *scarcity of power*. In this sense, classical politics is similar to the classical *laissez-faire* economics of capitalism, whose underlying premise is that there is a scarcity of wealth and resources so each person should strive for the largest possible share of what is available.

3. Because of the premise of the scarcity of power, classical politics, like classical capitalism, is competitive and aggressively

hostile. The aim of each nation is not only to acquire more power but actively to prevent its competitors from acquiring any. Thus the premise of scarcity yields the corollary premise of the *enemy*. The world becomes an arena of enemies and potential enemies and allies and potential allies; hence, the concept of alliances between nations, the art of diplomacy, and the utilization of war as an instrument of foreign policy.

4. Given the constant awareness of an enemy competing for power, classical politics can be characterised psychologically as a system predicated upon *suspicion and fear*, along with the secrecy and mistrust such attitudes imply. The characteristic ethos is that of amoral reliance upon the 'reason of state' or 'national security' to legitimise whatever actions a particular nation feels it must take to protect itself.

5. In the competition for power, classical politics puts value upon '*sinews of strength*': territory, natural resources, a population sufficient for an army and labour, a favourable balance of trade and payments, and the acquisition of wealth and strength. The emphasis is upon the tangible and the observable, not upon the intangibles of ideals and morality. The major exception to this is the cultivation among the young in particular of patriotism and national honour as ideals for which one should be prepared to sacrifice life.

6. Fundamental to classical world politics is the notion of *nation-states*. Anything less has no substantive value because it has little to show for itself in terms of the accepted criteria of what constitutes sinews of power. Hence the constant pressure in recent times towards nationalistic movements and the carving out of new nations. Once this has been achieved, the drive of the new nation is not towards either internal freedom or external cooperation but towards self-sufficiency economically and militarily. All else is generally subordinated to this task, for within self-sufficiency is independence and national security.

7. Fundamental to the notion of nation-states is the notion of *national sovereignty*, meaning that each nation refuses to acknowledge a source of authority outside itself. Any participation in treaty or multi-national organisations is only done if it accords with perceived self-interest or if it is compelled to do so by a superior power.

8. Closely connected with national sovereignty is *national interest*, an internal dynamic within each nation that seeks to discern what it needs and how best to obtain it. Lord Palmerston made the remark once during a Parliamentary debate over the question of an alliance between England and Turkey that "England has no

permanent friends, England has no permanent enemies, England has only permanent interests". This statement forms the essence of classical world politics.

9. As each nation pursues its own self-interest it must somehow attempt to ensure that it will not be destroyed by its competitors. This means that when any nation gets so powerful that it threatens its enemies with possible extinction or subjugation, these enemies must attempt in some way to regroup to restore the balance. Thus classical politics is a system based on a notion of *equilibrium*. To ensure this equilibrium, the ability to make war is essential. Only by being able to inflict unacceptable damage on anyone perceived as a threat does any nation feel secure enough to continue its competition for the limited amounts of resources, in order to obtain which the other nation is upsetting the equilibrium.

10. *War* is thus the ultimate referent of classical politics. It is the grounding principle which ensures that the enemy in the pursuit of power can be either neutralised or defeated; it is the basis upon which the suspicion and fear rest; it is the defence behind which nation states continue existing and competing.

The Age of Overkill has brought the classical system of world politics to an end. While the first principle of the classical world was that of the *scarcity* of power, the reality of nuclear arsenals is that of a *surplus* of power. The tragic paradox is that while these weapons are not suitable to the classical political system, the nation-states with nuclear arsenals are using them to defend interests and to maintain the paranoia *produced* by the classical system. Furthermore, the classical political system is so deeply engrained that even while knowing that the entire planet is being threatened, the nations cannot stop their escalation to develop more weapons, more sophisticated guidance systems, more accurate missiles.

It is quite clear that the current battle between the US and the USSR is not essentially one of ideologies, although the conflict that divides them is couched in ideological terms. It is not primarily a conflict between capitalism and communism, democracy and dictatorship, or individual rights and collective tyranny. If we examine the issue closely what emerges is a geopolitical rivalry between two superpowers caught in classical imperial conflict. This can be seen by examining a list of fears and grievances of these two countries.

Beginning with the Soviet Union:

1. The Soviets fear an American inspired invasion and thus insist on nuclear parity for defence against a first strike by the US.

2. The Soviets are fearful of more invasions. They insist that Eastern Europe be kept under Soviet control as a buffer zone.

3. The Soviets panic when their *cordon sanitaire*—the Warsaw Pact—is threatened either internally or externally.

4. The USSR feels it must not be bottled up in the Baltic and held back at the Dardanelles in the Black Sea.

5. The USSR feels besieged by NATO and US to its West; by China and US to its East and South; and by the US and Canada across the Pole to its geographic North.

6. The Soviets are vulnerable because they are not self-sufficient in many raw materials or high technologies. Of late, they have not even been able to produce sufficient food for themselves.

7. The Soviet Union no longer retains its hegemony over the world socialist movements. It does have a measure of influence in the Third World, but it is unable to match the US financial aid.

The US has its own list:

1. It fears a Soviet attack with nuclear weapons from which it could not recover. Thus it intends to 'stay ahead' in the arms race to deter that eventuality and to be able to inflict a nuclear first strike against the USSR from which the Soviets could not recover.

2. Unlike the USSR, the US is not landlocked but sealocked—separated from Europe and Asia by two vast oceans. The US fears for its trade and communication links as the USSR develops greater sea power and a bigger merchant fleet.

3. The US fears it would be isolated if Russian control spread over all of Europe.

4. The US depends on foreign supplies for 20 of the 36 minerals it regards as strategic. The US fears that Soviet influence in the Third World might cut off valuable raw materials and markets, sparking off a resource war against the US.

5. Although the US considers the Pacific and Atlantic oceans as its *cordon sanitaire*, the missiles the Soviet Union possesses now can penetrate that geographic immunity.

6. Vietnam, Iran, Afghanistan, Poland, El Salvador, and other recent experiences have brought home to the US the fear of strategic impotence, despite possessing a massive nuclear arsenal: hence the development of the concepts of 'limited' nuclear war and 'theatre' and 'tactical' nuclear weapons as a way to make the force of US power felt.

7. The Administration in the US is vulnerable to shifts in national public opinion.

What one finds in examining the Soviet and American lists is that

Paranoia of the USA and the USSR (Ingram Pinn © *Sunday Times*)

they are predominantly geopolitical, i.e. with ideologies reversed
—a communist US and capitalist USSR—the rivalries would remain
essentially the same. Moreover, if communism or capitalism had
been adopted by *both* superpowers we would have had essentially
the same result. One need only look at the rivalry between the
USSR and China or between China and Vietnam or between the
US and the EEC to see that both sides being 'communist' or
otherwise makes little difference. Ideology is at best only one
factor. Of greater importance are historical and economic
conditions, geopolitical realities and cultural and religious
orientations.

While the essential conflict between the imperial powers is
primarily *geopolitical*, the dominant mentality on both sides seeks
to shore up its positions and extend influence through *ideological*
distinctions.

The ideological differences are accentuated in order to keep the
geostrategic rivalry in focus. While the geostrategic rivalry is
primarily military and economic, the ideological distinctions are
primarily political and intellectual. Ideology is in the realm of
mentality. Indeed, the ideological distinctions between East and
West and the threat of the 'other' has been so deeply internalised
within both American and Soviet cultures that the very *self-identity*
of many people today is bound up with the ideological
assumptions of the Cold War. Ideology is indispensable for
keeping 'us' united against 'them'.

The US, for instance, identifies itself as the leader of the 'Free
World' against the 'Communist menace'. 'We' are on this side of
the 'iron curtain'. 'They' are on the other side. Only this
pre-existent need for bonding-by-exclusion, conditioned by
centuries of classical politics, can explain this fixation of the US
with the Soviet Union. Against the USSR, one's identity is not as
a black or woman or Baptist: one is a 'free' citizen.

Besides serving as a unifying device, the ideology of
anti-communism also serves the purpose of keeping internal
dissent down, whether from the trade unions, the universities, or
the churches. Who wants to be labelled 'soft on communism'?

The USSR has similar problems. Like the US, it is not composed
of a single nationality but of over a hundred disparate ethnic
groups from Siberia to the Black Sea. Bonding in the USSR comes
from not only the notion that it is the heartland of the world's first
socialist revolution but from the fact that it is surrounded from
Mongolia to the Arctic ice cap by a string of American-backed
alliances. More than anything, it fears 1,000,000,000 Chinese in
alliance with Western imperialism.

Perhaps because the external threat is more real and the

memories of invasion more immediate, the USSR uses this bonding against the other in directly disciplinary terms. The threat of the 'other' has been used from Lenin to Andropov to legitimise every form of repression. Any critic of the State is 'anti-Soviet', every impulse towards democracy 'counter-revolutionary'.

This device of uniting one's own group against the 'enemy' on the one hand and then using the spectre of the 'enemy' to justify repression at home on the other, is what keeps the ideological underpinnings of the nuclear arms race moving as fast as the baroque arsenals can be built. It is an ancient mechanism of social control, as old as that of classical politics. The advent of nuclear technology has breached the system itself. But it still works. It works only because our mentality has not kept pace with our technology. Weapons of the 1980s are being justified on the basis of ideologies of the 1940s. Otherwise they will have no justification. Although the nuclear arsenals of both sides have now *outpaced* both the classical political system and the original assumptions of the Cold War, nevertheless the ideology has remained the same.

Herein is the greatest cause for pessimism in the present crisis—that the mentality of both parties to the conflict are responding to *ancient* historical situations rather than to *actual* human needs. We are showing that we started out as uncivilised humans and have become sophisticated animals.

This point needs to be explained because it is so fundamental. It is well known that human ancestry is firmly rooted in animal origins—this is the conclusion of several centuries of anthropological research into the evolutionary history of our species. What has been emerging with an almost equal clarity has been the *predatory* nature of our origin. This is to say, that since our emergence from the apes we have been predators whose natural instinct has been to use violence to gain what we want.

Remembering the different characteristics of the classical political system, it is interesting to note the different instincts we have inherited from our primate ancestors. Robert Ardrey, in his book *African Genesis*, points out that these include the establishment and defence of territories; an attitude of perpetual hostility for the neighbouring territorial holder; the formation of social units as the principal means of survival; an attitude of amity and loyalty for those within one's own group and mistrust and suspicion for those in other groups; and a varying but universal hierarchical system to establish dominance and submission within the group to ensure both the efficiency of the group and the promotion of natural selection. Upon this deeply buried multifarious primate instinctual complex were added the necessities and opportunities of the hunt.

Ardrey exemplifies this through illustration of the lion. The non-aggressive primate, he says, rarely dies in defence of its territory; however, among the causes of lion mortality tabulated in the Kruger reserve of South Africa, death from territorial conflict is the second largest contributing factor. The non-aggressive primate seldom suffers much beyond humiliation in its quarrels for dominance; the lion, on the other hand, dies of such conflicts more than from any other cause. The forest primate suppresses many individual demands in the interest of the collective but still retains a measure of individuality; no collective in the animal world, however, can compare with either the organisation or the discipline of the lion pride or the hunting pack of the wolf. We can only presume, observes Ardrey,

> that when the necessities of the hunting life encountered the basic primate instincts, then all were intensified. Conflicts became lethal, territorial arguments minor wars. The social band as a hunting and defensive unit became harsher in its code whether of amity or enmity. The dominant became more dominant, the subordinate more disciplined. Over-shadowing all other qualitative changes, however, was the coming of the aggressive imperative. The creature who had once killed only through circumstance killed now for a living.[5]

In short, building upon anthropological evidence generally, particularly upon the evidence uncovered by Leakey in the Olduvai Gorge and Dart in southern Africa, Ardrey asserts that the human species "originated as the most sophisticated predator the world has ever known". War, he says, "has been the most natural mode of human expression since the beginning of recorded history, and the improvement of the weapon has been man's principal preoccupation since Bed Two in the Olduvai Gorge".[6]

Robert Bigelow, in his book *The Dawn Warriors: Man's Evolution Towards Peace*, elucidates both the deep-seatedness of our aggressive drives and their close connection with our feelings of cooperation and group support. He begins his book, appropriately enough, with an image of the very phenomenon we are considering:

> A hydrogen bomb is an example of mankind's enormous capacity for friendly co-operation. Its construction requires an intricate network of human teams, all working with single-minded devotion toward a common goal. Let us pause and savour the glow of self-congratulation we deserve for belonging to such an intelligent and sociable species. But without an equally high potential for ferocity, no hydrogen bomb ever *would* be built. Perhaps our co-operation has something to do with our ferocity.[7]

Bigelow offers the thesis that these two apparently contradictory aspects of human nature are in fact complementary. He points out that early human societies were organised in socially cooperative groups, much as the upper primates such as the baboon are today, but on a much higher level of complexity. The cooperation was confined, however, almost exclusively to individuals who belonged to the same group. Cooperation between groups was essentially non-existent, and the individuals of each group regarded all other groups as foreign and as potential threats to their survival.

Effective communication became necessary for effective group action. This, in turn, required developed brains. Those groups with the most highly evolved brains and consequently the greatest capacity for effective communication and cooperation in attack and/or defence, survived longest. The ingredients of evolution—genetic variability and natural selection—determined that survival went to that new combination most able to learn social cooperation for defence and offence against threats of would-be predators—both human and non-human. Those groups failing to cooperate effectively were slaughtered or driven into less hospitable lands. Cooperation was not substituted for conflict. Cooperation-for-conflict, considered as a single hyphenated word, was demanded—for sheer survival.

As the human race developed, the advantage of *inter-group* cooperation was seen, a difficult step to take in that it required cooperation with previous enemies and foreigners. As soon as the first two human groups formed a military alliance against a third party, however, the single group was faced with grave peril. Bigelow asserts this inter-group cooperation-for-conflict was a central factor in quickening the pace of human evolution.

Cooperation-for-conflict at the inter-group level resulted in the contending armies becoming larger, the weapons more devastating, the casualties higher. As history has progressed the restricted areas of inter-group cooperation-for-conflict have gradually expanded. Humans have gone from hunter-gatherer groups, to tribes, to city states, to kingdoms, empires, until today whole blocs of nations exist in alliances such as the Common Market or NATO or the Warsaw Treaty Organisation. War has simultaneously become bloodier and more destructive. We are thus today cooperating as never before. We are also divided and competing without precedence. And we have armed ourselves to the point of being able to blow the entire planet into oblivion. We have reached the point in our evolution where we will either move toward *uniting* the planet or *destroying* it.

The psychiatrist Elias Canetti defines paranoia as "an illness of power in the most literal sense of the words".[8] It is an illness that seeks power not only over life but over death, but because it is involved with an identification with the very death it is attempting to conquer, it can use no other weapon to fight death than the threat of death. Therefore paranoia ultimately results in destructive behaviour to others as well as to one's own self. While paranoia ordinarily seeks to divert death to others in order to spare the one who is paranoid, Canetti makes the point that "once (a person) feels himself threatened, his passionate desire to see *everyone* lying dead before him can scarcely be mastered by his reason".

This is a most profound insight, for it goes a long way towards explaining why it is that out of mutual mistrust, the Russians and the Americans have built up such huge nuclear arsenals that they now threaten every single person on the planet with death immersion. The current world situation—with each human being not threatened merely with one death but with arsenals that can destroy each man, woman and child *scores* of times over—this situation should be understood as acute paranoia, something that should be dealt with before it culminates in the double suicide that acute paranoia makes inevitable if left untreated.

The difficulty with both diagnosing and treating paranoia, however, is that it is often hard to discern.

The paradox within a society gripped by paranoia is that the society can appear to be in many ways 'perfectly normal'—so normal that the frenzy seems almost absent, gnawing at the conscience of certain individuals but not enough to arouse them from their stupor. Even the craziest person is not completely crazy, a point even truer of hysteria where nothing appears to be really wrong beyond a few 'excesses' here and there, coupled with the paralysis of normal functions to mitigate these excesses. In mass movements, therefore, we can expect many parts of the psychic body politic to appear entirely normal even while the overall analysis can only be that the collective is in the grip of hysteria.

This is an important point to internalise because it means that in cases of possession, when entire nations are transformed from civilised human beings to barbaric murderers as Germany was during World War II, many individuals caught up in this maelstrom are not *individually* transformed; rather, most continue living quite normal lives and if challenged about being part of a 'hysterical mob' would probably deny it, certainly deny their participation in it.

The Swiss psychologist Carl Jung commented on this phenomenon of individual normalcy within the grip of collective hysteria:

> Look at all the incredible savagery going on in our so-called civilised world: it all comes from human beings and their mental

condition! Look at the devilish engines of destruction! They are invented by completely innocuous gentlemen, reasonable, respectable citizens who are everything we could wish. And when the whole thing blows up and an indescribable hell of devastation is let loose, nobody seems to be responsible. It simply happens, and yet it is all man-made. But since everyone is blindly convinced that he is nothing more than his own extremely unassuming and insignificant conscious self, which performs its duties decently and earns a moderate living, nobody is aware that this whole rationalistically organised conglomeration we call a state or a nation is driven on by a seemingly impersonal but terrifying power which nobody and nothing can check.[9]

This apparent normalcy within a situation that can be described only as hysterical or paranoid is made possible by psychological defence mechanisms, which although complex, *must be understood* if we are to make sense of our present crisis.

A paper delivered by Professor Horst-Eberhard Richter of West Germany at the Second Congress of the International Physicians for the Prevention of Nuclear War, in April 1982, explored this area.[10] The psychological effects of the threat of nuclear war differ from country to country, he said, but there are common discernible patterns. Opinion polls in the United States indicate that 68% of the American public are concerned about the chances of nuclear war. Similar polls in Great Britain indicate that 70% of the public are not only concerned about such a war but expect to experience a nuclear war within this decade. In West Germany, 48% of the public believes a third world war is possible or probable. Young people in particular are pessimistic about the future. A poll taken by the American Psychiatric Association of Boston teenagers reveals that almost all believe their lives would be cut short by nuclear war. In West Germany, over 50% of the young people between 18 and 24 believe the world will be destroyed by nuclear war.

The question that must be asked about this pessimism is why are people not out on the streets screaming about it? Why does this oppressive nightmare remain, for the most part, unspoken?

When asked, most people state their belief that it is useless for them to try to exert any influence over today's calamitous political events. Most people believe their needs and fears are not considered or even recognised by the politicians. This is a primary reason why so few people vote in the United States. Polls reveal that only used car salesmen are mistrusted more than politicians. In West Germany, 78% of the people believe that most politicians do not know what the common people are thinking. Among younger people, the percentage is 86. The demoralisation that many people feel at being a helpless object of political decisions made by those one elects but has no influence over leads to the most common social ill of our time: depression and apathy. Apathy is not a result of not caring. It is the result of not feeling one can either express or receive affirmation for one's needs or fears. Apathy is frozen violence. It is unspoken frustration underneath the veneer of numbness and depression. It is a state of affairs that bears little resemblance to the proper function of the representative democracy which we have pledged ourselves to defend to death.

Not everyone is trapped in the paralysis of apathy and depression. Signs of disquiet have been and are increasing. One expression of this disquiet has been the peace movement. The peace movement is the result of people giving expression to their concerns about the future. While only a minority have broken through their apathy and organised themselves in protest against the current momentum toward war, they are channelling the pressures which burden the entire society. The youth invariably make up the most vocal component of the peace movement. Their sensitivity to social conflict and their awareness of injustices have not been dulled yet by age. Indeed, it is because of their age that they react so dramatically to threats to their future. After all, they have the longest future before them.

Because the peace movement is often identified with the young and discontented, it is possible for a great part of the older generation to channel some of its hidden fear—shared *by* the peace movement—*at* the peace movement. This allows the older representatives of the establishment in society to defend their threatened self-reliance. However, rather than solving the problem, it only engenders more protest. This dynamic is similar to the situation of a family burdened by conflict, where the parents conceal their worries from the children, who meanwhile react with dramatic symptoms. Instead of clearing up the conflict by openly sharing the concerns of the entire family (the only way to achieve a constructive solution), parents often react defensively and *discipline* rather than share with their children.

Similar irrational processes plague the peace movement. Up till now, the peace movement has found it difficult to express its concern and outrage in a relevant way which does not threaten those who make up the establishment. Their alarm about nuclear war is genuine and legitimate. Yet many in the peace movement find themselves suspected, harassed, and discriminated against by the very people to whom they make their appeal. The establishment reveals that it is more interested in hiding its fears than eradicating their causes.

This process of social disintegration becomes dangerous and potentially violent when fear is *suppressed* by those who bear the responsibility for political decisions and *expressed* by a popular movement which cannot take part in that process.

Between these two polarised factions lies the 'silent majority', which becomes temporarily interested in every conceivable issue from the marriage of Prince Charles to Lady Diana to the outcome of the local sporting match, but hardly ever about the probability of nuclear war. This avoidance could be due to a certain melancholy pleasure one obtains by contemplating one's inevitable doom. It could also be due to the psychological mechanism of *denial*. Often sick people ignore their diseases; healthy people never quite believe they will die. Do we have a similar attitude toward nuclear weapons?

Denial occurs when the fear of being unable to bear the thought of nuclear warfare pushes *even the fear of the threat itself* into the background. To hold the reality of nuclear war before one's eyes is like looking directly into the sun.

Denial, therefore, provides a temporary relief to psychic health on an individual basis no matter how irrational and dangerous it may be in political terms. Thus, as Jung points out, it is easy to maintain apparent individual normalcy within the grip of collective hysteria.

Yet the question remains how this denial is possible at all in light of the constant protest of the peace movement, the information freely available about the planning, production and deployment of new weapons of mass destruction, about the increases in the defence budget and the constant barrage of propaganda about the 'Russian threat'?

Professor Richter suggests five factors in this denial. The first is that nuclear weapons have effects which quite literally defy human imagination. The horrible becomes abstract if it lies beyond what we can conceive of. Thus we call anything which could ignite a possible nuclear war 'inconceivable', 'incredible', or 'indescribable'.

The second factor is that of habituation. Those living by railway tracks cease to hear the sound of the trains after a while. The fact that we have lived since 1945 under the threat of nuclear annihilation without that annihilation being unleashed has dulled the awareness of many and the perception of most.

The third factor arises from the first two. There is the widespread albeit naive belief that something cannot happen simply because it is too unreasonable. This factor paralysed the survival instincts of many Jews during the Nazi period. Gas chambers for genocide were too senseless to believe. In the nuclear situation, likewise, to threaten to use 'overkill' weapons seems so totally beyond belief that many deny the existence of the problem for this factor alone. In defiance of history, there is a prevailing assumption that reality could never be completely senseless.

The fourth factor is the notion held by many people that world politics is essentially the continuation of the kind of behaviour that all people experience in their daily relationships. The psycho-analyst Erich Fromm gave this as one of the reasons why numerous Jews could not bring themselves to emigrate from Nazi Germany. Many Jews kept up their normal personal contacts with Germans in their neighbourhoods right up to the end. It seemed completely unbelievable to many of them that the Nazis could ever carry out their criminal schemes of genocide. Similar criminal policies exist now, only the targets are all of us and the weapons are nuclear. Yet because the notion of megadeath is contrary to the way we correlate personal everyday experience, we ignore it.

The final factor contributing to the denial of the reality of nuclear war amongst the 'silent majority' is the mechanism of displace-ment. This again is an unconscious process which can best be explained by example. A girl learns that her mother is dying. She suddenly has the fear that she will come across a dead bird on her way to school. She begs to be allowed to stay home from school so that she will be spared the encounter with the dead bird. From a clinical perspective it is clear that the girl has displaced her fear of the death of her mother onto the idea of a dead bird.

The mechanism of displacement provides an explanation for the recent preoccupation of many people with anything in their lives that could threaten their body or property. Across the United States and Western Europe there has been an excessive concern about wholesome nutrition, body weight, cholesterol levels and proper exercise. Striving for material security and physical health has become a collective obsession. For many people, what is being invented are large numbers of dead birds.

Despite these various symptoms of denial, the overwhelming majority of people see the dangers of nuclear war quite clearly. However, most hold fast to the idea that it is only the *other* side's weapons which are to be feared. The more warheads their own side produces, the safer they feel. 'Our' nuclear weapons are good and necessary for deterring the 'enemy', who is viewed as the sole aggressor.

The psychic relief brought about by portraying the enemy as the devil is known as *projection*. We transfer our own aggressiveness onto the 'enemy'. Each superpower sees in the *other* an image of its *own* aggressiveness, ambition and desire for total supremacy. In this atmosphere of mutual projection it is impossible for each side to assess realistically the threat which it poses to the 'enemy' or the 'enemy' poses to it. This results in a faith in which 'we' have a defensive, peacekeeping nuclear deterrent, while 'they' have offensive lethal nuclear bombs.

In our time, the Soviet Union is 'The Enemy'; the Russians are 'the devil'. By seeing the Russians as a threat, people fix their fear on an object which their minds are able to comprehend.

Viewing the Russians as 'The Enemy' allows people in the West to perceive themselves as innocent victims of persecution. This absolves them from having anything to do with the creation of the menace of nuclear war. It is all 'the Russians' fault': they are the aggressors; they are the expansionists; their nuclear weapons are offensive, they are aimed at us.

Fear of the Russians is easily transformed into hate. This allows people to transform a passive position of being victimised by the Russians into an active one of fighting back. 'After all, the communists in Moscow, who are conspiring to invade my country and destroy my way of life, deserve to be destroyed.' This mentality is the foundation stone of the doctrine of 'deterrence'. It permits all our weapons, all our preparations, all our defence expenditures to be viewed as justified reactions to a hostile enemy.

This mentality also allows individual members of the Western public to avoid the feeling of being an outsider. By fixing one's fear and hate upon the 'Soviet threat' one can feel secure and in agreement with one's own political leaders and with the prevailing mood of public opinion. Locked into this mentality, the more weapons 'we' have, the more secure 'we' make ourselves feel against 'them'.

The same psychic relief is of course felt by members of the Soviet public who view the Americans as devils. Moreover, the same can be said about those dissenting minorities, in the East as well as the West, who see their own society as devilish and idealise the other side uncritically. Although these groups think of themselves as part of the *peace* movement for the most part, their claim to be working for peace is unjustified. They distort the truth just as blindly as those who can only live with the threat of nuclear war by using a stereotyped scapegoat projection as a crutch. Dissenting political groups who devilise their own country and idealise the other side have not really dealt with the threat, they have only shifted their projections onto another party.

Once projection is complete, and *both sides are doing it*, it then becomes the sacred duty of both to have the biggest guns and the most destructive weapon systems in order to defend themselves against the evil they see on the other side. While in the grip of the *problem*, therefore, each group, by projecting its shadow upon the 'enemy', psychologically absolves itself from any guilt and can continue the build-up of destructive weapons systems under the illusion that this is in fact the *solution*. Therefore German companies during World War II could calmly discuss improved models of gas chambers within the meetings of their boards of directors, even competing amongst themselves for the government contracts to build them; and German soap companies could go so far as to argue for more Jewish children to be gassed because they had discovered that making soap from corpses of young Jews was cheaper than making it by normal means. And likewise today: companies fiercely compete for nuclear weapons contracts; and the public passively accepts a nuclear deterrent against the hated Russians, even as the German public accepted gas chambers against the hated Jews.

The great tragedy of post-war Europe is that the willingness to own up to one's own aggression and recognise the inner existence of one's own shadow has not come about. We are forever forgetting this truth, says Jung,

> because our eyes are fascinated by the conditions around us and riveted on them instead of examining our own heart and conscience. Every demagogue exploits this human weakness when he points with the greatest possible outcry to all the things that are wrong in the outside world. But the principal and indeed the only thing that is wrong with the world is man.[11]

The fanaticism of the Germans against the Jews has been replaced by the anti-Sovietism of the West in general and the US in particular. Only this time the weapons are not gas chambers but nuclear arms and the other side is not meekly submitting to slaughter but is equally well equipped, hostile and dangerous, caught up in its own anti-Americanism. The conflagration that broke out in Germany was the outcome of psychic conditions which are universal. While the Germans threatened only a single people with genocide, the nuclear arms race threatens the entire human race with extinction.

The current situation is like two men in a rowboat in the middle of the ocean. One man says to the other, 'Because I don't like you, I'm going to punch a hole in your end of the boat.'

It was the British physicist and naval officer P.M.S. Blackett who first predicted that immense nuclear stockpiles could be tolerated by people only if they were convinced that they were protecting themselves from a truly demonic opponent. "Once a nation bases its security on an absolute weapon, such as the atom bomb," he said, "it becomes psychologically necessary to believe in an absolute enemy."[12] The German physicist Max Born seized on this idea, saying, "to quiet the consciences of human beings concerning military plans which conceive of the killing of tens or hundreds of millions of men, women and children on the other side—and on one's own side, which is not even mentioned—the other side must be viewed as essentially corrupt and aggressive".[13] Blackett and Born spoke these words in the 1950s. They have long since been proved true. *Absolute weapons require an absolute enemy.*

The Russians are believed to be the 'greatest threat to world peace' by 75% of the public in virtually all of the 16 nations in the NATO alliance. We collectively live under a persecution complex in which all measures taken by the Soviets are perceived as essentially aggressive and hostile and threatening. Even when they offer to lessen the tensions, as Brezhnev did in 1980 when he unilaterally withdrew 1,000 tanks and 20,000 troops from East Germany, we suspect that the Russians are scheming to take advantage of us unawares. The persecution complex is such that whenever the peace movement rises in protest, the charge is made that its protest is being orchestrated and financed by the Kremlin. This criticism of the peace movement is matched by an equally uncritical idealising of whatever one's own government is doing. To view the Russians as the 'Enemy' and the peace movement in the West as their agent is balanced by the insistence that one's own country stands for goodness, justice and freedom. The imperialistic and aggressive actions of one's own political system are virtually impossible to be discerned once the enemy has been designated. In fact, the sense of persecution absorbs the concentration of the Western public so much that many are blind to the ways in which the West itself is being endangered by the 'precautions' it is taking against the USSR.

Tragically, the projection and persecution mentality is now being inflamed by the official deterrent policies of both sides. They start with the assumption that a nuclear war can be prevented by threatening one's opponent at least to the same degree that one's own side *seems* threatened, all the while secretly working for a 'Final Weapon' that will *really* terrorise the 'enemy'. One can only make such threats if both sides stay in the armaments race.

Deterrence resides, not in the weapons built, but in the minds of those building them. Therefore, the psychological arms race must keep pace with arms production. If the projection and persecution complex does not keep abreast with the production schedules then deterrence itself is endangered and, according to this philosophy, so is peace. If either side were to relax its determination to set the apocalypse in motion, this could trigger the aggressive designs of the 'enemy', who is poised and waiting for 'our' resolve to weaken. Thus the factors of denial, projection, paranoia, and the persecution complex are essential ingredients of any credible deterrent policy. Where the 'Russian threat' must be real is not so much in *Soviet behaviour* as in *the hearts and minds* of Western societies.

The paradox of the socio-psychological situation in which we live is that our governments are telling us that our peace is threatened by the outbreak of a peace-loving attitude. Only suspicion, mistrust, hatred and fear can guarantee our security. Our peace cannot endure trust. These emotional responses needed to sustain the policy of deterrence were hardened long ago, and most people are not even aware of their basis. Moreover, the hatred and suspicion are expressed in concepts and language which have become both abstract and technical, thus enabling those caught up in the grip of the persecution complex to keep their hostile emotions deeply buried beneath the surface. The consequence has been that 'peace' has become merely an absence of war. Peace has become a technicality, the automatic residual result of a quantitative relationship between the destructive capacities of different weapons.

Our nuclear weapons have absorbed our aggression. They are the phallic symbols of our age. Our paranoia, our fear, our sexuality have become material. Instead of looking at our own motives, we look at the Cruise missiles, the SS–20s, the Trident submarines, the Backfire bombers. Somewhere in the numbers count is the 'peace' we seek. Our weapons, rather than we ourselves, have become the primary actors on the international chessboard.

The speed of rockets, deployment schedules, accuracy of warheads and first strike capabilities are the indicators of how we maintain the peace. The moral or political will of the peoples hiding behind these weapons is made irrelevant. The result has been that the military technocrats dominate the discussions of arms control. The question of peace is no longer how do we live together in mutual tolerance but how do we make the data balance out, so that in the end a stalemate results from a mutual balance of terror instilled from both sides.

The fact that we could achieve this balance of terror at a much lower level of armament is ignored. The ever increasing escalation in the arms race demonstrates that there are forces at work that will push the balance upwards until it can be pushed no more and an explosion must occur. Yet the revelation of just these decisive emotional factors is taboo. It is like two hostile groups being in a room, waist deep in petrol. The leader of one group has sixteen matches; the leader of the other has eighteen. Each leader is saying to his respective group, 'If only we had two more matches...'

In the nuclear debate we are being asked to be 'reasonable' and limit our discussion to the numbers count. The motives of hatred and mistrust are treated as irrelevant side effects of objective events. Therefore, it occurs to only a few that the denial, the paranoia, the persecution complex, the fear must be eradicated *first* before the reduction in the numbers of weapons can be made possible and meaningful.

Albert Einstein was one of the first to realise the solution to the problem he had engendered. He said, "Everyone sees that under the present conditions a serious military conflict (in fact, even the preparations for a *possible* military conflict) must lead to the annihilation of all mankind; nevertheless, men are unable to replace cunning and mutual threats with benevolent understanding".[14] The only way out of this predicament, he said, was to realise that "the precondition for a real solution of the security problem is a certain mutual trust by both parties, a trust which cannot be replaced by any kind of technological measures".

What Einstein is saying is that *we must come to terms with the Soviet Union before nuclear disarmament will be possible*. We must stop devilising them and seeing them as the Absolute Enemy because we possess the Absolute Weapon. Mutual trust can only be gained through mutual understanding. We must learn to extend to the Russians the simple recognition that our common humanity unites us far more powerfully than our differences divide us.

The irony of our common heritage is that it has also led to common fears. We have constructed, as a deterrent against one another, weapons systems which cannot destroy the 'enemy' without destroying 'ourselves'. Nuclear weapons, if used, will destroy our common heritage. They will not destroy our common fears.

Our technology has made the issue of the 'Russian threat' coterminous with the question of human survival. We are no longer faced with the question of war or peace, victory or surrender. We are faced with the question of existence or non-existence. There can be no such thing as nuclear 'war' between the superpowers. There can only be nuclear annihilation.

Although the arguments we hear against the Russians are couched in military, geostrategic and civil libertarian terms, the nuclear arsenals we have built make all such discussions obsolete, for, if used, our weapons would devastate the one species on earth that has even developed the *notions* of liberty or shaped the scales of justice. All of human history, all of civilization, all of the future are now being put in jeopardy because of our paranoia of 'the Russians' and their paranoia about 'the Americans'. We have allowed our fear of other human beings to deaden our love for life. That is what 'better dead than red' really means.

How can we save ourselves?

Einstein made the point after World War II that the atom bomb changed everything in the world *except* human consciousness. And thus, he said, we drift toward 'unparalleled catastrophe'. What we must change, therefore, is the way we think about life in light of the weapons we have created. We must have the courage to change our attitudes. It will indeed be difficult. It is not impossible.

The experience and reflection of George F. Kennan are helpful. He was the US ambassador to the Soviet Union immediately after the Second World War. While in Moscow, he sent the famous 'long-telegram' to President Truman stating that there was an "inherent tendency" in the Soviet Union to expand; that the totalitarian government of Stalin would repress human rights in whatever areas the Soviets took over; and that only a strong US military presence would stop Soviet totalitarian expansion. He believed in the Riga axiom, that the Soviets could only be countered by direct military and political confrontation. Any negotiations were an "appeasement". These hard-line views, shared by many others, played a major role in the development of the Cold War.

George Kennan came to see that these views were not only inaccurate but dangerous. In a speech given in 1980 to the Second World Congress on Soviet and East European Studies, he stated that the time had come for a new look at the USSR.[15] Kennan recognizes that the Soviet Union is still a totalitarian regime "in its high sense of orthodoxy, its intolerance for contrary opinion, its tendency to identify ideological dissent with moral perversity, and its ingrained distrust of the heretical outsider."

This totalitarian nature of the Soviet government sparked fear in the West right from 1917, says Kennan, because of the world-revolutionary commitment of the early Leninist regime. The period of the intensive pursuit of world revolution was brief, however, ceasing to be given any priority by 1921; but the *rhetoric* of world revolution remained substantially unchanged throughout the 1920s and 1930s. Moreover, the Kremlin maintained small factions of local Communist followers over whom it exerted the strictest discipline in all of the nations that eventually joined the NATO alliance. The Soviet Union endeavoured to use these local communist parties as a means for the explanation and pursuit of its aims, and demanded their allegiance even when this conflicted with loyalty to their own governments. Kennan considers this combination of totalitarianism at home and the use of strictly controlled communist parties abroad as the main cause of the high degree of tension and mistrust which prevailed in the relations between the Soviet Union and the West.

This mistrust was only deepened after World War II when the Soviet leaders persisted in the traditional Russian tendency to over-insure in military matters and maintaion forces along their western borders which were much larger than anyone in the West could justify. This situation was only made worse by Western strategists, politicians and military leaders who exaggerated the strength and numbers of Soviet forces to compel their parliaments and congresses to give larger military appropriations; while at the same time, the Western press fueled the mistrust by dramatising these exaggerations as a means of capturing public attention. Once caught up in the anti-Soviet hysteria, few remembered the Wars of Intervention or the Nazi invasion or the US encirclement from which the Soviets were trying to *defend* themselves with their large forces. People were made to see the Soviet leaders as motivated by global ambitions at the expense of the independence and liberty of other peoples, without any regard for international peace and stablility.

Out of all these ingredients was brewed the immensely disturbing and tragic melange we have come to call the Cold War: the frantic competition in the development of nuclear armaments; the blind dehumanization and devilisation of the other side; the systematic distortion of the adversary's intentions and motivations; and the inevitable replacement of political considerations by military ones in the calculations of diplomacy.

Kennan suggests three conceptual shifts that would enable us to extricate ourselves from this moral and political quagmire. The first is that the world-revolutionary fervour that marked the early stages of Soviet power is essentially gone. Moscow no longer figures as a great inspirational source of social revolution. It no longer has the allegiance of communist parties abroad, and it is no longer considered by nations who are communist as the vanguard of the revolution. In fact, it seems clear that the primary political objective of the Soviet Union is not war but détente, not revolution but peaceful coexistence.

What this means, and this is the second point, is that the conflict between the superpowers is largely geo-strategic and military, not ideological. When couched in military categories, the Soviet Union is no match against the overwhelming military, economic and scientific might of the United States. 'The Soviet leadership', says Kennan, 'has no intention, and has never had any intention, of attacking Western Europe.' There are areas of conflict to be sure, and instances of Soviet aggression, particularly in Eastern Europe and Afghanistan. But there have also been instances of US aggression, especially in Latin America and Indo-China. Both superpowers have their spheres of influence. All this is normal between nations and empires and has been true since recorded history began. There is no credible geo-strategic or political reason for the maintenance of armed forces on a scale that envisages the total destruction of an entire people, not to mention the immense attendant danger to the attacker itself and to countless millions of by-standers. Such a capability can only come from fear—sheer ignorance and fear. It can have no positive aspirations.

The third point is that our present overkill capabilities are devoid of a rational basis. What is more, they do not *need* a rational basis. The military-industrial complex simply feeds upon itself and provides its own momentum. That is why our predicament is so dangerous.

"No one will understand the danger we are in today", says Kennan,

> unless he recognizes that governments in this modern world have not yet learned to cope with the compulsions that arise for them not just from an adversary's cultivation of armed force on a major scale but from their own as well. I repeat: peoples and governments of this present age have not yet learned how to create and cultivate great military establishments, and particularly those which include the weapons of mass destruction, without becoming the servants rather than the masters of that which they have created, and without resigning themselves helplessly to the compulsive forces they have thus unleashed.

This is what happened in the First World War. Historians are still at a loss to find conflicts of interests serious enough between the European nations involved to warrant the sacrifices and miseries of the war that ensued. The politicians and the generals were simply carried along by the momentum of the weapons race in which they were involved. The resulting carnage introduced chemical and biological warfare techniques to the world and left 50 million dead or wounded.

Such a situation not only can happen again, it *is* happening. We are all being carried along *at this moment* towards a new military confrontation—a confrontation which can end in nothing less than mutual extermination. History offers no instance of a build-up of massive armaments by rival powers which did not end up in the outbreak of war. There is no reason to believe that our measure of self-control is any greater than that of our forebears. We have no greater wisdom at our command than our ancestors had. We only have more powerful weapons.

George Kennan has made the conceptual shifts necessary to come to terms with both the imminence of nuclear war and therefore the imperative to hold out the olive branch to the Soviet

Union. The man who began his career as an architect of the Cold War ended his address with the following plea to the decision-makers of the two superpowers:

> For the love of God, of your children, and of the civilization to which you belong, cease this madness. You have a duty not just to the generation of the present—you have a duty to civilization's past, which you threaten to render meaningless, and to its future, which you threaten to render non-existent. You are mortal men. You are capable of error. You have no right to hold in your hands—there is no one wise enough and strong enough to hold in his hands—destructive powers sufficient to put an end to civilized life on a great portion of our planet. No one should wish to hold such powers. Thrust them from you. The risks you might thereby assume are not greater—could not be greater—than those which you are now incurring for us all.[16]

If George Kennan could change his mind about the Russians, we all can. It will take a measure of insight into the *reality* of the Soviet Union behind the *myths* of the 'Russian threat'. It will also take a willingness to accept the minor risks involved in the disarmament process in order to avoid the supreme ones involved in our current compulsion to unleash nuclear annihilation upon ourselves. With Kennan, we must recognise that the problem of nuclear technology is common to the ideological worlds of both West and East. Its solution will require each others *co-operation*, not each others *enmity*. Moreover, this will come, at least initially, not form the leaders of the peoples. It will come, as it must, from the *peoples* themselves. As Einstein said, the answer to our nuclear crisis will resound from the Village Square. When President Eisenhower spoke about the dangers of the military-industrial complex, he also said that the day would dawn when the people of the world would demand peace so strongly that the governments would have to get out of their way.

Ambassador Kennan took thirty-five years to change his mind. We haven't got that sort of time. Our time is now. We have only to overcome our ignorance and apathy to express our strength.

REFERENCES AND SOURCES

1 'THE RUSSIANS ARE COMING'

1 In R. J. Lifton, *Death in Life: Survivors of Hiroshima*, Pelican, Harmondsworth, 1971, p.76.
2 *The Observer*, 1 Jan. 1978, p.3.
3 *The Sunday Times*, 3 May 1981, p.35.
4 Robert McNamara, "The Declining Strength of the Soviets", (interview with R. Scheer), *The Guardian*, 9 Aug. 1982, p.7.

2 KNOW YOUR ENEMY
Is the USSR Preparing to Wage War Against the West?

1 *The Wall Street Journal*, 23 Mar. 1982, p.1.
2 V. D. Sokolovsky, *Soviet Military Strategy*, trans. H. F. Scott, Crane Russak, New York, 1972, p.15.
3 "Why the Soviet Union Thinks It Could Fight and Win a Nuclear War", in *Commentary*, Jul. 1977, p.34.
4 *International Herald Tribune*, 15 Mar. 1981, p.2.
5 Clausewitz, *On War*, ed. and trans. M. Howard and P. Paret, Princeton Univ. Press, Princeton, 1976, p.92.
6 Lt. Col. Ye Rybkin, "On the Nature of a Nuclear Missile War", cited in W. R. Kintner and H. F. Scott, *The Nuclear Revolution in Soviet Military Affairs*, Univ. of Oklahoma Press, Norman, 1968, p.109.
7 T. K. Jones, Joint Comm. on Defense Production Hearings, *Defense Industrial Base: Industrial Preparedness and War Survival*, 17 Nov. 1976, Govt. Printing Off., Washington DC, p.185.
8 R. Pipes, "Why the Soviet Union Thinks It Could Fight and Win a Nuclear War", in *Commentary*, Jul. 1977, p.34.
9 Leonid Brezhnev, in speech at Moscow Peace Cong., 29 Oct. 1973. Quoted in *Pravda*, 30 Oct. 1973.
10 *The Observer*, 14 Mar. 1982, p.15.
11 M. Djilas, *Conversations with Stalin*, Penguin, Harmondsworth, 1963, p.90.
12 *Pravda*, 28 Jun. 1972; 28 Mar. 1973; 21 Jan. 1974, etc.
13 Lt. Gen. P. Zhilin, "Military Aspects of Detente", in *International Affairs*, Moscow, Dec. 1973, p.25.
14 W. Colby, Senate Foreign Rel. Comm. Hearings, *United States/Soviet Strategic Options*, January, Mar. 1977, p.142.
15 E. Crankshaw, *Khrushchev's Russia*, Penguin, Harmondsworth, rev. ed. 1962, Foreword.

Why is the USSR in Eastern Europe?

1 *Myths and Realities of the 'Soviet Threat'*: Proc. of an Inst. for Policy Stud. Conf. on US-Soviet Rel., 14, 15 May 1979, p.9.
2 *Time*, 6 Apr. 1981, p.17.
3 *Fiscal Year 1980 Arms Control Impact Statement*, Mar. 1979, pp.54–55.
4 *The Guardian*, 11 Mar. 1982, p.3.
5 *The Sunday Times*, 21 Feb. 1982, p.1.
6 In D. Campbell, "The 'Deterrent' Goes to War", in *New Statesman*, 1 May 1981, p.8.

What About Poland?

1 A. Starewicz, "The Heart of the Matter", in *Polish Perspectives*, Warsaw, May 1981, p.13.
2 *Ibid.*, p.14.
3 *Time*, 4 Jan. 1982, p.13.
4 *Ibid*, p.14.
5 *Op. cit.*
6 *Ibid.*, p.17.
7 *Ibid.*, p.18.
8 In *The Sunday Times*, 21 Feb. 1982, p.9.
9 *International Herald Tribune*, 21 Jan. 1982, p.4.
10 In C. Levinson, *Vodka-Cola*, Gordon Cremonesi, London, 1979, p.234.
11 *Op. cit.*
12 *Ibid.*, p.235.
13 *International Herald Tribune*, 11 Jan. 1982, p.5.
14 *Op. cit.*

What About Afghanistan?

1 Inder Malhotra, "Afghanistan: The Phoney Cockpit", in *Surge International*, Sep.–Dec. 1981, p.21.
2 *Ibid.*, p.24.
3 *The Economist*, 8 Aug. 1981, p.32.
4 *International Herald Tribune*, 20 May 1981, p.2.
5 *Op. cit.*
6 *Afghanistan: The Soviet Invasion and its Consequences for British Policy*, 5th Report from the Foreign Affairs Comm., House of Commons, 1979–80, p.IX.
7 In Jenny Pearce, *Under the Eagle: US Intervention in Central America and the Caribbean*, Latin Amer. Bur., Nottingham, 1981, p.9.
8 *Op. cit.*
9 *Ibid.*, p.10.
10 In Theo Westow, "The Ideology of National Security", in *The New Blackfriars*, Feb. 1980, p.10.
11 In Jenny Pearce, *Under the Eagle, op. cit.*, p.216.
12 *Ibid.*, p.217.
13 *International Herald Tribune*, 15 Feb. 1982, p.3.
14 *Op. cit.*
15 Jenny Pearce, *Under the Eagle, op. cit.*, p.240.
16 *The Wall Street Journal*, 3 Mar. 1981, p.1.
17 *The Los Angeles Times*, 4 Dec. 1979, p.6.
18 Jenny Pearce, *Under the Eagle, op. cit.*, p.227.

19 *Op. cit.*
20 *Ibid.*, p.250.
21 *International Herald Tribune*, 25 Feb. 1982, p.1.
22 *Ibid.*, 3 Mar. 1982, p.1.
23 *Ibid.*, 14 Mar. 1982, p.3.
24 *Op. cit.*
25 *Ibid.*, 17 Mar. 1982, p.2.
26 *The Observer*, 7 Feb. 1982, p.7.
27 *International Herald Tribune*, 18 Feb. 1982, p.1.

Do the Russians Want to Rule the World?
1 *Krasnaia zvezda*, 4 Feb. 1965, p.31.
2 In Sir W. Hayter, *Russia and the World*, Secker, London, 1970, p.4.
3 *Pravda*, 5 Jun. 1973.
4 Kissinger, "Statement to Senate Finance Comm.", Dept. of State Bull., Apr. 1974, p.323.
5 R. W. Herrick, *Soviet Naval Strategy: Fifty Years of Theory and Practice*, U.S. Naval Inst., Annapolis, Md., 1969, p.149.
6 In P. J. Mooney, *The Soviet Superpower: The Soviet Union 1945–80*, Heinemann, London, 1982, p.136, 137.
7 *Ibid.*, p.136.
8 In D. Horowitz, *From Yalta to Vietnam: American Foreign Policy In The Cold War*, Pelican, Harmondsworth, 1969, Preface.
9 *International Herald Tribune*, 8 Feb. 1982, p.4.
10 *Op. cit.*
11 *Op. cit.*
12 *Ibid.*, 16 Feb. 1982, p.2.
13 *Ibid.*, 27 Jul. 1982, p.2.

3 NUCLEAR STRENGTH

What About the Cruise Missiles and the SS–20s?

1 *Official Text*, US Embassy, London, 12 Jun. 1981, p.1.
2 Nino Pasti, *Euro-Missiles and the General Balance of NATO and Warsaw Pact Forces*, World Peace Coun., Helsinki, 1979.
3 *NATO Review*, NATO Inf. Serv., Jun. 1977, p.25.
4 *Annual Defence Dept. Report, Fed. Year 1978*, US Defense Dept., Washington DC, p.148.
5 *NATO Review*, NATO Inf. Sers., Jun. 1979, p.31.
6 *Analysis of Arms Control Impact Statements Submitted in Connection with the Fiscal Year 1978 Budget Request*, US Defense Dept., Washington DC, Apr. 1977, p.90.
7 *The International Herald Tribune*, 21 Mar. 1980, p.3.
8 Pasti, *Euro-Missiles, op. cit.*, p.45.
9 *Op. cit.*
10 *International Herald Tribune*, 27–28 Jun. 1981, p.1.
11 *Op. cit.*
12 *Ibid.*, 18 Jan. 1982, p.3.
13 *Ibid.*, 30 Nov. 1981, p.2.
14 *Ibid.*, 9 Jun. 1982, p.1.
15 *Ibid.*, 30 Nov. 1982, p.2.

16 *Ibid.*, 6–7 Feb. 1982, p.3.
17 *Ibid.*, 30 Nov. 1982, p.2.
18 *Official Text*, US Embassy, London, 17 Oct. 1981, p.7.
19 *New Statesman*, 31 Oct. 1981.
20 *The Guardian*, 23 Nov. 1981, p.7.
21 *International Herald Tribune*, 27–28 Jan. 1982, p.2.
22 *Newsweek*, 30 Nov. 1981, p.12.
23 *Op. cit.*
24 *Op. cit.*
25 *Ibid.*, p.14.

Do the Soviets Have Nuclear Superiority Over NATO?
1 Brochures available form the British Ministry of Defence.
2 "Sizing Up the Enemy", in *New Statesman*, 26 Sep. 1980, p.11.
3 See *Ibid.*
4 D. Campbell, "The Deterrent Goes to War", in *New Statesman*, 1 May 1981, p.8.

Do the Soviets Have Bigger and Better Bombs?
1 Paul Nitze, "Deterring our Deterrent", in *Foreign Policy*, Winter 1976–77, pp.198–9.
2 *The International Herald Tribune*, 9 Nov. 1981, p.2.
3 *The Observer*, 3 Jan. 1982, p.13.
4 G. A. Trofimenko, *SSHA: Politika, Voyna, Ideologiya*, Izdatel'stve Mysl', Moscow, 1976, p..323.

Do They Have Better Civil Defence?
1 *The New York Times*, 3 Jan. 1977, p.13.
2 Senate Foreign Relations Comm. Hearings, *United States/Soviet Strategic Options*, Jan., Mar. 1977, Govt. Printing Office, Washington DC. p.163.
3 In Fred M. Kaplan, 'The Soviet Civil Defense Myth', Part 2 in *Bull. of the Atomic Scientists*, Apr. 1978, p.42.
4 *Op. cit.*
5 C.I.A., *Soviet Civil Defense*, Washington DC, Jul. 1978.
6 Joint Econ. Comm. Hearings, *Allocation of Resources in the Soviet Union and China*, 1977, Washington DC, Jun. 1977, Pt. 3, p.26.
7 L. Goore, *War Survival in Soviet Strategy: USSR Civil Defence*, Univ. of Florida, Coral Gables, 1976.
8 A. Altunin, "The Main Direction", *Voyennye Znaniia* (Military Knowledge), Oct. 1976.
9 L. Goure, *War Survival in Soviet Strategy, op.cit.*, Chap. on "Problems and Shortcomings".
10 House Armed Serv. Comm. Hearings, *Civil Defense Review*, Washington DC, 1978, p.248.
11 C.I.A., *Soviet Civil Defense*, Washington DC, Jul. 1978, p.10.
12 Joint Comm. on Defense Production Hearings, *Civil Preparedness* Rev., Apr. 1977, pp.20, 68.
13 *Grazhdanskaya Oborona* (Civil Defense), Moscow, 1974, as trans. by Oak Ridge for Energy Research and Development Assoc. and Defense Civil Preparedness Agy., pp. 107–112.

14 Office of Technology Assessment, *The Effects of Nuclear War*, 3rd ed., Washington DC, 1979, p.76.
15 Fred M. Kaplan, *Dubious Spectre: A Skeptical Look at the Soviet Nuclear Threat*, Inst. for Policy Stud., Washington DC, 1980, p.36.
16 A. Tucker and J. Gleisner, *Crucible of Despair: The Effects of Nuclear War*, Menard, London, 1980, p.57.
17 *The Guardian*, 22 Jul. 1982, p.2.
18 *New Statesman*, 17 Jul. 1982, p.5.
19 *The Guardian*, 31 May 1981, p.8.
20 *Newsweek*, 26 Apr. 1982, p.28.
21 *Time*, 29 Mar. 1982, p.21.
22 *Newsweek*, 26 Apr. 1982, p.27.
23 *Op. cit.*
24 *The International Herald Tribune*, 8 Jul. 1982, p.3.
25 *Op. cit.*
26 *Time*, 29 Mar. 1982, p.23.

Does the United States Have a 'Window of Vulnerability' That Is Open to Soviet Attack?

1 C. Paine, "Running In Circles with the MX", in *Bull. of the Atomic Scientists*, Dec. 1981, p.5.
2 *Op. cit.*
3 J. E. Anderson, "First Strike: Myth or Reality", in *Bull. of the Atomic Scientists*, Nov. 1981, pp.6–11.
4 Henry Kissinger, in *International Security*, Sum. 1976, p.187.
5 Paine, "Running in Circles with the MX", *op. cit.*, p.6.
6 *International Herald Tribune*, 25 Mar. 1982, p.3.
7 *Op. cit.*

4 CONVENTIONAL STRENGTH

Are the Russians Stronger Than We Are?

1 Harold Brown, *Dept. of Defense Annual Report, Fed. Year 1980*, Washington DC, p.11.
2 Interview with Adm. Gene LaRoque, in *Challenge*, May–Jun. 1980.

Do the Soviets Outspend the West?

1 C.I.A., *A Dollar Cost Comparison of Soviet and US Defense Activities*, Washington DC, Jan. 1979, p.20.
2 A. J. Alexander, A. S. Becker, W. E. Hoehn, *The Significance of Divergent US–USSR Military Expenditures*, Rand Corp., Santa Monica, Feb. 1979, p.9.
3 SIPRI, *Yearbook*, Taylor and Francis, London, 1981, p.152.
4 *International Herald Tribune*, 13 May 1981, p.1.
5 *Op. cit.*

Will the Soviets Invade?

1 Interview, in *Challenge*, May–Jun. 1980.

5 STAR WARS

Do the Soviets Have 'Killer Satellites'?

1 J. Parmentola and K. Tsipis, "Particle Beam Weapons", in *Scientific American*, Apr. 1979, p.57.

2   *The Boston Globe*, 2 Jun. 1977, p.6.
3   In C. Simpson, ''Satellites: New Moons Unite the World'', in *Science Digest*, Dec. 1981, p.28.
4   *International Herald Tribune*, 29 May 1979, p.1.
5   *Newsweek*, 21 May 1979, p.13.
6   In C. Simpson, 'Satellites', *op. cit.*, p.28.

Are the Soviets Ahead in the Space Race?
1   *International Herald Tribune* 24 Feb. 1982, p.2.
2   *Op. cit.*
3   *Newsweek*, 27 Apr. 1981, p.19.
4   *Op. cit.*
5   *International Herald Tribune*, 7 Jun. 1982, p.1.

6 HUMAN RIGHTS
Isn't the USSR Just One Big Gulag Archipelago?
1   In R. Conquest, *The Great Terror: Stalin's Purge of the Thirties*, Macmillan, London, 1968, Preface.
2   *Prisoners of Conscience in the USSR: Their Treatment and Conditions*, Amnesty Int'l. Rep., London, 1980.
3   In A. J. P. Taylor, Introduction, in John Reed, *Ten Days That Shook the World*, Penguin, Harmondsworth, 1982, p.XI.
4   *Ibid.*, p.XVI.
5   *Ibid.*, p.252.
6   US Congress, *Congressional Record*, 57, part 2, p.1103.
7   *Washington Post*, 22 Jan. 1919.
8   Univ. of Chicago, Jos. Regenstein Lib., Spec. Coll., Samuel Northrop Harper Papers, Box 57, Folder 12: *The American-Russian Chamber of Commerce, Russian American Relationships in 1917, Feb. 15, 1918*.
9   *Ibid.*, Box 57, Folder 4: *An American Policy for Russia, Advocated by the American-Russian Chamber of Commerce, Sep. 1918*.
10 Catherine Breshkovsky, *A Message to the American People*, New York, 1919, p.13.
11 Lenin, *Collected Works*, Progress Pubs., Moscow, 1964, Vol.28, p.3.
12 US Congress, *Congressional Record*, 57, Pt. 2, pp.1392, 1394.
13 *Ibid.*, Pt. 4, p.3377.
14 *Ibid.*, Pt. 1, p.342.
15 *Ibid.*, Pt. 2, p.1101.
16 *Ibid.*, Pt. 2, p.1167.
17 Lenin, *Collected Works*, *op. cit.*, Vol.30, p.154.
18 W. S. Graves, *America's Siberian Adventure, 1918–1920*, New York, 1931, p.356.
19 Herbert C. Hoover, *Memoirs*, New York, 1951–52, Vol.1, p.411.
20 *The Bullitt Mission to Russia: Testimony Before the Committee on Foreign Relations, United States Senate, of William C. Bullitt*, New York, 1919, pp.89–90.
21 US Dept. of State, *Papers Relating to the Foreign Relations of the United States: 1920*, Washington DC, 1936, Vol.3, p.717.
22 *Ibid*, pp.463–68.
23 US Congress, *Congressional Record*, 64, Part 4, p.4168.

24 H. R. Knickerbocker, *The Red Trade Menace: Progress of the Soviet Five-Year Plan*, New York, 1931.
25 US Congress, *Congressional Record*, 72, Part 4, p.4526.
26 Lenin, *Collected Works*, Vol.29, pp.67, 68.
27 David Lane, *Politics and Society in the Soviet Union*, Martin Robertson, Oxford, 1977, p.76.
28 In *Myths and Realities of the Soviet Threat*: Procs. of an Inst. for Policy Stud. Conf. on US-Soviet Relations, 14, 15 May, 1979, p.13.
29 In Arthur Bryant, *The Turn of the Tide: 1939–1943*, Collins, London, 1957, p.472.
30 Winston S. Churchill, *The Gathering Storm*, Cassell, London, 1948, pp.284, 286–87.
31 Dr. Oleg Rzheshevsky, *Lessons of World War II*, Novosti, Moscow, 1979, pp.15ff.
32 In Konrad Heiden, *Hitler: A Biography*, London, 1936, p.264.
33 In Alastair Hamilton, *The Appeal of Fascism*, London, 1971, p.139.
34 In Nicolai Tolstoy, *Stalin's Secret War*, Cape, London, 1981, pp.86–87.
35 In F. A. Voigt, *Unto Caesar*, London, 1939, p.277–78.
36 In W. G. Krivitsky, *I Was Stalin's Agent*, London, 1939, pp.38, 39.
37 G. Watson, "Rehearsal for the Holocaust?", in *Commentary*, Jun. 1981.
38 In *Ibid.*, p.60.
39 In Rzheshevsky, *Lessons of World War II*, *op. cit.*, p.28.
40 In *Ibid.*, p.29.
41 In Alan Clarke, *Barbarossa: The Russian German Conflict 1941–45*, Penguin, 1966, p.70.
42 Rzheshevsky, *Lessons of World War II*, *op. cit.*, p.34.

How Should the West Respond?

1 In J. Power, *Against Oblivion: Amnesty International's Fight for Human Rights*, Fontana, Glasgow, 1981, pp.62–65.
2 In *Ibid.*, p.69.
3 *Op. cit.*
4 *Towards 1984*, Agenor publication, Brussels, 1980, p.34.
5 In *Kriminalistik*, Jun. 1974; trans. and quoted in *Ibid.*, p.35.
6 *New Statesman*, 5 Mar. 1982, p.7.
7 *Ibid.*, p.8.
8 *Ibid.*, p.9.
9 In Robert Jungk, *The Nuclear State*, trans. Eric Mosbacher, London, 1979, pp.118, 19.
10 *Intensified Nuclear Safeguards and Civil Liberties*, Nuclear Reg. Comm. Cont. No. AT(49–24)–0190, Washington DC, 31 Oct. 1975, p.1.
11 In Jungk, *Nuclear State*, *op. cit.*, p.132.
12 In *Ibid.*, p.142.

7 THE RISE AND FALL OF THE 'SOVIET THREAT'

1 NSC–68 was declassified in 1975. See T. H. Etzold and J. Lewis, eds., *Containment: Documents on American Policy and Strategy, 1945–1950*, Colombia Univ. Press, New York, 1978, pp.385–442.
2 Dean Acheson, *Present At Creation*, Norton, New York, 1969, p.374.
3 *Common Sense and the Present Danger*, Comm. on the Present Danger publication, p.2.

4 A. Wolfe, *The Rise and Fall of the 'Soviet Threat': Domestic Sources of the Cold War Consensus*, Inst. for Policy Stud., Washington DC, 1979, pp.7–32.
5 Nikita Khrushchev, *Khrushchev Remembers*, Deutsch, London, 1971, p.103.
6 H. Kissinger, *American Foreign Policy*, 3rd ed., Norton, New York, 1974, pp.89, 59.
7 V. Belov, A. Karenin, V. Petrov, *Socialist Policy of Peace: Theory and Practice*, trans. D. Shvinsky, Progress, Moscow, 1979, p.254.
8 *Pravda*, 9 Jun. 1976, p.1.

8 DOMESTIC REASONS FOR THE 'SOVIET THREAT'

The Scientists

1 Lord Zuckerman, *Science Advisers, Scientific Advisers and Nuclear Weapons*, Menard, London, 1980, p.5.
2 *Ibid.*, p.10.
3 G. Kistiakovsky, *A Scientist at the White House*, Harvard Univ. Press, Cambridge, 1976.
4 Harold York, *Race to Oblivion*, Simon and Schuster, New York, 1970.
5 Herman Scoville, *Missile Madness*, Houghton Mifflin, Boston, 1970.
6 R. Aldridge, *The Counterforce Syndrome: A Guide to US Nuclear Weapons and Strategic Doctrine*, Inst. for Pol. Stud., Washington DC, 1979, pp.26–31.
7 *San Jose Mercury*, 20 Jan. 1974, p.3.
8 *Hearings on Military Posture and House Resolution 11500*, House Armed Serv. Comm., 18 Feb. 1976, Pt. 5, p.78.
9 *United States Military Posture for Federal Year 1978*, Dept. of Defense, 17 Jan. 1977, p.24.

The Corporations

1 *US Congressional Record*, 95th Congress, 1st Sess., 28 Mar. 1977. CXXIII, Pt. 8, p.9269.
2 Mary Kaldor, *The Baroque Arsenal*, Deutsch, London, 1982, p.32.
3 In Jo L. Husbands, *The Long Long Pipeline: Arms Sales and Technological Dependence*, unpub., Center for Defense Inf., Washington DC, 1978.
4 In Mary Kaldor, *The Baroque Arsenal*, op. cit., p.65.
5 In *Ibid.*, p.69.
6 *Defense Procurements in Relationship Between Government and Its Contractors*, Hearing of the Sub-committee of the House-Senate Joint Econ. Comm., 2 Apr. 1975, p.2.
7 J. Fred Weston, ed., *Defense-Space Market Research*, MIT Press, Cambridge, 1964, p.28.

The Military

1 National Planning Assoc., *National Policy for Aviation: A Special Committee Report*, Planning Pamph., Nos. 50–52, Washington DC, 1946.
2 Boeing Company, *Boeing Annual Report*, 1948.
3 *Survival in the Air Age*, A Report by the President's Air Policy Comm., Washington DC, 1 Jan. 1948, p.21.
4 In Daniel Yergin, *Shattered Peace*, Houghton Mifflin, Boston, 1978, p.341.

5　In Thomas Powers, ''But Never Danger Today'', in *The Atlantic*, Apr. 1980, p.106.

6　*The Guardian*, 17 Feb. 1982, p.4.

The Politicians

1　*Public Papers of the Presidents of the United States, John F. Kennedy, 1961*, US Govt. Printing Off., 1962, p.68.

2　*Ibid.*, p.232.

3　Robert S. McNamara, *The Essence of Security—Reflections in Office*, Hodder, London, 1970, pp.57, 58.

4　Robert S. McNamara, ''The Declining Strength of the Soviets'', (interview), *The Guardian*, 9 Aug. 1982, p.7.

5　*International Herald Tribune*, 24 Mar. 1982, p.2.

6　*Newsweek*, 22 Mar. 1982, p.36.

7　*Time*, 29 Mar. 1982, p.20.

8　*New Statesman*, 5 Feb. 1982, p.14.

The Strategists

1　Colin Gray and Keith Payne, ''Victory is Possible'', in *Foreign Policy*, Sum. 1980.

2　*The Fiscal Year 1968–72 Defense Program and 1968 Defense Budget*, Hearings before joint committee of the Senate Armed Services Committee and the Senate Subcommittee on Department of Defense, Appropriations, Govt. Printing Off., Washington DC, 23 Jan. 1967, p.36.

3　In James Fallow, *National Defense*, Random House, New York, 1981, p.151.

4　*Official Text*, US Embassy, London, 7 Feb. 1981.

5　In Christopher Paine, ''Running in Circles with the MX'', in *Bull. of the Atomic Scientists*, Dec. 1981, p.10.

6　Gray and Payne, ''Victory is Possible'', *op. cit.*

7　*Official Text, op. cit.*

8　*International Herald Tribune*, 25–26 Apr. 1981, p.3.

9　*Ibid.*, 26 Jan. 1982, p.1.

10　*Ibid.*, 6, 7 Feb. 1982, p.3.

11　*Ibid.*, 18 Jun. 1982, p.3.

12　*Ibid.*, 16 Aug. 1982, p.1.

9　THE SOVIETS STRIKE BACK

War Communism

1　In Arthur Alexander, ''Decision-Making in Soviet Weapons Procurement'', in *Adelphi Papers*, (a publication of the Int'l. Inst. of Strategic stud.), Wint. 1978/79, p.2.

2　*Allocation of Resources in the Soviet Union and China*, hearings before the Joint Econ. Comm., in Subcomm. on Priorities and Econ. in Govt., Washington DC, 23 and 30 Jul. 1977, p.41.

3　*Ibid.*, 26 Jun. and 9 Jul. 1979.

4　In A. Alexander, *Armor Development in the Soviet Union and the United States: A Report Prepared for the Director of Net Assessment Office of the Secretary of Defense*, Rand R–1880–NA, Santa Monica, Sep. 1976, p.10.

The Metal Eaters
1 Nikita Khrushchev, *Khrushchev Remembers*, Deutsch, London, 1971, p.519.
2 Yakovlev, *Aim of a Lifetime*, trans. V. Vezey, Progress, Moscow, 1972.
3 In A. J. Alexander, *Research and Development in Soviet Aviation*, Rand R–589–PR, Santa Monica, Nov. 1970, p.22.

10 CAN THERE BE PEACE?
1 In Lord Zuckerman, *Science Advisers, Scientific Advisers and Nuclear Weapons*, Menard, London, 1980, p.11.
2 *Op. cit.*
3 In Lewis F. Thomas, "Unacceptable Damage", *New York Rev. of Books*, 29 Sep. 1981.
4 Max Lerner, *The Age of Overkill: A Preface to World Politics*, London, 1964, pp.20–23.
5 Robert Ardrey, *African Genesis*, Collins, London, 1961, p.317.
6 *Ibid.*, pp.26, 324.
7 Robert Bigelow, *The Dawn Warriors: Man's Evolution towards Peace*, London, 1969, p.3.
8 Elias Canetti, *Crowds and Power*, Gollancz, London, 1962, pp.227, 230, 448.
9 C. G. Jung, *Collected Works*, ed. William McGuire, trans. R. F. C. Hull, Routledge, London, 1958– , Vol.XI, paragraph 86.
10 *Proceedings, 2nd Congress of the International Physicians for the Prevention of Nuclear War*, Boston, 1982.
11 Jung, *Collected Works, op. cit.*, Vol.X, paragraph 441.
12 In Richter, *op. cit.*
13 *Op. cit.*
14 *Op. cit.*
15 George Kennan, *Politics and the East-West Relationship*, an Address to the 2nd World Cong. on Soviet and E. European Stud., in Garmisch, Germany, pub. by the Amer. Comm. on East-West Accord, Washington DC, Nov.–Dec., 1980.

Index